Decolonising Knowledge for Africa's Renewal

Endorsements

Decolonising Knowledge is not an idle and luxurious yearning - it is an urgent clarion call. If Africans are to produce home-grown solutions to our own challenges, first we need to be liberated intellectually from the clutches of narrow Western outlooks. Not that there is anything wrong with Western education, but it is only one side of the coin of knowledge. To be a fully rounded provider of solutions in the 21st century, one needs to have a well rounded education. The cry from students to have 'decolonised education' comes from a deep seated and well grounded fear that the current body of knowledge they are being pumped full of may well not provide solutions to our pressing challenges.

The call for decolonising knowledge is a call whose time has come.

Prof Phinda Mziwakhe Madi, School of Management, University of Johannesburg

Decolonising Knowledge for Africa's Renewal appropriates Africa's historical legacies and the impact of colonisation, appreciates her current structural and economic realities, re-configures her remaining cultural renaissance challenges, and imagines a better future. It is a beautiful thread in a reconstructive tapestry that patiently weaves passionate, practical and scholarly strands that address the dehumanisation and erosion of African cultures. At best this book is a timely resource for leaders, academics, practitioners and activists interested in Africa's social and economic advancement and embracing African wisdom.

Rev Vusi M Vilakati, Methodist Church of Southern Africa

Coming hot on the heels of the #RhodesMustFall student campaign, which has gone global, Professor Vuyisile Msila has brought together some of Africa's leading scholars to put the decolonisation struggle into its proper African Renaissance and Pan-Africanist context. The overriding argument made by the distinguished scholars in this book is that tackling global coloniality entails a deeper understanding of its existential, epistemological, spatial, spiritual and linguistic reach across the Pan-African world. This book goes to the heart of 21ˢᵗ century global justice struggles and demonstrates the enormous responsibility of African academics in pursuing a complex dialogue and shaping the Pan-African world's destiny on the terms of Pan-African peoples.

Dr Steve Sharra, Academic and author, Catholic University of Malawi

The relevance and significance of the call for an African Renaissance on the African continent is well attested to in a substantial body of literature concerned with philosophical, developmental, educational, language and ideological issues. In adding to this corpus, the present volume represents, in its concern with the problem of colonising knowledge for Africa's renewal, an insightful and critical contribution to the continuing debates on these multifaceted issues. This comprehensive collection of essays on the Africanisation of knowledge will be of interest to academics, policy makers, educators and curriculum specialists.

Emeritus Professor Philip Higgs, Indigenous Knowledge Specialist, University of South Africa

The book is a timely critical reflection on the undercurrents of the long-standing and recently renewed calls for the decolonisation of knowledge as it is manifest in the modern university in Africa, which university has its roots both in the global imperial expansion of colonial/western/ modern knowledge tied to globalisation of the Kantian-Humboldtian University born after the European Enlightenment. It was supplanted onto African soil as part of the "civilizing" mission of the colonial empires. This had terrible ramifications for African sovereign control over its ways of being and knowing, as well as for the survival of diverse knowledges that should dot the world for all. As this book shows, demands for the decolonisation of knowledge emanate from the tragedy of deferred dreams for liberation and shattered expectations of freedom that have come up against the gloomy reality of the neo-colonial conundrum of post-colonial Africa, evident in the continued hegemony of Western ways and the subjugation of other ways.

Professor Siphamandla Zondi, Department of Political Sciences, University of Pretoria.

First published in 2017

ISBN: 978-1-86922-672-5
eISBN: 978-1-86922-673-2 (ePDF)

Published by KR Publishing
P O Box 3954
Randburg
2125
Republic of South Africa

Tel: (011) 706-6009
Fax: (011) 706-1127
E-mail: orders@knowres.co.za
Website: www.kr.co.za

Printed and bound: HartWood Digital Printing, 243 Alexandra Avenue, Halfway House, Midrand
Typesetting, layout and design: Cia Joubert, cia@knowres.co.za
Cover design: Marlene de Villiers, marlene@knowres.co.za
Editing & proofreading: Jennifer Renton, jenniferrenton@live.co.za
Project management: Cia Joubert, cia@knowres.co.za
Index created with TExtract / www.Texyz.com

Decolonising Knowledge for Africa's Renewal

Examining African Perspectives and Philosophies

Vuyisile Msila (Editor)

kr ▸
publishing

2017

Contents

About the editor iii

About the contributors iv

Acknowledgements ix

Foreword: The Case for a Decolonised/Africanised Africa: *Sabelo J. Ndlovu-Gatsheni* x

Editor's Preface: *Vuyisile Msila* xvi

PART 1: PHILOSOPHY, RENAISSANCE AND PAN-AFRICANISM 1

Chapter 1: Tradition and the Foundation for African Renaissance: *Polycarp Ikuenobe* 2

Chapter 2: African Philosophy and African Renaissance: *Vuyisile Msila* 21

Chapter 3: Where did Azikiwe and Awolowo miss it? Rethinking Pan-Africanism and African Renaissance today: *Fred E F. Ayokhai & Peter W. Naankiel* 35

PART 2: IDENTITY, CONFLICT AND DEVELOPMENT 53

Chapter 4: The Pan-African Identity: Why Conflict and Community Identities Continue to Undermine Collectivism: *Wendy Isaacs-Martin* 54

Chapter 5: Engaging with the African Ground: Towards a New Research Paradigm for Conflict Studies in Africa: *Andries Velthuizen* 73

Chapter 6: Emerging 'Positive Masculinity' in the DRC: African Renaissance or Symptoms of Covert Gender Inequalities? *Francis Onditi & Abu Bah* 87

Chapter 7: The Struggling Urban Woman: Gendered Identities (Re)defined and (Re)interpreted in a New Social Environment: *Vuyisile Msila* 113

Chapter 8: Inventing Mythologies; Rational Conflict in a State of African Polity: *Saaba Sakana* 129

PART 3: HIGHER EDUCATION, AFRICANISATION AND LANGUAGE 145

Chapter 9: University Student Activism on Malawi's New Language-in-Education Policy: Singing the African Renaissance Tune: *Gregory Kamwendo* 146

Chapter 10: The Double-Edged Word: African Languages under Siege: *BXS Ntombela* 161

Chapter 11: Internationalisation and Africanisation of Master of Public Health Curricula in South Africa: Implications for Curriculum Transformation: *Jacqueline Witthuhn* 181

Chapter 12: A Critique of Africanised Curricula in Higher Education: Possibilities for
the African Renaissance: *Mago Mndawe*   201

PART 4: IDEOLOGY, YOUTH, MUSIC AND LEADERSHIP   **223**

Chapter 13: Towards Africa's Renewal: Decolonisation, Black Consciousness and the
Youth: *Vuyisile Msila*   224

Chapter 14: Duende in Maskandi Music: *Mxolisi Nyezwa*   237

Chapter 15: African Renaissance: Learning from some African Indigenous Leadership
Practices: *Vitallis Chikoko*   257

Chapter 16: Concluding Comments: Towards a new African society: *Vuyisile Msila*   271

Index   **279**

About the editor

Vuyisile Msila is the Head of the University of South Africa's Institute for African Renaissance Studies, and was also appointed Director: Leadership in Higher Education in March 2017. He has also been appointed as Director: Leadership in Higher Education in 2017 March. Msila was a Fulbright Fellow at Michigan State University where he completed a Masters Degree in Curriculum Theory and Teaching, and also has a Masters degrees in Education Management as well as in Conflict Management and Transformation. Msila taught at the Nelson Mandela Metropolitan University and the University of Johannesburg before joining the University of South Africa. He was also part of the research team that conducted a national longitudinal study, evaluating the effectiveness of the School of Management and Leadership qualification in South Africa. A C3 National Research Foundation (NRF) rated researcher, Msila received Unisa's Chancellor's Award for research in 2013. His recent books include *Africanising the curriculum: Indigenous perspectives and Critical theories* (Ed with M. Gumbo, 2016, Sun Press) and *Ubuntu: Shaping the current workplaces with (African) Wisdom* (2015, Knowres). One other book will be published in June 2017 - *Africanisation and the Curriculum: Lessons from practice* (Ed with M. Gumbo). Msila is also a regular newspaper columnist for *Mail and Guardian, Sunday Independent* and other Independent newspapers in South Africa

About the contributors

Fred Ekpe F. Ayokhai

Fred Ekpe F. Ayokhai holds a PhD and MA (History) from Nasarawa State University, Keffi, Nigeria. He also holds a PGDE from the Usmanu Danfodiyo University, Sokoto, and a BA (Hons) in History from the Bendel State University, Ekpoma, Nigeria. He is currently a Senior Lecturer at the Department of History and International Studies, Federal University Lafia, Nigeria, where he teaches West African History and International Relations. He is also the Acting Head of the Department. He was previously at the Taraba State University as a faculty member at the Department of History and Archaeology.

Fred has published in several prestigious national and international academic journals, and contributed chapters to various academic books within and outside Africa. He is also the lead editor of a book, *Concepts in Historiography: Essays in Honour of Olayemi Akinwumi*, published by Oasis of Greatness Publishers Ltd, Benin City, Nigeria. His research focus spans African development and economic history, with a special interest in gender, economy, peace, conflict and security studies. He is also interested in historiography, research methodology and African indigenous knowledge systems. He is currently engaged in co-editing several academic books and is on the editorial board of several journals within and outside Nigeria, including the *Lafiya Journal of Arts* on which he serves as editor, and the *Lafia Journal of Africa and Heritage Studies*, on which he serves as managing editor. Email: ayokhainekpe@yahoo.com.

Abu Bah

Abu Bakarr Bah is professor of sociology at Northern Illinois University and Faculty Associate at the Center for NGO Leadership and Development. He is also Editor-in-Chief of African Conflict & Peacebuilding Review (ACPR) published by Indiana University Press, and Senior Fellow at the Canadian Centre for the Responsibility to Protect. He was born in Sierra Leone and received his doctoral degree from the New School for Social Research (New York) and undergraduate degree from the University of Sofia in Bulgaria.

Abu's research interests include peace and conflict, democracy, and development. His books include *International Security and Peacebuilding: Africa, the Middle East, and Europe* (Indiana University Press, 2017) and *Breakdown and Reconstitution: Democracy, the Nation-State, and Ethnicity in Nigeria* (Lexington Books, 2005). His articles have been published in journals such as *African Affairs*, *Journal of International Peacekeeping*, *Critical Sociology*, *International Journal of Politics, Culture, and Society*, and *Africa Today*.

Bah is a recipient of the 2014 and 2016 Carnegie Foundation African Diaspora Fellowships, the 2012 Council of American Overseas Research Centers Multi-Country Research Fellowship, and the 2015 Northern Illinois University Outstanding International Educator Award. He is a frequent guest on international media programmes such as Al Jazeera and China Radio International. He has also been an invited speaker at major institutions such as Stanford University, the University of Illinois at Urbana Champaign, the University of South Florida,

Virginia Commonwealth University, the Global Center for Pluralism (Canada), and the Social Science Research Council (New York).

Vitallis Chikoko

Vitallis Chikoko is a Professor of Educational Leadership at the University of KwaZulu-Natal. He holds a PhD in Educational Leadership and Governance from the University of KwaZulu-Natal, and was an awardee of the Spencer Foundation Scholarship for his PhD and the DAAD Scholarship for his MA degree. Vitallis currently supervises research at both the master and PhD levels. He has graduated 11 PhDs and 35 MEds. He is co-editor of the book *Education Leadership, Management and Governance in South Africa,* published by Nova Publishers in 2011.

Vitallis is a member of the following academic and professional bodies: The Educational Management Association of South Africa; The British Educational Leadership, Management and Administration Society; and The Commonwealth Council for Educational Administration and Management. Email: Chikokov@ukzn.ac.za.

Polycarp Ikuenobe

Polycarp Ikuenobe holds a PhD in philosophy from Wayne State University, Detroit, USA. He is currently a Professor of Philosophy at Kent State University, Ohio, USA. His research and teaching interests include African philosophy; philosophy of law; social, moral, and political philosophy; informal logic; and philosophy of race. In 2016 he received the Kent State University Outstanding Research and Scholarship Award. He is the author of *Philosophical Perspectives on Communalism and Morality in African Traditions* (2006), and more than 60 refereed journal articles and book chapters. E-mail: pikuenob@kent.edu.

Wendy Isaacs-Martin

Wendy Isaacs-Martin has a Doctorate in Religion and a MA in Political Studies. She is a National Research Foundation (NRF) rated researcher at the University of South Africa (Unisa) in the Archie Mafeje Research Institute (AMRI), where she works as an Associate Professor. Her research focuses on identities – national, ethnic, social – and on the application of the scapegoating mechanism in societies. She has written extensively on identities in book chapters and accredited journals. She has appeared in the media to offer her expertise, and has penned several opinion pieces on identities in South Africa, the continent and the globe. She has supervised numerous master and doctoral theses, and assisted post-doctoral Fellows. Email: isaacw@unisa.ac.za.

Gregory Hankoni Kamwendo

Gregory Hankoni Kamwendo is Dean of the Faculty of Arts at the University of Zululand in South Africa, as well as the current Treasurer of the South African Humanities Deans Association (SAHUDA). He specialises in Sociolinguistics and Language Education, and has a special interest in language policy and language planning issues. He has recently been appointed to serve on the editorial board of *Current Issues in Language Planning*, a well-respected international peer-reviewed journal. He is also a fellow of the African Union's Academy of Languages (ACALAN). Kamwendo has published in several journals, including *Language Policy*; *Journal of Multilingual & Multicultural Development*; *International Journal of the Sociology of Language*; and *Language Problems & Language Planning*. Gregory has written over 38 peer-reviewed journal articles and over 20 book chapters, and has presented at numerous conferences. Email: KamwendoG@unizulu.ac.za or hankoni2004@yahoo.co.uk.

Mago W. Mndawe

Mago W. Mndawe is an Associate Professor in Environmental Education, specialising in Inclusive Education and Curriculum Studies in the College of Education at the University of South Africa (Unisa). Mago holds a Doctor of Environmental Education, Didactics (DEd) degree from Unisa. Currently he is Manager: Teaching Practice, at the same college and university, before which he was Head Teacher and Assistant Director of a primary school and an Environmental Education Centre respectively. His specialisation includes indigenous knowledge systems and multi-disciplinary methodologies in knowledge creation. He has published articles in these disciplines and supervised both MA and doctoral students in these fields under the name Maila Mago W. Email: mailamw1@unisa.ac.za or mndawmw1@gmail.com.

Peter Wilfred Naankiel

Peter Wilfred Naankiel holds an MA (History) from Benue State University, Makurdi, Nigeria, and a second MA (International Law and Diplomacy) from the University of Jos, Nigeria. He also holds a BA (Hons) in History from the University of Jos. He is now a PhD candidate at the Benue State University in Nigeria. He is currently a Lecturer at the Department of History and International Studies, Federal University Lafia, where he teaches African History and International Relations, amongst others. He has published in several prestigious national and international academic journals, and contributed chapters to several academic books within and outside Africa. His research focus spans social, economic, and diplomatic history. He is also interested in development and gender studies, alongside conflict and security studies. Email: naankiel@gmail.com.

Berrington Ntombela

Berrington Ntombela holds a Doctorate in English Language Studies and is a Senior Lecturer in the Department of English at the University of Zululand. He has worked in various institutions overseas as a Lecturer, Senior Lecturer and Head of Department. He has published research articles in numerous peer-reviewed journals in the field of English language teaching, and has also published chapters in books. He has presented scholarly papers at national and international conferences in South Africa, the Sultanate of Oman, Malaysia, Japan, and Australia. His research interests are sociolinguistics, discourse analysis, imperial linguistics, and literary criticism. He supervises master and doctoral theses, and also serves as an examiner.

Berrington is the current recipient of the University of Zululand's Vice Chancellor's Excellence Awards for Teaching and Learning. Berrington is the author of a book entitled *Hither and Yonder River*, published by AuthorHouse in 2014. His latest poems are published by Kalahari Review under the title *When I speak*. Email: ntombelab@unizulu.ac.za.

Mxolisi Nyezwa

Mxolisi Nyezwa holds a MA degree in Creative Writing from Rhodes University. He is currently the editor of *Kotaz Literary Journal* and the Managing Director of Imbizo Arts of South Africa. He also lectures on Rhodes University's Creative Writing Programme. In 2009, Mxolisi was the winner of the prestigious Thomas Pringle National Award for Poetry. His three volumes of poetry are widely lauded in South Africa and beyond. These include *Song Trials* (2000), published by Gecko Poetry; *New Country* (2008), published by UKZN Press; and *Malikhanye* (2008), published by Deep South. E-mail: imbizo.arts@gmail.com.

Francis Onditi

Francis Onditi is an Adjunct Assistant Professor of Peace, Conflict and War Studies at the Department of International Relations (IR), United States International University-Africa, Nairobi, Kenya. Currently he also works for the United Nations Entity for Gender Equality and the Empowerment of Women Regional Office in Nairobi on Leadership and Political Participation. Previously he was a Resident Policy Researcher with the International Peace Support Training Centre (IPSTC) and a non-resident Advisor to the Eastern African Standby Force (EASF). Francis holds a Doctor of Philosophy (DPhil) degree from Masinde Muliro University of Science and Technology, Kenya, prior to which he was educated at the University of Nairobi's Institute for Development Studies (IDS), graduating with BA and MA degrees in Geography. Francis specialises in policy analysis and social modelling in subjects related to civil-military relations, the political economy of African peace and security institutions, global politics, geopolitics, African studies and gender issues. He has published in several refereed journals and policy briefs, the most recent being, 'The Quest for a Multidimensional African Standby Force' in *The African Conflict and Peacebuilding Review*. Email: onditifrancis8@gmail.com.

Amon Saba Saakana

Amon Saba Saakana is an independent scholar and writer, and has a PhD in Drama/Cultural Studies from the University of London and a diploma in Egyptian Archaeology from The Institute of Archaeology at the University of London. He is widely anthologised in books in the USA and UK, and is the author of *Jah Music: The Evolution of the Jamaican Popular Song* (1980) and two volumes of Caribbean literary studies, *The Colonial Legacy in Caribbean Literature* (1987; 1997). His forthcoming books (2017) are *Kmt in the Italian Renaissance* (philosophy) and *Ntr Nfr Wa, The Perfect One: Groundings in the Nubio-Kmtan African Paradigm* (kemetology). Saakana has been the recipient of both the Hansib and Xpress awards for his contribution to publishing in the UK. Amon is the founder and commissioning editor of Karnak House, a publisher dedicated to excellence in African publications. Email: karnakhouse@aol.com or letters.perrekhinstitute@aol.com.

Dr Andreas Velthuizen

Dr Andreas Velthuizen is the Senior Researcher and Acting Head of the Institute for Dispute Resolution in Africa, College of Law, Unisa, where he is conducting trans-disciplinary research in endogenous knowledge management for dispute resolution, violent conflict prevention and restorative justice. In this regard he has published 13 articles in accredited journals, co-authored one book, and presented at academic conferences and workshops on every continent. His qualifications include a D Litt et Phil degree from Unisa for his dissertation entitled: *The Management of Knowledge: A Model for the African Renaissance.* His current focus is on the research and development of community sites of knowledge, specifically by means of community-engaged participatory research on the endogenous conflict and dispute resolution practices of post-conflict societies. Dries is also involved in the training of officials on the SLP Management of Democratic Elections in Africa (MDEA), as well as policy and strategy writing for public service institutions. Dries is rated as an established researcher by the National Research Foundation (NRF) in South Africa and is a Paul Harris Fellow of Rotary International.

Jacqueline Witthuhn

Jackie Witthuhn has over 25 years' experience in the public and private healthcare sectors, in which she worked at a director level for the Gauteng Health Department and managed a Health Promotion Consultancy before joining Monash South Africa (MSA) six years ago. Jackie holds a Doctorate in Education, with her doctoral thesis titled, *Internationalisation and Africanisation of the Master of Public Health curriculum in South Africa: a case study.* She is actively involved in curriculum development and transformation at MSA, where she serves as a member of the curriculum team and the curriculum transformation team. Jackie also represents the School of Health Sciences on the MSA Teaching and Learning Advisory Committee. She is a Senior Lecturer in the School of Health Sciences and lectures in the areas of health promotion, health programme planning, and evaluation and policy. She has published several peer-reviewed articles, including articles on National Health Insurance in South Africa, as part of the Oxfam Monash Team. Her latest accepted publication is in the *African Journal of Health Professions Education*: 'Factors that enable and constrain the internationalisation and Africanisation of the Master of Public Health curriculum in South African higher education institutions'. Email: Jacqueline.Witthuhn@monash.edu.

Acknowledgements

The editor would like to thank all the contributors who authored and subsequently submitted their valuable work to appear in this volume. Their contributions will help in advancing the necessary debates of our time. I would also like to thank all the reviewers of the chapters; their input has greatly enhanced this volume.

Prof Sabelo Ndlovu-Gatsheni's reading of the manuscript and his writing of the foreword also helped in the improvement of this volume. His expertise and comments enabled the editor to improve the sequence of the chapters, thus his recommendations were well received.

Finally, the editor is grateful to the publisher, Knowledge Resources, for creating and bringing to completion such a wonderful product.

Foreword: The Case for a Decolonised/Africanised Africa
Sabelo J. Ndlovu-Gatsheni

Decolonising Knowledge for Africa's Renewal is part of the re-emerging progressive literature that is signalling the importance of the decolonial turn in social sciences and humanities. The book is divided into four important parts. The first part focuses on African philosophy, African tradition and Pan-Africanism as anchors of the African Renaissance and the basis for decolonising knowledge. The second part of the book is focused on the complex subjects of identity, conflict and development. This includes such topical themes as masculinity, gender, community identity, collectivism, and the paradigm of conflict studies subjected to rigorous academic analysis, with a view to decolonise concepts and theories to enable new and decolonised knowledge for the African Renaissance to emerge. The third section covers higher education, Africanisation and the complex question of language. The last section brings to the fore the issues of ideology, youth, music, and leadership as they relate to the decolonisation of knowledge and the broader agenda of Africa's renewal, encapsulated by the philosophy of the African Renaissance. This is a book that boldly grapples with the complex change that is upon us, particularly the epistemological struggles predicated on the demands for decolonisation and Africanisation. The various essays contained in this book provoke two major questions: 'What is decolonisation?' and 'What is Africanisation?' This introduction responds to these fundamental questions as it introduces the broader terrain within which the theme of decolonising knowledge and the renewal of Africa arises.

When we agitate and fight for decolonisation today, we are no longer engaged in the politics of supporting one particular local elite to take over the state, as was the case with the anti-colonial movements of the 20th century. The decolonisation struggle of today takes into account the vastness of colonialism, i.e. the way it colonised space, time, nature, being, power, spirituality, gender, aesthetics, and knowledge. If indeed colonialism was this vast, then decolonisation must of necessity be a vast project, tracking colonialism and coloniality in all the crevices and corners where it is hiding, particularly in its institutionalised forms.

Thus even when we agitate and fight for Africanisation, we are no longer satisfied with the cosmetic changes of faces in parliament, the composition of new national anthems, the hoisting of new flags, or the changing of colonial names of countries, roads, airports and streets. While we acknowledge these forms of trying to 'move the centre' we strongly believe that the centre remains unmoved. There is thus a need to escalate our struggles beyond anti-colonial articulations into proper anti-systemic movements capable of tackling global coloniality on a world scale. This paradigmatic shift entails turning ourselves into new subjects who are capable of shifting political theory into another direction away from Eurocentrism. This shift can only be possible if we can introduce new vocabularies/concepts that are usable in unmasking invisible crimes taking place in the knowledge domain so as to produce restitutive knowledge.

The core message cascading from *Decolonising Knowledge for Africa's Renewal* is that any genuine decolonisation has to be restitutive in nature. In South Africa in particular, knowledge restitution is currently overshadowed by land restitution. This is because material dispossession/ economic extractivism is always the most visible crime of colonialism, but the reality is that land restitution cannot be separated from knowledge restitution. There are inextricable entanglements of ontological extractivism, material extractivism and epistemic extractivism as colonial/imperial technologies of subjectivation.

What unfolded in 2015 in South Africa under the banner of the Rhodes Must Fall campaign empirically revealed the entanglements of ontological, economic and epistemic extractivism as central leitmotifs of colonialism/apartheid/coloniality, in which the 'premier' University of Cape Town was implicated and complicit. What sparked the Rhodes Must Fall movement was the continued existence of the offensive statue of the British imperialist Cecil John Rhodes at the centre of the University of Cape Town. Among the justifications for keeping the statue of Rhodes at the centre of the university were that he had donated land and money to the university, as well as that the removal of the statue was tantamount to the erasure of history.

This is simply a colonial argument that is as offensive as it is insensitive; it reveals many issues that are hidden at its centre. In the first place, this narrative ignores the fact that Rhodes was involved in 'ontological extractivism' in the form of the dehumanisation and colonisation of indigenous people of their humanity, before dispossessing them of their land, mines and other materials. In the second place, there is clear 'theft of history' in the narrative of Rhodes as a donor who donated land and money to build the University of Cape Town. The fate of the San, the Khoi Khoi and the Xhosa people who experienced enslavement, genocide, dispossession, dehumanisation, and displacement is erased from history, as we are all summoned to pay homage to Rhodes as a benevolent imperialist/capitalist worth a statue at the centre of the University of Cape Town.

In short, the whole politics and agitation for the removal of the Rhodes statue spoke volumes about the complicity of the University of Cape Town in coloniality, dispossession, the dehumanisation of dispossessed black people, and the theft of history. It is therefore not surprising that what started as localised agitation for the removal of Rhodes' statue expanded into a broader student struggle for the decolonisation of the universities, curriculum change and transforming racist and patriarchal institutional cultures, as well as intense demands for free, decolonised, relevant and quality education.

The connection between ontological and epistemic extractivism are not hard to reveal. In the first place, how the 'human' is theorised from the North (Europe and North America) directly contributed to the writing of black people out of the human family in order to deny them humanity itself. The 'North' is used not to mean a simple geographical space, but a constituted power system with a specific language and a particular epistemology[1]. We can go as far back as the age of 'Cartesian conceptions' of being and the rise of scientific racism, as well as to how the majority of European philosophers and thinkers questioned the humanity of black people. If we do so we succeed in identifying the foundational dismemberment of black people from the human family[2].

What emerges clearly from this analysis is the very process of ontological extractivism involving the dispossession of the very humanity of the black people who produced such questionings: whether black people are real human beings; whether they have souls, history, civilisation, an alphabet, rationality, development, human rights, democracy and ethics. The imperial/colonial/apartheid logics of the social classification of the human species in accordance with race and their racial hierarchisation is still in existence long after the dismantlement of direct/juridical colonialisms[3].

What sustained the colonial/imperial denial of humanity went hand in glove with a denial of history as a major lever of dehumanisation and a core foundation of the colonial model of the world. What decolonisation is targeting today are epistemicides committed by colonialism. (Epistemicides speak to the process of the killing and appropriations of other knowledges, and are accompanied by linguicides (the killing of languages of the colonised)). Ngugi wa Thiong'o, in his book entitled *Something Torn and New: An African Renaissance*[4], articulated very well the logic of epistemicides and their methodology: "Get a few natives, empty their hard disk of previous memory, and download into them a software of European memory."

The church, school and university continue to play leading roles in the commission of epistemicides. The forced conversion of African people to Christianity, for instance, is an important form of commission of epistemicides. Once a people have been subjected to genocides, epistemicides and linguicides they develop a confused sense of self, a crisis of consciousness, and a crisis of identity[5]. The long-term consequences manifest themselves in terms of what is known as 'alienation'. As a concept, alienation speaks to a deliberate separation of the mind from the body; Africans from their history, culture, languages, religion, land and everything else, plunging them into limbo. This crisis, which is engulfing Africans today, is well articulated by Ngugi wa Thiong'o in his *Decolonizing the Mind*[6]. To Ngugi wa Thiong'o, what colonialism does is detonate a 'cultural bomb' on the African mental universe in its endeavour to cause alienation:

> The effect of the cultural bomb is to annihilate a people's belief in their names, in their languages, in their environment, in their heritage of struggle, in their unity, in their capacities and ultimately in themselves. It makes them see their past as one wasteland of non-achievement and it makes them want to distance themselves from that wasteland. It makes them want to identity with that which is furthest removed from themselves; for instance with other peoples' languages rather than their own. It makes them identify with that which is decadent and reactionary, all those forces which would stop their own springs of life. It even plants serious doubts about the moral rightness of the struggle. Possibilities of triumph or victory are seen as remote, ridiculous dreams. The intended results are despair, despondency and a collective death-wish[7].

Ngugi wa Thiong'o, in *Globalectics: Theory and the Politics of Knowledge*[8], spoke of alienation in terms of the dislocation of the African mind "from the place he or she already knows to a foreign starting point even with the body still remaining in his or her home-land. It is a process of continuous alienation from the base, a continuous process of looking at oneself from the outside of self or with the lenses of a stranger. One may end up identifying with the foreign base as the starting point toward self, that is from another self toward one self, rather than the local being the starting point, from self to other selves". The long term consequences are summed up by Ngugi wa Thiong'o in *Moving the Centre: The Struggle for Cultural Freedom*[9], as the "present conditions of a continent's disbelief in itself". The African Renaissance, as part of the broader decolonisation initiatives, is meant to bring confidence and restore African genius.

Where is the university in all this? How can the university as an institution play a leading part in restitutive initiatives? While the university has played a leading role in producing the "present conditions of a continent's disbelief in itself", the Rhodes Must Fall movement has fully exposed the complicity of the university in epistemicides and alienation, and challenged it to repent and begin to play a restitutive part. For the university to do so there is need to change the very idea of a 'university in Africa' into an 'African university.' This fundamentally means firstly changing the very identity and long-standing practices of the university from that of an alien (offshore) institution to an African institution, grounded in the realities of its location and being sensitive to the African people's plight and demands.

What the Rhodes Must Fall movement reignited in 2015 is a long-standing struggle that began with the agitations of such Africans as Edward Wilmot Blyden in the 19th century, which was carried over by nationalists such as Kwame Nkrumah and such organisations as the Association of African Universities in the 20th century. Why the struggle continues today to pre-occupy such movements as Rhodes Must Fall and #FeesMustFall is because the anti-colonial initiatives of the 1960s and 1970s did not grapple with the very epistemological foundation of higher education[10]. What is needed is not a reformation of higher education but a revolution. For example, adding writings of African scholars into the existing curriculum amounts to accommodating African thought into that which it sets out to subvert.

African thought has to be at the centre of the university. Africa as a legitimate epistemic site from which to see and experience the world has to be the hallmark of the university. Ngugi wa Thiong'o, in his latest book entitled *Secure the Base: Making Africa Visible in the Globe*[11], noted that: "We cannot afford to be intellectual outsiders in our own land. We must reconnect with the buried alluvium of African memory—that must become the base for planting African memory anew in the continent and the world."

What we must consciously do, according to Ngugi wa Thiong'o[12], is to return to our people as our base. He elaborated that: "A return to the base, the people, must mean at the very least the use of a language and languages that the people speak. Any further linguistic additions should be for strengthening, deepening and widening this power of the languages spoken by the people."

We have to take various practical steps if we are to decolonise knowledge and ultimately achieve an African Renaissance. Yes, we have to return to the base, and this means practically taking the African archive as the starting point in our work of changing the idea of the university. In the Ngugian sense that return must fundamentally entail thinking from where we are—from Africa specifically and the global South in general. The second step is to seriously shift the geography and biography of knowledge as flagged by the Caribbean Philosophical Association (CPA), whose motto is "Shifting the geography of knowledge". This is important because what today masquerades as the 'global knowledge economy' has a specific hegemonic centre from which it circulates—that centre is Europe and North America. Our actions and praxis has to involve a consistent process of 'moving the centre'.

It must be clear to all academics that the knowledge that took us to the current phase of crisis can never be the same knowledge that pulls us out of this crisis and takes us into the future. This means practically that we have to vigorously shift not only the 'geo' of knowledge, but also the 'bio' of knowledge. Biography of knowledge speaks to the identity and consciousness of the producer of knowledge[13]. In a practical sense, we have to change the giants on whose shoulders we stand. Most of the current giants on whose shoulders we stand are long-dead white men, including some overtly racist ones like Georg W. Hegel. If for this long, we have been standing on the shoulders of dead white males, then this means that our shifting of the geography and biography of knowledge has to involve de-patriachisation and deracialisation.

In the wise words of Cathrine Odora Hoppers and Howard Richards, in their slim but important book entitled *Rethinking Thinking: Modernity's 'Other' and the Transformation of the University*[14], we have to seriously 'rethink thinking' itself. Without a deliberate effort to rethink thinking, and even unthink some inherited ideas, we cannot begin to change the idea of the university so that it ceases to serve as a site of epistemicides and linguicides. Our work in rethinking thinking must begin with accepting the limits and problems of the current knowledge, as well as the forms of power and subjectivity it sustains. Hoppers and Richards[15] defined rethinking thinking in this enlightening way:

> The casting of light at last onto subjugated peoples, knowledges, histories and ways of living unsettles the toxic pond and transforms passive analysis into a generative force that valorises and recreates life for those previously museumised. […]. It is a process of engaging with colonialism in a manner that produces a programme for its dislocation. This dislocation is made possible not only by permitting subalterns direct space for engaging with structures and manifestations of colonialism, but also by inserting into the discourse arena different meanings and registers from other traditions.

This is very important because those of us who are working at the university are currently under strong pressure to respond positively to the definitive demands and enter into the academy those descendants of the racialised, enslaved and colonised peoples who are today loudly proclaiming that they are human beings born into valid and legitimate knowledge systems which they cannot find at the university. They also proclaim loudly that they are human beings whose education is worth investing in.

We need also to borrow a leaf from the indigenous people of Latin America and the Caribbean, as well as the feminist movement's important philosophy and pedagogy of "learning to unlearn in order to re-learn"[16]. This is very important because universities are inhabited by a majority of academics and their students, as well as academic leaders, who have imbibed and naturalised Eurocentric epistemology, resulting in them manifesting slave and colonial mentalities. It is my sincere hope that through the process of learning to unlearn in order to re-learn, some of those stuck in Eurocentrism will break out of epistemic deafness/a refusal to change epistemologically so as to play a meaningful role in the change that is thrust upon us. At the centre of the process of 'learning to unlearn in order to re-learn' is the process of inextricable linking of 'being', 'existence' and 'doing', so as to produce knowledge that is contextually relevant[17]. There is also an emphasis on a community learning from the accumulated knowledge and wisdom found in society, not just in the academy. Shifting from the Cartesian subject-object relations to the subject-subject model is part of the process of learning to unlearn in order to re-learn[18]. Fundamentally, through learning to unlearn in order to re-learn, we are basically searching for relevance. In conclusion, the decolonial change that is thrust upon us is a struggle for re-humanisation, restoring dignity and re-building institutions that recognise the humanity of all of us.

References

[1]Ndlovu-Gatsheni, S. J. 2013a. *Empire, Global Coloniality and African Subjectivity*. New York and Oxford: Berghahn Books.
[2]Ndlovu-Gatsheni, S. J. 2013b. *Coloniality of Power in Postcolonial Africa: Myths of Decolonization*. Dakar: CODESRIA Book Series.
[3]Ibid.
[4]Ngugi wa Thiong'o. 2009. *Something Torn and New: An African Renaissance*. New York: Basic Civitas Books.
[5]Ndlovu-Gatsheni, S. J. & Zondi, S. 2016. *Decolonizing the University, Knowledge Systems and Disciplines*. Durham, NC: Carolina Academic Press.
[6]Ngugi wa Thiong'o. 1986. *Decolonizing the Mind: The Politics of Language in African Literature*. Oxford: James Currey.
[7]Ibid.
[8]Ngugi wa Thiong'o. 2012. *Globalectics: Theory and the Politics of Knowing*. New York: Columbia University Press.
[9]Ngugi wa Thiong'o. 1993. *Moving the Centre: The Struggle for Cultural Freedoms*. Oxford: James Currey.
[10]Ndlovu-Gatsheni, S. J. & Zondi, S. 2016. *Decolonizing the University, Knowledge Systems and Disciplines*. Durham, NC: Carolina Academic Press.
[11]Ngugi wa Thiong'o. 2016. *Secure the Base: Making Africa Visible in the Globe*. London, New York and Calcutta: Seagull Books.
[12]Ibid.
[13]Ndlovu-Gatsheni, S. J. 2013a. *Empire, Global Coloniality and African Subjectivity*. New York and Oxford: Berghahn Books.
[14]Hoppers, C. O. & Richards, H. 2012. *Rethinking Thinking: Modernity's 'Other' and the Transformation of the University*. Pretoria: UNISA Press.
[15]Ibid.
[16]Tlostanova, M. V. & Mignolo, W. D. 2012. *Learning to Unlearn: Decolonial Reflections from Eurasia and the Americas*. Columbus: The Ohio State University Press.
[17]Ibid.
[18]Ibid.

Editor's Preface

Vuyisile T. Msila

The calls for the decolonisation of knowledge in Africa and the diaspora have been appeals that demonstrate why Africa needs to take her rightful place as she demotes the colonisers' culture and domination. During 2015 and 2016, South African higher education students stood up to power to demand not only a free education, but also a decolonised, African-focused system. The demands for decolonisation of knowledge are the ultimate call for freedom. Without the decolonisation of knowledge, Africans may feel their liberation is inchoate and their efforts to shed Western dominance all come to naught. The debates for an African Renaissance and decolonisation have been intensifying over the past decade. Ngugi Wa Thiong'o, Zeke Mphahlele, Mbulelo Mzamane, Thandike Mkandawire, Catherine Odora-Hoppers and Bantu Biko are some of the Africans who have written about the need to decolonise knowledge. The call for decolonisation is largely being equated with the search for an African identity that looks critically at Western hegemony. During the time of colonisation, the coloniser disrobed the African of indigenous values, heritage and way of life. As the African was recovering from the shock of denudation, she was bestowed a new colonial identity under a new foreign garb. The African was made to believe that this was a way of life that was opposed to the barbarity of her forebears; she was given a life that was more modern and more agreeable – to the West! The process of colonisation made a son to rebel against a father, a daughter to disown her mother's people's ways. It made chiefs sell their own people, but the more the colonised tried to wear the borrowed robes, the more they found themselves in a state of nothingness. Over the years, the African has realised the indelible mark left by colonisation, hence now she realises the need to reverse this through the decolonisation process.

The influences of colonialism have complicated the life of the African, as they have determined the various aspects of his life. Kwasi Wiredu[1] opines that decolonisation should begin here, as Africans divest "African philosophical thinking of all undue influences emanating from our colonial past". Wiredu[2] also highlights foreign/colonial language as one aspect that has philosophical relevance. He points out, "the African who has learned philosophy in English, for example, has most likely become conceptually Westernised to a large extent not by choice but by the force of historical circumstances. To that same extent he may have become de-Africanized. It does not matter if the philosophy learned was African philosophy". Language carries with it culture, identity and in this case colonising nuances that reflect myths and colonial misconceptions. Decolonisation is about battling it out to dispel myths and shed colonial fallacies. Chinweizu[3] explicates this well when he states that decolonisation does not mean ignorance of foreign traditions, "it simply means denial of their authority and withdrawal of allegiance from them". In addition, Frantz Fanon[4] maintains that for decolonisation to be attained we need a controlled violence, which will help Africans to achieve a desired national identity in a post-colonial state. Any African Renaissance will need this decolonisation process.

Apart from being a means to gaining an African Renaissance, decolonisation creates a path towards redeeming Africans from colonial anguish and from physical and mental bondage. Bantu

Biko[5] argued lucidly that Western culture changed the Africans' outlook as they were deemed unable to run their affairs:

> We were required to fit in as people tolerated with great restraint in a western type society. We were tolerated simply because our cheap labour is needed. Hence we are judged in terms of standards we are not responsible for. Whenever colonisation sets in with its dominant culture it devours the native culture and leaves behind a bastardised culture that can only thrive as the rate and pace allowed by the dominant culture. This is what happened to African culture.

Biko sought the black people to understand their origins; to understand black history and affirm black identity[6]. These are all embedded in the struggle to decolonise and search for African values and identities. The project of Eurocentrism has destroyed many of the above values, as Africans tended to embrace Western ways or modernity as the only absolute truth. There is no way that Africans can move forward in the present without decolonising their ways of viewing their world. Pan-Africanism, Black Consciousness and the African Renaissance strive for the return of an empowered African.

The former South African president, Thabo Mbeki, pointed out that the African Renaissance is the hope of a decolonised Africa[7]. Decolonisation gives Africa a face, vision and hope. Without this vision, Africans will not attain true freedom from the shackles of Eurocentrism. Africa and the diaspora have never before been under this pressure to look at how the motherland can utilise the continent's solutions to Africa's challenges. The African Renaissance has begun; its destination will be determined by the tempo of the decolonisation process. .

Ndlovu-Gatsheni[8] argues for a need to move towards African futures as Africans embrace decolonisation. Furthermore, he declared a need to release the African genius by intensifying the processes of decolonisation. He contended that:

> The spirit and language of liberation informing socialisation of modern global power should be uncompromisingly anti-Eurocentrism, anti-subject-object paradigm, anti-imperial, anti-colonial, anti-racist, anti-patriarchal, and anti-fundamentalism and anti-hegemonic. Only after this genuinely decolonial struggle has been won can African people be able to create African futures within a pluriversal future in which diverse but common futures are possible.

Ndlovu-Gatsheni argues that coloniality has a negative and disempowering effect on the endeavours of Africans creating their African futures[9]. Africans need a sense of empowerment and identity if they are to shirk oppression, which along with loss of dignity, language, and culture are the strong pillars of colonialism. Under coloniality the victims lose their voices and continue to embrace a consciousness that reminds them of their inferiority. The struggle to decolonise is an endeavour to obliterate this victimhood; it is a struggle to create a memory monument of the battles for justice waged by African heroes. South Africa and many other African states seek to attain nation-building based on fairness, justice and peace, yet this will be futile if the ghost of colonisation still looms large. It is also a decolonisation movement that will ensure the formerly colonised becomes equanimous as they disown victimhood and assume a rightful place as Africa seeks to attain her renewal.

The concept 'decolonisation' conjures not only a picture of Africa's renewal but Pan-Africanism as well; decolonisation helps us unpack the ideals of Pan-Africanism. Pan-Africanism was a vision that African intellectuals such as Kwame Nkrumah, Patrice Lumumba and Julius Nyerere envisaged as an ultimate destination after the decolonisation of Africa. On the African continent and in the diaspora, Pan-Africanism became a philosophy that paved a way towards Africa's renewal, as espoused by Amilcar Cabral, Cheik Anta Diop and several other African intellectuals. Pan-Africanism is critical in achieving a decolonial state of mind and the African Renaissance. Van Grassdoff[10] argues that:

A renewed version of Pan-Africanism should therefore be regarded as the second pillar of the African Renaissance at the centre of which should be the quest for a Pax Africana, African unity and the forging of African solidarity. It is a call for a 'deep renaissance' which does not build on oppressive structures of the European colonial legacy but rather re-constructs, transforms and actively re-builds Africa according to African priorities and values which, beyond economic and political liberation, implies intellectual and mental independence.

Pan-Africanism preaches solidarity amongst those of African descent because there is a belief that they share common interests as they share ancestry. Many argue that true Pan-Africanists constantly search for a decolonised Africa; they lead the revolution for an anti-colonial, liberated Africa. Horace Campbell[11] pointed out that Pan-African movements will face a number of challenges for the next hundred years, mentioning three aspects that will be critical, i.e. firstly, to make an impact on the African people in transforming the national consciousness; secondly, to make an impact on world opinion "with respect to Africans at home and abroad"; and thirdly, to realise the spirit of dignity for the renewal of human spirit. Additionally, for Campbell:

Pan-African liberation is not only linked to the quest for a new social system, but also one in which the development of the productive forces is not simply linked to the production of goods but also the creation of new human beings. This perspective of the transformation of gender relations, free men, women and children, of cultural freedom, of harnessing the positive knowledge of the African past now forms part of the conception of the struggle for Pan-African liberation in the twenty first century[12].

The essays in this book explore perspectives that create theories on social reality. The contributors address several connected themes that define what Africa and the diaspora require for a society devoid of colonialism that is ready for a renewed Africa. The discussions we develop and the philosophies we adopt on Pan-Africanism and decolonisation are due to a bigger vision, and for many of us the destination is an African Renaissance. An African Renaissance is a huge project that will need Africans to meet and converse constantly. They need to meet in *imbizos* across the continent to discuss the reclaiming of the continent. These meetings need to include many role-players, which the various viewpoints in this book reflect. As Okumu[13] argues, everyone has a role to play in realising the African Renaissance, including government, churches, universities, schools and cultural organisations. The success of African people will be evident in decades to come with the realisation of this renewal. To this end, it is appropriate to cite Okumu, who answered the question of how well can we measure the impact of an African Renaissance:

...it would be wrong to measure the success or failure of an African Renaissance purely in terms of economic growth... The success of an African Renaissance will also be shown by the quality of life of the African people, in terms of greater community and opportunity, improved access to healthcare and education, and a flowering of the literary, visual, and performing arts[14].

The authors in this volume try to demonstrate how we can improve this quality of life of African people by digging deep and utilising the African philosophy. Africans owe this betterment to themselves, for they cannot wait to be liberated but need to seize freedom. They need to set the agenda of an African Renaissance they want and the Pan-Africanist vision they seek to follow. In his book, *The White Man's Burden*, William Easterly[15] shows the paradox of the West's help for Africa, in that the West's endeavours to help the continent have done more harm than good. The chapters in this volume mainly look at this quandary, i.e. how do Africa and her people help themselves as they explore alternative philosophies to enhance the quality of life of all Africans?

The book's chapters are as follows:

In Chapter 1, Ikuenobe sets the tone for the book by elucidating the basic arguments that explore the question of what tradition is and what Western modernity is. The author argues that there is much good that Africa can learn from African tradition, which he refers to as the basis of the African Renaissance. Various arguments in the book explore this; different contributors in this volume dig deep to glean from African philosophy that which acknowledges the invaluable nature of African tradition. Ikuenobe raises the point that there was much rationality in traditional societies and elders were thinkers and reflective intellectuals. In search of an African Renaissance, Ikuenobe argues, we can no longer deny the African epistemological traditions.

Msila in Chapter 2 continues where Ikuenobe leaves off, examining the dichotomy between the dark Africa of Joseph Conrad in *Heart of Darkness* and "Western civilisation", revealing why Africa should and will experience the African Renaissance. African philosophy has been referred to as ethnophilosophy to disparage the indigenous knowledge systems. Like Ikuenobe, Msila argues that African philosophy provides an opportunity for the emancipation of Africans. Although Nyerere's *Ujaama* might not have been flawless, philosophers like him demonstrated that African thought can be used as a basis for carving a society's identity and a foundation for an African Renaissance.

In Chapter 3 Ayokhai and Naankiel critically appraise Nnandi Azikiwe and Obafemi Awolowo's philosophies. The authors show how the two political thinkers interconnected although they were different. The authors also demonstrate that Azikiwe and Awolowo's thoughts both sought to address Pan-Africanism. The two political thinkers' differences were mainly due to personal ambitions; as a result of their respective ambitions they resorted to the utilisation of aspects such as ethnicity and religion to realise their goals. Furthermore, the authors also show that the duo was largely biased towards the conservative, pro-Western ideology of capitalism and imperialism. They contend that Azikiwe and Awolowo contributed to Nigeria's failure. The authors also explore how the two failed, thus leaving Nigeria in a state of decadence. Finally, the authors show how the two betrayed the ideals of Pan-Africanism and the African Renaissance.

In Chapter 4, Isaacs-Martin investigates the Pan-African identity and how its essence is challenged in the face of armed conflict. The chapter seeks answers to the questions of how and why identities are undermined within the nation-states, which makes the concept of a Pan-African identity an impossibility. Isaacs-Martin explains that Africa is afflicted by a number of challenges that include poor governance and a lack of social trust. These lead to a complex state in which it may not be realistic to create a supranational identity. Despite these challenges, the concept of Pan-African identity remains a symbol that acts as an opposition to colonial ills.

Velthuizen in Chapter 5 focuses on research paradigms that can be applied to conflict studies in African contexts. Velthuizen approaches this discussion from the perspective of phenomenology as a philosophy; a transdisciplinary approach to research and a research methodology that is participatory and engaged. The author searches for new research paradigms that facilitate the study of conflict, people security and peace making in Africa. Velthuizen also argues that new ways of researching peace and security should reveal new horizons beyond racial and physical boundaries set by divisionary thinking brought to Africa by Western colonialism. Finally, the author proposes a new focus on African conflict studies that includes the study of poetics to challenge historic dominant discourses and pose an alternative to these discourses. Velthuizen uses his research experience with the San people of South Africa, a subject of his research for three years, to inform these arguments.

Onditi and Bah in Chapter 6 focus on masculinity in the fragile society of a post-colonial Congo. The authors employ the theory of multiple hegemonic masculinities, which reflect a society's ideal of how male behaviour should be. The chapter shows how society shaped by social-cultural structures informed by colonialism affects masculinity. The authors maintain that an African Renaissance should reflect a need to empower African people regardless of gender and ethnic affiliation. They also point out that the link between positive masculinity and African Renaissance is weak because "positive masculinity" does not espouse a renewal of African values that promises to transform the African society positively.

In Chapter 7, Msila looks at how the rural women's role is defined and redefined when they get to the city seeking a better life. Despite the socialisation in a society dominated by men, this chapter looks at how some women try to fight dependence on males when they get to the cities from rural areas. It is not easy because obstacles abound, but it is women who will be able to withstand the society dominated by male stereotypical views. In this chapter there is also an exploration of African feminism, which explores how this can help women to be empowered to stand on their own in a discriminating society.

Saakana traces the story, *Contending of Hor and Setekh*, based in KMT 3150-3200BCE in Chapter 8. The term 'Kemet' (spelt KMT) is said to mean the land of the black people. The ancient Egyptians are believed to have used this as their original name in reference to their country. The post-colonial societies of modern Africa have shown a penchant for a predatory appropriation of personal and family enrichment at the expense of the population. In this paradigm one labels the manifestation as a colonial inheritance, but Africa's long history has within it some excellent examples of how state control inevitably illustrates the benefits of trade, power and conquest. In this essay, we look at the mythological canonisation of the first royal family of KMT consisting of four siblings: Wsir (Osiris), Setekh (Seth), Isata (Isis) and Huthor (Hathor), within whom the state has pitted Osiris, the eldest son who inherited the throne from a mythical father (Geb, the earth) and mother (Nut, the sky), against his represented greedy, oppositional, and recalcitrant brother Setekh, who murdered him. The state has so portrayed a national conflict over the rights to rule by two factions: Setekh representing the established mediating power of trade nearly one thousand years before the incursion of Wosir, who defeats the indigenes, replacing them but rationalising their bloody victory by first dividing the land in two (as it was before), then by incorporation, and ultimately rejection and separation. For an African Renaissance, long heralded under the reign of Amenhotep 1 (2050 BCE) as *Wehemu Mesu* (repetition of the birth = Renaissance) to take place we must first *sankofa*, or return to the source of our beginnings and examine our histories microscopically in order to programmatically move forward with clarity and understanding.

The author points out that this moral drama has implications for the political arena found in Africa today. The story "remains a timeless code of moral conduct lesson for modern African leaders and those in distant, formerly enslaved and colonised lands".

Kamwendo in Chapter 9 focuses on a critical aspect of student activism as they confront the language policy in Malawian higher education institutions. The chapter traces how the Malawian higher education students fought the Education Act of 2012, which stipulated that English would be a medium of instruction. The students also fought for the right to use the indigenous Chichewa in higher education. The arguments here are similar to those in the following chapter by Ntombela. Kamwendo talks about what is referred to as a voice from below, arguing that the students' activism fits in well with the African Renaissance agenda. He further argues that the students are prepared to contribute to the liberation of society from linguistic imperialism. The arguments in this chapter illustrate that the time has come for indigenous languages in Africa to surface and challenge the dominance of English in institutions of higher learning.

In Chapter 10, Ntombela continues the language debates raised by Kamwendo in the previous chapter. While Kamwendo's arguments are based on a Malawian case study, Ntombela uses South Africa as a focal point for his debate. Ntombela portrays the picture of the multilingual reality in South Africa, tackling a crucial topic in African Renaissance – indigenous languages and their usage in African societies. He argues that although post-apartheid South Africa has 11 official languages, the nine indigenous languages still struggle to be recognised because official documents continue to exclusively use English and Afrikaans. The African philosophy will continue to struggle as long as the marginalisation of indigenous languages pervades. Ntombela argues for the end of the stigmatisation of African languages - a culture that was also supported by the system of apartheid education. He shows that the rise of the English language has been very detrimental to the development of indigenous languages. This author also adds that real decolonisation will begin with the embracing of indigenous languages.

Witthuhn in Chapter 11 explores two crucial concepts in the area of African philosophy and higher education; internalisation and Africanisation. The author shows why Africa needs to examine these terms in an age rampant with calls for an African Renaissance and relevant institutions of higher learning. Using the two concepts simultaneously, Witthuhn shows that Africanisation does not mean excluding experiences from outside Africa in education. She states that Africa can benefit from good experiences from outside her shores. With Africa receiving more international students every year, there is much need to accommodate internalisation. Witthuhn then applies this theory into why the programme Master of Public Health needs to be Africanised and decolonised.

In Chapter 12, Mndawe argues for the need to Africanise education. The author maintains that an Africanised curriculum that looks at the African contexts will be able to address the inadequacies of Eurocentric curricula. Furthermore, Mndawe directly joins the topical debates on the Africanisation and decolonisation of current education, and looks at what Africa has missed from not having African philosophy in its curricula. He further describes the need for indigenous knowledge systems to be a starting point as Africans shape the curriculum. Africanised curricula will also be able to address the issues of relevance that learners need. When education is relevant it enables the role players to pragmatically apply the curriculum in their everyday life. The Africanisation of education also supports the economic and political advancement of Africans. Mndawe adds that Africanisation will be enhanced by other cultures whilst using the African vision as a beacon.

In the 13th chapter, Msila explores Black Consciousness and youth as a means to embrace a new philosophy of decolonisation and black renaissance. The youth in South Africa, for example, have shown that they want to be involved in transforming their society. The call for #FeesMustFall at higher education institutions in 2016 was also a call for decolonising education and bringing African philosophy into higher education. The chapter argues that the African Renaissance needs emancipated youth; the author shows that black people need to shed victimhood as they employ Black Consciousness tenets to confront their challenges and grab social transformation, which will lead to the much needed renaissance.

Nyezwa, in the penultimate chapter, analyses maskanda music and the ways in which it emanates from African philosophy and black cultures. Nyezwa displays the various elements of how this genre supports protest culture – the maskanda artists sing about social problems, besides love and other life aspects. This chapter explores the crucial role of the arts in African philosophy. The chapter also uses arguments that show the need to replace Eurocentric art, as black art is used to explore various aspects of society. The maskandi artists use indigenous languages when they sing; the indigenous languages used support the tenets of African philosophy, which propounds that the use of indigenous languages must take centre stage as Africans attempt to define their identities and culture.

The final chapter focuses on the critical aspects of African leadership. From this chapter we learn that the African Renaissance and all that is discussed in this volume can come to naught without intentional leadership. Chikoko presents himself as an Afro-pessimist, who believes that although Africa may be experiencing a myriad of problems, she will rise with intent, conscientious leadership in her institutions. Chikoko acknowledges many effective practices that can be replicated in our life today, and underscores these qualities, emphasising hard work and wisdom. What makes this chapter more useful is that the author uses much empirical evidence from his study of SADC countries, including Zimbabwe and Zambia. The qualities still found in traditional societies and the intellectuals in villages demonstrate hope for the future.

References

[1]Wiredu, K. 1998. Toward decolonising African philosophy and religion. *African Studies Quarterly*, 1(4): 17.
[2]Ibid.
[3]Chinweizu. 1987. *Decolonising the African Mind*. Lagos: Pero Press.
[4]Fanon, F. 1963. *The wretched of the earth*. (Translation by Constance Farrington.) New York: Grove Press.
[5]Biko, S. 1987. *I write what I like*. London: Heinemann.
[6]Ibid.
[7]Mbeki, T. 1998. *Africa – the time has come*. Cape Town: Tafelberg.
8Ndlovu-Gatsheni, S. 2015. *Global coloniality and the challenge of creating African futures*. A Paper presented at CODESRIA 14. Dakar, Senegal. 08-12 June 2015.
[9]Ibid.
[10]Van Grassdoff, E. 2005. *African Renaissance and discourse ownership in the Information Age: The Internet as a factor of domination and liberation*. Berlin: Lit Verlag.
[11]Campbell, H. 1996. Pan-African renewal in the 21st century. *African Journal of Political Science New Series*, 1(1): 84-98.
[12]Ibid.
[13]Okumu, W. A. J. 2002. *The African Renaissance: History, Significance and Strategy*. Trenton: Africa World Press.
[14]Ibid.
[15]Easterly, W. 2006. *The White Man's Burden*. London: Penguin.

PART 1

PHILOSOPHY, RENAISSANCE AND PAN-AFRICANISM

Chapter 1

Tradition and a Foundation for African Renaissance

Polycarp Ikuenobe
Department of Philosophy, Kent State University

1.1   Introduction

Many aspects of African cultural 'unscientific' traditions have been criticised as the causes of Africa's backwardness and lack of civilisation or development. (Wiredu[1]; Bodunrin[2]; Hountondji[3]). A lack of development has also sometimes been attributed to African people's irrational mentality and uncritical attitudes, partly because of their acceptance of dogmatic cultural traditions and beliefs (Wiredu[4]; Bodunrin[5]; Oruka[6]). This has led to a clarion call for Africa's renaissance to civilise, develop, and adopt Western modern ways of life and thinking, which include liberal democracy, individualism, capitalism, and technological and scientific methods (Wiredu[7]; Appiah[8]; Bodunrin[9]; Hountondji[10]). Western modernity is assumed to be inherently honorific, and is considered an imperative and normative standard for judging the quality of a society or people. Some argue that the only way for Africans to develop is to make a clean break, and do away completely with its backward traditions (Appiah[11]; Wiredu[12]; Bodunrin[13]). These include its values, thoughts, and ways of life, such as communalism, authority of elders, oral tradition, and the metaphysical beliefs in witches or spiritual entities, which are characterised as superstitions.

To this end, African philosophers have been asked to provide an autochthonous African rational philosophical basis for its renaissance. I argue that a legitimate African philosophy that could provide the intellectual and rational basis for an African Renaissance must involve a synthesis of the positives of Western modernity and African tradition; it cannot involve a clean break with traditions. I argue that the characterisation of Western modernity as a normative basis for evaluating African tradition illicitly assumes the inherent honorific nature of modernity, as well as the inherent pejorative nature of tradition. This assumption begs the question as to whether Western modernity is necessarily good and African tradition is necessarily bad. I argue that modernity is not necessarily good, and tradition is not necessarily bad. Those who assume this inherent honorific view of modernity engage in a kind of reductionism, which reduces modernity illicitly, simply and solely to the positive elements of its epistemological dimension, scientific method, and technology, to the exclusion of its negative elements.

1.2   Criticisms of African Traditions

Many philosophers have criticised traditional African beliefs and modes of thinking by calling for the modernisation of their thoughts in terms of a legitimate African philosophy. They argue that these thought systems, which they have derogatorily called *ethnophilosophy,* cannot provide a basis for an authentic African philosophy that could anchor an African Renaissance. This is because these beliefs and thoughts are dogmatic, unscientific, authoritarian, and lacking in analytical rigour (Bodunrin[14]; Hountondji[15]). However, some African philosophers have argued that Africa can articulate a philosophy for its renaissance by relying *solely* on the positive aspects of African traditions[16]. Critics have suggested that this approach is not feasible because African traditions are either too remote to retrieve and rely on, or that they have been destroyed by colonialism[17]. Others have suggested that African traditions are too negative or irrational to have anything positive to offer for Africa's renaissance[18].

These views have engendered a number of issues. The first is whether there is a legitimate African philosophical thought system. The second is whether an African philosophical thought could include, or be based on, African traditional ideas and thoughts. The more pertinent issue, however, is whether such traditions can engender development or renaissance in Africa. In other words, is it possible for Africa to develop in a way that suits its situation or solves its problems without relying on some positive elements of its cultural traditions? The idea of transitioning from 'tradition' to 'modernity' presupposes a distinction between 'modernity' and 'tradition'. Is there such a distinction? What is the basis? What is modernity? What are the features that characterise modern philosophy, modernity, its modes of thinking, and ways of life?

Modernity is usually characterised as a set of ideas, beliefs, and modes of thought that employ scientific, logical, rational, rigorous, written, critical, and analytic methods. These ideas determine certain ways of life that indicate modernisation. 'Modernity' is also used to describe a period in the history of Western thought systems that began in the 17th century, and the set of principles, methodologies, schools of thought, and ways of life that represent this period. 'Modernisation' involves adopting these ideas for social, political, and economic development, and modernity is now generally considered the paradigm ways of living, thinking, and doing things. Modernisation is used as an imperative that calls on Africa to transform its tradition, and move away from it for Africa's development.

Wiredu[19] expressed this imperative for Africans as follows: "what you do is to *modernise*". For him, modernisation involves the infusion of scientific method into the dogmatic, irrational, authoritarian, and anachronistic traditional African thought systems. Thus, Wiredu[20] argued, "The habits of exactness and rigour in thinking, the pursuit of systematic coherence and the experimental approach so characteristic of science are attributes of mind which we in Africa urgently need to cultivate not just because they are in themselves intellectual virtues but also because they are necessary conditions for modernization". This suggests that the epistemic features of modernity, seen as intellectual virtues, are inherently good. He underscored this point by arguing that "logical, mathematical, analytical, experimental procedures are essential in the quest for the knowledge of, and control over, nature ..."[21]. Bodunrin[22] made a similar point by arguing that Africa needs the scientific and epistemological domain of modernity in order to develop. He noted that, "Whether we like it or not we will have science and technology. We have to acquire the thought habits needed to cope with life in a technological age". Usually, the honorific nature and necessity of science and technology are assumed without critical examination.

This is the sense in which, according to Gyekye[23], the notion of modernity has gained a normative status, "in that all societies in the world without exception aspire to become modern, to exhibit in their social, cultural, and political lives features said to characterise modernity". The apparent implication is that Africa can develop only by adopting the epistemological features of modernity. This imperative view of modernisation (as contrasted with tradition) implies that: (1) modernity is inherently good, it is not subject to critical examination, and it has no negatives; and (2) tradition is inherently bad and irrational, it has no positives, it has nothing to offer for Africa's development, and it is something that Africans must do away with completely. Thus, some philosophers criticise traditional African thought systems, simply and solely because they are seen–whether rightly or wrongly–as failing to meet the standards of rationality inherent in modernity (Wiredu[24]; Bodunrin[25]; Appiah[26]). It is assumed that only Western modernity is rational; this reflects the 'exclusivism' and parochialism of modernity and Western philosophy.

Based on this characterisation of tradition, critics have argued that Africans do not have a philosophy or thought system. This is because what is usually identified as the methods and subject matter of African philosophy are traditional thoughts, which are non-scientific, dogmatic, oral, irrational, mythical, non-analytic, and accommodative. The view is that any idea, belief, or thought is considered a philosophy only if it involves the conceptual, critical and rigorous analysis of principles, ideas, concepts, and problems. These critics argue that a scientific method, which is the rational basis for a legitimate thought system, philosophy, knowledge, or inquiry, is completely lacking in African traditions. Many of these critics ignore the historical facts that there were sophisticated civilisations and epistemological systems that existed before European modernity. As Harding[27] argued, Europe borrowed ideas and methods from other civilisations, including what are now called African traditions, via various European voyages of discovery.

Critics have also argued that African thought systems, ideas, and beliefs are meaningful, true or justifiable only for Africans; they are descriptive of specific cultures, and as such, they are culturally relative. It is also along this line of criticism that Appiah[28; 29] distinguished, on the one hand, between formal, rational, universal thought in terms of which modernity and modern philosophies are usually couched, and on the other, African traditional folk philosophy or cultural, relative, dogmatic thought. One absurd implication of this criticism is that one's culturally shaped conceptual scheme, experiences, beliefs, values, and the available evidence in one's society have no bearing on the rationality of a belief or the basis for its acceptance. This suggests that such cultural systems cannot engender development. This suggestion is obviously wrong as the developments in Japan and some other Asian countries have shown. These countries have developed without losing their traditional ways of life and cultures; rather, they have used their cultural traditions as the foundation for development of their distinct civilisations.

The essence of this criticism of African traditional beliefs as being irrational and irrelevant to development is that they lack the universal rationality, validity, and applicability of scientific and modern ideas. Oruka[30] underscored this criticism by arguing that, "Reason is a universal human trait. And the greatest disservice to African philosophy is to deny it reason and dress it in magic and extra-rational traditionalism". He suggested that African traditions are irrational and that a philosophy that will help Africa to achieve renaissance cannot be based on such irrationality. For Gyekye[31], the practical implication of this criticism is that the irrational, dogmatic, and unscientific elements of African cultural traditions have drawbacks or pitfalls, which Africans must avoid in their efforts to achieve renaissance. However, we cannot deny that some positive aspects of African cultural traditions, which are not universal, are necessary for African ways of life and Africa's renaissance.

As Annis[32] argued using examples, cultures and social contexts are relevant to the rational acceptance and justification of beliefs. Moreover, for Harding[33], cultures are the rational contextual toolboxes and bases for science, technology, and knowledge production. She discussed, for instance, the different methods of scientific inquiry in the West as opposed to Japan. This suggests that some socio-culturally relative aspects of European ideas, which are necessary for their modern ways of life, may not be reasonable in other cultural traditions. Africans and all peoples must rely on their own cultural traditions and ways of producing and applying knowledge. Perhaps the criticism of African traditions and their inherent negative features, which imply that they have nothing to offer Africa's efforts to develop, is specious. Similarly, the suggestion that African philosophers who embrace Africa's tradition also have nothing to offer such modernisation efforts, is specious. Critics argue that the proper role for African philosophers is to examine critically in order to identify why Africans must get rid of their traditions, instead of romanticising them. Sogolo[34] captured this view thus: "the major dilemmas of modern Africa today cannot be accounted for by romanticizing the past".

1.3   African Renaissance and Modernity

This raises the question of the nature and role of African philosophy for Africa's renaissance. Wiredu[35] argued that the effort to make African philosophy applicable and relevant to Africa's development involves "the broad sense of the word in which philosophy is, so to speak, a guide to the living of life...". In his view, a philosophy that can provide a guide to living life must rely on critical analysis, rationality, and the scientific method that will lead to principles that have universal applicability. This suggests that Africa's renaissance must involve articulating and adopting relevant intellectual, political, and social principles for Africa's development, and that Africa's cultural traditions cannot provide the basis for this. So, the characterisations of and distinctions between tradition and modernity, as well as the call for modernisation, raise the issue of whether African tradition has any connection to, or can in any way be blended with, modern Western thought systems, methods, and ideas. In my view, yes! I suggest that a more reasonable idea of African Renaissance must involve blending the positive features of modernity and tradition, and getting rid of their negative features.

In order to determine which elements of Western modernity to accept or get rid of, Africans must examine the different dimensions of modernity and the elements of each. They are the following: (1) the epistemological scientific dimension, which involves empiricism, positivism, foundationalism, reliance on reason, objectivity, analysis, and critical reflection; (2) the logical dimension, which involves the universality of the formal standards of reasoning, and the idea that linguistic concepts can capture the essence of things and reality; (3) the social and political dimension, which involves liberalism, democracy, rule of law, secularism, and the protection of individual rights and freedoms; (4) the moral dimension, which involves the moral sanctity of autonomy, voluntarism, individualism, and dignity of individual choice or conception of the good; (5) the metaphysical dimension, which involves physical ontology, atomism, realism, materialism, denial of idealism, and spiritualism; and (6) the economic dimension, which involves capitalism and *laissez faire*.

It is easy to see how these different elements and dimensions of modernity are mutually coextensive and supportive, such as the connections among the moral, political, and economic dimensions. We can also see the connections among the logical, epistemological and metaphysical dimensions regarding the nature of singular reality and universal truth that reason in scientific inquiry must discover. These dimensions shape and influence approaches and principles in the moral, political and economic dimensions. An examination of these dimensions will indicate that they all have positive and negative elements. Such critical analysis will help to determine which of these positive elements Africans should draw from as a basis for their renaissance.

In articulating the historical basis of the features of modernity, Russell[36] argued that it involves "the diminishing authority of the Church and the increasing authority of science". This feature involves rejecting religious authority and dogmatism—features which are said to characterise African tradition. It also involves accepting the authority of science and technology, and the adoption of the scientific method, which involves reason, experimentation, empirical testing, critical analysis, exactness, rigour, and systematic or methodological skepticism. It further involves accepting ideas or theories as tentative because they are persistently subject to critical examination. It is argued that the virtue of this method is manifested in its results, which include the industrial revolution and the advent of technology.

Russell[37] noted that a scientific method does not focus on the value of the outcome, but rather on the skillfulness with which one uses a process, which is founded on the notion of the neutrality, universality, objectivity, and sovereignty of reason. Modernism involves the view that there are universal and absolute truth claims that are embedded *exclusively* in reason. Scientific inquiries and theories seek to bring rationality, unity, simplicity, universality, and objectivity to ways of doing things and thinking about, explaining, and understanding phenomena in the world.

Another element of the modern mode of inquiry and thought is that it "has retained, for the most part, an individualistic and subjective character"[38]. This element is related to the first, in that the rejection of religious dogmas or the authority of the church has opened up numerous chosen areas of inquiry by individuals, the growth of knowledge, and the ability of individuals to think for themselves and articulate universally valid criteria for knowledge. This means that one must accept beliefs on the basis of one's own individual rational consideration of the evidence, as opposed to what is dictated by any community, the Church, or their dogma. This idea is manifested in Descartes' skepticism and foundation of knowledge in terms of *cogito*, and Kant's view of rationality, as the maxim, which tells one to 'think for oneself'. This is expressed by Hardwig[39] as follows: "the core of rationality consists in preserving and adhering to one's own independent judgment". The idea of individual rights, autonomous choice, rationality, and the conception of the good are underpinned by metaphysical voluntarism.

Most intellectuals who argue for modernity and use it as the standard for evaluating and criticising tradition ignore other elements of modernity, focusing mainly on its epistemological scientific dimension by reducing modernity to only this dimension and its positive features. Recently, intellectuals have been focusing on the political element of modernity in their advocacy of liberal democracy as the mode of governance. Liberalism has its foundation in the moral sanctity of individual autonomy; it provides a basis for justifying modern political, economic, and social conditions for individuals to freely make rational choices and formulate a conception of the good that they want to pursue and the life they want to lead.

1.4   The Liberal Perspective

Liberalism also has implications for the capitalist and *laissez faire* elements of the economic dimension of modernity. Liberalism implies that individuals are free to create and accumulate wealth in order to achieve economic prosperity. It is with respect to the idea of the sanctity of the individual, free choice, and property that modern liberalism is opposed to communalism, which is a feature of African tradition. Communal tradition assumes that the community is morally and logically prior to the individual, in that an individual's dignity derives from, and his choices are made meaningful or circumscribed by, the community. Communalism is viewed and criticised as specifying common ownership and a community's conception of the good, which is supposedly imposed on individuals, i.e. individuals are not at liberty to decide whether or not to choose such a conception. This criticism insists that the community vitiates one's individuality, rights, and autonomy, thus it is authoritarian.

Although Wiredu[40] used this modern liberal perspective to criticise African communal tradition, he also observed, "That our traditional culture was authoritarian is a distinctly modern comment". The suggestion is that this modern criticism illicitly assumes the obvious reasonableness of its liberal principles of individualism and autonomy. The problem is that this criticism over-emphasises individual autonomy and freedom to the detriment of the community, the values of caring, mutuality, and the need for communal interests and responsibilities. This begs the question about the value of rugged individualism and autonomy. It assumes without question that autonomy and individualism are intrinsically good, such that the individual and his autonomy have moral priority over, and may not be limited by, the community, common good or interest. The inherent goodness of individual autonomy has been questioned by the merits of the idea of 'relational autonomy' in African traditions, which emphasise the connection between one's choice and social relationships. This is usually ignored, according to Ikuenobe[41], when African traditions are criticised. He argues that autonomy is a tool and its goodness depends on what it is used for and how it is used in a context.

1.5   Distinction Between 'Modernity' and 'Tradition'

Many authors have articulated that the features of modernity are logically distinct from, and mutually exclusive of, the features of tradition. Usually, the features of 'modernity' are said to apply almost exclusively to the West, i.e. they are lacking in Africa. In Skorupski's view, traditional cultures are non-literate and they do not hold their belief based on empirical evidence, hence they are irrational. Sogolo[42] criticised this idea by arguing that these features cannot be used to adequately characterise traditional cultures, because some literate cultures may be characterised as traditional. He also argued that, "It is difficult to find an entire belief-system that is devoid of any rationality. A particular belief may be said to be irrational but often the man who subscribes to such a belief may also embrace others that are rationally grounded"[43].

In Sogolo's view, rationality can only be ascribed to a particular belief, but not an entire belief system or the person holding a belief, because a person can be irrational regarding one belief but not another. He argued that it is absurd to use rationality and the evidentiary basis for which individuals hold beliefs as a basis for characterising a culture or an entire belief system as traditional or modern. Gyekye[44] argued that to suggest that Africans do not have a rational basis for their traditional thoughts is to imply their inability to make sense of, or conceptualise, their experiences. It denies them a sense of humanity, if indeed rationality is a universal biological and cognitive feature of humans. Rationality is behind the ideas, thoughts, beliefs, and actions of every person, and is involved in the cognitive aspects of one's life. The characterisation that African traditional cultures are irrational raises questions about the nature of rationality.

Rationality involves, broadly, the cognitive *process* of reasoning, conceptualising, and justifying, which requires the application of evidence and concepts to beliefs, problems, issues, ideas, and things. This reasoning process is, in some fundamental sense, *similar* (not the same) among all peoples. I am not suggesting that all humans conceptualise and reason in exactly the same way such that the outcome of their reasoning is the same; my point is that all human beings conceptualise, reason, reflect, and evaluate their reasoning as a basis for understanding and explaining reality, and living a meaningful life. They may do them differently; reasoning could be inductive or deductive, and deductive reasoning could be good in the sense of validity or soundness. The quality of reasoning may be different, but the relative quality does make any reasoning categorically rational or irrational. Rationality is, categorically, a matter of degree. It involves a spectrum: with rationality and irrationality at both extremes, and various degrees of rationality in between. It is quite insulting and unreasonable to say that African traditions or Africans within their traditions are irrational.

It is either that these critics have a wrong or parochial view of rationality, or they improperly apply the concept to Africans and their beliefs. Lehrer[45] argued that one of the capacities that is uniquely human, amongst all humans, is the ability to meta-mentally ascend, that is, there is an ability to consider, reflect, and evaluate the contents of the mental states we form naturally, such as beliefs and desires. Wiredu[46] also made a similar point in arguing that there is a biological basis for universal human rationality and its associated norms. If this is true, and Africans are biologically human, then it is specious to argue that reason is only unique to science in modern Western culture and is lacking in African traditions. This denial involves the suppression of African epistemological, critical, and rational traditions. Ikuenobe[47;48] has argued that the much criticised African traditional beliefs such as witchcraft and authoritarian structures have rational pragmatic bases.

Traditional Africans were rational, critical, and reflective. According to Wiredu[49], elders in traditional African societies who were real thinkers were "not afraid to criticise, reject, modify, or add to traditional philosophical ideas". He went on to say that these "philosophers of old must have had some elaborate and persuasive reasons for their doctrines"[50]. Such critical reasoning and persuasive reasons must involve rationality. As Sogolo[51] also argued, the denial of rationality to the entirety of African traditions involves a specious attempt to generalise about the rationality or irrationality of a culture and its people. Such an attempt, which Sogolo[52] argued is similar to Karl Popper's characterisation of societies as 'closed' with respect to traditional cultures and 'open' with respect to modern cultures, also involves an unreasonable idealisation of cultures. Such idealisation cannot pick out clearly or instantiate any particular culture.

However, Sogolo[53] does admit that Popper's description of a closed society as semi-organic, communal and non-individualistic, with members who share common kinship, aspirations, needs, interests, and goals, may be an accurate description of a village community in African traditional society. One may also argue that this kind of community that Popper describes is not unique to, and does not necessarily only describe, African traditional communities, as such communities exist in modern Europe. For instance, this description may capture the Kibbutz communes in Israel, or rural villages in Greece or Italy. Are these Israeli, Greek, or Italian communities modern or traditional communities within modern Europe? This bolsters Gyekye's[54] argument that modernity and tradition do not involve a polarity; every society has elements of modernity and tradition, such that one is not a rejection of the other.

Sogolo[55] indicated that Horton's characterisation of tradition and modernity, and his distinction between them, are similar to Popper's view, in that for Horton, traditional, closed, unreflective, and dogmatic cultures do not show awareness of alternative ideas. Modern societies are open and have scientific orientation, in that they critically and reflectively seek alternative beliefs, and they always examine their theories against alternatives. In the views of Horton and Popper, traditional cultures are protective of their ideas, which makes them closed, dogmatic, and unreflective. Modern cultures critically examine their beliefs; their scientific attitude of openness to other views involves the potential to be destructive of existing beliefs. These characterisations are echoed by Appiah's ideas of Western 'formal philosophy', which is modern, and African 'folk philosophy' or ethnophilosophy, which is traditional.

Sogolo[56] criticised Horton's features as being inadequate in distinguishing clearly between traditional and modern cultures, because "as far as he is referring to individuals, both traits and attitudes cut across all societies, whether traditional or modern". Most of the features used to characterise modernity and tradition may aptly describe only particular individuals and their attitudes with respect to specific beliefs. Again, the attitudes of some individuals regarding particular beliefs cannot be used to generalise about or characterise cultural belief systems to which those particular individuals or beliefs belong.

Sogolo[57] argued that Gellner has observed that some scientists do have attitudes that are used to characterise traditional cultures, in that these scientists are unimaginative and dogmatic in their thinking and do not consider alternative theories. Thomas Kuhn[58] made a similar point that "normal science often suppresses fundamental novelties because they are necessarily subversive of its basic commitments". Sogolo[59] indicated that there is anthropological evidence in the works of Jack Goody and Evans-Pritchard, which indicates that some instances of traditional African cultures may provide counterexamples to Horton's characterising features of African tradition.

In spite of Sogolo's[60] view that "every thought system contains [elements of] both the traditional and the modern", he nonetheless suggests that modern Western culture is somehow distinct from African cultures:

> It is true that the West is predominantly science-oriented, but it is also true that there are Westerners who still entertain Western traditional thought, that is, that they still explain their experiences by drawing on non-natural phenomena. ... In the same way, we may admit that Africans are predominantly pre-scientific in thought without denying that some Africans explain their day-to-day events in scientific paradigms...[61].

This view, which suggests that African traditions have some rational and scientific elements, except that these elements are *not predominant*, is contentious. How do we determine such *predominance*? On what basis? It appears Sogolo[62] makes the same mistake that he soundly criticised, which is the idealisation or generalisation about cultures that implies that a feature (science-oriented) is predominant in one culture (Western) as opposed to another (African).

In characterising African tradition and Western modernity, the honorific nature of modernity and its scientific method is usually assumed without critical examination. In this sense, Sogolo[62] fails to drive to the proper logical conclusion his critique of the characterisations of, and the dichotomy between, modernity and tradition. This is because he falls into the same trap of ignoring the negatives and accepting without questioning the idea that modernity is inherently positive. The negative aspects of modernity can be highlighted by considering its criticisms by postmodernism. Postmodernism in philosophy involves a rejection of the ideas and methods in modern thought, including *foundationalism* about justification and knowledge; *essentialism* about concepts and what they denote; and *realism* about things or objects. Postmodernism also involves articulating multiple different ways of life and discourse, modes of thought or thinking, ways of knowing, understanding, and of interpreting reality and experiences.

Thus, postmodernism gives credence to the legitimacy of different cultural epistemological and philosophical traditions. According to Appiah[63], postmodernism involves a:

> rejection of the mainstream consensus from Descartes through Kant to logical positivism on foundationalism (there is one route to knowledge, which is exclusivism in epistemology) and of metaphysical realism (there is one truth, which is exclusivism in ontology), each underwritten by a unitary notion of reason.

Appiah articulated the contrast between postmodernism and (its critique of) modernism thus: "Modernism saw the economisation of the world as the triumph of reason; postmodernism rejects that claim, allowing in the realm of theory the same multiplication of distinctions we see in the cultures it seeks to understand"[64]. Annis[65] argued that the problem with foundationalism in modernity is that it ignores the multiplicities of the relative contextual social and cultural elements' justification and rationality. Postmodernism seeks to identify the problems with such exclusivism in the different dimensions of modernity. Postmodernism also reminds us that we should not over-romanticise modernity and the method of science, to the detriment of the merits of the contexts of cultural traditions.

Harding[66] bolstered this postmodernist point by arguing that modern science ignores the traditional cultural aspect of inquiry and knowledge production, and the different modes of thinking in different aspects of one's life. Thus, it is pertinent to indicate that whether or not one has a scientific orientation depends on the realm of one's life or nature of a belief. In the religious or metaphysical realm - whether in Africa or the West - beliefs and thinking are non-scientific and the canons of science do not apply. It is absurd and a categorical mistake to expect scientific canons to apply, because religious and metaphysical beliefs do not make empirical claims and they are not subject to scientific testing. With respect to other aspects of life, in Africa or the West, individuals are usually scientifically oriented. There are obviously aspects of life in African traditions where people rely on empirical testing, evidence, and practical rationality.

1.6   Tradition and the Basis of African Renaissance

As Sogolo[67] argued, it reasonable to say that "the African blends the traditional with the modern". Gyekye[68] also indicated that all cultures are eclectic; they are a blend of elements of both 'modernity' and 'tradition'. Some elements are 'traditional' because they have a long history; they have been preserved over time and passed down. Some elements are 'modern' and scientific, in that some beliefs, based on internal and external stimuli, have been critically examined, tested, modified, or changed. This scientific and modern nature of culture and modes of life is rarely appreciated. According to Boxill[69],

> People do not normally think of their own culture as an experiment in living. They do not suppose that their culture's mores and practices are hypotheses about how life should be lived and that in following these mores and practices they are behaving somewhat like scientists subjecting hypotheses to empirical tests. Normally they act as their culture dictates because they don't think about it, or because they believe that alternatives are wrong, or sometimes because they cannot conceive of alternatives. Still a culture is an experiment in living in the sense that things happen as a result of people following its mores and practices, and people do learn from how and why these things happen. This is why cultures change.

We must understand science broadly to involve the empirical testing of hypotheses, knowledge production, and application.

In this broad sense of science, all cultures are scientific and rational, otherwise individuals cannot live meaningfully or make sense of their lives, and their cultures cannot change or make progress. No culture is stagnant. Yes, there may be different degrees of progress or change; no-one can deny that some aspects of African cultural traditions have been 'modernised', changed or modified. Moreover, all traditional cultures have elements of authoritarianism and conservatism; it is usually a matter of degree. For instance, many Judeo-Christian traditions have endured in the West, but some have been modified or 'modernised'. Hence, based on the features provided, a clear-cut distinction cannot be made between 'tradition' and 'modernity', and these features do not aptly describe African and Western cultures.

Harding[70] has argued that what was erroneously considered irrational and un-scientific in traditional African cultures is now seen as scientific and rational. For instance, the use of herbs for treating illnesses was considered unscientific, but now scientists realise that herbs have bio-chemical and pharmaceutical compounds that have effects on human physiology to cure ailments. The denigration of African traditions as being inferior to Western modernity based on their said contrasting features is wrong headed. As Wiredu observed, instead of comparing African superstitious beliefs or unscientific attitudes with similar beliefs or attitudes in the West, intellectuals usually compare Africans' superstitious beliefs with Western scientific beliefs, and then proceed to conclude that Africans' beliefs and their underlying thinking are inferior to Western beliefs and thinking. According to Wiredu[71] such a comparison is inappropriate, because "instead of seeing the basic non-scientific characteristics of African traditional thought as typifying traditional thought in general, Western anthropologists and others besides them have tended to take them as defining a peculiarly African way of thinking".

Wiredu[72] insisted that we must distinguish between *pre-scientific superstitious forms of thinking* and *scientific empirical forms of thinking*, both of which exist in African traditions and in the West. The idea of critical inquiry and seeking empirical evidence as the basis for one's beliefs is neither uniquely scientific nor Western. Such thinking and attitudes exist in African traditions (Olela[73]; Gyekye[74]; Keita[75]; Harding[76]). It is questionable whether traditional thoughts are 'pre-scientific', per Wiredu, or 'predominantly unscientific', per Sogolo; it depends on how broadly or narrowly we understand science. As Harding[77] argued, "the suppression of other cultures' knowledge traditions also contributed to producing the illusion that only European sciences were and could be universal ones". This suggests that the West narrowly defines what science and modernity are as a way of elevating their thoughts as universally true and rational, in order to exclude, denigrate, and suppress other non-Western forms of knowledge—a form of exclusivism.

One problem that Africa faces in its efforts to adopt Western modernity is the exclusivism of modernity, which prevents the continent from incorporating important positive elements of its tradition. Gyekye[78] has identified some positive and negative elements of African traditions. This idea of using modernity to evaluate and critique tradition, which indicates exclusivism, implies that modernisation must involve Western science as the only rational way of thinking, and that Africa must make a clean logical break with its traditions. Such exclusivism prevents multiplicities of views, traditions, and methods that would allow the different (epistemological, political, metaphysical, logical, economic, and moral) dimensions of modernity to coexist or blend with Africa's traditions or methods in its modernisation efforts. This implies that Africa must accept the inherently good and rational modernity (with its scientific method) or nothing else, because the alternative - irrational and dogmatic tradition - is inherently bad.

Besides the fact that this exclusivism involves a false dichotomy, the imperative of modernisation also raises the following questions: (1) Is Western modernity inherently good? (2) Is African tradition inherently bad? (3) Must Africa's renaissance uncritically adopt wholesale, Western modernity? (4) Must Africa's renaissance involve a clean break with tradition? (5) Is it possible for Africa's renaissance or development to draw from, rely on, or blend with, the good elements of its tradition? (6) Must Africa's renaissance rely solely on African traditions?

The issues of the inherent goodness of modernity and the inherent badness of tradition are pertinent, because whenever one argues in favour of African traditions or articulates their valuable features, the retort usually offered by critics is that we should not romanticise Africa's traditions. There are few efforts to highlight and balance the good over the bad in African traditions; most of the time only the bad aspects are emphasised. This is usually not the case with modernity; many intellectuals highlight only its positive features. Perhaps they assume that even if modernity has negatives, those are outweighed by the positives, such that they are not worth highlighting.

The overemphasis on only the positive features of modernity gives the illusion of its inherent goodness, which is then used as a standard for evaluating African tradition or Africa's development. This emphasis begs the question about the inherent goodness of Western modernity and science, as contrasted with the inherent badness of African tradition. I appreciate the tremendous positive results of science and technology, but we must not romanticise these positives by ignoring their negative and debilitating effects. Consider the calamitous consequences of science and various technologies on the environment - air pollution, contamination of food, and the chronic and debilitating illnesses they have caused. In addition, Western scientific methods are extremely adversarial, individualistic, competitive, and alienating, and they sometimes engender unproductive conflicts. Sometimes this method encourages knowledge or discovery for its own sake, without consideration for its humanistic and moral effects or implications. We cannot ignore the extreme negative selfish consequences of modern individualism and the permissiveness of liberalism.

Rugged individualism, egoism, and extreme capitalism have engendered a number of negative moral and social effects, such as greed, exploitation, and a lack of caring and sympathy for others, as well as some social pathologies that correlate with pervasive incidences of extreme deviant, criminal, and violent behaviours. These facts remind me of a profound statement made by my spouse years ago when she came newly to the United States. Based on the pervasiveness of moral decadence, violence, selfishness, indifference, lack of caring, and social pathologies she saw, she said, "If what I see here is modernisation, then I don't want Africa to be modernised". The implication is that Africa should maintain some moral and social aspects of its cultural traditions. One may criticise this statement by saying that the problem is not modernisation *per se*, but the manner in which Africans modernise, the values of modernisation they choose to adopt and internalise, and how they apply these values in their behaviours.

One might also argue that the moral and social pathologies we find in the United States do not exist in many European and Scandinavian countries that are modernised. This is precisely my point! The negative aspects of modernity and science indicate that Africa must be circumspect in their view of modernisation, or how and what they modernise; they must adopt the positives and avoid the negatives. When many people rave about Western modernity and science but ignore their negatives, no one ever reminds them that they are romanticising modernity. Yet, whenever one talks about the positive features of African tradition, critics are quick to say that one is romanticising it. Why is there an asymmetry in the characterisations of, and attitudes towards, Western modernity and African tradition? This asymmetry involves seeing only the good in modernity and not the bad, but seeing only the bad in tradition and not the good.

The failure to see the negatives in modernity and the positives in tradition is an error that Africans must be aware of in order to avoid it in the efforts to achieve renaissance. What the African Renaissance needs is a balancing act. This involves a critical evaluation of Western modernity in order to harness the good and avoid the bad. Many of the elements of modernity we find in Africa today are their negatives or the bastardisation of the positives, such as some pervasive moral and social pathologies that did not exist in African traditions. Can Africa develop by extricating the good of modernity from its bad? Yes! Africa must determine what to develop; the strategy by which it wants to develop in order to achieve its renaissance by avoiding the negatives of modernity. This must involve the synthesis or blend of the good in both tradition and modernity. As Bodunrin[79] argued, "No doubt many things are worth preserving in our traditional culture— especially in the moral sphere—but we stand in danger of losing these if we do not take pains to separate these from those aspects that are undesirable". These valuable aspects of tradition must be retained in order for Africa's renaissance to be meaningful.

Such a renaissance cannot involve a clean break with tradition, but it must draw from its positives. For instance, African tradition involves communal (*Ubuntu*) moral values and social structures, which involve caring, humility, fraternity, and mutuality, which provide the basis for social harmony. We can appreciate the merits of traditional African communalism when it is compared to the social and moral pathologies that are engendered by the extreme rugged individualism of Western modernity. Sogolo[80] argued that one important precondition for Africa's development must be social harmony and a form of individual and social discipline. He believed that African communal traditions, values, and attitudes have stabilising effects, and they have something to offer today in engendering social harmony and discipline[81].

Communalism, which is usually considered a pejorative feature of African tradition, may have contributed to social harmony and discipline. In communal societies, an individual is seen as a social and corporate being whose life is inseparable from his community and ways of life, which have positive values that are conducive to peace and harmony. In Sogolo's[82] words, "It could be that man's uncritical attitude to traditional institutions, his willingness to accept them and the ease with which he internalises conventional norms, are society's techniques for survival. It is for this reason that some philosophers attribute rationality to social institutions". This suggests that there is a rational foundation for African traditional beliefs and communal practices, and that social institutions have wisdom that is better than, or may override, individualistic feelings and rational judgments. Perhaps it is more appropriate regarding the above comment to describe the people's *accepting attitude* toward traditional institutions or authority as a willingness to rationally compromise or achieve consensus per Wiredu[83], rather than an 'uncritical attitude' that is seen as a negative feature of African tradition. This attitude is not uncritical! Such "willing attitude of acceptance", in Wiredu's[84] view, usually engenders consensus and social harmony.

The pertinent issue, as Sogolo[85] indicated, is, "What remains controversial is the connection between that past and contemporary political development". Sogolo[86] argued for the 'transformational blending' of some traditional elements of African cultures into the modern, by indicating that in some parts of Africa, "traditional, social and political institutions have given birth to new forms"[87]. This is instructive in terms of how Africa can achieve renaissance by *not* breaking completely with tradition. Africa can blend tradition and modernity by critically reflecting on and 'modernising' relevant, valuable, and practically applicable aspects of tradition. Sogolo[88] indicated that critics of tradition who argue that Africa must make a clean break with its traditions seem to do so because "traditional social institutions are seen not as the creations of individual intellect but of some 'blind' mechanisms". This implies that traditional cultural, social, and political institutions were not rationally designed or created, thus they cannot be rationally reconstructed, critically examined, or modified for current adaptation.

As critics argue, there is little to be gained from romanticising African tradition or trying to reconstruct it; not only was that tradition bad, but there is also a practical problem of reconstructing it. African traditional past is far too removed in time; it is lost historically and it no longer exists to be reconstructed, or it has been completed destroyed or irretrievably corrupted by colonialism. The alternative view is that such reconstruction can indeed be done because these traditional values and social and political structures, such as communalism and traditional rulership, still exist. According to Sogolo[89], many political theories that have sought to provide a viable social and political structure for modern Africa "start from the base that traditional African societies are structurally communalistic", with "the hope of formulating a new social and political formula that reflects the uniqueness of African society". This suggests that Africa's renaissance and efforts to develop its social and political structures must be guided and informed by traditional values and principles.

Sogolo[90] went further to say that, "some of the social and political ideals, freedom, democracy, equality, justice, etc., which we seek to attain [in Africa today] are intrinsically part of our traditional African social structures and that what we need are suitable institutions for realizing these virtues". Moreover, there are suggestions that traditional African cultures had democratic communal structures and practices that may be harnessed and modified for Africa's renaissance (Wiredu[91]; Ramose[92]; Ake[93]). Those who argue that Africa's renaissance ought to make a clean break with tradition indicate that those traditional structures were based on kinship, theocracy, and authoritarianism, and were hardly democratic (Eze[94]; Otubanjo[95]). They insist that the democratic governance needed in Africa cannot be built on these theocratic, tyrannical, authoritarian and kinship systems.

15

Sogolo[96] described as "fruitless" the debate regarding whether the traditional African social and political systems were authoritarian or democratic, and insisted that there are positive features of tradition that Africa can draw from in order to develop. He added that, "My impression, however, is that the past of African politics was far more decent than what exists today"[97]. This raises the question of whether African traditions that are said to be in the 'past' are really in the 'past'. Are they so irretrievably removed from the present, or are they, as Sogolo[98] indicated, a 'past' (tradition) that coexists or blends with the 'present' (modern)?

Wiredu[99] argued that the past and present coexist by indicating that many people still hold and exhibit traditional African communal ethos and sensitivities, the values of consensus and common good, and other-regarding attitudes of caring. Moreover, Ekeh[100] has argued that there is something good about African traditional 'past', which, he suggested, coexists with the present. His distinction between the 'civic public' and 'primordial public' suggests that the former represents the modern, while the primordial public represents tradition. Communal moral norms apply in the primordial public of tradition, but are absent in the civic public of modernity. These norms contributed to social harmony in African communities.

The efforts to break cleanly with tradition and the inability to blend some modern European structures with traditional structures are creating serious social, moral, and political problems in Africa, which are manifested in mass corruption. Ekeh[101] argued that some modern social structures (migrated social structures), such as democracy, were brought to Africa by colonialism without the necessary moral systems that sustained them in Europe, and were not engrafted to traditional moral systems. Wiredu[102] also observed that the Western moral foundation for democracy, such as "those finely designed parliamentary palliatives, which in the United States or the United Kingdom, for instance, do mollify the opposition to some extent, are in Africa often nonexistent, or equivalently, existent only on paper". Perhaps the lack of efforts to blend modern structures to traditional African structures is attributable to the mentality that modernity is inherently good and that tradition is inherently bad, and that modernisation must make a clean break with tradition.

1.7 Conclusion

I have argued that an African Renaissance cannot involve a complete break with tradition. It is not true that tradition offers nothing good for Africa to draw from. I indicate that communalism (*Ubuntu*) could provide the foundation for Africa's renaissance. Some moral and social elements of this communal tradition still exist in Africa today. The values of consensus and caring are not in the past; they still hold sway in people's minds and attitudes. These sensitivities and ethos could provide a way of resolving conflicts and harmonising divergent interests for the sake of common good and harmony. The modern Western individualistic attitudes that were imported from Europe have engendered the persistent and pervasive social and political conflicts in Africa. Thus, it is imperative for Africa to blend its positive traditional values with modernity as the basis for its renaissance.

References

[1]Wiredu, K. 1980. *Philosophy and an African Culture*. London: Cambridge University Press.
[2]Bodunrin, P. O. 1984. The Question of African Philosophy. In R. A. Wright (Ed.). *African Philosophy: An Introduction*. New York: University Press of America, pp. 1-23.
[3]Hountondji, P. 1996. *African Philosophy: Myth and Reality*. Indianapolis: Indiana University Press.
[4]Wiredu, K. 1980. *Philosophy and an African Culture*. London: Cambridge University Press.
[5] Bodunrin, P. O. 1984. The Question of African Philosophy. In R. A. Wright (Ed.). *African Philosophy: An Introduction*. New York: University Press of America, pp. 1-23.
[6]Oruka, O. 1987. African Philosophy. In G. Floisted (Ed.). *Contemporary Philosophy: A New Survey, Vol. 5: African Philosophy*. Dordrecht: Martinus Nijhorff, pp. 47-65.
[7]Wiredu, K. 1980. *Philosophy and an African Culture*. London: Cambridge University Press.
[8]Appiah, A. 1992. *In My Father's House: Africa in the Philosophy of Culture*. New York: Oxford University Press.
[9] Bodunrin, P. O. 1984. The Question of African Philosophy. In R. A. Wright (Ed.). *African Philosophy: An Introduction*. New York: University Press of America, pp. 1-23.
[10]Hountondji, P. 1996. *African Philosophy: Myth and Reality*. Indianapolis: Indiana University Press.
[11]Appiah, A. 1989. *Necessary Questions: An Introduction to Philosophy*. Englewood Cliffs: Prentice Hall.
[12]Wiredu, K. 1980. *Philosophy and an African Culture*. London: Cambridge University Press.
[13]Bodunrin, P. O. 1984. The Question of African Philosophy. In R. A. Wright (Ed.). *African Philosophy: An Introduction*. New York: University Press of America, pp. 1-23.
[14]Ibid.
[15]Hountondji, P. 1996. *African Philosophy: Myth and Reality*. Indianapolis: Indiana University Press.
[16]Ikuenobe, P. 1998. A Defense of Epistemic Authoritarianism in Traditional African Cultures. *Journal of Philosophical Research*, 23: 417-440.
[17]Bodunrin, P. O. 1984. The Question of African Philosophy. In R. A. Wright (Ed.). *African Philosophy: An Introduction*. New York: University Press of America, pp. 1-23.
[18]Appiah, A. 1989. *Necessary Questions: An Introduction to Philosophy*. Englewood Cliffs: Prentice Hall.
[19]Wiredu, K. 1980. *Philosophy and an African Culture*. London: Cambridge University Press.
[20]Ibid.
[21]Ibid.
[22]Bodunrin, P. O. 1984. The Question of African Philosophy. In R. A. Wright (Ed.). *African Philosophy: An Introduction*. New York: University Press of America, pp. 1-23.
[23]Gyekye, K. 1997. *Tradition and Modernity: Philosophical Reflections on the African Experience*. New York: Oxford University Press.
[24]Wiredu, K. 1980. *Philosophy and an African Culture*. Cambridge University Press, London.
[25]Bodunrin, P. O. 1984. The Question of African Philosophy. In R. A. Wright (Ed.). *African Philosophy: An Introduction*. New York: University Press of America, pp. 1-23.
[26]Appiah, A. 1989. *Necessary Questions: An Introduction to Philosophy*. Englewood Cliffs: Prentice Hall.
[27]Harding, S. 1998. *Is Science Multi-Cultural?* Indianapolis: Indiana University Press.
[28]Appiah, A. 1989. *Necessary Questions: An Introduction to Philosophy*. Englewood Cliffs: Prentice Hall.
[29]Appiah, A. 1992. *In My Father's House: Africa in the Philosophy of Culture*. New York: Oxford University Press.
[30]Oruka, O. 1987. African Philosophy. In G. Floisted (Ed.). *Contemporary Philosophy: A New Survey, Vol. 5: African Philosophy*. Dordrecht: Martinus Nijhorff, pp. 47-65.
[31]Gyekye, K. 1997. *Tradition and Modernity: Philosophical Reflections on the African Experience*. New York: Oxford University Press.
[32]Annis, D. 1982. The Social and Cultural Component of Epistemic Justification–A Reply. *Philosophia*, 12(2): 51-55.
[33]Harding, S. 1998. *Is Science Multi-Cultural?* Indianapolis: Indiana University Press.
[34]Sogolo, G. 1993. *Foundations of African Philosophy*. Ibadan: University of Ibadan Press.
[35]Wiredu, K. 1980. *Philosophy and an African Culture*. London: Cambridge University Press.
[36]Russell, B. 1945. *A History of Western Philosophy*. New York: Simon and Schuster.
[37]Ibid.
[38]Ibid.
[39]Hardwig, J. 1985. Epistemic Dependence. *Journal of Philosophy*, 82: 335-49.
[40]Wiredu, K. 1980. *Philosophy and an African Culture*. London: Cambridge University Press.
[41]Ikuenobe, P. 2015. Relational Autonomy, Personhood, and African Traditions. *Philosophy East & West*, 65(4): 1005-1029.
[42]Sogolo, G. 1993. *Foundations of African Philosophy*. Ibadan: University of Ibadan Press.

[43]Ibid.

[44]Gyekye, K. 1984. Akan Concept of a Person. In R. A. Wright (Ed.). *African Philosophy: An Introduction*. New York: University Press of America.

[45]Lehrer, K. 1997. *Self Trust*. New York: Oxford University Press.

[46]Wiredu, K. 1996. *Cultural Universals and Particulars: An African Perspective*. Bloomington: Indiana University Press.

[47]Ikuenobe, P. 1995. Cognitive Relativism, African Philosophy, and the Phenomenon of Witchcraft. *Journal of Social Philosophy*, 26(3): 143-160.

[48]Ikuenobe, P. 1998. A Defense of Epistemic Authoritarianism in Traditional African Cultures. *Journal of Philosophical Research*, 23: 417-440.

[49]Wiredu, K. 1980. *Philosophy and an African Culture*. London: Cambridge University Press.

[50]Ibid.

[51]Sogolo, G. 1993. *Foundations of African Philosophy*. Ibadan: University of Ibadan Press.

[52]Ibid.

[53]Ibid.

[54]Gyekye, K. 1997. *Tradition and Modernity: Philosophical Reflections on the African Experience*. New York: Oxford University Press.

[55]Sogolo, G. 1993. *Foundations of African Philosophy*. Ibadan: University of Ibadan Press.

[56]Ibid.

[57]Ibid.

[58]Kuhn, T. 1962. *The Structure of Scientific Revolution*. Chicago: University of Chicago Press.

[59]Sogolo, G. 2014. Ethical and Socio-Cultural Foundations of National Security. *African Journal for Security and Development*, 1(1): 85-94.

[60]Ibid.

[61]Ibid.

[62]Ibid.

[63]Appiah, A. 1992. *In My Father's House: Africa in the Philosophy of Culture*. New York: Oxford University Press.

[64]Ibid.

[65]Annis, D. 1982. The Social and Cultural Component of Epistemic Justification–A Reply', *Philosophia*, 12(2): 51-55.

[66]Harding, S. 1998. *Is Science Multi-Cultural?* Indianapolis: Indiana University Press.

[67]Sogolo, G. 2014. Ethical and Socio-Cultural Foundations of National Security. *African Journal for Security and Development*, 1(1): 85-94.

[68]Gyekye, K. 1997. *Tradition and Modernity: Philosophical Reflections on the African Experience*. New York: Oxford University Press.

[69]Boxill, B. 1998. Majoritarian Democracy and Cultural Minorities. In A. M. Melzer., J. Weinberger, and M. R. Zinman (Eds.). *Multiculturalism and American Democracy*. Lawrence: Kansas University Press, pp. 107-119.

[70]Hardwig, J. 1985. Epistemic Dependence. *Journal of Philosophy*, 82: 335-49.

[71]Wiredu, K. 1980. *Philosophy and an African Culture*. London: Cambridge University Press.

[72]Ibid.

[73]Olela, H. 1984. The African Foundations of Greek Philosophy. In R. A. Wright (Ed.). *African Philosophy: An Introduction*. New York: University Press of America, pp. 77-92.

[74]Gyekye, K. 1997. *Tradition and Modernity: Philosophical Reflections on the African Experience*. New York: Oxford University Press.

[75]Keita, L. 1984. The African Philosophical Tradition. In R. A. Wright (Ed.). *African Philosophy: An Introduction*. New York: University Press of America, pp. 57-76.

[76]Harding, S. 1998. *Is Science Multi-Cultural?* Indianapolis: Indiana University Press.

[77]Ibid

[78]Gyekye, K. 1997. *Tradition and Modernity: Philosophical Reflections on the African Experience*. New York: Oxford University Press.

[79]Bodunrin, P. O. 1984. The Question of African Philosophy. In R. A. Wright (Ed.). *African Philosophy: An Introduction*. New York: University Press of America.

[80]Sogolo, G. 2014. Ethical and Socio-Cultural Foundations of National Security. *African Journal for Security and Development*, 1(1): 85-94.

[81]Ibid.

[82]Ibid.

[83]Wiredu, K. 1996. *Cultural Universals and Particulars: An African Perspective*. Bloomington: Indiana University Press.

[84]Ibid.

[85]Sogolo, G. 1991. The Futures of Democracy & Participation in Everyday Life: The African Experience. In B. Van Steenbergen., R. Nakarada., F. Marti, and J. Dator (Eds.). *Advancing Democracy and Participation Challenges for the Future*. Barcelona: Centre UNESCO De Catalunya, pp. 55-59.

[86]Sogolo, G. 1993. *Foundations of African Philosophy*. Ibadan: University of Ibadan Press.

[87]Ibid.

[88]Ibid.

[89]Ibid.

[90]Ibid.

[91]Wiredu, K. 1996. *Cultural Universals and Particulars: An African Perspective*. Bloomington: Indiana University Press.

[92]Ramose, M. 1999. *African Philosophy Through Ubuntu*. Harare: Mond Books.

[93]Ake, C. 1996. *Development and Democracy in Africa*. Washington DC: Brookings Institution.

[94]Eze, E. 1997. Democracy or consensus? Response to Wiredu. In E. Eze (Ed.). *Postcolonial African philosophy: A Critical Reader*. Oxford: Blackwell, pp. 313-323.

[95]Otubanjo, F. 1989. Themes in African Traditional Political Thought. In J. A. A. Ayoade and A. B. Agbaje (Eds.). *African Traditional Political Thought and Institutions*. Lagos: Center for Black and African Arts and Civilisation, pp. 1-14.

[96]Sogolo, G. 1991. The Futures of Democracy & Participation in Everyday Life: The African Experience. In B. Van Steenbergen., R. Nakarada., F. Marti., and J. Dator (Eds.). *Advancing Democracy and Participation Challenges for the Future*. Barcelona: Centre UNESCO De Catalunya, pp. 55-59.

[97]Ibid.

[98]Ibid.

[99]Wiredu, K. 1996. *Cultural Universals and Particulars: An African Perspective*. Bloomington: Indiana University Press.

[100]Ekeh, P. P. 1983. *Colonialism and Social Structure. An Inaugural Lecture*. Ibadan: University of Ibadan Press.

[101]Ibid.

[102]Wiredu, K. 1996. *Cultural Universals and Particulars: An African Perspective*. Bloomington: Indiana University Press.

Chapter 2

Of African Philosophy and African Renaissance: Redeeming Education

Vuyisile Msila
Institute for African Renaissance, University of South Africa

2.1   Introduction

In the novel *Heart of Darkness*[1], the author Joseph Conrad portrays an image of Africa that is dark; a stark contrast to Europe. The Congo drawn is debased, backward and its inhabitants ignorant brutes. Regarding this portrayal, Chinua Achebe[2] wrote:

> *Heart of Darkness* projects the image of Africa as "the other world", the antithesis of Europe and therefore of civilisation, a place where man's vaunted intelligence and retirement are finally mocked by triumphant bestiality. The book opens on the River Thames, tranquil, resting, peacefully "at the decline of day after ages of good service done to the race that peopled its banks." But the story will take place on the River Congo, the very antithesis of the Thames.

This novel demonstrates and justifies why Africa cannot experience a renaissance; Africa is dark; it is like the beginnings of the world. It is uncouth and is without any philosophy. Conrad's novel[3] elicits the themes tersely, where Marlow continually reflects how the colonialists think. They regard black Africans as objects, as sub-humans. When one native, "a savage", dies in Marlow's ship, the latter finds no reason to mourn. The book's plot and central themes demonstrate how African ways are exploited and changed. Like all colonisers, the Belgians get into the Congo seeking to enlighten, civilise and educate the Africans, however the coloniser maimed and murdered the indigenes in order to seize power. Men like Kurtz and Marlow get into Africa to ravage it and rob it of its identity and culture[4]. In short, *Heart of Darkness* is an example of a novel that shows how imperialism instils certain fallacies upon Africans, such as when Kurtz points out that whites are like supernatural beings to the black Africans. When a black African man is dying, Marlow offers him biscuits. Subsequently, when he eventually dies, Marlow contemplates that "he was a savage who was no more account than a grain of sand in a black Sahara"[5]. So brutal is the treatment of Africans here that one sees how the colonisers reduced the natives to nothingness; no ethos, no character, just a shell. Africa when compared to Europe was not a continent inhabited by "civilised" people. There are many other works of art that portray Africa as such. The problem argued by philosophers such as Walter Rodney[6] is that the interpretation of the underdevelopment of Africa as ordained by God has been accepted by African people because of the cultural and psychological crisis suffered. Rodney[7] contended that:

> The moment that the topic of the pre-European African past is raised, many individuals are concerned for various reasons to know about the existence of African 'civilisations'. Mainly, this stems from a desire to make comparisons with European civilisations. This is not the context in which to evaluate the so-called civilisation of Europe. It is enough to note the behaviour of European capitalists from the epoch of slavery through colonialism, fascism and genocidal wars in Asia and Africa. Such barbarism causes suspicion to attach to the use of the word 'civilisation' to describe Western Europe and North America. As far as Africa is concerned during the period of early development, it is preferable to speak in terms of 'cultures' rather than 'civilisations.'

In their introduction in Chapter 3, Ayokhai and Naankiel shed light on Europe's "civilisation" that saw the colonisers seizing slaves from Africa. Amongst others, the calls for an Afrocentric education in institutions of learning in Africa have been necessitated by the need to present Africa as a continent that is also worthy. Apart from the constant calls for a free education in South Africa, higher education students have been clamouring for a system of education that underscores African philosophy and indigenous knowledge systems. Basil Bernstein[8] acknowledges how biases in education become an economic and cultural threat to democracy, but he pointed out that "education can have a crucial role in creating tomorrow's optimism in the context of today's pessimism". The African philosophy has a potential to address the ideals of tomorrow's education. This chapter explores some of the themes explored by Ikuenobe in Chapter 1. Like Ikuenobe, I do focus on tradition versus Westernisation, the so-called modernity. I look at what is missed when the focus is on Western education only, and this is also to some extent in discussions raised by Mndawe in Chapter 13.

In a struggle to change education in Africa, we need a system that is pragmatic and undergirded by a philosophy from Africa. Furthermore, this calls for rich indigenous heritage and knowledge systems from a fecund ground, which Africans can utilise to enhance their values and the African worldview. Education needs to be a focus because this is where the future in this modern world is built. Transformational strategies in emancipatory classrooms will demonstrate that learners will benefit not only from Western philosophies, but immensely from African philosophies as well. The African philosophy explicates African epistemologies from whose content the learners derive their experiences. Higgs[9] argued that:

> Educational discourse in South Africa certainly stands in need of this liberation from ideological hegemony which derives its power from the hegemony of Western Eurocentric forms of universal knowledge. People cannot be empowered if they are locked into ways of thinking that work to oppress them. Nor can people be empowered if they do not have access to those indigenous forms of knowledge which provide them with their identity as persons.

From a young age African learners should be answering bigger questions; they should be probing the meanings of being African and why it matters. They should be taught to understand the ravages of colonialism and why formal education needs to address such issues. These questions call for the development of African philosophy from the school level, thus enabling the youth to be able to dabble in the endeavours to decolonise knowledge.

2.2   African Philosophy and Decolonisation

The concept *African philosophy* is sometimes understood to be a contentious term. Janz[10] defined it as a philosophy produced by African people; it presents African worldviews. Anyanwu[11] defined African philosophy as an area of study that concerns itself with the way in which African people of the past and present make sense of the world in which they live. From time immemorial, however, Africans have reflected on their ways of life. Janz[12] also argued that a philosophy will count as an African philosophy if it involves African themes including personhood, space and perceptions of time, or uses methods described as characteristically African. Furthermore, Janz contended that any philosophy produced by Africans, by people of African descent or others engaged in the analysis of their works, will be deemed African philosophy. Yet Gyekye[13] rejected the idea that an African philosophy is comprised of the work of Africans writing on philosophy; he stated that it must arise from African thought and relate to the culture from which it emanates. In addition, Gyekye pointed out that the critical analyses of certain traditional African modes of thought are crucial in developing a distinctively African philosophy[14]. Intellectuals who embrace Pan-Africanism cannot marginalise African philosophy, for African philosophy is, among others, about identity, beliefs and culture. Furthermore, Mkandawire[15] claimed that intellectuals have played a pertinent role in shaping ideologies and societal visions. One may argue that this includes the necessary African philosophy. African philosophy is one aspect that seeks to chart ways; a map towards an accentuated Africanism and African Renaissance.

The struggle for advancing African philosophy is a noble effort that all intellectuals should strive for, especially those in pursuit of Pan-African ideals or an African Renaissance. Ideally, the African philosophy will dispel the myths about Africa; it will repudiate Marlow's views cited in the opening paragraph of this chapter. In the same vein, Mkandawire[16] pointed out that "one task of ideas in both the enslavement and colonisation of Africa was to dehumanise the enslaved and the colonised by denying their history and denigrating their achievements and capacities". Mkandawire also added that the coloniser's claims to universalism for his culture and values, thus devaluing other cultures, triggered resistance. The search for an African philosophy and African Renaissance is also part of the resistance to give Africa what is duly hers.

A true African philosophy is not only about the valorisation of an African past, however, it also seeks answers where Africans may have diverted from their "rightful" paths. It should also make amends where Africans are entrapped in colonial ways, because during the time of colonisation Africans suffered through mimesis that destroyed their worldviews. Chinweizu[17] criticised the diseased mimetic behaviours among the colonised Africans in Africa and the diaspora. During the decades of colonisation, Africans sold one another for pieces of gold and mirrors, they enslaved others as they assumed new and foreign religions, they turned their backs on their brethren as the race towards capitalistic gains became inevitable, and propelled their ways of life. Colonialism destroyed the Africans' identities as they began to doubt their past and their values. Yet it is a great paradox today that it is Western philosophy that will enhance the struggle to rebuild the African philosophy. As Africans contemplate African philosophy, they will be aware of the ravage created by the colonial "civilisation". Yet the African philosophy should not be merely perceived as a response to colonial culture, for this will be a grievous fault. Africans have a magnanimous agenda; that of magnifying Africa's role in the world. In fact, there are three critical aspects about African philosophy: unravel, teach and redress. Unravelling the hidden past and history is basic to any African philosophy this century. After this, Africans need to teach one another before they will be able to redress the colonial damage whose main agenda was to obfuscate the African mind.

African philosophy may not be as structured as the Western philosophy if one uses Western spectacles, but all African societies had this. The tribe taught the best of its orators, warriors and queens from this philosophy. African philosophy is a way of life that inspires Africans to live using history and identity. It is an inspiration that enables Africans to define themselves. Today, African philosophy seeks to defeat Western notions of what Africa is and who her people are. This is no lesser philosophy, for many have noted how African philosophy is relegated to ethnophilosophy by those who want to demean and denigrate it. The philosophy of African thinkers such as Mazisi Kunene, Tiyo Soga, Eskia Mphahlele and Charlotte Maxeke is no lesser than that of Hegel, Kierkegaard or Foucault. The African philosophy exposes the truth that Africans are able to look critically at their own epistemologies. Because they were not using the same Western labels, people including black African scholars trivialised these. Even today there are myriad African scholars who doubt the practicability of including African philosophy across the curricula in higher education institutions as well as in basic education. Africans had art, ways of seeing, humanhood, and ways of interpreting life, dependability and ethical living with the environment. All these when looked at critically formed part of the African philosophy.

Kimmerle[18] noted that he found three distinct themes in African philosophy:

(a) The basic concept of vital force differing from the basic concept of being, which is prevalent in Western philosophy.
(b) The prevailing role of the community, differing from the predominantly individualistic thinking in the West.
(c) The belief in spirits, differing from the scientific and rationalistic way of thought, which is prevalent in Western philosophy.

Furthermore, Kimmerle explored how communalism shapes the African philosophy, yet he cautioned us about authors who are against the idealisation of African philosophy. Kimmerle[19] maintained that:

> The most fervent criticism is formulated by VC Simiyu, a Kenyan political scientist. He speaks of the "democratic myth in African traditional societies". He makes clear that hate and struggle were not unknown in these societies. Moreover, to presuppose one and the same structure everywhere proves to be a too simplistic way of speaking about traditional social life in Africa.

The above can be linked to what Ezekiel Mphahlele, a renowned Africanist, stated in a speech in 1963, when he underscored the point that we need not romanticise Africa. Mphahlele[20] opined:

> I feel insulted when some people imply that Africa is not also a violent continent. I am a violent person and proud of it because it is often a healthy human state of mind; some day I'm going to plunder, rape, set things on fire, I'm going to cut somebody's throat; I'm going to subvert a government; I'm going to organize a coup d'état; yes, I'm going to oppress my own people; I'm going to hunt the rich fat black men who bully the small weak black men and destroy them; I'm going to become a capitalist, and woe to all who cross my path or who want to be my servants or chauffeurs and so on…

Simiyu and Mphahlele demonstrate that it will be a detriment to think of Africa as pure and flawless. These are some of the caveats that African philosophers need to heed as they chart the various tenets that would strengthen the continent. Yet Africans will hardly attain victories without the decolonisation process. When the colonised has not achieved a mindset, the changes will be superficial.

Wiredu[21] argued for the need for decolonisation if Africans will succeed in their quest for African philosophy. He also pointed out that we need a conceptual decolonisation, which is "the elimination from our thought of modes of conceptualisation that came to us through colonisation and remain in our thinking owing to inertia rather than to our own reflective choices"[22]. Furthermore, Wiredu contended that Africans should use African languages in formulating their philosophy. The use of foreign, Western languages in formulating African philosophy by Africans may be a huge hindrance. "The main antidote to that impediment, as far as I can see, is for African philosophers to try to think philosophically in their own vernaculars, even if they still have to expound their results in some Western language"[23]. Decolonisation starts with the language, as per an argument that was also advanced by Cheik Anta Diop[24]. Language has an immense impact on philosophical formulations. Wiredu[25] perceived studies on African philosophy as aids to decolonisation. He also stated that decolonisation in African philosophy means "divesting African philosophical thinking of all undue influences emanating from our colonial past"[26]. Oelofson[27] also wrote about the need for African philosophy to decolonise the mind as it develops concepts with roots in Africa. She referred to this understanding of African philosophy as "philosophy-in-place". Oelofson also cited Tabensky, who argued that African philosophy should be "a quest for health" and a search for authenticity. She posited:

> I believe that African philosophy, as a result of this aim, results in empowering Africans through articulating philosophical positions which take the context and cultural particularities of African places into account. This empowerment in turn leads to a reclamation of the intellectual space denied to Africa during the racist project of colonisation.

African philosophers have been referred to as ethnophilosophers, which is a concept that has been disputed by various philosophers from Africa (Wiredu[28]; Imbo[29]; Osha[30]). Wiredu[31] has contended that the Western philosophers have always highlighted the peculiar nature of the Africans' philosophy, and have seen this to signify a peculiar African way of thinking. Wiredu argued that there is much to learn from African traditional cultures, although educated Africans should not uncritically adhere to traditional African beliefs and practices[32]. The emergence of ethnophilosophy, which was instituted to show the unique nature of African philosophy, was started to advance colonial beliefs. Osha[33] pointed out that ethnophilosophy has been disregarded because of various reasons, which include (a) it is perceived as a colonial product; (b) it seeks to de-agentialise the subject people and agents; and (c) it is patronising in its claims to "give voice to the voiceless and power to the powerless"[34]. Furthermore, a number of Western trained African philosophers have claimed that describing beliefs of a group of people can hardly be referred to as philosophy[34], yet it was this beginning that served to goad these philosophers to find alternatives; some pointed out that this was a starting point of the modern discussions of African philosophy[35], but ethnophilosophy has always been criticised by Western philosophers. Janz[36] claimed that:

> …ethnophilosophy does not have a critical edge, but is merely descriptive; it is anonymous, in the sense that no particular person holds any specific views, but they are ascribed as a group; ethnophilosophy overgeneralises to all Africa, and thus covers over deep internal differences; ethnophilosophy is fraught with all the problems that any ethnographic research has in capturing meaning.

One of the major contentions when it comes to ethnophilosophy is that it is too collective to be a philosophy. There are also various implications that seek to demonstrate that Africans cannot rationalise. Western philosophy tends to gauge the strength of ethnophilosophy by comparing it with "Western Philosophy". The paradox in this, however, is that this is the persisting colonisation of black African thought. Philosophy will always be influenced by questions that people have as they search for wisdom, and the Africans' experiences are different in many aspects from Western experiences. Echekwube[36] argued that:

> The African has carefully entrenched around himself a galaxy of divinities in a hierarchical order and he has a host of spirits who play very important roles in his daily life…They (African philosophers) have written enormously of such problems as reincarnations, predestination and the after-life.

Echekwube[37] also rightly demonstrated why the world needs a philosophy such as the African philosophy, pointing out that the African world-view is integrative of both Western and Eastern philosophies – African philosophy has set goals and seeks "to show how they can be integrated into the scheme of things in order to realise a richer world culture, a type of civilisation which can begin to bring about the much desired peace on earth"[38]. Whilst philosophers such as Paul Houtntondji[39] characterised ethnophilosophy as pseudophilosophy, it remains an area of a group of philosophers who want to see philosophy decolonised. African philosophers will continue using rituals, myths and symbols as sources of knowledge. To deny the life-worlds of people because of over-emphasis on critical analysis would be to rob the Africans of means to record their culture and identity. "The lesson from all this and the answer to the question of whether ethnophilosophy is really philosophy, seems to be that whether philosophy should be written or unwritten, modern or traditional, depends on the values with which one starts out"[40]. In this volume, several authors have used the principles from African philosophy in generating knowledge. This does not in any way make their chapters less inspiring or less "scientific". Van

Niekerk[41] also cited Oruka, who posited that even those African philosophers who claim to be on the right path regarding the question of African philosophy may have been helped by the provocation of ethnophilosophy. When African philosophers discuss African Renaissance in African education, African philosophy supplies much of the foundation of the debate.

2.3 African Renaissance, African Philosophy and Education

The years 2015 and 2016 will go down in history as the years that South African university students strengthened their fight for free education. Coupled with this was a fight for the decolonisation of the curriculum; the students wanted an education that is Africa-centred and undergirded by African philosophy. There might be less consensus now as to what kind of higher education we will have if African philosophy is introduced, but we can be certain of the need for Africans to revisit their history. Africans need to see the damage caused by colonialism in Africa, and education is well placed in exploring how African philosophy can be utilised. Rodney[42] argued that education, both formal and informal, is crucial in any type of society for the "preservation of the lives of its members and the maintenance of the social structure". Furthermore, Rodney[43] contended that education can also be responsible for social change. The institutions of learning in Africa still bear much character from colonial education, which has denuded anything African in its visage. When the African students demand decolonised education, it is a call for a system that responds to the African experience. Regarding the colonial educational experience, Rodney claimed that:

> Another aspect of the colonial educational and cultural patterns which needs investigation is the manner in which Europeans' racism and contempt was expressed not only by hostility to African culture but by paternalism and by praise or negative and static social features. There were many colonialists who wished to preserve in perpetuity everything that was African, if it appeared quaint or intriguing to them.

Today people have realised the importance of formal education in combating the colonial legacy. The call for African philosophy is a means of endeavouring to move towards an emancipating and relevant education. Chumbow[44] pointed out that education is not only a social service, but a much required national investment. Hountondji[45] declared that what is crucial today is not to study African cultures, but to live them. He argued that there is more need to practice African cultures and transform them in the meantime. Hountondji also pointed out that the teaching of African languages should give way to teaching in the African languages, instead of using English to discuss the structures of Yoruba. Universities should lead in this – "this will obviously require an enormous amount of preparatory work which only the universities can undertake"[46]. Hountondji stated that we should avoid "exhibiting ourselves to ourselves and so looking at ourselves through the eyes of others". In bringing forth African philosophy, the institutions of higher learning should be emancipatory in how they do their business. In Africa, we need to seriously rethink the role of education as we bring in the African philosophy. These are all pertinent arguments for achieving the African Renaissance in education.

In the *Heart of Darkness,* Marlow never saw any possibilities of a renaissance for a dark Africa[47.] The word renaissance in African Renaissance conjures hope, progress, resilience and the defeat of colonialism. In the context of Africa's history, the African Renaissance will embrace African philosophy for the emancipation and overcoming of blind intellectual subservience to Western ways of knowing. When Cheikh Anta Diop[48] coined the concept in 1946, he defined this term as encapsulating the renewal of culture and economy in Africa. He perceived the African Renaissance as a way in which Africans can rediscover themselves in arts, architecture and language. He pointed out that "the development of our indigenous is the prerequisite for a real African Renaissance"[49]. Diop added that for the African child, education is a difficult exercise as they have to understand the meaning of words in a foreign language, whilst also trying to grasp the accompanying reality of the words. In South Africa, the current calls for scrapping the Afrikaans language to replace it with English may be misinformed, as what this means is that Afrikaans may be used less but English will be elevated to the detriment of African languages. This language debate is pursued more by Ntombela in Chapter 11 and to some extent by Kamwendo in Chapter 10.

The call for an African Renaissance in education is an awareness of not only African languages and African philosophy in education; it is a call for a system based on the history and experiences of Africans. African notions have undergone much strain after the ills of colonialism, enslavement and denigration over the years. The call for an African Renaissance is to reclaim that African potential, which can only come about if actively reclaimed. Many people believe that the African Renaissance can be attained in full with the attempt to embrace Pan-Africanism. This indeed makes sense, as a Pan-African people unified by history can find in the African Renaissance a stronger cause. The African experiences so many challenges because of a number of circumstances, however Pan-African unity can enable Africans to strive for a future of enlightenment; of going back to African roots. Africans need a renewal in language use, in heritage, in economy, in forming institutions that are collective in approach and in being intent on fighting corruption and poverty. Africa will not prosper when there are such ills. Education should attempt to defeat some of these ills for people to really appreciate the ultimate goals of an African Renaissance.

What will delay an African Renaissance is the lack of maturity that is necessary to be receptive to African ideals. Intellectuals in higher education institutions, for example, need the wisdom of intellectuals from the communities. The renaissance needs to encompass the various knowledges from different societal strata. Theorising about the poor but excluding them will only bring superficial viewpoints. This can symbolically be perceived when the grassroots people stand up to demand service delivery in their communities. No one can express their problems better. Nabudere[50] asserted that:

> The struggle against imperialism in Africa was a struggle for African independence and to that extent for an African Renaissance. This struggle at the cultural level could not have taken on a political form until the whole continent was freed from colonialism and this struggle against apartheid represented a stage in raising the anti-imperialist consciousness of the African people and

their unity as African people in the diaspora and at home on the African continent. Up to this point, Pan-Africanism played a significant role in developing the unity of purpose.

The struggle for an African Renaissance needs the coming together of all intellectuals to combat coloniality and power. The role of intellectuals in society has never been so crucial, especially in Africa at a time when all need the renaissance in society. The development of ideas in Africa will be dependent upon the direction given by its intellectuals. The hierarchy of intellectuals is very important in society, and it is these intellectuals who will speed up or slow down the process of transformation and decolonisation. From rustic life in hamlets, intellectuals nurture life to give even more life to society. In villages, the people will bring forth information on when best to reap and sow seeds. Intellectual work is knowledge production and it is not only schools that develop knowledge producers. The African Renaissance needs different kinds of people to generate knowledge for a global world. Where Africa is today is a time in history where Africans seek intellectuals who stand for the oppressed in society. In Africa, the colonised have always had intellectuals who support the colonial and imperialist notions of living. In a transforming society, intellectuals should lead the knowledge base with ideas that seek to challenge the status quo. For an African Renaissance, we need various progressive intellectual groups from society. Three kinds of intellectuals may strive to bring about change for an African Renaissance - the *Idyllic Intellectuals* (these are equal to Gramsci's organic intellectuals); the *Revolutionary Intellectuals* (these include mainly the workers who are intent on fighting imperialism and worker oppression); and finally, the *Erudite Intellectuals* who we find in the ranks of university staff and other knowledge production fields. Some will straddle between two or more of these "intellectual roles".

From the debates above, it is clear that in Africa the philosophy will show how it can be an antidote to colonialism as it elevates African thought. The African philosophy will also be incomplete if it does not explicate blackness, oppression, the meaning of Western philosophy, as well as the liberation of the black African from the shackles of history. Institutions of learning, for example, fail to begin here. Before one can understand Althusser or Derrida, we may also need to read a Krune Mqhayi, a Kwame Nkrumah, a Leopold Senghor or a Cheik Anta Diop. As Africa seeks to transform education there is no better way than starting from asking more about questions that seek answers from African philosophy. Ruch and Anyawu[52] pointed out that African philosophy was spurred by frustration:

> The frustration according to Ruch and Anyawu was due to historical events such as slavery, colonialism and racism that generated frustration with European philosophy. This eventually led to angry questions and then responses and reactions out of which African philosophy emerged. These reactions led to a great debate and then to more questions and reactions… The frustration was borne out of colonial caricature of Africa as culturally naïve, intellectually docile and rationally inept; the caricature was created by European scholars such as Kant, Hegel and much later, Levy-Bruhl. It was the reaction to this caricature of Africa that led African scholars returning from Europe into philosophising.

The call for an Afrocentric education by the student movement in South Africa is a frustration that seeks the African to be revived in education. For many decades, all over Africa, African education has been anything but African. This movement correctly looked at how African philosophy, among others, can reshape education. However, this has hardly been debated by administrators and academics, which does not portend well for it seems to imply that we are in a society that is not ready for Afrocentric education. In a theory I have just developed, I speak of four proclivities of African philosophy. I perceive these as elements or factors crucial in attaining African philosophy. These are:

Communication – African languages
Connectedness – Nature and environment
Collective dialecticism – Community, academies
Critical self-scrutiny - Intellectualism[53]

All these inclinations challenge the colonial debate. These four try to attend to the frustration in institutions of learning. Education in Africa is below where it should be if it fails to respond to the African milieu, hence the need for an African philosophy. The huge need we have, however, is to start talking about the African philosophy at tertiary institutions. The Department of Basic Education in South Africa needs to play its role right from grade R throughout the school career. The debate on introducing Mandarin in schools is an unfortunate decision in a country where school children battle to master any of the nine indigenous languages, yet we all know the case of politics over pedagogy.

2.4   African philosophy: Did Nyerere miss the mark?

The late Tanzanian President Julius Nyerere introduced in his country an idea of socialism based on the philosophy of *Ujamaa* or familyhood[54]. *Ujamaa* has since been described as an African philosophy that Nyerere wanted to use in overcoming the ill effects of individualism introduced by the coloniser in Africa. *Ujamaa* is a concept derived from the KiSwahili language, referring to communalism among villagers, that was a socialist system of village cooperatives which aimed to lead to equal opportunities and villagers being able to be self-sustaining. *Ujamaa* was criticised by some who regarded it as a philosophical idealism and led Tanzania to squander developmental opportunities, while Ibuwoh and Dibua[55] argued that beyond the socialist rhetoric, *Ujamaa* was based on a fallacy of developmentalism that involved:

> …the objectification of African peasants and rural dwellers as hapless victims of underdevelopment who needed to be emancipated to higher levels of social and material well being, where these better standard of living was defined in terms of the Westernisation of the peasantry. As a result, the Ujamaa's commitment to the modernisation paradigm resulted in a situation where improving the conditions of the peasants meant alienating them from their cultural and social realities in favor of transplanted Western ways of life.

Nyerere's *Ujamaa* was a philosophy that sought to bring all Tanzanians together, thus creating stability. Nyerere was also basing *Ujamaa* on the aspects of equality and unity[56]. The African philosophy will always seek to achieve this unity and stability, yet the challenge will be to overcome Westernisation as one does that. What was beneficial about the philosophy of *Ujamaa* was its attempt to include all Tanzanians, young and old, formally educated and not. In fact, this should be the basis of an African philosophy. Nyerere, in his inaugural speech in 1962, spoke of the need for every Tanzanian to be a teacher who teaches about *Ujamaa* wherever they are. Crucial to his pronouncements about *Ujamaa*, Nyerere explained that everyone is an expert, thus the people should not wait for experts to tell them what *Ujamaa* is all about. "*Ujamaa* is a way of life and there are no experts better qualified than yourselves to expound the way of life. We are all of us *Ujamaa* experts"[57].

Despite the strong challenges that Nyerere's *Ujamaa* stood against, he tried to bring forth an African philosophy, but any African philosophy needs leadership and visionaries to uphold it. This is an argument raised by Chikoko in Chapter 16. Although others could see flaws in *Ujamaa*, many Tanzanian citizens understood and owned Nyerere's vision. Kilby[58] cited Shivji, who talked about the way in which Nyerere united the nation and ensured political stability in those early days of freedom. Nyerere introduced a powerful dimension by also introducing KiSwahili as a lingua franca, thus rejecting European languages to unify the Tanzanian nation. This created a sense of community in the African sense. Kilby[59] maintained that Nyerere's philosophy was not sustained because of a lack of leaders who were visionaries. Nyerere used cultural heritage to draft his philosophy of *Ujamaa*. Echekwubu cited Madimbe, who observed that Nyerere's socialism was pragmatic and rejected capitalism, supporting communalism and self-reliance[60]. Furthermore, Echekwubu argued that African socialism emphasises societal integration, economic growth and continental independence. Arguably, this is a kind of African philosophy that the continent needs.

There will still be many other challenges faced by African philosophy, like with any other field of study whose pronouncements may sometimes be contested, yet African philosophy is required for social, political and cultural grounding. Makumba[61] posited that "African philosophy should take a positive approach to the current circumstances and turn what appears to be a culture clash into a breeding ground for a double-edged political philosophy, one that seeks a dynamic cultural retrieval…".

2.5 Conclusion

The struggle for an African Renaissance and the African philosophy is the beginning of emancipatory education in Africa. These will create opportunities for Africans to perceive their world and appreciate the ecology and landscape of the continent, while also being able to enhance the African economy in a global world. African intellectuals have a task to position Africa well in the global world. The African Renaissance will not necessarily make Africa unique because there are many elements that Africa shares with the world, yet the positive elements such as the African philosophy that give Africa its identity will enhance Africa's renaissance. Many Pan-African leaders, both past and present, realised Africa's strength as its unity, which augured well for a prosperous continent. Nyerere knew that in building a strong Tanzania he needed to unite her people, and that there would be positive outcomes for Africa in general. Patrice Lumumba in Congo and Anton Lembede in South Africa are some of the leaders who saw hope in an African Renaissance. The Pan-Africanist thinker Mmangaliso Sobukwe also saw the immense role of education in Africa, labelling it a "barometer of African thought". This is an apt expression when we think of the education needed in Africa today; a system of education that will be able to guide the African as it becomes a compass for intellectual ideas on the continent. Certainly, we can no longer embrace or believe in the images of Africa as portrayed by characters such as Marlow and Kurtz in the *Heart of Darkness*.

References

[1]Conrad, J. 1973. *Heart of Darkness*. New York: Penguin.

[2]Achebe, C. 1977. An image of Africa: Racism in Conrad's Heart of Darkness. *Massachusetts Review*, 18: 782-794.

[3]Conrad, J. 1973. *Heart of Darkness*. New York: Penguin.

[4]Ibid.

[5]Ibid.

[6]Rodney, W. 2009. *How Europe underdeveloped Africa*. Abuja: Panaf Publishing.

[7]Ibid.

[8]Bernstein, B. 2000. *Pedagogy, Symbolic Control and Identity: Theory, Research, Critique*. Lanham: Rowman, Littlefield Publishers.

[9]Higgs, P. 2003. African philosophy and the transformation of educational discourse in South Africa. *Journal of Education*, 30: 5-18.

[10]Janz, B. B. 2009. *Philosophy in an African Place*. Plymouth: Lexington Books.

[11]Anyawu, K. C. 1989. *The substance of African Philosophy*. Auchi: African Philosophy Projects Publications.

[12]Janz, B. B. 2009. *Philosophy in an African Place*. Plymouth: Lexington Books.

[13]Gyekye, K. 1995. *African Philosophical Thought; The Akan Conceptual Scheme*. Philadelphia: Temple University Press.

[14]Ibid.

[15]Mkandawire, T. 2005. African intellectuals and Nationalism. In T. Mkandawire (Ed.). *Rethinking Politics, Language. Gender and Development*. London: Zed Books, pp 10-55.

[16]Ibid.

[17]Chinweizu. 2016. *On Negrophobia: Psychoneurotic Obstacles to Black Autonomy: or why I love Michael Jackson*. Retrieved from: http:www.africawithin.com/chinweizu/on-negrophobia.htm. [Date accessed: December 12, 2016.]

[18]Kimmerrle, H. 2006. *Ubuntu and Communalism in African Philosophy and Arts*. Retrieved from: http://rozenbergquarterly.com/ubuntu-and-communalism-in-african-philosophy-andart. [Date accessed: December 11, 2016.]

[19]Ibid.

[20]Mphahlele, E. 1963. On Negritude in Literature. The Rand Daily Mail, Johannesburg, June 7, 1968. In A. L. McLeod and M. B. McLeod (Eds.). *Powre above Powres: Representative South African Speeches, the Rhetoric of Race and Religion*. Mysore, India: University of Mysore.

[21]Wiredu, K. 1995, Conceptual decolonisation in African philosophy. In O. Oladipo (Ed.). *Selections and introductions: Conceptual decolonisation in African Philosophy – four essays*. Badan: Hope Publications.

[22]Ibid

[23]Ibid

[24]Diop, C. 1996. *Towards the African Renaissance: Essays in culture and development, 1946-1960*. (Translation by E. P. Modum). London: The Estate of Cheikh Anta Diop and Kamak House.

[25]Wiredu, K. 1998. Toward decolonising African philosophy and religion. *African Studies Quarterly*, 1(4): 17.

[26]Ibid.

[27]Oelofson, R. 2015. Decolonisation of the African mind and intellectual landscape. *Phronium*, 16(2): 130-146.

[28]Wiredu, K. 1995. How not to compare African Thought with Western Thought. In A. G. Mosley (Ed.). *African Philosophy: Selected Readings*. New Jersey: Prentice Hall.

[29]Imbo, S. O. 1994. *An Introduction to African Philosophy*. Lanham: Rowman & Littlefield.

[30]Osha, S. 2011. *Post-ethnophilosophy*. New York: Rodopi.

[31]Wiredu, K. 1995. How not to compare African Thought with Western Thought. In A. G. Mosley (Ed.). *African Philosophy: Selected Readings*. New Jersey: Prentice Hall.

[32]Ibid.

[33]Osha, S. 2011. *Post-ethnophilosophy*. New York: Rodopi.

[34]Janz, B. B. 2009. *Philosophy in an African Place*. Plymouth: Lexington Books.

[35]Ibid.

[36]Echekwube, A. O. 1994. *An Introduction to African Philosophy*. Ibadan: Kraft Books.

[37]Ibid.

[38]Ibid.

[39]Hountondji, P. J. 1983. *African Philosophy & Myth Reality*. Bloomington: Indiana University Press.

[40]Imbo, S. O. 1998. An Introduction to African Philosophy. Lanham: Rowman & Little.

[41]Van Niekerk, M. 2000. Understanding trends in African thinking: A Critical Discussion. In P. H. Coetzee and A. P. J. Roux (Eds.). *Philosophy from Africa: A Text with Readings*. Oxford: Oxford University Press.

[42]Rodney, W. 2009. *How Europe underdeveloped Africa*. Abuja: Panaf Publishing.

[43]Ibid.

[44]Chumbow, B. S. 2005. The language question and national development in Africa. In T. Mkandawire (Ed.). *African Intellectuals: Rethinking Politics, language, Gender and Development*. London: Zed Books.

[45]Hountondji, P. J. 1983. *African Philosophy & Myth Reality*. Bloomington: Indiana University Press.

[46]Ibid.

[47]Conrad, J. 1973. *Heart of Darkness*. New York: Penguin.

[48]Diop, C. 1996. *Towards the African Renaissance: Essays in culture and development, 1946-1960*. (Translation: Egbuna P. Modum.) London: The Estate Cheikh Anta Diop and Kamak House.

[49]Ibid.

[50]Nabudere, D. W. 2001. The African Renaissance in the age of globalisation. *African Journal of Political Science*, 6(2): 11-27.

[51]Nyerere, J. K. 1970. President's Inaugural Address. *Freedom and Unity: A selection from writings and speeches*. Dar es Salaam: Oxford University Press.

[52]Ruch, E. A. & Anyawu, K. C. 1981. *African Philosophy: an introduction to the main philosophical trends in contemporary Africa*. Rome: Catholic Book Agency.

[53]Msila, V. 2016. *Of African Philosophy and African Education*. Paper presented at NMMU Book Launch. Port Elizabeth, 03 May 2016.

[54]Nyerere, J. K. 1970. President's Inaugural Address. *Freedom and Unity: A selection from writings and speeches*. Dar es Salaam: Oxford University Press.

[55]Ibawoh, B. & Dibua, J. I. 2003. Deconstructing Ujamaa: The Legacy of Julius Nyerere in the quest for social and economic development in Africa. *African Journal of Political Science*, 8(1): 59-83.

[56]Nyerere, J. K. 1970. President's Inaugural Address. *Freedom and Unity: A selection from writings and speeches*. Dar es Salaam: Oxford University Press.

[57]Ibid.

[58]Vilby, K. 2007. *Independent? Tanzania's challenges since Uhuru*. Uppsala: Nordiska Afrikainstitutet.

[59]Ibid.

[60]Echekwube, A. O. 1994. *An Introduction to African Philosophy*. Ibadan: Kraft Books.

[61]Makumba, M. M. 2007. *An introduction to African Philosophy: Past and Present*. Nairobi: Paulines Publications Africa.

Chapter 3

Rethinking Pan-Africanism and the African Renaissance today: Where did Azikiwe and Awolowo miss it?

Fred Ekpe F. Ayokhai, Department of History and
Peter Wilfred Naankiel, Department of History, Federal University Lafia, Nigeria

3.1   Introduction

The fact that Africa is the cradle of humanity is no longer in contestation, yet Africa lies on the lowest rung of the ladder of human development. This fate is absurd given the universal logic of the historical transformations of the existential experiences of humanity. This absurdity lies not only in the fact that she had led the course of human civilisation prior to the age of the slave trade, but also because of her abundant wealth of human and material resources. The veracity of her claim to the wealth of human and material resources is already established in the attention she attracted from the rest of the world, especially the West, since the 15th century. This absurdity of horrendous poverty in the midst of fabulous wealth has been attributed to the dynamics of her exploitative and dehumanising relations over the centuries[1]. To explain the state of underdevelopment in Africa, the epochs in Afro-Western relations since the 15th century are often divided into the slavery/slave trade, and colonial and neo-colonial/post-independence phases.

The area that came to be known as Nigeria was indeed an integral part of these processes of Afro-Western relations and the consequent underdevelopment. In fact, the Nigeria area was such a strategic part of the slave trade that a part of the area became known as the 'Slave Coast'. The significance of the Nigeria area did not wane, even at the expiration of the slave trade. Indeed, the colonial enterprise in the area was propelled by the equally strong economic motive of 'legitimate commerce'. This is substantiated by not only the incorporation of the area into the European colonial estate, but also by the fact that one of the earliest protectorates established in the area was named the 'Oil Rivers Protectorate', thus denoting the major object of European trade interest. The fact that the river Niger, from which the name of the country, Nigeria, was coined, provided the major means of transportation for expatriating the commodities of European trade interests, further corroborates the economic thesis in Afro-Western relations. Even in the post-independence era Nigeria has remained an area of strategic importance to the West, largely because of her huge population which provides a ready market for Western industrial finished goods and her Niger Delta region which is a source of supply of the cheap crude oil that powers its industries. However, writers such as Shivji[2] have written about capital accumulation, which refers to profits gained by a country from natural resources that do not facilitate the construction of a domestic industrial sector. Arguably, the latter also applies to Nigeria.

The aim of this chapter is to demonstrate that Afro-Western relations across time have been conceptualised and executed within the framework of human thoughts and actions. African political leaders have been in the driving seat of this process; how they perceived and reacted to the actions of their Western counterparts in these processes of relations have gone a long way in determining the nature of the emergent Afro-Western relations and the place of African polities in the global system. In fact, without a crop of African leaders who had a hunger for freedom, the liberation of the continent from the claws of colonial rule would have been unattainable. This chapter therefore argues that leadership was not only a critical variable in the liberation of Africa from colonial rule, but also remains central to the attainment of the African Renaissance at this critical juncture of post-independence nation-building and development in African history. Specifically, this chapter:

1.   rethinks the contributions of Nnamdi Azikiwe and Obafemi Awolowo regarding the development of Pan-African nationalist thoughts and the African Renaissance movements during and after the decolonisation of Nigeria;

2.   describes the nature and type of Pan-Africanist ideas and thoughts that Azikiwe and Awolowo espoused, and explains their implications for the African Renaissance in the context of decolonisation and post-independence national regeneration in Nigeria;

3.   demonstrates the nexus between the emergent typology of Pan-Africanist thoughts and the failure of the African Renaissance project in post-independence Nigeria within the context of the establishment of democratic political systems, economic development, and peace in a rapidly globalising world;

4.   highlights the weaknesses in the Pan-Africanist and African Renaissance thoughts of Azikiwe and Awolowo, with a view to explaining the intersection between Nigeria's slow progress in attaining democratic political systems, sustainable economic development and social stability; and

5.   makes a recommendation for the extrication of Nigeria from the negative outcomes of the weak Pan-Africanist and African Renaissance thoughts of Azikiwe and Awolowo, which resulted in the entrenchment of the prependal politics, predatory leadership culture, economic quagmire, social crisis and parasitic state system that characterised her post-independence existential realities.

3.2   Afro-Western Relations through the lens of Nigeria

The 15th century witnessed a reversal of the place and role of Africa in the global system, and therefore marked a watershed in Afro-Western relations in the Nigeria area. By 1471, Portuguese ships had reconnoitred the West African coast as far south as the Niger Delta, and in 1841 emissaries from the King of Portugal visited the court of the oba (king) of Benin. For a time, Portugal and Benin maintained close relations and the trade in slaves constituted a significant part of these. Later the trade in slaves extended to the south-western coast of Nigeria and neighbouring parts of the present-day Republic of Benin, which together became known as the 'slave coast'. When the West African coast began to supply slaves to the Americas in the last third of the 16th century, the Portuguese continued to look to the Bight of Benin as one of its sources of supply. The Portuguese monopoly on the West African trade was, however, broken by the rising naval power of the Netherlands in the late 16th century. The Dutch thus took over the Portuguese trading stations on the coast that were the sources of slaves for the Americas, however French and English competition was later to undermine the Dutch position. Although the slave ports from Lagos to Calabar saw the flags of other European maritime countries and North American colonies, Britain became the dominant slave trading power in the Nigeria area in the 18th century; its ships handled two-fifths of the transatlantic traffic and Nigeria kept its important position in the slave trade throughout the great expansion of the transatlantic trade. Slightly more slaves came from the Nigerian coast than from Angola in the 18th century, while perhaps thirty percent of all slaves sent across the Atlantic came from Nigeria in the 19th century. In the 18th and 19th centuries, the Oyo kingdom and the Aro confederacy were responsible for most of the slave exports from Nigeria. Over the period of the slave trade, it is estimated that more than 3.5 million slaves were shipped from Nigeria to the Americas. The outbreak of the industrial revolution in Europe, as well as the abolition of the slave trade and its substitution with 'legitimate commerce', led to the dawn of another epoch in Afro-Western relations in Nigeria in the late 19th century.

The new phase of Afro-Western relations in most of the area of West Africa, which later came to be known as the Colony and Protectorate of Nigeria, was established between 1861 and 1960 when it was gradually but steadily conquered and put under British colonial rule. Between 1886 and 1899, much of the area witnessed a spell of company rule under the Royal Niger Company. In 1900, the Southern Nigeria Protectorate and the Northern Nigeria Protectorate passed from company hands to the Crown. The process of conscripting the various peoples and societies into the colonial fiefdom of Britain entailed brutal military subjugation, dehumanising psychological disorientation, and gruesome material exploitation in a manner hitherto unprecedented in that area.

For the area south of Nigeria, the process of colonisation began in 1861 with the British establishing the Colony of Lagos, from where the colonists progressed steadily to establish the Oil Rivers Protectorate (later re-designated the Niger Coast Protectorate) in 1884 and subsequently conquered the hinterlands. The eventual 'unitarisation' of the Southern Protectorate and the Colony of Lagos took place in 1906, after Lugard declared the polities of northern Nigeria a British protectorate in 1900. The defeat of the Sokoto Caliphate, which took place in 1903, marked Britain's effective occupation and establishment of colonial rule over the northern Nigeria area. However, the amalgamation of the southern and northern territories eventually gave birth to the Colony and Protectorate of Nigeria in 1914. The British held sway over the administration of the colonial enclave, Nigeria, but protracted and persistent struggles forced them to grant the Richards Constitution of 1939, which was replaced by the Macpherson Constitution of 1951, which was, in turn, supplanted by the Lyttleton Constitution in 1954. This process of constitutional reform forced the British to throw in the towel and grant the country independence on 1st October, 1960.

The era preceding World War II marked the defeat of African military resistance to the colonial enterprise, but the post-World War II era witnessed the reawakening and re-dedication of Africans to their historic responsibility of reclaiming and preserving their group existence, collective dignity and material subsistence. The era was dominated by Pan-African nationalism, thinking, ideas and actions. The post-WWII period thus marked a watershed in Pan-Africanist and African Renaissance movements. In the context of the colonial subjugation and exploitation of Africa, decolonisation and national liberation struggles are conceived as part of the movement for African Renaissance; an attempt to redeem the African persona, restore his dignity and liberate his material resources, including his territory, from the marauding white colonists and neo-colonists. In the Nigeria area of the British West African colonies, several individuals took the lead in developing, interpreting and advocating for the Pan-African nationalist and renaissance thinking that inspired, propelled and gave force to the myriad of socio-political activities, which eventually culminated in the liberation of the Colony and Protectorate of Nigeria from the British colonisers, and transformed it into an independent member of the comity of nation-states. The ideas, thoughts and actions of Nnamdi Azikiwe and Obafemi Awolowo were foremost in this process in Nigeria. The ideas and thoughts of these Pan-Africanists are yet to be subjected to a systematic comparison, while their intersection with African Renaissance thoughts and actions in post-independence Nigeria have been equally neglected. The next section of this chapter undertakes a comparative study of the contributions of Nnamdi Azikiwe and Obafemi Awolowo to the development of Pan-Africanist and African Renaissance thoughts since the decolonisation struggle began in Nigeria.

3.3 Pan-Africanism and African Renaissance: Continuing the Legacy of African Struggle

Pan-Africanism or Pan-African consciousness dates back to 1900 and the pioneering works of Edward Blyden (1832 – 1912)[3]. Pan-Africanism, which means 'all Africans', metamorphosed from being a worldview into a social and political movement. It "seeks to unify and uplift both native Africans and those of the African Diaspora as part of a global community"[4]. It was originally conceived as the ideology of unity of all black African cultures and countries by Trinidadian Henry Sylvester Williams[5]. Although Pan-Africanism began in the West Indies, the concept expanded to include all black African-descended people worldwide who were dispersed to the United States of America, the Caribbean, Latin America and parts of the Middle-East, including South Asia, through the Atlantic and the Islamic/East African slave trades and later immigration. Recently, the concept has expanded to also include the Dravidian blacks of India, the Siddi, the Kanikar, the Tamil and the Kamil, the Andamanese Island Negroes and the black aboriginal populations of Australia, Melanesia and New Guinea, among others. Therefore, Pan-Africanism has come to encompass all African communities everywhere in the world. The colonisation of the African continent by European powers in the late 19th century provided the impetus for the rapid and widespread development of Pan-African consciousness. Pan-Africanism came to include the various movements in Africa which profess as their objective the unity of Africans and the elimination of colonialism and white supremacy from the continent. The first Pan-African congress was held in London in 1900; other congresses followed in Paris in 1919, London in 1923 and New York in 1927. African organisations in London also joined to form the Pan-African Federation, which demanded African autonomy and independence for the first time.

With the convocation of the First Conference of Independent African States in Accra, Ghana, in 1958, Pan-Africanism was launched as an intergovernmental movement, yet Ghana and Liberia were the only sub-Saharan countries in attendance. As independence was attained by more African countries, other interpretations of Pan-Africanism emerged to include the Union of African States (1960), the African States of the Casablanca Charter (1961), the African and Malagasy Union (1962), and the African-Malagasy-Mauritius Common Organisation (1964). Similarly, Pan-Africanism became associated with black nationalism, for instance, during South Africa's apartheid regime there was a Pan-Africanist congress that dealt with the oppression of black South Africans.

The primary focus of the Pan-Africanist movement has remained Africa, while the different struggles in the various blocs of the continent for the liberation of the black world have been characterised by measures of cooperative tactical endeavours and ideological exchanges between Africans in the diaspora and those on the continent. Put succinctly, Pan-Africanism has come to represent the dynamics of Africans' thought processes, ideology, philosophy and struggles for the emancipation of black races everywhere since the dawn of the 20th century. There is no gainsaying the fact that this has had implications for an African Renaissance, and it will continue to have implications for an African Renaissance as we progress into the 21st century and beyond. Nevertheless, the understanding and expression of an African Renaissance has varied among African people, leaders and from place to place, hence the need to compare in a systematic manner the Pan-Africanist thoughts of Nnamdi Azikiwe and Obafemi Awolowo, and their implications for the African Renaissance project in Nigeria. For this reason, the upcoming section discusses the contributions of the duo to the development of Pan-Africanist and African Renaissance thoughts and activities within the context of the decolonisation struggle, the establishment of democratic political systems in post-independence Nigeria, and the achievement of sustainable economic development. We also evaluate their impact on the nature and type of nation-state as leaders of thought and politics.

Before we begin the task of examining the legacies of the political thoughts of these Nigerian leaders, it is important to explore the meaning of 'African Renaissance' in some detail to establish the context of its operationalisation in this study. To this end, we shall briefly examine some of the dominant perceptions about an African Renaissance.

In recent times, the concept of 'African Renaissance' was popularised by Thabo Mbeki when he predicted the rebirth of Africa in the 21st century in a 1997 speech to a gathering of American investors and leaders of the Southern African Development Community (SADC). At that occasion he declared, "Those who have eyes to see, let them see. The African Renaissance is upon us. As we peer through the looking glass darkly, this may not be obvious. But it is upon us"[6]. To Mbeki, the African Renaissance is "the third moment" in Africa's contemporary historical cycle, which dates from Ghana's independence in the 1950s. It is therefore a definite period of time in the historical process of Africa. According to Mbeki:

The third wave of re-birth in our continent can only, in reality, begin to show its full potential in the context of our preparation and entry into the 21st century. It is not the 20th, but rather the 21st century which is likely to be the historical era of the African Renaissance[7].

To President Bill Clinton, an African Renaissance entails the spread of democracy, economic growth and peace in Africa[8], while in Louw's[9] view, an African Renaissance connotes a revival of an Africa of hope and prosperity. It may thus imply a "positive vision of Africa as a peaceful, democratic and market-orientated region that will attract foreign trade and investment, as well as the return of thousands of talented Africans and billions of flight capital now in safe havens abroad". Similarly, it has been considered that an African Renaissance offers an "alternative to the prevailing European concepts of, and structures for, African and global order". In this regard, sovereign rights must, therefore, give way to more enduring and universal human rights, while national governments remain the principal guarantors of the security and wellbeing of the people of Africa. To realise this end, African governments need to increasingly hold one another accountable; a community of nations, rather than an alliance of states, could thus provide "the basis for advancing peace and prosperity throughout Africa and for enhancing Africa's influence in world affairs"[10].

Mbeki also identified two epochs in Africa's rebirth to include: i) the period of the liberation struggles of the immediate post-World War II years, which culminated in the political liberation of the continent from the domination of colonial and racial regimes; and ii) the post-cold war era which resulted from the collapse of the USSR in 1989 and the consequent surge of more open political and economic interaction on a world scale.

The objective of "the third moment" is:

...to empower African peoples to deliver themselves from the legacy of colonialism and neo-colonialism and to situate themselves on the global stage as equal and respected contributors to, as well as beneficiaries of all the achievements of human civilisation. Just as the continent was once the cradle of humanity and an important contributor to civilisation, this renaissance should empower it to help the world rediscover the oneness of the human race.

One of the most fundamental elements which constitute the content of this renewal is the construction of a growing and sustainable economy capable of assimilating the best characteristics, contribute to and take advantage of the real flows of economic activities around the world[11].

He also identified political renewal as the second element of African renewal. In this regard, he observed that the process of political renewal had actually started with the establishment of democratic political systems in most nations of Africa[12].

Mbeki thus observed that although the aspirations encapsulated in an African Renaissance are not new in view of the continent's antecedents of the struggles for emancipation, new conditions brought about by the completion of the decolonisation process, the end of the cold war and the acceleration of the process of globalisation now exist to facilitate their attainment[13].

This study illuminates the meaning of an African Renaissance offered by Thabo Mbeki, as it embraces all areas of human endeavour such as the political, economic, social, technological, environmental and cultural spheres of Africa's revival[14]. However, it must also be noted that this study considers an African Renaissance to be only a strand of Pan-Africanism, whose existential context in terms of periodisation, socio-political and economic dynamics vary slightly from the former. The goals and objectives of both thoughts and movements are consistent with each other. The latter is, therefore, considered a continuation of a thought process and social movement that have their roots in the interwoven objective conditions of Africa's history since the epoch of the slave trade. Therefore, we do not think that both concepts embody different ideologies. In fact, both Pan-Africanism and the African Renaissance are one and the same ideology expressed in interwoven but slightly different historical contexts. Instead, it is the individual leadership actors in the saddle of governance that may express divergent ideological pathologies and consequently diversify the processes of the realisation of the objectives of the African Renaissance. It is on this basis that we consider the African Renaissance as an attempt to revive, recreate and rebirth the pre-slave trade glorious era of Africa in the globalising world of the 21st century and beyond. It is, therefore, a continuation and extension of Pan-Africanism in the context of the political, social and economic dynamics of post-independence Africa.

3.4 Rethinking Pan-Africanism and African Renaissance Today: Exploring the Thoughts and Actions of Azikiwe and Awolowo

Having situated the context of our concepts, we shall proceed to give a sketchy biography of the personalities in focus in this study, with a view to understanding the making of their respective thoughts. Nnamdi Azikiwe was born on November 16, 1904, in Zungeru, Nigeria, and died on May 11, 1996, in Enugu, Nigeria. He was a prominent nationalist figure and the first president of independent Nigeria (1963–66). Azikiwe, fondly called Zik, attended various primary and secondary mission schools in Onitsha, Calabar, and Lagos. He arrived in the United States in 1925, where he also attended several schools. Azikiwe earned multiple certificates and degrees, including bachelor's and master's degrees from Lincoln University in Pennsylvania and a second master's degree from the University of Pennsylvania. In 1934 he went to the Gold Coast (now Ghana), where he founded a nationalist newspaper and was a mentor to Kwame Nkrumah (later the first president of Ghana), before returning to Nigeria in 1937. In Nigeria he founded and edited newspapers and also became directly involved in politics, first with the Nigerian Youth Movement and later as a founder of the National Council of Nigeria and the Cameroons (NCNC) in 1944. In 1948, with the backing of the NCNC, Azikiwe was elected to the Nigerian Legislative Council. The NCNC became increasingly identified with the Igbo people of southern Nigeria after 1951 and he later served as premier of the Eastern region between 1954 and 1959[15].

Azikiwe led the NCNC into the important 1959 federal elections, which preceded Nigeria's independence, and was able to form a temporary government with the powerful Northern People's Congress (NPC). However, the deputy leader of the NPC, Abubakar Tafawa Balewa, took the key post of prime minister, while Azikiwe received the largely honorary posts of president of the Senate, governor-general, and, finally, president.

During the Nigerian civil war (1967–70), Azikiwe backed his fellow Igbo and travelled extensively in 1968 to win recognition and help for Biafra from African and other countries. In 1969, however, realising the hopelessness of the war, he threw his support behind the federal government. After Olusegun Obasanjo turned the government over to civilian elections in 1979, Azikiwe ran unsuccessfully for president as the candidate of the newly formed Nigerian People's Party (NPP). Prior to the 1983 elections, the NPP became part of an unofficial coalition of opposition parties known as the Progressive Parties Alliance (PPA). The coalition failed to agree on one presidential candidate and decided to field both Azikiwe, representing the NPP, and Obafemi Awolowo, representing the United Party of Nigeria (UPN). The coalition had largely deteriorated by the time of the election, and neither Azikiwe nor Awolowo won.

An important figure in the history of politics in Nigeria, Azikiwe had broad interests outside that realm. He served as chancellor of the University of Nigeria at Nsukka from 1961 to 1966, and he was the president of several sports organisations for football, boxing, and table tennis. Among his writings are *Renascent Africa*[16](1937) and an autobiography, *My Odyssey*[17] (1970).

Obafemi Awolowo, also known as Chief Obafemi Awolowo or simply Awo, was born on March 6, 1909, in Ikenne, Colony and Protectorate of Southern Nigeria. He died on May 9, 1987, in Ikenne, Nigeria. He was a Nigerian statesman who was a strong and influential advocate of independence, nationalism, and federalism. He was also known for his progressive views concerning social welfare.

Obafemi, the son of a peasant, first studied to be a teacher and later worked as a clerk, trader, and newspaper reporter, while organising trade unions and participating in nationalist politics in his spare time. In the 1930s he became an active member of the Lagos Youth Movement (later the Nigerian Youth Movement), and rose to become its secretary for the Western Province. During that time he came to bemoan the ethnic divisions within the nationalist movement and the growing political inequalities between some of Nigeria's ethnic nationalities and regions.

Awolowo went to London in 1944 to study law, and while there he founded the Egbe Omo Oduduwa (Society of the Descendants of Oduduwa) to promote the culture and unity of the Yoruba people, one of the largest ethnic groups in colonial Nigeria, and to ensure a secure future for them. During that period Awolowo also wrote the influential *Path to Nigerian Freedom* (1947)[18]. In 1947 Awolowo returned to Ibadan to practice law, and the following year he established the Egbe Omo Oduduwa in Nigeria. In 1950–51 he founded a political party, the Action Group, with some of the Egbe's members as its nucleus, and in the process became the party's first president. In 1951 the party won the first elections held in the Western Region, one of the colony's three administrative divisions, and Awolowo later served as leader of government business and minister for local government structure, the latter for which he established elective councils. From 1954 to 1959, he was premier of the Western Region. After a disappointing showing in the hard-fought 1959 elections and after the two other major parties had formed a coalition, he became leader of the opposition in the federal House of Representatives. Meanwhile, he tried to build the Action Group into an effective nationwide party by making alliances with ethnic groups in other regions. Awolowo supported his party's efforts to accelerate Nigeria's progress toward self-government by pushing the British to commit to an early date for independence.

After Nigeria achieved independence in 1960, Awolowo began to modify his earlier position, leaning toward socialism and advocating a neutral foreign policy rather than his earlier pro-Western position. With dissension growing in his own party over both ideology and administration, Awolowo fought to maintain ascendancy. Although he managed to prevail at the annual party conference in 1962, one year later he was tried and convicted of conspiracy to overthrow the government and was sentenced to 10 years in prison. He was released after a military coup took place in July 1966 - the second coup to occur that year. Later that year Awolowo was a member of the National Conciliation Committee, which attempted to mediate a rift between the federal government and the Eastern Region which was inhabited predominantly by the Igbo people. Mediation attempts failed, and he eventually threw his support behind the federal government when the region seceded as the Republic of Biafra, sparking civil war (1967–70). During the conflict, Awolowo was federal commissioner for finance and vice chairman of the Federal Executive Council. In the mid-1970s he was chancellor of the University of Ife (now Obafemi Awolowo University) and Ahmadu Bello University.

When the 12-year ban on political activity was lifted in 1978 in preparation for a return to civilian rule, Awolowo emerged as the leader of the Unity Party of Nigeria. He ran for president in the elections of 1979 and 1983 but was defeated both times by Shehu Shagari. Following a military coup at the end of 1983, parties were once again banned, and Awolowo retired from politics. An important figure in Nigerian history, Awolowo's ideals and accomplishments continue to influence Nigerian politics. He wrote several books, including *Awo: The Autobiography of Chief Obafemi Awolowo*[19] (1960) and *Thoughts on Nigerian Constitution*[20](1966).

More than anything else during the careers of both Azikiwe and Awolowo in the post-independence era, Nigeria succeeded in building a notorious reputation not only for failing to live up to the social, political and economic aspirations of her citizens, but also for disappointing Africa's expectations of her leadership role in global politics and the confidence of the international community in her potential to transform her huge human and abundant material resources in a manner that would place her in the league of developed societies. Nigeria has not only failed to provide inspiration for Africa's prospects of development, but has also remained one of the continent's worst and biggest development challenges for the world. This is illustrated by the fact that within the first decade of her independence, the major constituent ethnic nationalities were already engaged in fratricidal and genocidal conflicts, while the atmosphere of politics was overly polluted by instability generated largely by intra-elite competition for power that led to the enthronement of military governance and the consequent obliteration of the culture of democracy. The net outcome of the successive military rulers was bad governance, a consistent and progressive deceleration of economic growth, and an escalation of social and human insecurity in a manner that inhibited the take-off of the nation-building process in Nigeria. At the heart of this process of social crisis were the power elite for whom both Azikiwe and Awolowo provided leadership and inspiration. The fact that they have been in this leadership saddle since the decolonisation struggle makes it inevitable to interrogate the colonial roots of Nigeria's paradox of failure. The right point to begin from, therefore, is to interrogate the political thoughts of the leaders on which Nigeria's decolonisation and post-independence statecraft were anchored. Both Azikiwe and Awolowo stand out in this regard.

One characteristic common to the Pan-Africanist thoughts of the duo of Azikiwe and Awolowo was that their perspectives on nationalism fell essentially within the domain of plaintive nationalism[21]. For most of the time that colonial rule prevailed, they merely pleaded for the accommodation of Africans in the governmental and administrative processes of Nigeria's colonial state. For instance, the political charter of the Nigerian Youth Movement (NYM) pledged itself to the goal of "a complete autonomy within the British Empire" for Nigeria, and pressed "for more use to be made of Nigerian barristers for judicial and legal appointments…."[22]. This is illustrative of the plaintive character of the Pan-African nationalism advocated by the duo when we take into account the fact that they were leading figures in the movement. The movement's economic charter reinforces this fact, as it pledged itself to "demand for our people economic opportunities equal to those enjoyed by foreigners", "protect all Africans in industry and to resist every attempt by foreigners to oust them…" and "to champion the good cause of the labourers employed under the railways, at the docks and workshops of the Government, at the colliery at Enugu, at the tin mines of the Bauchi plateau and on the gold fields", while its cultural and social charter committed to "urge on the Government to make elementary education progressively free and compulsory…".

At the individual level, Azikiwe[23] advocated that there should be two stages (the preliminary and the intermediate) in the evolution of the Nigerian state. He argued that the preliminary stage of ten years should be marked by:

> …a conscious process of Nigerianisation in all aspects of our political and administrative life. The economy of the country should be planned in order to adjust and adapt it to the conscious process. At this stage, 200 scholarships should be awarded to the sons and daughters of Nigeria annually, for five years, to enable them proceed abroad for specialized training in all branches of human endeavour…. If Britain means to reduce the period of tutelage during which period this country must suffer political servitude, then it should realize that only by this country producing trained men and women in all aspects of human endeavour can political progress be accelerated…

He further elaborated on this position when he stated that:

> …during the First Stage, Nigeria should be ruled by non-Nigerians, and Nigerians should undergo a period of tutelage which should prepare them for self-government. The key positions in the Nigerian State should be shared between Nigerians and non-Nigerians, and the former would act in an administrative capacity in concert with the latter[24].

At the intermediate stage, he opined that Nigerianisation "makes it necessary for non-Nigerian appointees in the Civil Service to act in an advisory and not in administrative capacity, in all aspects of Nigerian political life". This stage should last for five years, he believed, after which "non-Nigerian political experts should 'hands off' our affairs administratively".

Similarly, Awolowo[25], while prescribing how local self-government was to be attained, recommended the elimination of "all Administrative Officers from the Native Administrations".

Although he did not recommend their replacement with African Administrative Officers, he nonetheless argued that the trusteeship role of the British colonial government in the political development of Nigeria would be better served by training and appointing educated Nigerians into substantive positions in the clerical, technical and administrative cadres of the Native Administrations.

In addition, in his essay *Argument for Empire*, Awolowo[26] made a plea for Nigeria to remain within the British Empire, but appealed that all acts of unfairness and injustice to Nigerians within it should be addressed. While criticising the average Briton's total ignorance of the colonies or some the grotesque ideas held about its inhabitants, he pleaded that there was:

> …a growing body of people among the white groups in the Empire, who are strongly opposed to all acts of unfairness and injustice towards the coloured groups, and are working strenuously for the wider and equal distribution of the good things of the Empire. The best interest of the coloured peoples, therefore, lie in co-operating whole-heartedly with this body of people, confident in the hope that in due course the beneficial influences of men of goodwill will prevail over the discordant and disrupting forces of snobbery, prejudice, and racial superiority.

Another point to be noted is that they did not only believe in cooperating with the colonisers once they provided accommodation for Nigerians in the colonial administration, but also believed that there were some elements within the colonial system who actually had good intentions for Nigeria. Undoubtedly, it was the pre-eminence of this kind of nationalist thinking that essentially molded the character of Nigeria's decolonisation. The disposition of both Azikiwe and Awolowo to colonialism and imperialism was clearly that of condonation. They believed that the colonisation of African peoples and societies was necessary to provide political tutelage for the indigenous elites; they were merely against the practices of injustice and unfairness within the colonial system and advocated the gradual transition of power to the Africans. This plaintive approach to African nationalism and renaissance failed to grasp the full essence of the exploitative capitalist ideology that underpinned the colonial enterprise. It is the weakness of this kind of political thinking that made it possible for them to see some of the colonisers as "men of goodwill" worthy of collaboration. This kind of disposition in their political thinking not only betrayed their ideological alliance with capitalism and neo-liberal ideology, but also their inherent bias against radical nationalism that resulted in the process of constitutional reforms, which characterised Nigeria's decolonisation struggle. In this way, they not only availed themselves as willing collaborators of the bourgeois class of metropolitan Britain, but also helped to foist and propagate the oppressive and exploitative ideology and system of imperialism and capitalism in Nigeria.

Further, and probably following from the above, these early Nigerian political thinkers were unanimous in their thinking on the role of Western education and the educated elite in Nigeria's transition to self-government. This can be gleaned from the role they prescribed for the educated elite in the process of political development outlined above. They believed that the destiny of Nigeria was in the hands of the educated elite whom they claimed were better equipped than the traditional elite to drive the process of self-governance on the simple account of Western education[27]. There is no doubt that the state of Nigeria in the 21st century has proven the contrary. Most analysts of Nigerian statecraft agree that the country has underperformed given her human and material potentials, and have found the educated ruling class culpable of providing one of the world's worst leadership. The fact that most Nigerian analysts advocate the restructuring of the country on the basis of the criteria that are etched in the country's pre-colonial history is an indication of the failure of the educated elite's ability to provide the quality of leadership necessary to transform her into a modern developed nation and civilised society. The fact that both Azikiwe and Awolowo prescribed and worked tirelessly to foist this ideologically twisted leadership class onto the governance structures of Nigeria is a sore point in the political thinking that has made a wreck of a nation out of Nigeria.

In addition, they believed that liberal democracy characterised by universal adult suffrage was the only viable strategy for attaining self-government and building a nation out of Nigeria. In fact, for Azikiwe, democracy as a political philosophy was not only "the goal of progressive humanity but also the 'indigenous political philosophy of Nigeria', in the main, is essentially democratic…"[28]. In the face of the military usurpation of political power, he advocated the political system of diarchy as a path to the attainment of liberal democracy in post-independence Nigeria. Similarly, Awolowo, in his book, *The People's Republic*[29], restated his belief in the potency of liberal democracy in driving Nigeria's course of progress (Awolowo, 1968). One thing in common to the duo is that while their political careers lasted, they demonstrated their commitment to the core values of democracy by making themselves available for elective offices and thus became the icons of Nigeria's democracy. However, we must not ignore the fact that the democratic experiments which they mediated failed in large part because they refused to concede defeat, and the political parties which they led embarked on acts of violence that threatened the corporate security of the country and therefore paved the way for the military takeover of power and the truncation of democratic development in Nigeria. For instance, the 15th January, 1966, military coup was largely an attempt to nip in the bud the political instability occasioned by the Action Group crisis, while the 1983 coup was a response to the violence that followed the loss of elections by the Unity Party of Nigeria in some states in the western part of Nigeria. This heritage of post-election violence appears to have become an entrenched culture in the politics of Nigeria, as the progress made in the democratic experiment of the fourth republic has been heavily tainted by post-election violence, particularly in many states in the northern part of the country. The failure of liberal democracy in Nigeria is thus a bad commentary on the neo-liberal ideology that informed the political thoughts of Azikiwe and Awolowo.

One other issue that has continued to dominate the political discourse since the decolonisation struggle is the ethno-regional and religious polarisation of the political parties and movements in Nigeria[30]. While the leadership of the independence movement professed Pan-Africanism as their abiding political philosophy, they nevertheless were divided along ethno-regional and religious allegiances in their quest to capture political power. This was largely responsible for the failure of Azikiwe and Awolowo to unite their respective political parties and their followers into a single political front, and present a formidable alternative to the northern elite that came to dominate post-independence Nigerian politics. This created a paradox of principle and practice in not only the leadership class, but also the followership. It also created a situation in which both leaders merely professed Pan-Africanism in principle, while in practice they were steeped in a struggle for political power in which the principal instrument of support mobilisation was ethno-regional and religious affiliations. They engaged in politics of expedience rather than ideology as they mobilised all the centrifugal forces within their reach in the quest for power at all costs. Again, this disposition points to the individualistic and primordial content of the ideological orientation of the political culture of capitalism and its underlying philosophy of the end justifies the means.

An examination of the political thoughts expressed in *The Official Programme* of the Nigerian Youth Movement *1938*, an association in which both Azikiwe and Awolowo were prominent members, in addition to Azikiwe's *Political Blueprint of Nigeria* and Awolowo's *Towards Local Self Government* and *Argument for Empire*, exposes the explicit content of decolonisation politics. In these documents, they express a strong preference for ethno-regional and religious sectarianism as the bases for the structural and administrative organisation and social inclusion in the colonial state of Nigeria. This consequently led to social cleavages in which nepotism and clientelism were elevated to the position of the grand norm in Nigerian politics. This resulted in the social instability that came to characterise the post-independence Nigerian state. The fact that Azikiwe and Awolowo held on to political control of their respective ethnic groups and regions of the country throughout their political careers, only on the basis of their ethno-regional affinities and the fact that their political rivalry arose essentially on the basis of their attempts to encroach on each other's sphere of political influence and control, are illustrative of this paradox of principle and practice not only in Nigeria's politics, but also in their respective political thoughts. They both did everything possible to exclude each other and others from their domains of primordial control at the expense of their pretensions to Pan-Nigerian and Pan-African ideologies.

The plaintive and conservative political views of both Azikiwe and Awolowo transcend the politics of post-independence Nigeria. Although relative to the views of their northern counterparts such as Ahmadu Bello, Tafawa Balewa and Shehu Shagari, the duo's thoughts are considered progressive within the context of Nigerian politics, but when evaluated against the context of Pan-African politics, their progressivism fails to stand the test. Nonetheless, they remained the most influential politicians and political thinkers who molded the dominant political views in Nigeria's first and second republic politics. Since their exit from the political turf of Nigeria, their political associates have continued to be very influential and their political thoughts and views have continued to influence the course of politics, even in the politics of the fourth republic. It is not likely that Nigeria's politics will witness a major departure from the paths of the legacies of political thoughts bequeathed by Azikiwe and Awolowo soon.

Although these Nigerian political thinkers did not engage the concept of an African Renaissance in the manner of Thabo Mbeki, it will be difficult to deny them any form of association with its ideals, especially in the context in which the concept was conceptualised earlier in this study. This is because the duo, within the limits of their ideological inclinations, aspired for the post-independence Nigerian state the same objectives espoused by the concept of African Renaissance. Beyond their aspiration for the liberation of Nigeria and the entire African continent from the shackles of colonisation, they also envisioned the rebirth of the continent through the building of democratic political systems, economic regeneration through sustainable economic development, and the attainment of peace and social stability. They also envisioned a change in Africa's place in the rapidly globalising world economy, so that it becomes free of the yoke of the international debt burden and reverses its role as a supplier of raw materials and importer of manufactured goods. While the duo did not possess the substantive political power to drive this process of national regeneration, they did make public their intention to give fillip to the process. Unfortunately they never succeeded in gaining the required political power at the national level in Nigeria, however at the regions where they presided over the affairs of government, they did not fail to demonstrate their capacity to midwife the development they envisioned. For instance, Awolowo consistently made a case for the need for a federal form of government in an independent Nigeria to safeguard the interests of each ethnic nationality and region as a panacea for sustainable unity in Nigeria. He also worked to improve education, social services, and agricultural practices, among other progressive policies. Notably, his administration introduced programmes that provided free health care for children and free universal primary education. The first television station in Africa was also established in the Western Region by his administration. By virtue of these policies, the other regions of the country are, to date, still trying to catch up with the pace of development in the defunct Western Region of Nigeria. Following the examples set by Awolowo's Western Region, the Eastern Region government under Azikiwe also made some progress, although to a lesser extent, in socio-economic development. Azikiwe, within the limits of the resources available to the Eastern Region's government, adopted most of the Western Region's policies, yet to date the southern part of the country is better developed than the Northern Region. Notwithstanding the fact that politicians of northern extraction have been in control of political power for the most part of the post-independence era in Nigeria, the country cannot claim any significant socio-economic development and therefore remains a major development burden to the world.

From the foregoing, it is difficult not to assert that, given the degree of the correlation between the political careers of Azikiwe and Awolowo on the one hand, and the failure of democracy, poor leadership, political instability, social insecurity and the deceleration of economic growth on the other, the heritage of the post-colonial state and the political system which the duo bequeathed to the country are not the least progressive. When we add this to the fact that they conceived the Nigerian state as a mere agglomeration of divergent ethnic nationalities and mutually antagonistic cultures which structure is unsuitable for the promotion of national integration and unity, we can only come to the conclusion that their leadership in politics and political thought was counterproductive for the attainment of the objectives of nation-building, peace-building and overall sustainable economic development within the ideological context of Pan-Africanism and African Renaissance in a rapidly globalising world. On this premise, we find the duo culpable in the failure of Pan-Africanism and the African Renaissance project in Nigeria, to the extent that their political thoughts influenced the political course of Nigeria.

3.5   Conclusion

This study undertook a retrospective examination of Pan-Africanism and the African Renaissance. It argues that although the existential contexts of both thoughts and movements are different, they are nonetheless interwoven. The African Renaissance is therefore an extension and continuation of Africa's struggle to extricate itself from the pangs of dependence, underdevelopment and indignity. While Pan-Africanism addressed these issues in the colonial context, the African Renaissance focuses on the same issues in the post-colonial setting. The study thus identified major points of convergence in the thoughts and ideas of Azikiwe and Awolowo, and argues that despite the rivalry and public perception of the acrimony between the two leading Nigerian political thinkers and politicians, they were not diametrically opposed in their Pan-Africanist and African Renaissance thinking. Rather, their differences were superficial and largely founded on the irreconcilability of their personal ambitions to wrest power at the centre than their commitment to the public good, hence their resorting to the mobilisation of primordial sentiments and centrifugal forces such as ethnicity, regionalism and religion.

The study also examined their thoughts and contributions to the decolonisation movement and the post-independence politics of Nigeria, and found their nationalist and renaissance thoughts plaintive, conservative and pro the Western ideology of capitalism and imperialism. It is the study's considered position that they largely contributed to Nigeria's failure to attain democratic political systems, economic development and social stability upon the attainment of independence on account of their legacies of political thought. On this note, it is argued that the duo's thoughts missed the points essential for the creation of the political environment necessary for the African Renaissance project in the post-independence Nigerian state. This is because they failed to mobilise their political support on the basis of the ideology of Pan-Africanism which prioritises social inclusion, but rather they resorted to the mobilisation of ethno-regional and religious differences to gain political capital to foster their personal and class ambitions. The study concludes, therefore, that there is a gross deficit of Pan-African ideological thinking and action among African leaders as illustrated by the ilk of Azikiwe and Awolowo. Nigeria, which prides herself as the leader of Africa, is grossly deficient of a leadership class with a heritage of Pan-Africanist ideology and African Renaissance thought. This has not only limited Nigeria's role and contribution to the African Renaissance, but Nigerian leaders have also inadvertently collaborated with Western powers, exacerbating the pangs of poverty through national and continental policies that promote Western progress at the detriment of African prosperity.

Although this study does not pretend to recommend the conditions necessary for Nigeria's renaissance, it nonetheless recognises that the political thoughts of political leaders are inevitable elements in the process of regenerating and liberating a nation from the burdens of oppression, conflict and underdevelopment. It is on this note that we suggest that further studies should be conducted into the political thoughts of Azikiwe and Awolowo, since they have continued to influence the course of politics in Nigeria in view of their strong influence on their political associates who have continued to dominate Nigerian politics. It is also recommended that contemporary Nigerian leaders rethink the contributions of Azikiwe and Awolowo to the development of Pan-African nationalist thoughts, in order to successfully re-engage the process of a post-independence African Renaissance and nation-building, and pilot Nigeria away from the path of disintegration that she is currently travelling. It is only in this way that Nigerian leaders can gain the trust of other African leaders and nations in order to enable the nation to assume her destined leadership role and responsibility effectively in the war against poverty in Africa, and restore the value and dignity of the African persona within and without the boundaries of Nigeria and the shores of the African continent. Unless this is done urgently, Nigeria will continue to grope in the darkness of political decadence, social disorder and economic malaise, thus failing not only herself but also the rest of the continent in the struggle to return Africa to its historic glorious position in a rapidly globalising 21st century world and beyond.

References

[1]Rodney, W. 1972. *How Europe Underdeveloped Africa*. Washington DC: Howard University Press.

[2]Shivji, I. G. 2011. The Struggle to Convert Nationalism to Pan-Africanism: Taking Stock of Fifty Years of Africa's Independence. *Pambazuka*, 1(544). Retrieved from: http://pambazuka.org/en/category/features/75620. [Date accessed: March 20, 2015].

[3]Blyden, E. W. 1872. *Africa for the Africans*. Washington DC: African Repository.

[4]Egbomuchie-Okeke, L. 2006. *The Political Thought of Africa*. Onitsha, Nigeria: Golden Value Books.

[5]Ibid.

[6]Mbeki, T. 1997. *Attracting Capital to Africa*. Address by Executive Deputy President Thabo Mbeki to Corporate Council on Africa's Summit, Chantilly, Virginia, USA. April 19 – 22, 1997.

[7]Mbeki, T. 1998. *The African Renaissance: South Africa and the World*. Address by Deputy President Thabo Mbeki, April 9, at the United Nations University, Tokyo, Japan. Retrieved from: http://unu.edu/unupress/mbeki.html. [Date accessed: September 9, 2016].

[8]Clinton, B. 1988. *America Needs a Strong South Africa*. Text of Bill Clinton's Address to the Great Hall of Parliament. *The Star*, Johannesburg, March 27.

[9]Louw, A. H. 2000. *The Concept of African Renaissance as a Force Multiplier to Enhance Lasting Peace and Stability in Sub-Saharan Africa*. Research Paper, Executive National Security Programme 02/2000, South African National Defence College. 17th October.

[10]Stremlau, J. 1999. African Renaissance and International Relations. *South African Journal of International Affairs*, 6(2): 61-80.

[11]Mbeki, M. 1999. *The African Renaissance*. Retrieved from: http://www.columbia.edu/cu/ccbh/souls/vol2num2art8.pdf. [Date accessed: September 09, 2016.]

[12]Mbeki, T. 1998. *The African Renaissance: South Africa and the World*, Address by Deputy President Thabo Mbeki, April 9, at the United Nations University, Tokyo, Japan. Retrieved from: http://unu.edu/unupress/mbeki.html. [Date accessed: September 9, 2016.]

[13]Mbeki, T. 1997. *Attracting Capital to Africa*. Address by Executive Deputy President Thabo Mbeki to Corporate Council on Africa's Summit, Chantilly, Virginia, USA. April 19 – 22, 1997.

[14]Department of Foreign Affairs. 2000. *Conceptual Framework for the African Renaissance*. Workshop circular, 17 July.

[15]

[16]Azikiwe, N. 1968. *Renascent Africa* (2nd ed.). London: Frank Cass & Co. Ltd.

[17]Azikiwe, N. 1970. *My Odyssey: An Autobiography*. Ibadan, Nigeria: Spectrum Books.

[18]Awolowo, O. 1947. *Path to Nigerian Freedom*. London: Faber & Faber.

[19]Awolowo, O. 1960. *Awo: The Autobiography of Chief Obafemi Awolowo*. Cambridge: Cambridge University Press.

[20]Awolowo, O. 1966. *Thoughts on Nigerian Constitution*. Ibadan: Oxford University Press.

[21]Ayokhai, F. E. F. & Naankiel, P. W. 2015. Rethinking Pan-Africanism and Nationalism in Africa: The Dilemma of Nation-Building in Nigeria. *Historical Research Letter*, 27: 1 – 9.

[22]Awolowo, O. (Ed.). 1960. *Awo: The Autobiography of Chief Obafemi Awolowo*. Cambridge: Cambridge University Press.

[23] Azikiwe, N. 1975. Political Blueprint of Nigeria. In G. C. M. Mutiso and S. W. Rohio (Eds.). *Readings in African Political Thought*. Nairobi: London Heinemann, pp. 100 – 103.

[24] Ibid.

[25] Ibid.

[26] Ibid.

[27] Ayokhai, F. E. F & Naankiel, P. W. 2015. Rethinking Pan-Africanism and Nationalism in Africa: The Dilemma of Nation-Building in Nigeria. *Historical Research Letter*, 27: 1 – 9.

[28] Azikiwe, N. 1975. Political Blueprint of Nigeria. In G. C. M. Mutiso and S. W. Rohio (Eds.). *Readings in African Political Thought*. Nairobi: London Heinemann, pp. 100 – 103.

[29] Awolowo, O. 1968. *The People's Republic*. Ibadan: Oxford University Press.

[30] Ayokhai, F. E. F. & Naankiel, P. W. 2015. Rethinking Pan-Africanism and Nationalism in Africa: The Dilemma of Nation-Building in Nigeria. *Historical Research Letter*, 27: 1 – 9.

PART 2

IDENTITY, CONFLICT AND DEVELOPMENT

Chapter 4

The Pan-African Identity: Why conflict and community identities continue to undermine collectivism

Wendy Isaacs-Martin

Archie Mafeje Research Institute (AMRI), University of South Africa

The subservient role which Africa plays in global politics makes her susceptible to all ideologies of international politics (Ani & Matambo, 2016:104).

4.1 Introduction

This chapter leverages on the context of armed groups on the continent in establishing the continued complexities of identity in direct contrast to the philosophical and political aim of promoting the Pan-African identity. Much has been made of the African identity and the collective experience of Africans in terms of being perpetual victims of colonialists, poor national governance and armed conflict. Africa remains a continent of distinct, often manipulated, identities subject to the interests of political leadership and those seeking access to political power and influence that includes controlling resource opportunities. Collectively these dynamics impact on identity structure and the manner in which it is internalised within the population. State, state-sponsored and non-state armed groups exacerbate any underlying differences in identity, and ultimately result in suspicion, distrust and conflict within and between communities long after armed groups have left, which can last for decades. In such spaces, local affinities, as argued by Lake[1], preside over notions of continental identity.

Franz Fanon's *The Pitfalls of National Consciousness*[2] demonstrate the persistence of localised identities within communities, where these identities are based overwhelmingly on social connections and the presumption of friendship[3]. The concept of a collective continental identity, such as Pan-Africanism, is an amorphous misnomer[4]; it is an illusion created by scholars such as Lake[5], who argued that in states such as Ghana, the contemporary diaspora Africans are seeking to define an identity that is transnational and transregional that extends beyond the nation-state as an alternative form of political organisation. However such organisation requires intellectual complexity that extends beyond the intergenerational community identity and does not include the overwhelming majority of Africans who are located in the rural areas and are struggling to access limited state resources. These notions ignore the overwhelming influence of cultural artefacts and historical experience within community identities, that to change requires an external stimulus.

The chapter does not attempt to investigate the African state ideologues who espoused the collective Pan-African identity, but rather this is an attempt to demonstrate the themes and concepts present in their interpretation. The focus is on why and how identities are undermined within the nation-states that makes the concept of a Pan-African identity an impossibility. That

Africa remains plagued by a lack of 'social trust' is influenced by a number of experiences on the continent, ranging from poor governance to ineffective leadership, structural adjustment programmes, corruption, the after-effects of the extensive slave trade and the persistent influence of international institutions[6].

To consider the notion of identity beyond the nation is problematic and fits with the liberal nationalist idea[7]. Beyond the universal inclusive ideals that are reflective of democracies, people also rely significantly on historical experience, birth, culture and religious affinities to attach themselves, therefore the Pan-African identity competes with the community identity, as well as the national.

The aim here is to argue that creating a supranational identity in Africa is unrealistic due to the absence of poor leadership structures, state institutions and accountability. Apart from the power dynamics, generational community structures, coupled with the national community, act to ensure that support can be assured, and limited, to these structures. Good governance, argued Mo Ibrahim[8], is the basis for development, and aid fails to propel Africa forward to ensure effective structures to sustain societies. Fanon[9] noted that the African experience is located locally and not at a continental level; a distinct lack of communication exists between the political leadership and the citizenry it is meant to represent. In a continent where conflict is persistent and pervasive, the notion of identity is reductive rather than collectively universal.

4.2   The Concept of Identity

The generational identity, loaded with concepts of historical experiences and cultural artefacts, informs communities and often larger groups. It is here that the notion of the nation is formulated. All states are nation-states; the lens that informs the identity of the state is the national community, even if liberal nationalists raise issues of human rights and individualism to outweigh the mindset of entrenched community identity. Spinner-Halev[10] argued that there is an instinctive competitive nature to communities, which leads to outright hostility when there is competition for resources and political power. Further, they commented that issues of self-esteem are an unstable foundation for a nation.

Yack defined communities from a narrow base as individuals who share loyalty and experience, as opposed to the abstract notion of community as defined in Anderson's *Imagined Communities*[11]. Communities are overwhelmingly seen through the lens of cultural artifacts, historical experiences and the contingency of birth. Cohen[12] argued that community boundaries such as these prevent entry to outsiders and preserve what members of a specific community regard as the unique experiences and identity of those who are members. The contemporary environment demonstrates that identities are reformed and thus overlap with existing older generational identities "in a transformative act"[13]. Generational communities that are overwhelmingly located in the contingency of birth provide the earliest forms of identity for their members, i.e. the individual is informed of their identity through community processes of information. This information does not need to be the truth or fact[14], as communities internalise what is central to their needs.

However communities are complex structures and encompass unique patterns of behaviour and insight[15]. Unfortunately, rather than the concept of the nation being like localised identities fading away to make way for grander identities that encompass more people, the reality is that community identities have not disappeared[16]. Even in the supernationalism of the former Soviet Union there was, and still is, a revival of ethnic nationalism and indigenous identities. The identities formulated in Africa, however, ran on a "counter-discourse" representing symbolic formation[17]. The contradiction lay in the indigenous cultures, and to a large extent national cultures, that are closed particularly when they are located in culture, religion and experience. The sense of community is still "necessary to people"[18]. In Africa many of the reinforced identities are "re-contextualised reconstructions of social systems" that may no longer exist and have essentially been wrecked[19]. De la Rosa[20] spoke of the 'glocal' identity in which the localised identities are heavily influenced by globalisation factors which no longer have any substance or values, but rather exist as a response to external factors that do not represent deep meaning but simply a group meaning. De la Rosa[21] asserted that there is a new trans-African identity that is internalised by groups outside of Africa in a desire to transcend the national, territorial and economic boundaries that are located within ethnicity but in a universally collective manner – thus the racial phenotype is not located solely in skin colour but rather mass culture that encompasses globalised issues of culture and political thought.

Unfortunately, although the interpretation of identity beyond the nation-state has been materialised, it is not with the intention of a larger informed identity. Rather it is a form of irredentism that is linked through exclusion and an inability to access state resources. So while such identities extend beyond the nation-state, they still encompass the community as its locus. It was argued by Ben-Israel in Ciisa-Salwe[22] that irredentism brings into play "biological and territorial sources of nationalism", and leads to the weakening of state borders as groups who share identities (language, religion, culture, kinship ties and socio-political leadership) would seek to self-determine.[1] Instead, the Pan-African approach was to reimagine the continent beyond national borders similar to a "federalised community", but recognise individuals as Africans thus challenging the normative approach of citizenship within a nation-state that is inclusive rather than exclusive. Whilst the notion of Pan-Africanism asserts the concept of "citizenship engagement", in reality the African environment, particularly in times of conflict, diminishes and eventually eliminates such engagement[23]. Rather, external stakeholders who oversee peace agreements in African states ignore not only many opposition voices, but certainly those of civil society[24].

4.3   The Pan-African Identity

How much of the Pan-African identity is guided by cultural and political influences and experiences, and does the average African citizen speak with the voice of the marginalised within his/her own nation or general consensus? This chapter draws partially on Fanon's *The Pitfalls of*

---

1   For a detailed discussion on irredentist movements in Africa since the 1960s refer to Ciisa-Salwe, C. M. (2000). Cold War Fallout: Boundary Politics and Conflict in the Horn of Africa, Haan Pub.

National Consciousness[25]as a lens through which to discuss notions of identity, therefore locating identities within and without the nation-state. The chapter focuses on ongoing conflict realities in Africa and what political opportunities, in terms of identity construction, are presented from these occurrences. It does not unpack the work of state ideologues such as Nkrumah, Nyerere and Senghor (the heads of Ghana, Tanzania and Senegal respectively) to expound on "post-national ideas and post-sovereign citizenship"[26]. For Nyerere, the *ujaama* presented an alternative understanding of the citizen that was located in the village, while for Senghor, the focus was on negritude and bringing about active citizenship. To discuss issues of identity requires political solidarity, and in Africa this is overwhelmingly founded in community identities, which according to the state ideologues require a collaborative approach.

To argue that the concept of identity is imposed by the colonial past is to remove the role of the current political leadership in Africa. However in times of conflict the voice of political leadership is silenced and given over to regional interest groups in the form of armed groups. These groups claim to serve community interests and therefore their marginalised identities[27], but conflict rather seeks to eradicate citizens and their voices.

The term 'Pan-Africanism' emerged at the first African Congress in London in 1900, along with the leading advocate of the ethos, W.E. Du Bois, who proposed an international political community of people of African descent[28]. Along with other thinkers such as Williams (who initiated the conference), James and Padmore (who convened the 1945 Pan-African conference in Manchester where issues of the colonial borders were denounced), Ciisa-Salwe[29]gave the concept "form and substance"[30]. Similarly, Blyden, who proceeded and influenced Marcus Garvey's thinking, created the link between Africa, the United States and the Carribean, and the notion of negritude later used by Senghor was initiated by him[31]. The argument was that while Europe has grown into nation-states with technological advancement and social development, Africa, like Asia and South America, suffered the consequences but not the benefits of these advances[32]. Yet notions of "black nationalism, black consciousness and black internationalism" were already prevalent by the 1850s in the United States[33], however there was also the neo-Pan-African identity, ensconsed in race, as advocated by Henry Winston[34]. Clarke[35] asserted that while the name originated in the 20th century, it has significant dimensions due to actions and thinking located in the 18th century.

The post-colonial Pan-African identity does not identify itself with the "shaping of the international but rather as the recipient of its rules"[36]. Pan-African thinking is located in 19th century America as a response to the continued exploitation and alienation of African-descended people, and resulted in the formation of the American Colonisation Society for the Establishment of Free Men of Colour of the United States in 1816[37].

For many the Pan-African idea is a colour issue, but for many indigenous Africans, identity is linked to a cultural origin. The Pan-African ideology developed in the 1900s diaspora of Africans to advance an ideological underpinning and 'self-governance', attributed to Marcus Garvey's thinking, was meant to confront the racial and economic exclusion experienced by black populations[38]. Garvey espoused the return of black people to Africa where they would be free from white domination, prejudice and exploitation. The Pan-African identity was seen through the lens of Garvey in the 1920s in the sentiment that all Africans suffered alientation, discrimination and humiliation[39]. He argued that the conflicts in Africa have resulted in the "affirmation of parochial primordial frivolities" to the "detriment of a trans-national identity"[40]. This has since developed into the notion that Africans must solve their own problems, particularly when it comes to conflicts on the continent. Yet with constant external sourcing in terms of ideology and economic, educational and political systems, to find the Pan-African identity without utilising alternative, preferably internal, solutions, will remain elusive.

The Pan-African movement called for the abolition of the territorial boundaries as agreed at the Berlin Conference of 1885 and instead promoted a unified Africa[41]. However the notion of Pan-Africanism has never been agreed upon and unified, as ascertained by the Brazzaville bloc (Malgache that sought an African cultural identity) and the Casablanca bloc (socialist leanings that considered socialism to support anti-colonialism and African independence), each of which were opposed to each other ideologically, and the third known as the Monrovia group[42].

Although the idea of Pan-Africanism was an ideological slant found primarily in the United States, in Africa Pan-Africanism found expression in armed conflict against colonialism and exploitation[43]. While Clarke argued that there was a shared sentiment of this identity, the objectives differed; he believed that Pan-Africanism is about restoring "African people to their proper place in world history", but more importantly about the "restoration of respect"[44].

The rationale of the Pan-African identity differs from that of the European white identity. European identity, not accommodating the Pan-European identity that was attempted by the ideals of Marx in unifying workers pre-WW1, was unified around a nationalism based largely on economics and industrialism. The notion of identity must be located in an identity that not only marks the historical experience, but also a way forward. Yet in Africa we find that identity ebbs are determined by economic circumstance and opportunities, which Fanon argued result in "a permanent seesaw between African unity" and the inevitable return of parochial identities and "chauvinism"[45]. He added that African unity is unlikely to be attained due to the notion of "territorialism". At independence, newly created states were faced with a legacy of disordered populations and land, and a desperate position to prevent irrendentism[46]. It was argued during the 1960s after independence for many states that the inherited borders would raise tensions and create conflict[47]. The desire to maintain the territorial boundaries undermined any prospect of Pan-Africanism, irrespective that they were arbitrary and artificial[48].

The Pan-African sense of identity is located in the historical experience of exploitation, racial marginalisation and social exclusion; the African experience is familiar and recognises it, but the community of cultural artefacts and birth contingencies remain salient. As Lake[49] (1995) noted in his research on diaspora Africans, many, but certainly not all, identified being African as a root identity of experience and origin – quite distinct from how indigenous Africans would identify themselves. Yet African states, argued Fanon[50] in *The Pitfalls of National Consciousness* in the *The Wretched of the Earth,* allowed race and tribe to supercede the nation and the state. Bloch-Hoell[51] argued that while there is an assumption of an African identity that would somewhat be located in a supranational tribe and race, there is a serious lack of analysis to support such a deduction. Rather, he argued it is a concept that is simply taken for granted. Instead the identity is "local, regional, seldom national and almost never related to the continent"[52]. In irony the nature of identiy is not constant, and is always "historically, geographically and sociologically conditioned"[53].

The nation is an "institutional form of community"[54], and Pan-African identity is a "political principle" that must be located within a community. In his chapter, *The Pitfalls of National Consciousness,* Fanon[55] related that the issue of limited identity is central to African politics. This crucial aspect allowed Fanon to argue that poor governance is scaffolded on this foundation of oppressed populations, thus providing a convincing account of why unity beyond the nation-state is unlikely. Yet conflict also brings its own dimension to social change due to forced migration[56].

Pan-Africanism is a "static ideology" that requires nationalism[57]. The resistance of various communities and nations were a defence of their populations against the forced slave trade, however the Pan-African ideology was already being derailed at the Pan-African conference in Tanzania, as Clarke[58] argued that "Africans came with separate programmes" that were not in the continent's interests. Clarke ultimately argued that there is a need for nation building in the context of the African identity that must preceed any universal collective position[59].

Africans retain a strong commitment to their national identities. In his research, Lake identified diasporic Africans as the group most informed by the Pan-Africanist notion of a single identity. Further, he pointed out that it is the diaspora Africans who are most influenced by the notion of the Pan-African identity; their identities are linked to a romanticised past and a seeking of a singular identity as a unified people. He opined that the willingness of diaspora Africans to support, for example, Ethiopia's independence from Italy's invasion in 1935, is indicative of Pan-African identity, and therefore he commented that there is a desire to demonstrate "historical linkages between Africa and its diaspora"[60]. Given the associations between smaller communities, where concerns of obligations and social friendships are linked because they are located in shared identity, there is an assumption that this can be transferred to a group of people due to their association with a continent. Lake argued that rather it is diaspora people who wish to assert a collective Africa, in spite of, as he maintained, the persistence of political and cultural hegemony that makes ethnicity salient.

Yet Lake added that political power is a key factor in determining identity in the African context. Many diaspora Africans consider race to be "a uniting factor", saying that it serves as "an expression of their commonality" with Africans on the continent[61]. Yet this is still a "mythic construction" in the context of the "historical, cultural and regional differences". The notion of the Pan-African identity can be juxtaposed with the universal white European identity, perceived as hegemonic, by their racial and economic exploitation, but this manner of universal collective identity creates "cultural and territorial sovereignty". However others such as Schnapper have stated that ideas of identity can only be effective when located in "national solutions"[62].

Instead Africa is represented by "soft states"[63]. This implies that they are predatory, corrupt and resource poor in terms of distribution and development. Benefits are distributed to the "ethnos rather than demos", and further complicated by an "autochthony discourse"[64]. Yet the ethnic diversity of most African countries is not the sole reason for weak African states[65].

The notion of the nation in Africa is argued to be a European transplant with a focus on territorial claims, however arguments to create a supranational identity do not take the various forms of nationalism into account, or particularly the notion of irredentism. The conflicts in Africa illustrate this point well[66]. Ibrahim[67]argued that Africa is riddled with "failed voices" that have no impact on external actors, along with no integration and no transparency. For the masses, the state has failed them; the state is derelict and predatory, serving a minority of elites to the detriment of its citizens as there are no longer common interests[68].

4.4   Undermining Collective Unity and Universal African Identity

Nationalism is not the dominant ideology of Africa, although it is supposed to be a popular ideology. The African incorporation into the nation state did not happen as it did in Europe; rather these were imposed identities overseen by a minority who would use force to uphold and maintain their political position. The myths of origin that form the "symbolic foundation of the nation" are absent and do not reflect a shared experience based on economic and social experiences, but rather as colonised and subjected as a cultural artefact and therefore a collective identity. Yet this experience is different amongst groups as well and is equally divisive[69]. The African version of nationalism is viewed through a lens of territorial borders and is "republican" and not "ethnic and romantic"[70]. And unlike their European counterparts, it is not Janus-faced but only futuristic.

Nation building in Africa, as in the majority of states, is located in the inclusion and exclusion of various groups. This has led to the hierarchical formation of group identity, where the recognition of certain groups allows them access to state institutions and resources to the detriment of excluded groups. Daley[71] argued that to maintain this structure, where the state often provides the most lucrative and sustainable form of employment and enrichment, this process is maintained through "violence and ideology". The divisive practices employed by colonial administrators continued into the independent governments, where those groups that were elevated in terms of access to education, social progression and state employment, continued the marginalisation of others. Armed groups often respond to these arrangements not by wanting to change the status quo in order to include all groups, but simply to assert themselves in these existing arrangements, further driving notions of separation and difference. In fact, it is acknowledged that the desire to build national identity after independence in Africa has been reduced and relapsed into colonial definitions of identity, and replaced with contested localised identities. Instead of inclusion, community identities have become lodged in their intergenerational identity with rigid boundaries to the exclusion of others as foreigners[72]. African identity has been reduced to intra- and inter-ethnic competition. The notion that it is the state's responsibility to provide access and security for all its citizens has been eroded and has been replaced with competition, often violent, to assert control of political authority and distribution.

State capture has become the sole interest of political elites[73] to the exclusion and disregard of citizens, and international organisations have instead taken on the responsibility of providing for citizens as "alternative service providers". Unfortunately these services become tools for all forms of leadership seeking control and influence over desperate populations.

It is argued that the African identity as conceived as opposition to the European concept is anachronistic. However Africans never shared an undifferentiated identity; the identity is relational and polychromatic rather than dependent on issues of culture and positional geography[74]. The African identity is no longer located simplistically in autochthony[75]. Eze asserted that our current political dynamism, in which globalism and glocalism[76] are influential, should be understood from the perspective of Africapolitanism. Rather than a fixed identity it acknowledges diversity and various international experiences – an application of African cosmopolitanism that moves beyond the essentialism of identity over pluralism, and that identity is hyphenated. Achille Mbembe unpacked Afropolitanism as the ability to see oneself apart from the foreigner[77]. Inclusive of this is the opinion that the role of the nation-state is diminishing due to globalism[78]. However, within this context, national and local identities are reinforced, rather than the original African elite who chose to centralise identity over the myriad of localised identities. Claude Ake[79] acknowledged that a second form of nationalism was located in discrimination against locals, i.e. internal xenophobia. The inclusiveness highlighted at independence has disappeared and been replaced by the exclusion of social groups[80]. But within the continent there is a move towards marginalising those who are not "sons of the soil", a term meant to distinguish those who have territorial and organic rights to the land regardless that denizens have been there for generations[81]. Often those from other parts of a country, although citizens, are not allowed to possess land in other parts of the territory. Opportunists use history to exclude groups they redefine as foreigners on their soil, and so gain political support and trust[82]. Pan-Africanism is an elite concept; for the poor, the arrival of foreigners is seen as competition for already scarce resources. Instruments of ideology and cohesiveness that may work in the urban areas do not necessarily not work in rural locations where resources are limited and often fought over.

The United Nations affirms the right to self-determination and for communities with political expression to seek economic, social and cultural development, but while respecting the sovereignty of states, this approach can significantly undermine the territorial integrity of existing state structures. Yet others argue, contrary to irredentism, that ethnic groups are "crammed within African states"; the resulting tensions due to the inability, or reluctance, of African governments to provide for all their citizens equally has forced them to retreat to their "ethnic enclaves" in order to access resources[83]. But this is not to suggest that intrinsically there is conflict in plurality. Rather it is suggested that the political processes that were evident in the various identities during colonial administration turned these innocuous differences into "ethnic cleavages", and the resulting poor policies of independent states exacerbated these[84].

African countries only receive a fraction of the financial spoils that resource extraction produces, and even less is transferred to state institutions[85]. Often coerced by large financial institutions to accept lower taxes and incentives, little is left for effective governance and state institutions are left open to manipulation by competitor interests.

Forms of 'aid' to Africa, from external stakeholders and various governments, along with expectations, heavily influence the political and social structures in African countries[86]. The persistence of the implementation of democratic principles to be 'supervised' by other governments often leads to increasing social, economic and political tensions for governments, bureaucracies and the governments. It has become a norm where external stakeholders play a role in establishing Africa's socio-political system[87], however this is not done in isolation of the local population – the personal ambitions of certain individuals effect these external processes.

The notion of conflict in Africa is often reduced to simple dynamics of ethnic differences, not considering the complexity of local factors and interests. The interests of external actors are placed first in the form of DDR programmes, democratic processes, and the inclusion of non-state armed groups and opposition groups into government and bureaucratic structures. It is assumed that the participation by all parties is the automatic replaying of European democratic principles and policies. This does not include the economic policies imposed, as envisioned by the Washington Consensus and created by the Bretton Woods institutions, that had disastrous effects on African economies[88]. While many African countries are peripheral participants in their economies, now given over to external stakeholders and enriching a small elite, this is not being discussed here. However it should be noted that the persistent poverty and underdevelopment feeds into the eventual conflicts and tensions that arise in many states. Actors that may or may not be supported by the state apparatus eventually become the 'leaders' amongst certain communities due to their ability to assist economically.

Although there have been interventions by neighbouring states in African conflicts, this has not led to long term peace. Often African countries themselves, as has been seen in the DRC and the CAR, have financial and resource interests and benefits to maintaining conflict and civilian discord. Armed groups in these environments often have external financial and logistical support by which to engage in conflict with the state.

To assure a Pan-African identity requires that there is effective and transparent state institutions. The irony is that to secure the supranational identity requires proper mechanisms and acceptance within national states. The manipulation of these institutions, to the extreme where these are either ineffective, corrupted or non-existent, undermines the potential for universal identity recognition. Instead the trend is to assert community identity structures upon which political systems in Africa have become dependent.

The genocide in Rwanda in 1994, the extreme violence in Liberia and Sierra Leone in the 1990s, as well as the continued fighting in the Democratic Republic of Congo, Libya and the Central African Republic, demonstrate, according to Ani and Matambo[89], that when external interests are not being met then attempts to intervene and offer effective support is delayed or withdrawn. While African states have attempted to intervene militarily and diplomatically to secure peace in unstable regions, a lack of resources results in funding dependency that is still overwhelmingly received from foreign states, which only offer support if the initiatives are approved in accordance with their interests, not those of the continent. This lack of resources allows for other non-state armed groups to ascend in states and challenge political leadership.

The demonstration of the varied identities in Africa is located not in the purpose of creating unity but rather disintegration, which Fanon described as the "stiffening of racism"[90]. He argued that the greatest obstacle to African unity, and therefore the Pan-African identity, is located within the African classes themselves; the "national bourgeoisie" who lack the impetus of an "embryonic industrial revolution".

Such mutualistic relations have been a consistent theme of African politics. Unable to secure significant funding from state structures, many bureaucrats and rural leaders sought to secure their financial largesse, and for many, although not all, access to political leadership. Their ability to link to rural grievances led shunned bureaucrats to seek alternative means to access wealth. These behaviours are seen as being ignored by international institutions such as the World Bank, which promotes "extractive industries in Africa even when they contribute nothing to development"[91]. These often lead to problematic parasitic behaviours by bureaucrats.

Generally speaking, rebel groups are not interested in accessing political power but rather they claim their ideology is located in the grievances of the rural populations (Pouligny[92]; Ani & Matambo[93]). Often the lack of security and state administration in the rural areas, and many urban, leads to the formation of armed groups of civilians. Gerlach[94] argued that in the rural areas, villagers and communities are subject to criminal activity from the state, as well as non-state actors and bandits. Vulnerable to these entities, farmers and other inhabitants are forced to arm themselves to protect the little they own. Self-defence units are formed in this manner, often in opposition to neighbouring communities, and tend to embrace a traditional cultural behaviour.

4.5 Warlords, Militias and Strongmen subverting Identity Structures

Fanon's argument of the co-opted rural leadership to suit the interests of the urban political establishment was first utilised by the colonial administrators. Societal organisations were kinship based and relied on subsistence agriculture that has morphed into ethnic identities. The complex web of kinship was virtually neutralised by the colonial establishment and its coercive powers. Urban areas, rather than the location of de-ethnicity, became the destination of re-ethnicity, as detailed by Adrien-Rongier[95]. However, on arriving in the cities without access to employment, many found themselves isolated in the ethnically-defined areas where their link to the rural areas was the only known acceptance they possessed.

The issue of conflict brings the salience of the 'tribal attitudes' to the forefront. Intellectuals are prone to blaming external interest groups for any conflict and reduce the acts of xenophobia as the actions of neighbouring and regional populations where "old interracial hatreds come to the surface"96. Such simplistic interpretations of conflict reduce nationalism in Africa as 'hollow' demonstrating that African unity can simply and inevitably "crumble into regionalism". The irony is that the political unfolding, in terms of conflict, on the continent is contradictory to the themes envisioned by Pan-Africanism, namely those of unity, reasserting dignity and alienation.

The 'big man' state system remains a fundamental part of African politics. Due to alliances to secure power, elites who are brought into the political structures can accumulate power to themselves along with financial resources, increasing them opportunity to take up arms if their interests are not met. Rather than serve the population, the aim is to centralise power around a leader and the state bureaucratic system. The persistent use of community leaders, as argued by Fanon[97], results in a competition for economic and political leadership that is detached from the interests of the population. Fanon articulated an extensive argument on the ineffectiveness of African leadership due to the continued usage of community identities to assert power and authority. He continued that urban leadership was located in the ideology of the former colonies, whereas the rural leadership made claims to African values, traditions and ethics.

Armed groups are often absorbed into larger groups, becoming coalition forces under the leadership of a warlord. However each group still maintains its own identity and is loyal to their particular commando, which often leads to problems when peace agreements are negotiated by external stakeholders. Armed groups, which are overwhelming sponsored by and answerable to individuals who are not in positions of direct political authority and legitimate leadership, proliferate where state institutions are fragile and ineffective[98]. In environments where survival is an ongoing struggle, there is a trend for these communities to seek support from warlords in the area to secure better weaponry. This creates competition between communities, but it also results in providing fighting resources for the warlords. In these remote areas, where there is little opportunity for the youth and the unemployed, the traditional culture of their community identity remains salient. It is often within this framework that many choose to join these armed groups, which comes with a stipend, a sense of belonging and purpose. As Ani and Matambo[99] asserted, the aim of many of these rebel groups is not to seek political change, but simply to destabilise the state security and authority and to benefit economically.

Constant interference claiming to assist political leadership and stability in Africa is usually a veil for economic interests, and remains a concern. The most recent event was the United Nations' Security Council's use of military force in Libya, which the African Union condemned, due to the parochial interests of the SC's permanent members and external interests, but was also complicated by African disunity[100]. The Organisation of African Unity, formed in 1963, asserted that territorial boundaries, as partitioned by colonial authorities, are inviolable and sovereign. The African Union, established in 2002, was established on the ideals of Pan-Africanism, but disunity amongst African leaders is part of the reason why there is an inability to bring about sustainable peace on the continent. Often 'hegemonic antagonisms' by countries such as Egypt, South Africa, Algeria, Nigeria and other regional states are reliant on their funding and support. Many African states are easily intimidated by the withholding of funds and therefore undermine the potential unity required, and many external funders purposely negotiate with individual governments to intentionally undermine unity[101].

Prejudices between the Soviet Union and Western thought was the largest obstacle to African unity, particularly as each attempted to extend their influence globally. Africa has been contested territory throughout history from outside forces and ideologies. Arab invaders, Western Europe, the eventual bi-polar ideological confrontations and the present inclusion of China and India have played themselves out on African territory to the detriment of its populations.

Overwhelmingly warlords are, or were, government employees[102], providing them with access to disgruntled present and past military personnel. The notion of identity is a means to secure support from communities, although the actions of warlords are seldom for their benefit[103]. As Ani and Matambo[104] noted, African elites are quick to blame external actors for the apparent problems in Africa, yet they do not possess the political will to confront these concerns. In contemporary Africa, the constant conflicts demonstrate tensions that would not realise in universal identities. The realities for ordinary Africans are displacement and migration within the continent. Governments, along with populations, are hostile towards refugees and sentiments of xenophobia are rife[105]. Often neighbouring citizens are regarded as 'foreigners', and increasing numbers of internally displaced people and the persistence of violence in various forms complicates issues of social acceptance and the ability to be included in existing communities[106]. Instead, their lives are dictated to by external humanitarian efforts that are often unfamiliar with, and naïve about, the socio-political environment. Governments renege on their responsibility to assist their citizens who then have no real home, as well as a lack of agency. Rather, it is external stakeholders who decide the social reality of displaced people, and much of these decisions are temporary yet have long lasting effects on these populations. The reality is that rather than moving toward identity universality, indigeneity becomes the salient identity, reducing citizens within their rightful sovereign home as outsiders. Indigeneity has become the norm to citizenship and displaced groups have become foreigners. In reality the IDP is regarded as a refugee; even within the state they are excluded from the political community, where they are rationalised as victims. Having lost their citizenship rights within their states they are often vulnerable to armed groups, state and non-state, and are frequently displaced further, denying them access to protection and resources.

However, while the ideology and the modus all claim to defend specific identities, religious or ethnic, the reality is that these groups are often comprised of a motley crew of professional soldiers, ex-soldiers, the ranks of the unemployed and youth gangs[107]. The interests of the fighters are thus varied; for those who are displaced by conflict, the problems of survival and belonging escalate. Often neighbouring states are reluctant to accept refugees and want to force repatriation by removing their refugee status, preventing them from participating in economic activities, requiring "spatial segregation", and threatening to make them stateless[108]. Refugee camps are situated near borders and have access to limited resources, hence displaced individuals find themselves in the position of being in "repatriation without integration" and "integration through marginalisation" as African countries have become more hostile toward refugees[109]. Even amongst IDPs, political elites may be hostile to particular ethnic groups and reluctant to assist them because indigeneity has become commensurate with entitlement. Camps often are ethnicised and armed groups find their way into the camps to intimidate ethnic groups. The positioning of camps is strategic as they can be used as "human shields against rebel incursions", yet IDPs wish to remain there as their land has either been destroyed by armed groups or it has been claimed by political elites[110]. Remaining at the location poses its own challenges with locals regarding land ownership, however, yet it is often the complicity of government that results in forced displacement and eventual destitution. For some reason, indigeneity does not provide the entitlements that it should once they have moved from their communities.

Often camps for IDPs become locations of new identities under alternative political leadership. Often humanitarian institutions inadvertently create new social identities and new power relations, where allegiance is given to warlords and strongmen who have gained authority over the camps[111]. Since the 1990s, IDPs and refugees in Africa have been met with increasing hostility as a threat to 'national harmony'[112]. These structures undermine the state's credibility with its citizens who now direct their concerns towards humanitarian organisations. In addition, tensions are created with IDPs as locals who now consider them foreigners attribute any economic difficulties to them. Even within the camps tensions exist between various groups, further fragmenting any unity of national identity and reducing it to community identities. These differences are maintained and can result in eventual marginalisation in and from society. Instead the IDPs find themselves in a camp-state within a nation-state.

The elites in Africa stoke conflict to suit their own needs. The persistence of poor personalised governance translates into individuals seeking to promote personal and group interests rather than that of the population. The use of ethnicity to secure political leadership encourages "regionalist ideals and separatism"[113].

4.6   Conclusion

The notion of the Pan-African identity is a multi-faceted response to socio, political and economic circumstances. It was first promulgated in the 1900s in response to the experiences of slavery and the right of return of those in the diaspora; in Garvey's opinion, all African people everywhere, to Africa. It was a response to the persistent marginalisation of African descended peoples in the Americas who were discriminated against and subject to an inferior position in society. The second phase was a centrapetal force, when economics and skills were needed in Africa and emigration, particularly to West Africa, was encouraged. For the emigré it was a way to experience and be immersed in their heritage and the romanticised notions of cultural belonging. The third phase was the desire to create a unified Africa in which solutions would be sought "by Africans, for Africans". The argument was that the Bretton Woods institutes suggested accelerated economic reforms in Africa that were not meant to facilitate development on the continent, but rather accelerate the profits of external stakeholders who invested little back into the African economies. The concept of the Pan-African identity is thus a response to these measures of discrimination.

While the notion of the Pan-African identity appears to be overwhelmingly placed at ideological levels, the reality is that the community structure identity remains salient. Frantz Fanon's *Pitfalls of National Consciousness*[114] offers lucid insight into the behaviours of African leadership that perpetuate the contemporary challenges and tensions on the continent. Although there is a collective understanding that the phenotype of Africans and being African is collective throughout the continent, identity salience remains at the level of birth contingency, a historical experience that is prescribed to a particular community, and cultural artifacts. These generational identities remain the strongest within the social experience. Research has shown that those who decide to emigrate to Africa from Jamaica and the United States are confronted with cultural identity patterns that consider them an outsider, regardless that they share a continental identity. This illustrates that the cultural identity remains the primary locus for communities and belonging, even when people chose to physically move away. This link provides unity during conflict.

Due to the prevalence of conflict on the continent, community identities remain the strongest amongst populations - even surpassing national identities. The nature of conflicts, like political structures, is located in the ethnic identities of communities. Political structures remain along ethnic and community lines, reinforcing the notion of community identities and loyalties. While this secures political leadership for elites it also encourages separate power structures to be formed outside of government. As the legitimate political leadership does not endeavour to create development and economic opportunities to benefit all citizens, there remains a focus on bloating bureaucracies instead with the supporters of particular ethnic identities. This creates an impression that largesse is identity dependent and thus leads to competition to access these resources.

This creates competition between ethnic and community identities. As is seen in African conflicts, although not isolated to Africa by any means, the allegiance to particular participants relies on the support of community identities. Those seeking to access political power, resources and personal enrichment use identities in order to secure support, which they argue is logical and expected. It was highlighted that supporting individuals in a particular identity assists with employment and access to resources that the state leadership reserves in a parallel relationship. As long as political leaders persist in outsourcing political responsibilities to community/traditional leadership structures, then the possibility exists for conflict and personal interests. This means that the realisation of a Pan-African identity will remain elusive.

The Pan-African identity remains, as per Anderson, an imagined community, in that communities are informed of their shared historical experiences and reminded of their obligations to members within their social group. However this imagined community is problematic in that it competes with other identities that are more intimate and familiar. Like the national identity, the unfamiliar stands in opposition to the familiar structures, and hence the community identity is salient. Those seeking to assert authority and power will exploit the community identity and reassert differences, however minor, between groups.

As long as the method to assume political power and resources occurs along community and ethnic lines, so the saliency of these narrowed identities will persist. In countries and regions where conflict has led to tensions between communities, the aftermath results in long-lasting suspicions and stereotypes. Therefore, while the intention to create a supranational identity of Pan-Africanism is important for psychological internalisation and as a buffer to Western ideas of identity superiority and economic interest, it must be considered that personal and marginal interests will continue to undermine such attempts. As long as community self-esteem issues exist there will be competition between groups to assert their primary identities over others rather than an attempt to share. Political and social leaders who have the greatest influence with which to promote supranational identities are reluctant to do so, as it would undermine the support, based on community and ethnic identities, upon which they depend. Unless restrictions are placed upon the manner in which political leadership is attained in Africa, particularly as it is influenced by external stakeholders, the reality of the Pan-African identity will remain elusive and a romantic aspiration for the continent. Ideas require more than ideology but a practical implementation, absent of high coercion, in which there is benefit to all parties involved when invoking fraternity and solidarity.

References

[1]Lake, O. 1995. Toward a Pan-African identity: Diaspora African repatriates in Ghana. *Anthropological Quarterly*, 68(1): 21-36.

[2]Fanon, F. 1963. *The wretched of the earth*.(Translation by Constance Farrington). New York: Grove Press.

[3]Yack, B. 2012. *Nationalism and the moral psychology of community*. Chicago: University of Chicago Press.

[4]Eze, C. 2014. Rethinking African culture and identity: the Afropolitan model. *Journal of African Cultural Studies*,26(2): 234-247.

[5]Lake, O. 1995. Toward a Pan-African identity: Diaspora African repatriates in Ghana. *Anthropological Quarterly*, 21-36.

[6]French, H. W. 2015. The Looting Machine: Warlords, Oligarchs, Corporations, Smugglers, and the Theft of Africa's Wealth. *Foreign Affairs*,94(4): 150-155.

[7]Spinner-Halev, J. A. T. & Elizabeth, M. 2003. National Identity and Self-Esteem. *Perspectives on Politics*,1(3): 515-532.

[8]Ibrahim, M. 2014. *Mo Ibrahim On How (And Why) Africa Should Solve Its Own Problems*.Retrieved from: http://www.forbes.com/sites/skollworldforum/2013/07/15/mo-ibrahim-on-how-and-why-africa-should-solve-itsown-problems. [Date accessed: November 7, 2016.]

[9]Fanon, F. 1963. *The wretched of the earth*. (Translation by Constance Farrington.) New York: Grove Press.

[10]Spinner-Halev, J. A. T. & Elizabeth, M. 2003. National Identity and Self-Esteem. *Perspectives on Politics*, 1(3): 515-532.

[11]Anderson, B. 2006. *Imagined communities: Reflections on the origin and spread of nationalism*. London and New York: Verso Books.

[12]Cohen, A. P. 2013. *Symbolic construction of community*.London and New York:Routledge.

[13]Bird, G. 2016. Beyond the nation state: the role of local and pan-national identities in defining post-colonial African citizenship. *Citizenship Studies*, 20(2): 260-275.

[14]Dretske, F. I. 1999. *Knowledge and the Flow of Information*. Cambridge, Massachussetts: MIT Press.

[15]Hall, S. 1993. Culture, community, nation. *Cultural Studies*, 7(3): 349-363.

[16]Ibid.

[17]Ibid.

[18]de la Rosa, F. J. U. 2011. Trans-African identity: Cultural globalisation and the role of the symbolic-aesthethic dimension in the present identity construction processes. *African Journal of History and Culture*,3(8): 128.

[19]Ibid.

[20]Ibid.

[21]Ibid.

[22]Ciisa-Salwe, C. M. 2000. *Cold War Fallout: Boundary Politics and Conflict in the Horn of Africa*. London: Haan Pub.

[23]Bird, G. 2016. Beyond the nation state: the role of local and pan-national identities in defining post-colonial African citizenship. *Citizenship Studies*, 20(2): 260-275.

[24]Pouligny, B. 2004. *The Politics and Anti-Politics of Contemporary Disarmament, Demobilisation and Reintegration Programs*. Paris, France: Secrétariat Général de la Défense Nationale.

[25]Fanon, F. 1963. *The wretched of the earth*. (Translation by Constance Farrington.) New York: Grove Press.

[26]Bird, G. 2016. Beyond the nation state: the role of local and pan-national identities in defining post-colonial African citizenship. *Citizenship Studies*, 20(2): 260-275.

27Sambanis, N. S., Skaperdas, S. & Wohlforth, W. C. 2015. Nation-Building through War. *American Political Science Review*, 109(2): 279-296.

28Chrisman, R. 1973. Aspects of Pan-Africanism. *The Black Scholar*, 4(10): 2-8.

29Ciisa-Salwe, C. M. 2000. *Cold War Fallout: Boundary Politics and Conflict in the Horn of Africa*. London: Haan Pub.

30Clarke, J. H. 1988. Pan-Africanism: A brief history of an idea in the African world. *Présence Africaine*, (1): 26-56.

31Ibid.

32Chrisman, R. 1973. Aspects of Pan-Africanism. *The Black Scholar,* 4(10): 2-8.

33Ibid.

34Ibid.

35Clarke, J. H. 1988. Pan-Africanism: A brief history of an idea in the African world. *Présence Africaine,* (1): 26-56.

36Bird, G. 2016. Beyond the nation state: the role of local and pan-national identities in defining post-colonial African citizenship. *Citizenship Studies*, 20(2): 260-275.

37Ciisa-Salwe, C. M. 2000. *Cold War Fallout: Boundary Politics and Conflict in the Horn of Africa*. London: Haan Pub.

38Ani, N. C. & Matambo, E. 2016. African Solutions in chains: external and internal causes of Africa's continued dependency fifty years on. *Journal of African Union Studies*, 5: 83-111.

39Chrisman, R. 1973. Aspects of Pan-Africanism. *The Black Scholar,* 4(10): 2-8.

40Ebijuwa, T.,& Gbadegesin, A. S. 2015. Mediating Ethnic Identities: Reaching Consensus through Dialogue in an African Society. *Cultura*, 12(1): 57-69.

41Ciisa-Salwe, C. M. 2000. *Cold War Fallout: Boundary Politics and Conflict in the Horn of Africa*. London:Haan Pub.

42Ibid.

43Clarke, J. H. 1988. Pan-Africanism: A brief history of an idea in the African world. *Présence Africaine,* (1): 26-56.

44Ibid

45Fanon, F. 1963. *The wretched of the earth*. Transl. by Constance Farrington. New York: Grove Press.

46Ciisa-Salwe, C. M. 2000. *Cold War Fallout: Boundary Politics and Conflict in the Horn of Africa*. London: Haan Pub.

47Ibid.

48Ibid.

49Lake, O. 1995. Toward a Pan-African identity: Diaspora African repatriates in Ghana. *Anthropological Quarterly*: 21-36.

50Fanon, F. 1963. *The wretched of the earth*.(Translation by Constance Farrington.) New York: Grove Press.

51Bloch-Hoell, N. E. 1992. African Identity. European Invention or Genuine African Character? *Mission studies,*9(1): 98-107.

52Ibid.

53Ibid.

54Balibar, E. 2012. The 'impossible'community of the citizens: past and present problems. *Environment and Planning : Society and Space,* 30(3): 437-449.

55Fanon, F. 1963. *The wretched of the earth*.(Translation by Constance Farrington.) New York: Grove Press.

56Bloch-Hoell, N. E. 1992. African Identity. European Invention or Genuine African Character? *Mission studies,* 9(1): 98-107.

57Clarke, J. H. 1988. Pan-Africanism: A brief history of an idea in the African world. *Présence Africaine,* (1): 26-56.

58Ibid.

59Ibid.

60Lake, O. 1995. Toward a Pan-African identity: Diaspora African repatriates in Ghana. *Anthropological Quarterly*, 21-36.

61Ibid.

62 Bird, G. 2016. Beyond the nation state: the role of local and pan-national identities in defining post-colonial African citizenship. *Citizenship Studies*, 20(2): 260-275.

63Eriksen, T. H. 2016. The Problem of African Nationhood. *Nations and Nationalism*, 22(2): 222-231.

64Ibid.

65Ibid.

66Vinck, P.,&Pham, P. 2010. Building Peace, Seeking Justice: A Population-Based Survey on Attitudes About Accountability and Social Reconstruction in the Central African Republic. Seeking Justice: A Population-Based Survey on Attitudes About Accountability and Social Reconstruction in the Central African Republic (August 3, 2010). University of Berkeley, California: Human Rights Centre

67Ibrahim, M. 2014. *Mo Ibrahim On How (And Why) Africa Should Solve Its Own Problems*.Retrieved from: http://www.forbes.com/sites/skollworldforum/2013/07/15/mo-ibrahim-on-how-and-why-africa-should-solve-itsown-problems.[Date accessed: November 7, 2016.]

68Ebijuwa, T.,&Gbadegesin, A. S. 2015. Mediating Ethnic Identities: Reaching Consensus through Dialogue in an African Society. *Cultura*, 12(1): 57-69.

[69]Eriksen, T. H. 2016. The Problem of African Nationhood. *Nations and Nationalism,* 22(2): 222-231.

[70]Ibid.

[71]Daley, P. 2013. Refugees, idps and Citizenship Rights: the perils of humanitarianism in the African Great Lakes region. *Third World Quarterly*, 34(5): 893-912.

[72]Cohen, A. P. 2013. *Symbolic construction of community.* London and New York: Routledge.

[73]Daley, P. 2013. Refugees, IDPs and Citizenship Rights: the perils of humanitarianism in the African Great Lakes region. *Third World Quarterly*, 34(5): 893-912.

[74]Eze, M. O. 2013. Pan-Africanism and the Politics of History. *History Compass*, 11(9): 675-686.

[75]Ibid.

[76]de la Rosa, F. J. U. 2011. Trans-African identity: Cultural globalisation and the role of the symbolic-aesthethic dimension in the present identity construction processes. *African Journal of History and Culture*, 3(8): 128.

[77]Ibid.

[78]Kersting, N. 2009. New nationalism and xenophobia in Africa: a new inclination? *Africa Spectrum*, 7-18.

[79]Ake, C. 1996. *Development and Democracy in Africa.* Washington, DC: Brookings Institution.

[80]Ibid

[81]Kersting, N. 2009. New nationalism and xenophobia in Africa: a new inclination? *Africa Spectrum*, 7-18.

[82]Ibid.

[83]Ebijuwa, T.,& Gbadegesin, A. S. 2015. Mediating Ethnic Identities: Reaching Consensus through Dialogue in an African Society. *Cultura,* 12(1): 57-69.

[84]Ibid.

[85]French, H. W. 2015. The Looting Machine: Warlords, Oligarchs, Corporations, Smugglers, and the Theft of Africa's Wealth. *Foreign Affairs*, 94(4): 150-155.

[86]Ani, N. C.,& Matambo, E. 2016. African Solutions in chains: external and internal causes of Africa's continued dependency fifty years on. *Journal of African Union Studies,* 5: 83-111.

[87]Reno, W. 1999. *Warlord politics and African states.* Boulder, Colorado: Lynne Rienner Publishers.

[88]Ani, N. C.,& Matambo, E. 2016. African Solutions in chains: external and internal causes of Africa's continued dependency fifty years on. *Journal of African Union Studies,* 5: 83-111.

[89]Ibid

[90]Fanon, F. 1963. *The wretched of the earth.* (Translation by Constance Farrington.) New York: Grove Press.

[91]French, H. W. 2015. The Looting Machine: Warlords, Oligarchs, Corporations, Smugglers, and the Theft of Africa's Wealth. *Foreign Affairs*, 94(4): 150-155.

[92]Pouligny, B. 2004. *The Politics and Anti-Politics of Contemporary Disarmament, Demobilisation and Reintegration Programs.* Paris, France: Secrétariat Général de la Défense Nationale

[93]Ani, N. C.,& Matambo, E. 2016. African Solutions" in chains: external and internal causes of Africa's continued dependency fifty years on. *Journal of African Union Studies,* 5: 83-111.

[94]Gerlach, C. 2010. *Extremely Violent Societies: Mass Violence in the Twentieth Century World.* New York: Cambridge University Press.

[95]Adrien-Rongier, M.F. 1981. Les" kodro" de Bangui: un espace urbain oublié(Bangui's' Kodro: A Forgotten Urban Space). *Cahiers d'études Africaines*, 93-110.

[96]Fanon, F. 1963. *The wretched of the earth.*(Translation by Constance Farrington.) New York: Grove Press.

[97]Ibid.

[98] Hills, A. 2007. Warlords, militia and conflict in contemporary Africa: A re-examination of terms. *Small Wars & Insurgencies,* 8(1): 35-51.

[99]Ani, N. C.,& Matambo, E. 2016. African Solutions" in chains: external and internal causes of Africa's continued dependency fifty years on. *Journal of African Union Studies,* 5(1): 83-111.

[100]Ekwealor, C. T., & Okeke-Uzodike, U. 2016. The African union interventions in African conflicts: unity and leadership conundrum on Libya. *Journal of African Union Studies,* 5(1): 63-82.

[101]Ibid.

[102]Isaacs-Martin, W. 2016. Political and Ethnic Identity in Violent Conflict: The Case of Central African Republic. *International Journal of Conflict and Violence*, 10(1): 26.

[103]Ibid.

[104]Ani, N. C., & Matambo, E. 2016. African Solutions in chains: external and internal causes of Africa's continued dependency fifty years on. *Journal of African Union Studies,* 5(1): 83-111.

[105]Daley, P. 2013. Refugees, IDPs and Citizenship Rights: the perils of humanitarianism in the African Great Lakes region. *Third World Quarterly*, 34(5): 893-912.

[106]Ibid.

[107]De Zeeuw, J. (Ed.). 2008. *From Soldiers to Politicians: Transforming Rebel Movements after Civil War*. Boulder, Colorado: Lynne Rienner Publishers.

[108]Daley, P. 2013. Refugees, idps and Citizenship Rights: the perils of humanitarianism in the African Great Lakes region. *Third World Quarterly*, 34(5): 893-912.

[109]Ibid.

[110]Ibid.

[111]Pouligny, B. 2004. *The Politics and Anti-Politics of Contemporary Disarmament, Demobilisation and Reintegration Programs*. Paris, France, Secrétariat Général de la Défense Nationale .

[112]Daley, P. 2013. Refugees, idps and Citizenship Rights: the perils of humanitarianism in the African Great Lakes region. *Third World Quarterly*, 34(5): 893-912.

[113]Fanon, F. 1963. *The wretched of the earth*.(Translation by Constance Farrington.) New York: Grove Press.

[114]Ibid.

Chapter 5

Engaging with the African ground: towards a new research paradigm for conflict studies in Africa

Andreas "Dries" Velthuizen

Institute for Dispute Resolution in Africa (IDRA), University of South Africa

5.1   Introduction

Thabo Mbeki, during his 'I am an African speech' in 1998, stated:

> I am born of a people who are heroes and heroines…whatever the circumstances they have lived through and because of that experience, they are determined to define for themselves who they are and who they should be.

This statement inspires the people of Africa to not only know what happened in their past, but to also be conscious of their present place and role in the world, as well as have an understanding of what the future might hold. In order to access, process, interpret and apply all this knowledge, there is a need for research paradigms that would facilitate knowledge production, including on conflict and peace in Africa. The need is for such a paradigm to reveal new peaceful horizons beyond the racial and physical boundaries set by divisionary thinking that causes Africa to remain in conflict and escape lasting peace.

Against this background, the question is asked 'What is an appropriate research paradigm that that can be applied to conflict studies in African contexts?' This chapter aims to identify specific variables that could be an integral part of a new grounded or engaged theory for conflict studies in Africa. This aim will be achieved by investigating conflict studies in Africa from the perspective of phenomenology as a philosophy, a transdisciplinary research approach and a research methodology that is participatory and engaged, discovering the lived experiences and consciousness of involved engagement with communities in Africa that are involved in violent conflict or recovering from it.

The chapter will start with explaining African phenomenology as a philosophical framework for research, trans-disciplinarity as an approach to research, and community engaged participatory research. The research activities of *trust building, knowledge-discovery* and *complementary interpretation* will be presented, illustrating how these activities were applied during my research with the San of South Africa, relating it to the conceptual framework. From the conceptual framework and case study, variables will be identified that will inform a new research paradigm for conflict studies in Africa and the possible impact thereof for new engaged theory for conflict studies in general.

5.2 A philosophical framework for a new research paradigm on African conflict studies

From different vantage points to new horizons

Heidegger[1] asserted that it is just human for individuals to interpret by discovering meaning in social contexts. The conditions in which phenomena such as conflict take place can be observed from a stepping-stone, which serves as a secure vantage point and foothold towards a full understanding of a phenomenon. From this vantage point, self-reflection and consciousness of the position of people in the world takes place, including the essence of the belief system of people, as well as the importance of cultural and historical context. A hermeneutic cycle enables the participant to listen to messages, interpret them, and pass them on to others. When other people are exposed to these experiences, it assists them in the understanding of the others.

In this cyclic process, Husserl[2] encourages us to break out of disciplinary constraints and systematic disciplinary practices. This breakout will free us from the prejudices of natural sciences, especially assumptions that were not thoroughly examined. Gadamer[3], meanwhile, presented to us the outcome of the "fusion of horizons" as the mediation between the immediate horizon of the interpreter and a new emerging horizon. This fusion is achieved through complementary reflection.

From the assertions of these Western philosophers, a research paradigm is offered as a process of observation and complementary reflection from different vantage points, where for instance different perspectives of researchers and the lived experience of the communities find each other and bring some merged understanding of violent conflict as a phenomenon.

The fusion of life-worlds through complementary reflection

Keeping in mind these assertions from Western philosophers such as Heidegger, Husserl and Gadamer, the philosopher from the African diaspora, WEB Du Bois[4], offered a "racialisation" perspective which claims that all Africans were made 'black' by Western thinking in a deliberate quest to assert supremacy and a specific identity on people of African origin. Consequently, African people move between two life-worlds and a double consciousness: the world as asserted by Western capitalism as opposed to reality as experienced by African people.

Senghor[5] further explained the epistemological differences between the African and the European, acknowledging the conceptual variation in reasoning. In the European tradition, reasoning is "mechanical and atomistic, functioning as an instrument of manipulation, dissecting the object to expose its hidden essence". In the African traditional model, reason takes place to cultivate and sustain an affective, living, reciprocal, relationship of energy and influence exchange. In this relationship there is no barrier between subject and object. According to Senghor, the African "keeps his senses open, ready to receive any impulse, and even the very waves of nature, without screen ... between subject and object".

It is in this understanding of a dichotomy and tension between European epistemology and African tradition that Du Bois[6] described self-reflection as "first sight", where people see themselves through their own eyes in relation to the whole life-world, uprooting stereotypes about skin colour and reconstructing the self and the world with creative discourses and symbols. Du Bois contrasted it with "second sight", meaning seeing oneself through the eyes of others. Schutz[7] identified a view of the world from the "first order construct" of the people studied and the "second order structure of the researcher", connecting a common sense world with scientific theory.

Laverty[8] described interpretation as the construct of variations through intuition, imaginative variation, and synthesis. Laverty[9] suggested that it is important for the researcher to start the research from personal self-reflection about his or her position in relation to other people involved in the research. The researcher should then reflect to ensure an understanding of the world as lived by the people to be researched.

This process of reasoning was recognised by a contemporary African scholar, Odora Hoppers[10], as a system of meaning, in other words a relationship between variables and the meaning attached to it that reflect essential interrelatedness and interdependence of all phenomena. Such a knowledge system of interpretation involves the 'co-evolution' of spiritual, natural and human worlds. In many African contexts, it infers to a relationship with nature, 'human agency' and human solidarity, which implies 'I am human because I belong'.

Henry[11] explained such self-reflection as the development of comparative cultural perspectives. From the perspective of African phenomenology, the author[12] pointed out the importance of descriptions of phenomena as the product of self-reflection, actively constituting the consciousness of African people. In this process, egos are displaced through "de-centring techniques" practiced in specific cultures and epistemic practices and from inside any discipline, producing knowledge in a trans-disciplinary way. According to Cox[13], interpretation takes plays after suspending judgement. The essence of meaning is discovered through comparative studies and bracketing away unexamined assumptions about the world, allowing a phenomenon to speak for itself.

These assertions by African scholars prompt the researcher in Africa to be conscious of the different life-worlds on the continent. It requires the researcher to not only think rationally, but to be able to feel impulse from the research subjects. The ability to both feel and rationalise can be enhanced through self-reflection about how the researcher and subjects in the present reality are interrelated and interdependent of all phenomena, including the life-worlds of other people. In this self-reflection it may be important to suspend judgement about what happened in the past or may happen in future, and rather focus on understanding the current reality of interrelated phenomena.

The call for free, creative, trans-disciplinary and empowering research strategies
Gordon[14] defined the core of human reality as freedom, which is not determined by any law or necessity from within or without:

> We are free to choose our existence with nothing to legitimate or guarantee it other than our choice. Consequently, we are primarily responsible for who we are and what we will become.

Odora Hoppers[15] reminds us of the reality in terms of atrocities and 'evil acts' in some places in Africa that cannot be subjected to expert assessments founded on the sociology of conflict only. A combination of literature and political theory, as well as an understanding of "a phenomenology of humiliation" that cause the dissonances in the narratives of the community and that of the researcher from outside the community, should always be considered. Odora Hoppers therefore called for a new theory of freedom.

Amina Mama[16] argued that intellectuals from Africa need to engage more proactively with the "methodological implications" of their own intellectual ethics. This engagement would require addressing the intellectual challenges of the "complicated and contradictory location in the world" of Africa, ensuring unique vantage points to pursue freedom through methodological and pedagogical strategies.

Paulin Houdontji[17] reminds us that African studies is not a discipline but a range of interrelated disciplines, and African studies are not simply to understand Western philosophy or other traditions from outside Africa, but also endogenous knowledge in Africa accumulated over a long time as part of knowledge production and appropriation. African studies should be part of a wider project focusing on self-knowledge; the priority is to develop an African-based tradition where questions are initiated and research agendas are set by African society. Africa should develop its own process of knowledge accumulation and not be reduced to a subject of study.

According to Ndlovu-Gatsheni[18], coloniality (a remnant of colonialism) is maintained as criteria for academic performance in books, in cultural patterns, in common sense, in the self-image of peoples, and in aspirations of the self. The coloniality of knowledge emphasises epistemological issues, the politics of knowledge generation, as well as questions of who generates which knowledge, and for what purpose. African studies often neglect to investigate the origins of disciplines and the destructive placing of the dynamic flux of experience into static, observable Euro-American centric blocs without meaning (epistemicides), in the interest of imperialism and colonialism. Endogenous and indigenous knowledge have been marginalised to such an extent that the people of Africa are currently burdened with irrelevant knowledge that 'disempowers' rather than empowers individuals and communities. Therefore, at the epistemic level, decoloniality is about epistemological disobedience premised on the domains of power, knowledge, and being. At the political level it is about a new critical theory, new meaning making, and action. At the methodological level, it 'rebels' against knowledge of 'equilibrium' and methods that operate as part of 'colonial matrices of power' that prevent transformation.

These assertions by African scholars confirm that currently, in Africa, scholars enjoy the freedom of knowledge accumulation and production. Furthermore, a current freedom of action exists for a new critical theory to make meaning of phenomena such as conflict in Africa, and to take action.

A new consciousness of aesthetic knowledge in African research
From his vantage point in the diaspora, Du Bois[19] encouraged the African people to use their poetry, storytelling, songs and music to creatively uproot and destroy stereotypes about them. He

asked Africans to reconstruct discourses that are creative and display a will towards self-elevation to a critical point when a person becomes 'I' and 'We'; a human being without racial identity.

Steve Biko[20] reminded us of the eagerness of Africans to communicate with each other through song and rhythm. In the African culture, music describes all emotional states; burdens and pleasures are shared through music, and games are accompanied by music. Music is inherent to African communication. It is never sung for individuals, but in groups, so everybody is reading the same thing from a common experience. Substance is found in togetherness. Music is part of a culture of defiance, self-assertion, group pride and solidarity. The common experience of oppression finds expression in music, dress and other aspects[21].

Henry[22] called it the "loving reconstruction of African consciousness" through poetics, moving beyond European philosophical approaches to phenomenology. In the discourse on phenomenology, poetics is a newcomer after creative writing about a subject; as professed by Derrida; existential analysis by Sartre; reduction through self-reflection by Husserl; the Dasein (the mode of being human) of Heidegger; the application of meditation by Hegel and the propositions of radical doubting by Descartes.

In a recent publication, a young African scholar named Robtel Neajai Pailey[23] confirmed that the purpose of African Studies as a field of scholarly inquiry is to interrogate epistemological, methodological, and theoretical approaches to the study of Africa, inserting the people of Africa as subjects, rather than objects. She found that African Studies remains colonised, misrepresented, homogenised and simplified in terms of essence. African studies are still dominated by "non-Africans", who position themselves as authoritative voices, as if Africa does not have its own intellectuals or knowledge production. In publishing about Africa, African scholarship is often disrespected and dismissed. Knowledge about Africa is more than just its history, politics and development processes; it is about appreciating Africa 'aesthetically' through the study of drama, fiction, visual art, and dance forms, produced and taught by Africans as an affirmation that Africans produce knowledge about their continent.

From these propositions, it is evident that African scholars are calling for creative discourses and appreciation of the knowledge articulated through aesthetics such as poetics and music, in a way that it creates a consciousness of the identity and unique knowledge that African people have about their continent. It is therefore important for both researcher and research subjects in Africa to access the knowledge about conflict and peace that resides in an aesthetic knowledge domain.

Trans-disciplinary approach to research

According to Max-Neef[24], 'trans-disciplinarity' is not a new discipline but a way of seeing the world as systemic and more holistic. Nissani[25] explained that all research takes place along a continuum, ranging from the two imaginary poles where pure disciplinary work is at the one pole, and a grand synthesis of all human knowledge at the other. The knowledge exemplars of research and education can be compared according to the number of disciplines involved; the 'distance' between them; the novelty and creativity involved in combining the disciplinary elements; and their degree of integration.

Nicolescu[26] asserted that trans-disciplinary education is founded on trans-disciplinary methodology, allowing us to establish links between persons, facts, images, representations, fields of knowledge and action. In this way we discover the "Eros of learning" during our entire life by continuously questioning the integration of beings and phenomena. In the natural world, trans-disciplinarity is coherent among different realities. Self-consistency ("a cosmic bootstrap") seems to govern the evolution of the universe, from the infinitely small elements to the infinitely large, from the infinitely brief to the infinitely protracted. It seems as if a flow of information is transmitted in a coherent manner from one reality to another in our physical universe.

Following the perspectives of Nissani[27], Max-Neeff[28], Nicolescu[29] and others, it can be inferred that the trans-disciplinary approach is essential to find solutions to wicked problems such as violent conflict. In the space among disciplines there is knowledge (normative, scientific, analytic and aesthetic) that may reveal new perspectives on the causes of conflict and how to find peace. Trans-disciplinarity opens new perspectives on how to deal with problems in a real world that moves beyond the constraints of disciplinary boundaries. Trans-disciplinary sense-making enables the researcher to do away with dichotomised and divisionary thinking while creating better societies.

Community engaged research
Community engaged research is "the process of working collaboratively with and through groups of people affiliated by geographic proximity, special interest, or similar situations to address issues affecting the well-being of those people"[30]. Community engaged research is different from traditional research in the sense that the research question is defined by the community or an organisation, which approaches the researchers to explore the research topic. However, a researcher may also initiate a partnership with a community[31].

The use of Community Engaged Participatory Research (CEPR) as a methodology in African contexts is not new. In fact, the positive experiences of several researchers show many advantages where violent conflict or human security challenges are experienced. South African researchers learned that community engagement is not just "consultation" and "involvement". Community engagement as a research activity proved to be a dynamic, participatory and reflexive dialogical process that embraces the building and sustaining of authentic relationships, inclusive of previously marginalised voices. It promotes close collaboration with community partners who share common goals and interests. Community engagement is grounded in the principles of justice, empowerment, critical self-reflection/enquiry and consciousness (awakening of critical self-awareness) through dialogue, as well as self-determination. It aims at trust building, the gathering of resources and allies, the enhancement of equal communication, as well as attaining outcomes that will bring improvement for all parties participating in the engagement. CEPR entails ongoing relationships between researchers and community representatives, so that the impact of interventions can be further researched. The relationship involves sensitivity. CEPR contributes to an emerging knowledge base for safety promotion in South Africa and the rest of the continent. Furthermore, CEPR creates harmonious and contextual community-centred learning that advances social justice, citizenship and democracy. Moreover, CEPR may result in constructs such as a sense of belonging, connectedness, shared values, and community cohesion and efficacy, guiding the community away from "individuation" and "self-aggrandisement"[32].

CEPR builds on the strengths and resources of the community with a commitment to action research and an emphasis on a dynamic relationship between theory and practice (praxis). CEPR is a partnership between research institutions and community members, sharing the findings of knowledge with all relevant stakeholders and applying it to the benefit of the community. As a long-term process, there is commitment to ownership and sustainability. CEPR is characterised by understanding and respecting the historical and current dynamics of the community; aligning community engagement with community agendas; establishing structures and processes to include diverse participation; fostering community ownership; as well as strengthening and sustaining communities[33].

The philosophical discussion for a new research paradigm on African conflict studies recognises different vantage points from which conflict in Africa is observed. This recognition opens the door for the fusion of knowledge from different life-worlds in Africa, by means of complementary reflection as part of emancipatory and innovative research strategies that use the new freedom of action to move from a static vantage point to eradicate the boundaries between 'life-worlds' created by historical events and disciplinarity. The purpose of the initiative is to engage with a domain where knowledge is expressed in aesthetic forms and appreciated by the researcher who engages with African people where they live today. Engagement initiatives would require a collaborative partnership based on trust and respect, including dialogue departing from self-reflection and an awareness of the importance of cognitive justice, empowerment of research partners, critical complementary enquiry and reflection. From this partnership emerges knowledge that is grounded in the common consciousness for the need for self-determination, ownership and sustainability.

5.3   Applying African phenomenology, trans-disciplinarity and participatory engagement with the San communities of South Africa

The Research Process

It is with this research strategy in mind that since September 2013, the Institute for Dispute Resolution in Africa (IDRA), in the College of Law at the University of South Africa (Unisa), has conducted CEPR with the San community of Platfontein. By the end of 2016 the research project was ongoing within the ambit of a project with the San Council of South Africa, which represents the broader San community of Southern Africa.

The San of Platfontein are part of the First People of Southern Africa, whose origins can be traced to the 'Mitochondrial Eve' from whom, according to Oppenheimer[34], all Africans originate. The San of Platfontein speak Kwedam and !Kun, which distinguishes them from other groups. The Khwedam speaking people (the Kwhe) are from the Kavango region of Namibia and the Cuando-Cubango province of Angola. Most of the !Kun were hunter-gatherers who lived in the remote savannah areas of Angola, Botswana and Namibia. During colonial rule by the Portuguese in Angola, men from both groups served as Portuguese soldiers. When Portugal withdrew from Angola in 1974, the San soldiers became part of the South African Defence Force who fought against insurgents in Angola. After the independence of Namibia in March 1990, they were settled in South Africa by the South African government. Currently they reside in a low-income village called Platfontein on the outskirts of Kimberley, the capital of the Northern Cape Province of South Africa[35]. (See http://dspace.nwu.ac.za/handle/10394/13079 for scholarly publications about the San of Platfontein.)

Figure 1: Location of the San of Platfontein

The purpose of the research with the San of Platfontein was to discover solutions for ongoing disputes in the community that tend to be violent. The research team followed a CEPR methodology that started with trust building and capacity building as part of a Preparatory Phase of six months (this relatively short period was possible because the Chief Investigator was well known to the community). A Knowledge Discovery Phase, a Design Phase and an Implementation Phase followed.

The Knowledge Discovery Phase took place with the participation of young San field researchers, who conducted interviews and focus groups with key knowledge holders. This phase included an Interpretation Phase, with a broad spectrum of specialists asserting meaning to the discovered knowledge, using techniques such as conflict mapping. During the Knowledge Discovery Phase, 260 research reports resulted from semi-structured interviews, focus-group meetings and interpretative conversations, as well as solution design workshops. These reports were captured and collated in what is called the San Dispute Resolution Oral Archive[36] (see http://uir.unisa.ac.za). Approximately 200 members from the community participated in the research.

The research team, consisting of a Chief Researcher, an Assistant Researcher from Unisa and eight San field researchers, used conflict mapping to process the wealth of information obtained from community members. Interpretative conversations were also conducted with the Elders and the leaders of the ‡Khomani San community of Andriesvale (230km north of the town of Upington, about 600km from Platfontein) and scholars from different disciplines.

During the Design Phase, the community members designed solutions together with the researchers and other specialists. This phase brought community leaders, scholars and practitioners from several disciplines together at a writers retreat and international conference to design dispute resolution architecture for and with the community. The findings of the research are therefore a synthesis of the results of several research activities[37].

The Implementation Phase, consisting of a series of dispute resolution interventions in Platfontein, aimed to empower the community to establish a dispute resolution capacity. The interventions were community driven, with the researchers acting as consultants. The overall goals were to enable the community to live in harmony. The first objective was to implement dispute resolution capacity building programmes in the community. An integrative approach between rediscovering the unique traditional forms of dispute resolution and the transfer of modern dispute resolution methods were followed. The second objective was to guide other stakeholders towards interventions that would contribute to dispute prevention and resolution in Platfontein[38].

What is important about this research is the trans-disciplinary perspective that was used throughout the process. With the San community, it was found that research into violent conflict was not possible within the limitations of disciplines such as political science, law and anthropology (the specialist fields of the researchers involved). Thorough investigation required borrowing methods from disciplines such as sociology, history, linguistics, archaeology and theology. Only then could the lived experiences of people of the San of South Africa be discovered.

Trust building

The San people see some researchers as ruthless people who just want to "suck out the inside fat", referring to the belief that the gecko (lizard) is capable of doing that to a person. There is also the San experience of the researcher as a chameleon, who changes colour any time during the research process, deviating from initial agreements.

During a recent conversation between San leaders and academics, the issue of trust between researchers and San communities was thoroughly analysed (South African San Institute, 2016). During this workshop, the participants discovered that trust building is enhanced by several aspects. "Entering through the right gate" (meaning the legitimate governance body of a community) or an official nodal point is considered to be of critical importance. Dealing with individuals is unacceptable to a community and creates suspicion. Furthermore, contracts should be entered into with formal instructions covering aspects such as patents, trademarks and copyright. Other aspects are informed consent that should be linked to individual consent (not that of the governing body only); compensating for work done but not paying for information; keeping your word; using appropriate language to explain everything; doing what is agreed upon initially and not something else, and adhering to the do-no-harm principle.

The participants agreed that trust building is about everybody treating everybody as equals, where no person is the subject or object of research, but equal partners in the research process. Equity in the research means recognition of the contribution of the community in the whole research process, honouring of contracts and traditional structures, and entering into the research process as trusted friends who can keep their word. Against the background of the historically humiliation of San identity, the principle of equality is of vital importance.

Throughout history, collective identity was affirmed by political forces and contested by most indigenous people of South Africa, namely the assertion of identity as 'Bosjeman' (by the Dutch), 'Bushmen' by the British, 'Boesman' in Afrikaans, and currently 'San', which is also contested by some groups of indigenous people as being derogatory. It is therefore of utmost importance that the correct vocabulary is used when researchers engage with African people.

Knowledge discovery: Fact finding, critical reflection and complementary interpretation
Looking at the community as a site of knowledge, the researcher should be able to work out how this knowledge can be accessed in a way that is acceptable to the community. Acceptability means that equitable collaborative partnerships are maintained, irrespective of the identities of the people involved. In the spirit of equity, knowledge is not a one-way access by the researcher, but an interaction where emphatic learning and capacity building takes place. Discovering the truth about violent conflict is about a holistic perspective of the conflict, considering all dimensions of the conflict. Holistic perspective means understanding the geographical, cultural and historic context of causes; the dynamics; the actors involved; and the consequences of the conflict. Furthermore, with the aim of truth discovery, the participants are able to challenge divisionary thinking characterised by subservient relationships and dominant narratives that tend to manipulate research findings. Moreover, from the perspective of the researcher, CERP enforced rigorous academic standards and met social responsibility at the same time[39].

In their research with the San, the researchers found that to undertake participatory research with communities they could meet all the usual requirements of good research, such as empirical investigation, mitigation of language and personality barriers, flexible application of research methods, as well as a rigorous processing of knowledge claims. The integrative and interactive nature of the research is ideal to verify the accuracy of knowledge claims in a cultural context. The equity of perspectives was achieved by listening to many different worldviews. Eventually the research succeeded in challenging hegemonic power relationships, paradigms and narratives, which ultimately assisted the researchers to develop a holistic perspective and judge what is true about the conflict.

Language barriers and dialogue between the researched and researchers proved to be a challenge; it was common that focus group meetings took place in four different languages. The participants communicated in their own languages, !Kun and Kwedam, with young researchers from the community translating it into Afrikaans for everybody to understand and occasionally into English for the benefit of visiting experts from other countries.

Velthuizen[40] found that the synthesis of knowledge requires not only cross-disciplinary interrogations of knowledge claims about the real world; in a trans-dimensional world, knowledge perspectives are subject to empirical observation, analytical procedure and application of normative wisdom, or what can be called holistic knowledge. Such a synthesis can be achieved by means of conflict mapping, where information about the conflict can be ordered into parts so that the meaning of each part can be examined.

In the case of research with the San, the 'Baobab Map' (a conflict analysis map) was developed by the field researchers to serve as an analysis tool around which different people could gather to discuss the meaning of the data visible on the map. The method followed for interpreting the data on the map can be described by means of concentric circles. First, during several workshops, community members gathered around the map to assert meaning to the aggregate data, and elders from the community added their narratives from their perspectives. During later events, a further circle of interpretation was added by involving members from other San communities who would look at conflict from their different perspectives. Further perspectives were added by joining all community members together with scholars and practitioners during a major conference and writer's retreat. A further process of peer review of publications added significant meaning to the knowledge and took it into the academic sphere.

The research with the San of Platfontein shows that a new research paradigm can be applied in African communities, which provides for the different vantage points and life-worlds of the researcher and those of knowledge holders in a community to merge in such a way that they become complementary. In this case, an innovative research strategy was followed that deliberately wiped out the boundaries between the 'life-worlds' formed by disciplinarity in the research and history of a community. Grounded in the knowledge by engaging with African people in their current circumstances, the strong indication is that a new research paradigm for conflict resolution in Africa will be collaborative partnerships with communities. The mutual engagement will be characterised by self-reflection by community members and researchers, continuous dialogue including aesthetic forms of communication, complementary joint meaning-making, and joint development of solutions to end conflict and ensure peace.

It is in the quest for self-knowledge, transformation and social innovation that a new paradigm for conflict studies in Africa emerges. It is a paradigm that seeks not only to discover and build knowledge for the sake of discovery, but to articulate a new lived experience where stories are told, music is played and art is displayed. It is a creative paradigm where people use their freedom to replace dominant discourses with own poetics, independent but part of a new emerging engaged theory for conflict/peace studies in Africa.

The CEPR with Platfontein illustrates how a new engaged theory for African research is developing that is also grounded theory, in the sense that theory is systematically generated from research in a specific episteme to break away from the dominant discourses of scholars who live outside Africa and write about Africa without being continuously engaged in it. Furthermore, a new engaged theory is about equity, where the voices of communities and scholars engaged with their knowledge are taking a leading role in questioning dominant assumptions about peace and conflict studies in Africa. Moreover, a new engaged theory should be the result of interconnected knowledge discovery, collective learning and knowledge production in a unique African way.

5.4   Conclusion

This chapter departed from a research problem that inquires, 'What is an appropriate research paradigm that can be applied to conflict studies in African contexts?' The aim was to identify specific variables that could be an integral part of a new grounded or engaged theory for conflict studies in Africa. This aim was achieved by viewing conflict studies in Africa from the perspective of the philosophy of phenomenology (specifically African phenomenology), a transdisciplinary research approach, and Community Engaged Participatory Research (CEPR) methodology. It was shown that from this vantage point, the discovery of lived experiences and consciousness of people in Africa who are involved in violent conflict or recovering from it, became possible. The research experience with the San people of South Africa was used to inform these arguments.

It was found that the most appropriate research paradigm will ultimately be an engaged and grounded theory; engaged in the sense that it was developed through engagement with communities as equal partners in research, and grounded in research results that were systematically generated in an African episteme to break away from dominant discourses that diminished African knowledge.

The content of engaged and grounded theory for conflict studies in Africa first of all requires authentic and equal relationships between researchers and communities as part of trust-building. Furthermore, a new research paradigm will allow people to discover knowledge from lived-experiences, including reconstructing a common identity based on interconnectedness, away from racial identities. Moreover, complementary reflective dialogue will be required that will be critical but culturally sensitive to ensure a thorough understanding of conflict, towards designing and implementing joint solutions together. However, it is when the focus of African conflict studies shifts from Western-dominated paradigms to own discovery and understanding, that social innovation and human security of communities will improve. If the focus of African conflict studies is based on the use of specific indicators to analyse and interpret the poetics of communities in conflict, peace and justice can be attained, replacing the dominance of certain discourses. It is foreseen that trans-disciplinary research that is conscious of African phenomenology and epistemology will contribute to positive change in the form of social justice and opportunities for self-empowerment for the people in African communities who are recovering from violent conflict.

References

[1]Heidegger, M. 1962. *Being and Time*. New York: Harper.

[2]Husserl, E. 1962. *Ideas: General Introduction to Pure Phenomenology*. (Translation by B. Gibson.) London: Collier/Macmillan.

[3]Gadamer, H. G. 1976. *Philosophical Hermeneutics*. Berkeley: University of California Press.

[4]Du Bois, W. E. B. 1969. *The Souls of Black Folk*. New York: New American Library.

[5]Senghor, L., & Kaal, H. 1962. On Negrohood: Psychology of the African Negro. *Diogenes*, 10(1): 8.

[6]Du Bois, W. E. B. 1969. *The Souls of Black Folk*. New York: New American Library.

[7]Schutz, A. 1962. Collected Papers I. *The problem of social reality*. The Hague: Martinus Nijhoff.

[8]Laverty, S. M. 2003. Hermeneutic Phenomenology and Phenomenology: A Comparison of Historical and Methodological Considerations. *International Journal of Qualitative Methods, 2*(3): 1-92.

[9]Ibid.

[10]Odora Hoppers, C. 2004. *Culture, Indigenous Knowledge and Development: The Role of the University*. Centre for Education Policy Development Occasional Paper 3.

[11]Henry, P. 2006. Africana Phenomenology: Its Philosophical Implications. *Worlds & Knowledges Otherwise*, Fall 2006. Retrieved from: https://globalstudies.trinity.duke.edu/wp-content/themes/cgsh/materials/WKO/v1d3_PHenry.pdf [Accessed April 3, 2017].

[12]Ibid.

[13]Cox, J. L. 2015. *The Phenomenology of Religion*. Interview by D. G. Robertson. Transcribed by M. Lepage. Retrieved from: http://www.religiousstudiesproject.com/podcast/podcast-james-cox-on-the-phenomenology-of-religion/ [Accessed: 3 April 2017].

[14]Gordon, L. 1995. *Bad Faith and Anti-black Racism*. Atlantic Highlands: Humanities Press.

[15]Odora Hoppers, C. 2004. *Culture, Indigenous Knowledge and Development: The Role of the University*. Centre for Education Policy Development Occasional Paper 3.

[16]Amina M. 2007. Is It Ethical to Study Africa? Preliminary Thoughts on Scholarship and Freedom. *African Studies Review, 50*(1): 1-26.

[17]Houtondji, P. J. 2009. Knowledge of Africa, Knowledge of Africans. *RCCS Annual Review,* 1: 7–10.

[18]Ndlovu-Gatsheni, S. J. 2013. Why Decoloniality in the 21st Century? *The Thinker* (48): 10-15.

[19]Du Bois, W. E. B. 1969. *The Souls of Black Folk*. New York: New American Library.

[20]Biko, N. M. 2004. *Steve Biko: I write what I like*. Johannesburg: Picador Africa.

[21]Ibid.

[22]Henry, P. 2006. *Africana Phenomenology: Its Philosophical Implications*. Retrieved from: https://globalstudies.trinity.duke.edu/wp-content/themes/cgsh/materials/WKO/v1d3_PHenry.pdf [Accessed 3 April 2017].

[23]Pailey, R. N. 2016. *Where is the 'African' in African Studies? African Arguments*. Retrieved from: http://africanarguments.org/2016/06/07/where-is-the-african-in-african-studies/ [Accessed 3 April 2017].

[24]Max-Neef, M. A. 2005. *Foundations of Transdisciplinarity*. Retrieved from: http://www.sciencedirect.com. Accessed 12 January 2016.

[25]Nissani, M. 1995. Fruit salads and smoothies: A working definition on interdisciplinarity. *Journal of Educational Thought,* 29(2):121-128.

[26]Nicolescu, B. 2005. *Towards Transdisciplinary Education and Learning*. Paper prepared for conference on 'Science and Religion: Global Perspectives', June 4-8, 2005. Philadelphia: Metanexus Institute.

[27]Nissani, M. 1995. Fruit salads and smoothies: A working definition on interdisciplinarity. *Journal of Educational Thought,* 29(2): 121-128.

[28]Max-Neef, M. A. 2005. *Foundations of Transdisciplinarity*. Retrieved from: http://www.sciencedirect.com. [Accessed May 10, 2016]

[29]Nicolescu, B. 2005. *Towards Transdisciplinary Education and Learning*. Paper prepared for conference on 'Science and Religion: Global Perspectives', June 4-8, 2005. Philadelphia: Metanexus Institute.

[30]CDC/ATSDR Committee on Community Engagement, Public Health Practice Program Office. 1997. *Principles of community engagement*. Atlanta, GA: Centers for Disease Control and Prevention.

[31]Southern California Clinical and Translational Science Institute (SC CTSI), Office of Community Engagement (OCE). 2013. *A Quick Start Guide to Conducting Community-Engaged Research*. Retrieved from: http://oprs.usc.edu/files/2013/01/Comm_Engaged_Research_Guide.pdf. [Accessed February 4, 2016].

[32]Eksteen, R., Abdulsamed, B., van Niekerk, A., Ghouwa I., & Lekoba, R. 2012. Ukuphepha: A Multi-Level Community Engagement Model for the Promotion of Safety, Peace and Health. *Journal of Psychology in Africa*, 22(4), 499–510.

[33]Lazarus, S., Duran, B., Caldwell, L., & Bulbulia, S. 2012. Public Health Research and Action: Reflections on challenges and possibilities of community-based participatory research. In J. Maddock (Ed.). *Public Health*. Retrieved from: http://www.unisa.ac.za/static/corporate_web/Content/About/Service%20departments/community%20engagement%20and%20outreach/documents/public-health-research-action_reflections-challenges.pdf. [Accessed April 3, 2016].

[34]Oppenheimer, S. 2004. *Out of Africa's Eden. The peopling of the world*. Johannesburg: Jonathan Ball.

[35]Hart, T., Jacobs, P., Ramoroka, K., Mangqalaza, H., Mhula, A., Ngwenya, M., & Letty, B. 2014. *Policy brief: Social innovation in South Africa's rural municipalities: Policy implications*. Pretoria: HSRC.

[36]Ibid.

[37]See https://dspace.nwu.ac.za/handle/10394/13079 for articles published.

[38]Velthuizen, A. 2012. A transdisciplinary approach to understanding the causes of wicked problems such as the violent conflict in Rwanda. *The Journal for Transdisciplinary Research in Southern Africa*, 8(1): 51 - 62.

[39]Velthuizen, A. G. 2014a. On truth-telling and storytelling: Truth-seeking during research involving communities with an oral culture and a history of violent conflict. *The Journal for Transdisciplinary Research in Southern Africa*, 10(3): 19-35.

[40]Velthuizen, A. 2015a. Listen to us—we know the solution: mapping the perspectives of African communities for innovative conflict resolution. *Conflict, Security & Development*, 15(1): 75-96.

Chapter 6

Emerging 'Positive Masculinity' in DR Congo: An indication of African Renaissance or Symptoms of Covert Gender Inequalities?

Francis Onditi
United Nations Entity for Gender Equality and Women Empowerment,
United States International University - Kenya

Abu Bah
Centre for NGO Leadership and Development, Northern Illinois University

6.1   Introduction

In the following chapter, Msila focuses on the challenges and opportunities for women in a South African province, whilst in this chapter we focus on masculinity. Much has been researched and written about masculinity in the Democratic Republic of Congo (DRC). The debate has been about the complications that hegemonic masculinity adds to the gender-based violence associated with the intractable armed conflict. Nevertheless, one thing that is not clear is the potential implications of 'positive masculinity' on gender equality. Studies of masculinity in relation to gender and power relations has a long history, dating back to at least the 1980s[1]. Raewyn Connell and James Messerschmidt defined hegemonic masculinity as those traits that various cultures ascribe to 'real men', and which not only set out such 'real men' from women and all other men, but also justify all men to generally be in a position of domination over women[2]. This is of course, what sociologists and African Studies scholars alike, refer to as 'patriarchal system' in which men control and dominate spaces of opportunities in the society. Various sources such as Connell[3], Ari[4], Machineripi and Khan[5], as well as Cosa[6], have shared similar conceptions of masculinity. The common elements believed to shape the African emancipation are relationships, embodiment, genealogy and heredity, socio-economic background and historical forces, educational background, individual will and self-assertion.

Globally, hegemonic masculinity manifests itself in varying forms, both geographically and in social spaces, which has led researchers to conceive the idea of multiple hegemonic masculinities (Connell & Messerschmidt[7]; Donaldson[8]). This characterisation puts no doubt to the fact that hegemonic masculinity is a representation of society's ideal of how male behaviour should be (Connell[9]; Connell[10]). In reality, its function is to legitimate the social ascendancy of men over women in all aspects of life, which is evident in many societies all over the world (Carrigan, Connell & Lee[11]; Connell[12]). In eastern DRC, for example, where conflict has existed for several years, hegemonic masculinity has emphasised the superiority of men over women at various levels of hierarchy; 'manly' men over the 'not-so-manly' men. In Christian-dominated communities such as the DRC, this social ascendancy is often portrayed through religious practices, the family institution, the mass media, business and even through government policies and practices[13]. In trying to enact the meaning of this term against misconception, Christine Beasley stressed that it is worth noting that the latter terms refer not so much to political legitimation, as to the degree of particular characteristics that at any one time may be associated with normative manliness (Beasley[14]; Bourdieu[15]). The various strands of thought that try to define an 'African' aim to address the issue of white supremacy that guarantees the socio-economic, civil and political dominance of white people, that vests the majority of power, minds, ideas and thoughts into the support and maintenance of the dominance of white people (Zeleza[16]; Diop[17]). However, some scholars have posted concerns that even in the 21st century, African people are yet to decolonise their minds towards an African *rebirth*[18]. In particular, Sabelo Ndlovu-Gatsheni posed that in order for the "Africa Future" to be attained, Africans must deal with what seems to be the Western-perpetuated modern power structures, sustained by what he called "global coloniality"[19].

It is under this masculine hegemonic optic that the women in African countries, such as DRC, have almost become the accomplices of *status quo*, fearing being rejected by society (Berry[20]; Cuvelier & Bashwira[21]). These hegemonic perceptions and conceptions of masculinity are the product of a long period of socialisation, similar to what scholars refer to as the collective conscience of perception, thought processes and action[22]. The diffusion of these traits include family, church, state, systematic ideologies, continued periods of violent conflict and other cultural practices (Addis & Mahalik[23]; Scott-Samuel, Stanistreet, & Crawshaw[24]). In addition, hyper-masculinity, often exercised by men in power, is a sign of deepened power relations[25]. DRC is a truly culturally mosaic country with four big socio-linguistic groups: Pygmies, Bantus, Sudanese and Nilotic speaking people[26]. These groups are further subdivided into more than 400 tribes, in which diverse cultures have been around since time immemorial[27]. In that socio-cultural context, men dominate women by holding important social positions, decision making power and privileges attributable to patriarchal society (Hollander[28]; Bard, Baudelet & Mossuz-Lavau[29]).

DRC has endured a history of mixed episodes. The most deplorable of this history was the influence of colonial administration by Belgium[30]. In the early 20th century, Belgian forces arrived and enslaved millions, while King Leopold ruled the country as his personal fiefdom[31]. During a painful independence struggle in the 1960s, the vast country almost disintegrated as regions fought each other[32]. The DRC is slowly recovering from a conflict known as Africa's first world war, which led to the loss of some five million lives between 1994 and 2003, yet many eastern areas are still plagued by violence as various rebel groups continue to operate there[33]. *The Guardian* estimated that in DRC, 45,000 people are killed each month. Since the beginning of the second Congo war in 1998, it is estimated that 5.4 million lives have been lost through armed conflict[34]. The intractable fighting between the government and a variety of rebel and sectarian groups has continued to devastate the country[35]. Although the UN Security Council has sent a significant number of troops to help the nation, conflict still exist in most parts of the country[36].

During these successive bouts of war and conflict, as well as the subsequent socio-economic impact of the last 30 years in that country, there has been an evolution of mixed forms of masculinity (Lwambo[37]; Baaz & Stern[38]). On the one hand, it has led to the subordination and patriarchal oppression of women, while on the other, men have relegated their responsibilities at the family level, leading to women being unable to access important services and opportunities such as education and health that would benefit the entire society[39]. This led to a change in the traditional roles played by men and women in society, where women have become the bread winners of the family, thus becoming financially empowered. In spite of these developments in the social ecosystems of families and societies in DRC, a fundamental problem has been that rather than this trend promoting equality between men and women, men are particularly affected by unemployment. In other less developed countries such as Peru, powerful stereotypes create social instability[40]. A similar trend is observed in DR Congo, where women feel obliged to take care of their families (regardless of size) without any support from the men[41]. This practice is, however, contrary to the African Renaissance philosophy as espoused by leaders such as the former South African President, Thabo Mbeki[42]. In his call for an African Renaissance, Mbeki encouraged Africans to be reflective of anti-colonial sentiment and mobilise their fellow Africans to unite against the tyranny of colonialism[43]. This form of societal change is anchored on African identity and independence from external influences.

While the focus of this chapter is on how society evolves around social-cultural structures and institutions such as masculinity and the associated power relations[44], it is important to understand that the exercise of patriarchal power in society occurs within, and is supported by, a system of male power, both at the domestic household level and in the public sphere. This is nowhere more evident than in DRC, where the specific form of patriarchal culture is closely knit to its socio-cultural and economic fabric; an environment that is reinforced by the interlinked vicious cycle of armed conflict. We begin this chapter with a reflection of the context in which this social evolution is taking place, and then frame the analysis of the emerging issues within the four concepts developed by Raewyn Connell[45]: 1) hegemonic masculinity; 2) gendered hierarchy; 3) social embodiment; and 4) geography of masculinity.

6.2 Contextualising Masculinity and Power Relations in DRC

Arguably, Democratic Republic of Congo can be classified as a fragile post-conflict state (Le Billon[46]; Burnley[47]). It is an extremely big and mineral rich country, with a total land area of 2,345,410 sq. km. that is similar in size to Western Europe. It is rich in diamonds, gold, copper, cobalt and zinc. The country also has supplies of some of the rarest minerals in the world, such as coltan, which is used for manufacturing electronic gadgets. Ironically, the country is riddled with bouts of conflicts and civil wars, and is trapped in the vicious cycle of exporting raw materials[48]. For the people of DRC, its resource wealth has rarely been harnessed for their benefit[49]. Another paradox is that despite the vast natural resources the country has hardly any roads or railways, yet ironically armed groups at all levels of administrative structures own sophisticated weapons to exploit civilians in mines and other socio-economic spaces[50]. As a result of being a near-failed state, the natural riches have attracted rapacious adventurers, unscrupulous corporations, vicious warlords and corrupt governments, and divided the population between competing ethnic groups[51]. Political economy analysis has framed the complexity of natural resource abundance amidst armed conflict as hegemonic masculinity (Baaz & Stern[52]; Meger[53]). This is due to atrocities performed by the powerful rebel and government forces through sexual and gender based violence (SGBV), constituting part of the "global assembly line" of capitalist production[54].

Literature throughout the Congo's first (1960-64) and second (1999) civil wars identified six major issues that seem to sustain hegemonic masculinity in the country (Barker *et al.*[55]; Hollander[56]). First is the fragility of DRC, particularly where violence has become an instrument of war, i.e. a new way of expressing masculinity. In Kinshasa and other big towns like Mbuji-Mayi and Kaluna, new groups of delinquent youth are somehow the expression of violent masculinity. It makes people believe that the violence towards women and girls is deeply rooted in the gender norms. This perspective brings out some parallels, which led Connell to see masculinity beyond the static and monolithic conceptions of biological status and the marital roles of men and women. Thus masculinity does not necessarily refer to 'sex', but rather the social fabrics and practices that shape the societal dynamics of power relations, material distribution and human embodiment. In other words, hegemonic masculinity has ideologically legitimated the global subordination of women to men[57]. However, it is important to note that Connell's thesis of hegemonic masculinity has been challenged on various grounds. The most widely read critique is that masculinity has moved beyond the theoretical model[58]. Progressively, the debate has moved into an empirically supported and widely employed conceptual frame for the relationship between women and men, narrations of manhood, and gendered cultures[59]. This frame fits well into the conceptualisation of this chapter as we explore how cultural norms and mores influenced the evolution of the "positive masculinity" in DRC (Shyaka[60]; Keuleers[61]).

Second, socio-economic and behavioural factors have an implication on the longevity of masculinity in DRC. The macroeconomic indicators are impressive in the country, and show an expansion of the economy. The development of the *Inga* hydropower project, at an estimated cost of $100 billion, is an indication of sustained economic growth[62]. However, the *principal paradox* is that this is not being translated into the wellbeing of the majority of people who do not have access to sufficient food. And despite the progress made in the judiciary as far as family protection, fighting against sexual violence and the equalisation of gender rights is concerned, as per Articles 14 and 15 in the Constitution, there are still some legal dispositions that favour masculine supremacy, especially in Articles 448, 449, 450, and 451 of the family code. Men must also be involved in fighting against and eradicating the violence against women, as well as gender inequality. In a study of middle income economies such as India, female youth expressed more gender-egalitarian attitudes than male youth, but reported greater restrictions to their independence than male youth[63]. When males and females engaged in behaviours contravening sex-specific gender norms, there were corresponding increases in mental health problems for both sexes[64].

Third, the cultural orientation of DRC plays a critical role in determining the gender evolution of men and women. In North Kivu province, for instance, work on the contradictory relationship between idealised hegemonic masculinity and the realities of human life indicate that both men and women seem to accept that hegemonic masculinity is part of life, and that the masculinity power is obtained through the creation and preservation of an exploitation against the vulnerable groups[65]. These norms have not changed despite the displacement of people and the hard economic circumstances which make it difficult and even impossible for many to acquire property.

The fourth factor is justice and gender. Despite the fact that the police are entrusted with the role of protecting people, some of them have been found guilty of sexual violence. Although the police take cognisance of the fact that injustices against girls and women is rampant in most parts of DRC, their knowledge of the physical and psychological impacts of sexual violence is not as it should be[66]. The on-going global efforts to demasculinise the military through training has received criticisms in both method and substance. It has to be recognised that norms are not only or best addressed by training or talking, but through other measures such as those identified above. One problem with the current training and workshop approach is that these events tend to be isolated, with soldiers going through a couple of days of training and then returning to their military units. Isolated events such as these will certainly not produce much change. It is only when norms enforcement mechanisms are integrated into day-to-day military life and instruction that there will be any palpable normative and behaviour change[67]. The other problem with current efforts is the underlying assumption that soldiers are living in a moral vacuum, and that they should be cured of their ignorance and pulled out of their moral morass by being educated in international regimes on human rights[68]. Moreover, discourses on masculinity, violence and ethics must also be situated within beliefs that are central to people's everyday lives[69].

Fifth, is the 'male hegemony' syndrome. Although women have made efforts to liberate their fellow women from the yoke of male domination, the optimal gender parity seem to be far from reality in DRC, as illustrated by this adage deep-seated among the Congolese people, "mwasi akotikala kaka mwasi ata aza monkonzi" (the woman remains a woman even if she is a chief). The persistence of this conception explains, among other factors, the reason behind the rejection of the bill by the Parliament of Congo advocating 30% of seats for women in the National Assembly. One of the majority MPs noted that, "A woman cannot have a say in the public for me why should she have it in the Assembly?" This illustrates the depth of hegemonic masculinity, profoundly instilled into our morals and social practices[70]. Even if there is a social change or things have started changing in DRC, it appears that efforts are still necessary to achieve a society with equal opportunities for both genders. This implies that in order to tackle the gender inequality and different forms of violence associated with them, the role of men is key, partly because DRC is a patriarchal society[71]. This is the reason why hegemony operates through the formation of exemplars of masculinity; symbols that have cultural authority despite the fact that most men and boys cannot fully live up to them. Hegemonic masculinity imposes an ideal set of traits which stipulate that a man can never be unfeminine enough (Martin[72]; Petersen[73]; Holter[74]). In this way, hegemony is not gained through necessarily violent or forceful means, but is achieved through culture, institutions, and persuasions[75]. It is evident that patriarchal forms of behaviour ensure that men dominate over women, which is inconsistent with the philosophy of African

Renaissance which espouses human civilisation[76], including increasing access to socio-economic and political opportunities by all people - men, women, boys and girls.

The sixth and final factor that sustains negative masculinity in DRC is how boys and girls are socialised. Michael Carter applied the identity theory to show how gender maintains a diffuse status characteristic across social situations[77]. When children are socialised by their parents, they are immersed in a world in which they have nothing to compare. The family during infancy and beyond serves not as a passive transmitter of culture, but rather as an active agent in screening in and out elements of culture[78]. This process of socialisation and gender construction is accomplished in two ways: 1) by means of *activities* (such as playing with others, visiting places, participating in sports, etc.); and 2) through *comment* and *comparison* (i.e. evaluating such activities and the people who do or do not participate in them)[79]. Through these processes, gender is constantly developed. In what he referred to as a *fundamental paradox*, William Ickes observed that the relationships of men and women with traditional gender roles are far from optimal[80]. In patriarchal societies such as DRC, the exposure of women to retrogressive practices such as exclusion, economic marginalisation and sexual violence is generally worse than in stable and progressive communities. In DRC, the availability of appropriate data to catalyse the debate on positive masculinity is lacking, making it difficult to gauge the positive qualitative change in the life of women[81].

The *principle paradox* reflected through the contextual issues in DRC reveal that whereas it is expected that men's perceptions subjugate women's space, the view is also shared among women that men are heads of the house. The most common responses from among the married women were that marriage gives a man parental rights over his wife. In view of this finding, we have argued in this chapter that as much as women remain victims of all forms of hegemonic masculinity, they are paradoxically complicit in these patriarchal tendencies, hence perpetuating gender inequalities. This is contrary to the ethos and principles of the African Renaissance, as espoused by some of the leading Pan-African icons such as former South African President Thabo Mbeki, Sir Cheik Diop of Senegal, and Prof. Ngugu Wa Thiongó of Kenya.

6.3   The Method of Studying Masculinity in Fragile Societies

An understanding of the DRC's socinternationalisation of curriculumultural universe, in reference to the deep-seated prejudices, proverbs, maxims, idioms and adages surrounding masculinity and relationships between man and wife, was crucial in obtaining the data that inform this chapter. The contradiction in Congolese society informed both our theorisation and our framing of the interpretation of our results. For instance, a Luba adage (one of the tribes in DRC) states that "mwaba wa mukaji nku tshikuku" (the place where the woman belongs is the kitchen). The Luba speaking community is known to be patriarchal with a strong hegemonic conception of masculinity, but there are in the same community other adages that praise the woman who manages to succeed in the society. They say, for example, "Mukaju wa kutemba ku bantu" (the woman, the model of humanity, an example to imitate). Although the social success of a woman emancipates and dignifies her, this does not confirm her superiority over a man.

This study could have not been conducted without first understanding the perception of masculinity, as influenced by both societal norms as well as individual conceptions of the roles between men and women. The research was thus informed by the basic understanding that masculinity is "an identity or sentiment/feeling" of being a man in function with what one knows of that gender and what the society says about that matter[82]. Besides societal norms, it is also the feeling of belonging to the male gender as a socially constructed norm. That is perhaps why Elizabeth Bantinter consented that to be a man means there is hard work to assimilate and accommodate that ideal type of male chauvinism[83].

With the understanding that issues of masculinity and gender are deeply embedded in societal norms and values, our study was based on focused group discussions and semi-directive interviews, complemented by a survey across four provinces. Key informants were chosen among local dignitaries, activists of associations and feminist movements, animators of NGOs dealing with human rights, trade unionists, religious leaders, teachers, students, pupils, and representatives of youth movements. In all, 160 men and 160 women participated in 16 focus groups organised for that purpose, by forming four focus groups of 20 people per province. In addition, 256 people (179 men and 177 women) were interviewed during the personalised and semi-directive interviews, 68 (of which 20 were women) in Bas-Congo, 22 (of which seven were women) in Equateur, 130 (of which 39 were women) in Kinshasa, and 36 (of which 11 were women) in South-Kivu (see Table 1).

Table 1: Distribution of respondents by province

Surveyed	Kinshasa	Bas-Congo	Equateur	South-Kivu	Total N	Total %
Men	738	469	103	318	2564	54,1%
Women	351	796	659	370	2176	45,9%
Total N	1089	1265	1698	688	4740	100%
Total %	23,0%	26,7%	35,8%	14,5%	100%	100%

Source: Survey data (2014-2015)

6.4   Gender Equality Stuck in Masculinity: The Principal Paradox?

In spite of the emerging elements of societal transformation towards men-women equality, human biology and social traction may still lead us to be attracted to the opposite creatures whose appearance and behaviour is stereotypically masculine or feminine. But, as some scholars observe, this attraction is caustic in light of a growing body of research that indicates that the relationships of men and women with traditional gender roles are far from changing, and are generally worse than those of androgynous men and women[84]. Earlier, William Ickes uncovered a similar finding, i.e. that the behaviour of men and women in human society may often display a paradoxical quality depending on the prevailing circumstances[85]. These paradoxical realities of life may reflect the conflict between how the society expects men and women to behave vis-a-vis the ingenuity of cultural and biological realities. This inconsistency in socio-biological realities and evolutionary images of gender is what we will refer to as the *principal paradox*, i.e. that traditionally masculine men and traditionally feminine women have relationships that are stable. For instance, the man who has committed himself to advocating for gender equality may be the same man who still unequivocally promotes fellow men at the expense of equally qualified women. Similarly, the woman who vows that she will never enter into the polygamous marriage her mother had, may be the same woman who cannot understand why she is ruinously attracted to a married man who abuses her. In order to gauge this hypothesis, the following themes were investigated: hegemonic masculinity, gendered hierarchy, social embodiment, and geography of masculinity. However, due to contextual and methodological factors, this chapter replaces 'geography masculinity' with 'social and spatial interactivity of masculinity'.

Hegemonic masculinity - Power relations
The question we posed here was, 'What is a man?', in the Congolese context. This question aimed to dig up the meaning and significance of masculinity as understood and lived by the communities under investigation. So as to answer the question, we collected commonly shared representations, as well as variations of those representations (see Table 2).

Table 2: Description of 'man' according to Congolese

Categorisation	Description
According to the capacity of reproduction or procreation	A man is a human being with physical features and sexual organs different from that of a woman; a being with a functioning male sex organ recognisable by erection, the production of viable sperms, and the presence of a woman and children around him.
According to social status	To be a man is to be a human male, fulfilling three functions or essential roles: first as husband and father who works (has a job); secondly as someone who provides for his family and shows respect for it, who can manage the family, have a house, a plot of land and take care of his family; and thirdly, someone who sacrifices himself for his people.
According to the management capacity, making decisions, domination and protection or security	To be a man is to have the ability to make decisions, to be firm and determined, and to not be set back even in the case of opposition, threats or resistance. It is someone who can manage different sectors and who takes risks for the wellbeing of his people. It is someone who received from God the power to rule over everything, including the woman in all instances.

Categorisation	Description
According to the level of autonomy	A man is someone who is independent; someone who doesn't beg so as to satisfy his needs. He represents God. He is a creature created in God's image, a fundamental difference with a woman who was not created in God's image.
According to the conscience of himself and self-esteem	A man is someone who really knows how to define himself in terms of the functions of which the society awaits from him.
According to the ability to accept challenges	A man is a physically strong being who is capable of fighting and winning battles.
According to qualities/attributes	A man is an intelligent being, rational, courageous, strong, and gifted.

Source: Field data (2014-2015)

The result clearly shows that the commonly shared representations put men as superior human beings, who are dominant and leaders of not only the household, but also the entire human ecosystem. As seen from Table 2, the variations of the meanings of masculinity are mainly based on sex and social and educational levels, but religious confession seems also to be a great influence. For women, particularly those influenced by religious values, a man is the person responsible and capable of taking decisions when there are problems; he is a strong being for whom a woman has been created; he must be the starting point of everything in the family; he must be the symbol of respect, responsibility and security. These descriptions are similar to the five classifications of Trujillo[86] regarding what is considered hegemonic masculinity: (1) "when power is defined in terms of physical force and control" (particularly in the representation of the body); (2) "when it is defined through occupational achievement in an industrial, capitalistic society"; (3) when it is represented in terms of familial patriarchy; (4) when it is "symbolized by the daring, romantic frontiersman of yesteryear and of the present-day outdoors man"; and (5) "when heterosexually defined" and centred on the representation of the phallus[87].

In one of the interviews in a village in Goma, a young man said:

> Anyone who pretends to be a man should be the real man, the protector and vital person in the family. If a man is sterile, impotent, or incapable of satisfying his wife in the bedroom, or when he has no money and is unable to satisfy the basic needs of the family, then he would not be a man with that capital. Men think that to be a man is to have the reasoning capacity coupled with the resolution of crucial problems facing the family; it is to be able to get out of difficult situations. (Interview with a resident of Goma, eastern DRC, June 2014).

In the suburbs and rural areas of Kinshasa, Bas-Congo, Equator and South Kivu, the man is power; the incarnation of protection of the woman and the family. A man must be capable of self-control and have certain values, in short, he must be a responsible person. In addition, the well-off respondents underlined protection and responsibility as being dominant aspects of masculinity, whereas the poor insisted it was decision making power and physical strength. This result concurs with Christopher Matthews's seminal piece on linkages between hegemonic masculinity and health issues, in which male violence against women is systematically condoned in the society and sometimes legitimised by the state[88]. Based on this linkage, it is easier to see how patriarchal social relations sustain power within and between social configurations of gender, perhaps as an extension of social class. In setting the tone of 'normal' and 'natural' notions about men and women, the hegemonic position confirms and thus reinforces these disparities across social classes (Connell & Messerschmidt[89]; Messerschmidt[90]).

In Kinshasa, particularly in the urban areas, there was a general conception that a man is the leader of the family. This position goes with its responsibilities (duties) and obligations towards the woman, the family and the community. The conception among the youthful population indicated that a man who is not capable of doing so cannot be a true man. Therefore, according to the Congolese, 'real' men are obliged to deploy a lot of effort and energy to merit that position. Those who cannot use violence as a means to prove themselves. In patriarchal societies, pervasive images of masculinity hold that 'real men' are physically strong, aggressive and in control of their work[91]. Yet the structural dichotomy between manual and mental labour means that no one's world fulfils all these conditions.

In DRC, the manual labourers work for others at the low end of the class spectrum, while management sits at a desk. Consequently, while the insecurities generated by these contradictions are personally dissatisfying to men, these insecurities also impel them to cling all the more tightly to sources of masculine identity validation offered by the image system. "For working-class males, who have less access to more abstract forms of masculinity-validating power (economic power, workplace authority etc.), the physical body and its potential for violence provide a concrete means of achieving and asserting manhood"[92]. In the DRC, societal normative practices are deeply embedded in a disciplinary culture that condones or even encourages violence. Examples of such negative masculinities include risk taking, self-sufficiency, physical toughness, emotional restrictedness, and avoidance of femininity[93]. Yet this development is not necessarily consistent with Wong et al.'s[94] finding that even college men defined "a man" as being centered on family and being responsible and accountable. This reminds us of the theorisation of what would entail a 'real' African Renaissance. To this end, the African 'rebirth', in President Mbeki's own words, will require rebellion against "the mixture of greed, dehumanising poverty, obscene wealth and endemic public and private corruption practice"[95].

Gendered hierarchy - women agency

In different socio-cultural contexts in Congo, like anywhere else, there is a traditional division of labour based on sex, with responsibilities, jobs and roles reserved for men and women (social production and salaried jobs for men and non-paying housework for women)[96]. This distribution of work is not natural or fixed; it changes with time and space. It is on the basis of this dynamic nature of gender roles that this study sought to find out how that kind of division of labour evolved and what the fundamental elements for that division are.

For the male respondents, hard labour is naturally and traditionally reserved for men in general, because women are physically weak. Heavy, dangerous or high risk work is thus reserved for men. This agrees with a study conducted in the USA, which found that a majority of the men surveyed (71%) had experienced financial stressors[97]. The hegemonic masculine perspective suggests that it is possible that the men viewed these stressors as threats to the self as providers for themselves and/or their families. Threats to hegemonic masculinity also occurred through some of the men's inability to exert social dominance and command respect through the demonstration of their authority.

In what seems to be a revolution of knowledge, the concept of hegemonic masculinity has attracted a great deal of criticism. To some scholars, the concept of masculinity is blurred, is uncertain in its meaning, and tends to deemphasise issues of power and domination (Collinson & Hearn[98], Hearn[99]). It is ultimately unnecessary to the task of understanding and contesting the power of men. The concept of multiple masculinities tends to produce a static typology. For Petersen[100], the concept of masculinity is flawed because it essentialises the character of men or imposes a false unity on a fluid and contradictory reality. Some versions of this argument criticise masculinity research because it has not adopted a specific poststructuralist tool kit, which would, for instance, emphasise the discursive construction of identities[101].

As seen in Table 3, the study established that in rural areas, hunting, digging, building houses, fishing and cutting down trees are for men, whereas women engage in sowing, weeding, harvesting and transportation. In town, driving heavy machines, carrying big loads and riding motorcycles are reserved for men, which is why men say that in addition to this work, they cannot do house chores like taking care of children, cooking or fetching water. The *principal paradox* is that whereas this social attribution of masculinity seems to disfavour women, the result from DRC indicates that both the men and women interviewed are in agreement that domestic work and household chores are essentially the domain of women (see Table 3).

Table 3: Distribution of household tasks between partners

	Women				Men			
Chores done	**Woman**	**Share**	**Home**	**Total**	**Men**	**Share**	**Home**	**Total**
Repair the house	73.7%	3.9%	22.4%	100	50.3%	9.5%	40.2%	100
Clean the house	97.7%	2.0%	1.3%	100	88.9%	8.1%	3.0%	100
Clean the bathroom	94.1%	3.9%	2.0%	100	83.2%	8.4%	8.4%	100
Wash the dishes	98.1%	1.3%	0.7%	100	93.7%	5.0%	1.3%	100
Wash the clothes	95.4%	4.0%	2.3%	100	80.5%	16.5%	3.0%	100
Wash the children	93.0%	5.0%	0.4%	100	77.1%	19.9%	3.0%	100
Shopping	92.3%	5.7%	54.4%	100	81.8%	14.9%	3.3%	100
Cooking	96.3%	3.3%		100	89.0%	9.3%	1.7%	100

Chores done	Women				Men			
	Woman	Share	Home	Total	Men	Share	Home	Total
Pay the bills	35.5%	10.1%		100	32.7%	17.8%	49.5%	100
Average	86.2%				75.2%			

Source: Field data (2014-2015)

As expected, 86.2% of household chores are done by women compared to men's 75.2% (see Table 3). Even if there are differences in the statements of men and women regarding the chores shared between them, these differences are not significant. Women said during the interviews and the focus-groups that there are some jobs perceived as specifically made for men or women. In an interview with a middle-age woman in Kinshasa, she said that, "...household chores are seen as the work of women, though you can find today men who can do it. But building, painting, or being an electrician for example remains the domain for men...". From this interview, it seems contradictory, however, to assume that respondents believe that the society has evolved towards gender equality. On the other hand, men accept the fact that women can take on the traditional tasks provided they do them properly. Today, with technological advancements and the use of machines, men and women do practically the same jobs and have equal opportunities, despite their biological differences. As expected, those among the respondents who had a more conservative or traditional conception about division of labour strongly opposed the move for equality between men and women. Some amongst them asked who would take care of the children if a woman is employed:

> Women should be educated so as to take care of the children and manage well the salary brought by the husbands. For some people the proliferation of juvenile delinquency nowadays may have roots in the change of roles in the family. Instead of staying at home, the woman is forced to struggle so as to survive. There is no gain by having money when your children are not well brought up. (Interview with a local resident in North Kivu, June 2014).

A similar statement was made by Pierre Bourdieu when he affirmed that "the truth about sexual domination is revealed when we see for example that a woman who managed to occupy the very high positions in the society (civil servant, permanent secretary in the cabinet etc.) have to pay for it in one way or another by setbacks on the domestic level (divorce, late marriage, permanent singlehood, problems or failure in the education of children etc.) and in the economy of symbolic goods, the success at the domestic level implies a partial or total sacrifice of the professional side"[102].

On the other hand, those who have a more progressive conception realise that a revolution is taking place, according to which there are no more tasks reserved exclusively for men or women. With better education and the socio-economic crisis, women today are doing what used to be men's jobs (e.g. stone breaking). Some interviewees admitted that Congolese society will not progress as long as so many men continue to prevent their wives from working; just the opposite of Western societies where women and men work without much segregation or preference. To achieve this there is need for a change both in labour and family laws, so that a woman may have the right to apply for a job and work in any field without the permission of her husband. Through these elements we realise an evolution of morality, despite a large number of respondents who are still attached to the tradition that sexualises work. It was interesting to observe examples of men who do household chores because their wives work and provide for the needs of the family. Today what matters most is the financial contribution of each partner and the household chores should not be left to the woman alone; the man has to collaborate.

In view of the emerging 'positive masculinity', some scholars have cautioned that women's rise in power has created a crisis in masculinity all over the world. In particular, in cultures in which the traditional male role as bread-winner and protector has declined and in which machine has replaced muscle, the pursuit of muscularity has become one of the few ways left for men to exhibit their masculine selves[103]. Thus men have developed muscles not for their usefulness, but for their representation of masculinity. By helping to differentiate masculinity from femininity, images of masculine aggression and violence – including violence against women – afford young males across class, race and geographical boundaries a degree of self-respect and 'security' within the more socially valued masculine role. In addition, as microeconomic shifts have contributed to a decline in both employment and real wages for working-class males in many economies, images of violent masculinity in the symbolic realm of media and advertising function, in part, to bolster masculine identities that have increasingly less foundation in the material world[104].

Moreover, the women's movement, in seeking equality, has been one of the most successful social movements of the past century. Feminist theories have been shaped by women's changing place in contemporary societies, and these theories have sometimes proved effective in changing both men's and women's consciousness and conditions[105]. Although masculinist men's movements sometimes decry feminism, generally men's studies treat feminism and feminist theory as scholarly big sisters, perhaps dull, dowdy, outmoded, or too restrictive, but nevertheless models to be followed and bettered[106]. Feminists ridicule masculinist men's studies and welcome pro-feminist efforts by men. The American feminist journalist Gloria Steinem announced that "women want a men's movement" if that means men will "become more nurturing toward children, more able to talk about emotions" and be less violent and controlling[107]. The English psychologist Lynn Segal regretted the "slow motion" of men toward gender equality, and mused that the literature of masculinity "uncannily mirrors" its feminist forebears: it "focuses upon men's own experiences, generates evidence of men's gender-specific suffering and has given birth to a new field of enquiry, 'Men's Studies'"[108]. But the feminist or masculinity graph has never been stable. For instance, by seeking to understand the causes, means and results of gendered inequality, feminist theories hope to develop effective ways to improve women's conditions, sometimes by making women more similar to men than they are now[109]. Within this societal rubric, it is common to observe the family institutions making men more similar to women as seen in the case of DRC, sometimes by validating women's traditional characteristics and sometimes by working towards the abolition or minimisation of the categories of gender altogether. But, more interestingly, simultaneously transforming ideologies and institutions, including the family, religion, schools, corporations, and the state.

Gender hierarchy seeks to explain not only why men hold a superior position to women, but also how each group influences the other. Research has documented the durability of non-hegemonic patterns of masculinity, which may represent well-crafted responses to racial/ethnic marginalisation, physical disability, class inequality, or stigmatised sexuality. Hegemony may be accomplished by the incorporation of such masculinities into functioning gender order rather than by active oppression in the form of degradation or violence[110]. This new emphasis on gender hierarchy seeks to take a more relational approach to women as well. In DRC, for example, we found out that women are central in many of the processes constructing masculinities, as mothers, schoolmates, girlfriends, sexual partners, wives, and workers in the gender division of labour. Gender hierarchies are affected by new configurations of women's identity and practice, so more attention has been given to the historical interplay of femininities and masculinities.

Dina Pinsky acknowledged the fact that there is a dearth of analysis on the role of patriarchy in the gender literature, which is perhaps the impact of undemocratic practices not adequately documented[111]. Patriarchal behaviours are manifested in various forms, including access to education facilities among girls and boys, and the arrangement of political structures that could facilitate or limit women's participation in political leadership. In the DRC, the survey revealed that although both men and women's level of secondary education completion stood at 40.2% (of those interviewed), when disaggregated along gender lines (see Table 4), the rate of women who had never been to school was 7.5% against 3.5% for men. The less educated population is more likely to be influenced by the traditional and religious rules in every sphere, especially those pertaining to the masculinity perception and attitudes relating to gender parity. Studies from advanced economies show a correlation between access to educational opportunities and desirable gender socialisation among men and women. Indeed, it is within such institutions that gender traits are reinforced (Jacobs[112]; Eccles et al.[113]; Freedman[114]; Eccles[115]).

Table 4: Level of Education

Level of education	Number	Percentage
Did not go school (illiterate)	252	5.3
Did not complete primary school	397	8.4
Completed primary school	303	6.4
Did not complete secondary school	1906	40.2
Completed secondary school	1086	22.9
Did not complete college	250	5.2
Completed college	246	2.6
Did not complete university	171	3.6
Completed university	129	2.7
Total	4470	100

Source: Field data (2014-2015)

In the developed world, gender socialisation is centered around family life and relationships are very important – sometimes more so than structural variables. In this case, gender socialisation can be operationalised in three distinctive ways - as forms of transmission from parents to children; which depend on personal attitude and resources (self-esteem, age, status); and also on family life (housework gender division)[116]. Masculinities are configurations of practices and ethos that are constructed, unfold and are dynamic[117]. Thus, as gender relations evolve and women's movements grow stronger, the dynamics of masculinities may see a complete abolition of power differentials and a more equitable relationship between men and women and between men and other men[118]. Although, this may seem positive, studies show that in *the short term, gender inequality reduces the rape rate, whereas in the long term, higher levels of gender inequality are associated with higher levels of abuse, such as rape*[119]. This finding, however, is inconsistent with the work of Richard Collier, who argued that linking 'masculinity' to 'crime' is "tautological", and that it does not create any logical sense. The African Renaissance should, instead, reflect the need to empower African people (regardless of gender and ethnic affiliation), while at the same time harness social capital bestowed on all men and women to grow and sustain African economies[121].

Social embodiment

Social embodiment defines how thoughts and behaviours are influenced by sensory, motor, and perceptual cues in the environment[122]. The study of the body's role in constituting psychological and social life is linked to embodiment cognition. Psychologists have found that intergroup relations have formative influences on human behaviour and its linkages with the entire ecosystem[123]. The importance of this area of inquiry is that embodiment cognition illuminates the interplay between embodied phenomenology and social communication in the development of common-sense knowledge, and promises productive directions for empirical and theoretical advancement. Some thinkers view embodiment from rights perspectives. To this end, there is broad agreement that self-ownership involves the right to control oneself, the right to exclude others from control of oneself, immunity from expropriation of these rights, the power to transfer these rights, and the right to compensation for the infringement of these rights (Van Parijs[124]; Vallentyne[125]).

The survey established that according to Congolese men, parents are responsible for health issues at home in general, and in particular the husband since he is the household leader. He should, in that position, assume his role as leader in all spheres of family life. If it happened that the parents had no money to take care of the health of the members of the family, they could have recourse from one of the adult children already working. This is motivated by the sense of decency. Some of the interviewed men also said that "it is not good for them to go to the hospitals where women are admitted since they can come across some scenes they would not like to see". This obliges them to have recourse to the female members of their families. It appears, according to the views of these men, that there must be a certain distribution of tasks in taking care of the health of the family members. According to men, the financial and moral burden of health care in the family is on the shoulders of the men, but the auxiliary work of dispensing this care would be the responsibility of the women. Interestingly, on this matter, both the men's and women's viewpoints converged. In fact, according to the female respondents, women are generally the ones to take care of the family as they are the ones who stay at home, but when it comes to the needed money, the men step in again and the *principal paradox* emerges.

Sexual violence in DRC has become normalised. This normalisation has found its way into the security institutions with diverse repercussions on women's careers[126]. Maria Baaz and Maria Stern found that male's "sexual needs" emerged as a given, known, natural driving force, which required "satisfaction" from women[127]. This is a common feature not only in the DRC security space, but is a common problem among military institutions worldwide[128]. Previous researchers found similar trends among men and women soldiers, for example Cynthia Enloe established that while soldiers sometimes stated that women had a role to play in the army, this role belonged to the "feminised" sphere of the armed forces, e.g. social work, health, administration, secretarial work and cooking[129]. Commanding and combat, male soldiers explained, demanded qualities that were considered stereotypically masculine and belonged decidedly in the military sphere, i.e. being courageous, level-headed, tough killers (Braudy[130]; Nadelson[131]). Even when such courageous women found their way into the front line on the battle field, soldiers repudiated women soldiers as either "masculine", or as unworthy.

Those interpreting the results in this article should be cautious that any social embodiment cues are context-specific. For instance, Lisa MacDonald and her team found out that the majority of family planning initiatives in Asia target only women[132], however women's lack of decision-making power, even with regard to their own health, hinders their ability to practice family planning. Experience shows that, given the right role models and enabling environments, men are willing to be more fully and positively engaged in reproductive health matters. Two approaches are thus suggested in order to ensure that both men and women are involved; engaging men and valuing women. Thus, in their very nature, male-centred methods of population control would ensure that men could and would play an active role in family planning.

Other than the linkages between thoughts, feelings and behaviours, embodiment cognition can also bring out personality-related individual differences[133]. Other critical individual differences might relate to people's varying levels of bodily ability. For example, to clarify mediating variables and mechanisms, it will be highly illuminating to examine physical abilities that tend to decay over the life span, after injury, or through declining physical health (e.g., vision, hearing, and physical strength). For example, might elderly people represent their social environments differently because they have limited physical capabilities? Furthermore, might a person's representation of his or her world change after a physical injury or declining health? Research by Bhalla and Proffitt[134] suggests that such variables can influence embodiment. They found that elderly people and individuals in declining health perceive hills as steeper, reflecting their decreasing ability to climb them. Future research of this type can explore to a much greater extent the manner in which embodied constraints on behaviour are innate and fixed or malleable across physical disabilities and the life span.

Social embodiment calls for a more rigid definition of what a hegemonically masculine man is and how the idea is actually carried out in real life. The pattern of embodiment involved in hegemony was recognised in the earliest formulations of the concept, but called for more theoretical attention. The importance of masculine embodiment for identity and behaviour emerges in many contexts. For example, in youth, skill in physical activity becomes a prime indicator of masculinity. This notion continues to manifest itself into many different health and sexual practices, such as eating meat or having multiple sexual partners. The emergence of transgender issues has made it particularly clear that embodiment must be given more focus in reconceptualisations. The circuits of social embodiment may be very direct and simple or may be long and complex, passing through institutions, economic relations, cultural symbols, and so forth without ceasing to involve material bodies[135].

In 2007, the government of Vietnam passed laws that promote gender equality in all areas of life, and detailed the responsibilities of organisations, institutions, families, and individuals in ensuring the health, economic, and social status of girls and women in Vietnam[136]. Despite these efforts, research shows that violence against women is still prevalent in Vietnam; studies have revealed that more than half (58%) of women who have been married reported having experienced violence. Other studies have recommended that empowerment, a process often used for women, is also important for men[137]. To construct and encourage a positive, non-violent version of masculinity, men need relevant knowledge, skills, mentoring, and peer support. It is a challenge for gender-based violence initiatives to work on increasing public awareness of the issue of violence against women, and reduce society's tolerance of it, without increasing stigmatisation of and objections to men in general, and to perpetrator men in particular.

Other studies on a similar subject in DRC reveal that as men try to enact masculine ideals of being breadwinners and family heads, the current political and economic context puts them under increasing pressure[138]. The effects of this malfunctioning in the society led to asserting masculinity, lack of productivity, and violence. The studies were critical of the fact that most initiatives aimed at combating sexual and gender based violence focus exclusively on supporting women, failing to recognise the interdependent and interactive nature of gender[139]. More interestingly, the study found out that 'hegemonic masculinity' significantly contributed to creating a general climate of violence and conflict, pointing to the need for holistic approaches that empower men to make non-violent life choices. In most of the provinces surveyed in DRC, observations showed that there were some anecdotes of positive masculinity traits among men. They included: 1) they are providers and household heads; 2) they should behave in non-violent ways towards household and community members; 3) they are responsible, good negotiators and problem solvers, which is a result of life-long socialisation and identity formation. Studies among students have concurred with the DRC case in many instances, for example regarding self-identity and embodiment, self-identity is an important foregrounding factor in the management of emotions, particularly as it relates to building resilience and selfhood (Aymer & Patni[140]; Rajan-Rankin[141]).

Social and spatial interactivity of masculinity

The implications of hegemonic masculinity on the status of women and gender in space and time has been a consistent theme in international development discourses. Charlotte Hooper described the deployment of masculinities in the arenas of international relations[142], and Connell proposed a model of "transnational business masculinity" among jet-setting corporate executives[143]. Because of this, Connell and Messerschmitt proposed that hegemonic masculinities be analysed using geopolitical optics at three levels: local, regional, and global[144]. The links between these levels are critical to gender politics, as interventions at any level giving women more power and representation can influence from the top down or from the bottom up. Additionally, adopting a framework that distinguishes between the three levels allows one to recognise the importance of place without making generalisations about independent cultures or discourses. In the DRC context, men are the central element in the ritual system and they preside over and make decisions at all levels. Despite the brightness of the woman in some areas, she is always relegated behind the man in the name of cultural constraints.

In regard to the politics of decision making in 'home' spaces, it is the father who has the final say at home, because he is the leader of the family. He gets that power from God and the customs and laws of the land. The woman has to submit herself to the man; even if she is more educated than the husband, she must accept the submission since, "in the married life the degrees of the wife are useless". That kind of statement is also commonly accepted by women. They (women) radicalise the position of men, saying that a woman cannot say or do anything without prior agreement and permission from her husband. That power of decision and control over the woman is exercised by the man in every sphere of life, regardless of the geographical location (see Table 5).

Table 5: Decisions within the family

Men N=2564			
Who makes decisions?	**Food and clothing**	**Big investment**	**Time with friends**
The husband	42.9%	52.1%	45.4%
The wife	15.9%	7.1%	8.4%
Both	20.7%	19.3%	23.8%
Someone else	9.7%	9.3%	9.5%
The husband and someone else	3.4%	2.8%	3.7%
N/a	7.4%	9.4%	9.2%
Percentage	100%	100%	100%

Source: Field Data (2014-2015)

Concerning decisions in households, the survey revealed that it is the husband who decides, at 42.9% for food and clothes, time to spend with friends at 45.4%, and 52.1% for big investments. The wife, in the areas where one would think she has the power to decide, for example food and clothes, is in very low position (15.9%). For men, domination and control over women is due to their incompetence, irrespective of their level of education, but women see it as part of married life. That is why for many women, to accept marriage means the acceptance of domination and control by their husbands. "The husband has to choose for her friends and control her all the time. A married woman should not be free at all. The marriage is a contract that gives to the husband the guardianship right over the wife". This explains why some women accept the domination of their husband despite them having less income. In the Congolese social and cultural context, a woman is only respected when she is married. The idea that the decision-making power of the husband is derived only from the fact that he is the family provider rather than cultural considerations, is losing ground.

The other factor is the marginalisation and subordination of women to men. Domination and control exercised by men by virtue of their masculinity has consequences such as the marginalisation, subordination and submission of women. They must side with their husbands' positions if they want to be well perceived by the society as a "good wife", recognising their low social status in the family as well as in the community. For men, the subordination and submission of women is natural. A good wife is one who submits to her husband and obeys him at all time; she has no viewpoint against that of her husband. Here men and women have advanced the religious norms to justify the marginalisation of the woman. Their point of view is that the woman is physically weak and psychologically a coward and very emotional; women think fast and most of the decisions they make are irrational and they regret that later. All these reasons "justify that men dominate women and always lead", and explain the prejudices according to which "Basi batongaka mboka te" (women are not capable of building the community). Among the respondents, some denounced the marginalisation of woman and said that they are simply "victims" who do not give women the space for freedom of expression. This sad reality is particularly felt by women in the rural areas of DRC.

Concerning rape, the results were surprising as women accepted at 45.9% (against 37.1% for men). It seems that sexual violence is perceived as a reality that is increasing in the country, especially in urban areas. The argument that a woman's dress can be the reason for rape was noted often by the respondents; an indecently dressed woman is said to arouse the appetite of men for sex. For the respondents, men are directly responsible for sexual based violence due to their ignorance of the consequences of their actions, whereas women are indirectly responsible through their dressing style or seductive walking. Then there is a need to sensitise the community to the legal implications in the case of sexual violence and health consequences. One of the ways to curb that violence is to organise sensitisation campaigns to help people become more aware, but the belief that a woman should not refuse to have sex with her husband is common amongst men and women. More than half of men (56.9%) agreed that a human should be beaten sometimes. The argument that a man can beat his wife if she refuses to have sex with him was more accepted by women (41.4%) than men (24.7%).

Table 6: Opinions regarding rape and gender based violence

Attitudes	Women N=2176				Men N=2564			
	Agree	Neutral	Disagree	Total	Agree	Neutral	Disagree	Total
There are occasions when women must be beaten.	38.6	16.6%	44.8%	100%	56.9%	14.4%	28.7%	100%
A woman should be patient and tolerate violence to safeguard her marriage or family.	35.6%	15.9%	48.5%	100%	35.5%	18.7%	45.8%	100%
A man can beat his wife if she denies him sex.	41.4%	12.7%	45.9%	100%	24.7%	20.9%	54.4%	100%
When a woman is raped, she has done something to seduce.	30.7%	13.8%	55.55	100%	38.3%	10.5%	51.2%	100%
In some cases, women want to be raped.	26.8%	11.4%	61.8%	100%	46.1%	9.5%	44.4%	100%
If a woman does not fight physically, you cannot call it rape.	48.0%	8.8%	43.2%	100%	46.1%	9.5%	44.4%	100%
In all cases of rape, you have to understand whether a woman had consented.	45.9%	10.4%	43.2%	100%	37.1%	15.0%	47.9%	100%
In all cases of rape, you have to ask if the woman had a bad reputation.	54.5%	8.0%	37%	100%	47.4%	10.1%	42.5%	100%

Source: Field data (2014-2015)

Regarding gender based violence (GBV), according to men, the differences between sexes cannot explain alone the violence that men exercise against women; there is always a root cause for men's violence towards women. The study found mixed reactions from men regarding gender based violence; men thought that it would be wiser to interview men individually so as to know why this man or that one had been violent. Women, on the other hand, thought that sexual differences are not the only reason for violence. For women, violence against women is not only physical, but is also manifested psychologically and economically.

In his meta-analysis of policies and strategies for gender equalisation in the South African Development Community (SADC), Newman Wadesango found that feminism is faced with the challenge of negotiating better prospects and greater gender inequalities[145]. Besides the issue of inadequate financial and human resources, there is a lack of political will and entrenched patriarchal attitudes[146]. This implies that because of entrenched patriarchal attitudes and a lack of commitment, the otherwise protective structures, such as police, encourage retrogressive practices such as female genital mutilation (FGM). Most countries in the region, DRC included, portrayed an inability to effectively enforce laws and policies on FGM and other gender-related malpractices, partly because the courts are male-dominated[147]. Moreover, women are currently handicapped by the division of labour in the family, which has created a series of psychological barriers for women to overcome[148]. The barriers are based on the belief that since husbands usually hold superior jobs to their wives, they are superior to their wives. It is believed that divorce is more devastating to the wife and the children than to the husband[149].

It is through the diversity of masculinity that men and boys can more easily see a range of possibilities for their own lives, and both men and women are less likely to think of gender inequality as unchangeable[150]. It also becomes possible to identify specific groups of men who might engage in alliances for change. Linden Lewis concluded that if one accepts that masculinity is not a fixed notion but one that is constantly changing and adjusting to new circumstances, then clearly there is a space within which men can navigate the new challenges that face them in the changing social environment of the Caribbean[151]. Likewise, for DRC, one cannot ignore the threats posed by a loss of income capability by some men resulting from a combination of factors, especially the vicious cycle of underdevelopment exacerbated by state fragility. What is abundantly clear is that the cause of conflicts as far as the gender relationship is concerned is money; the person who has the monopoly over money in the family controls the other members of the family. Thus, progress on the gender front, particularly in underdeveloped economies such as DRC, will more likely be determined by, among other factors, financial independence. This is consistent with Joe Cossa's observation that the only way Africa will attain an African Renaissance is by creating space for of both men and women in socio-economic, cultural and political activities of the society[152].

6.5   Conclusion

From the findings and discussions, it seems unlikely that gender equality can be attained given the anecdotes regarding 'positive masculinity' observed in the Democratic Republic of Congo. This implies that the African Renaissance, as espoused by Thabo Mbeki, may not be renewed though social movements, such as the one advocated by women across the continent. This is because the liberation of African states and their socio-economic fabrics, as well as institutional values, can only be realised through an African-centered engagement that is capable of confronting social inequalities. However, the lack of consistency and transformational men and women in DRC seems to suggest that the emerging 'positive masculinity' may not bring about socio-economic change on the gender front. Therefore, the linkages between 'positive masculinity' and an African Renaissance are weak, because the anecdotes of 'positive masculinity' do not espouse a renewal of African values that promise to transform the African society positively. In view of this finding and analysis, one must therefore concur with the sociologist William Ickes that equality between men and women is far from optimal, especially in societies that are deeply rooted in cultural mores, reinforced through cyclic state fragility and weak resilience among both men and women.

Given the links between an African Renaissance and the attainment of social transformation such as gender, as championed by Ali Mazrui, it is unlikely that *African rebirth* will be realised by singly focusing on weak social evolutionary clichés such as the 'positive masculinity', instead, efforts should be made to strengthen social movements as a 'force' to re-energise the call for the African Renaissance.

References

[1]Connell, R. W. 1987. *Gender and Power: Society, the Person, and Sexual Politics*. Malden: Polity Press.

[2]Connell, R. W., & Messerschmidt, J. W. 2005. Hegemonic Masculinity: Rethinking the Concept. *Gender and Society*, 19(6): 829-859.

[3]Connell, R. W. 2005. *Masculinities*. Berkeley, CA: University of California Press.

[4]Africa Portal of ARI. *Gender and Peacekeeping. Case Studies: The DRC and Sierra Leone*. Retrieved from: https://www.africaportal.org/partner/africa-research-institute-ari?page=1. [Date accessed: October 16, 2016.]

[5]Machineripi, G., & Khan, K. 2015. Constructing nationalist masculine identities? Heroism and legitimacy in Joshua Nkomo's The Story of my Life. *International Journal of African Renaissance Studies*, 10(2): 190-203.

[6]Cossa, J. 2009. African Renaissance and globalisation; A conceptual analysis. *Ufahamu: A Journal of African Studies*, 36(1): 1-25.

[7]Connell, R. W., & Messerschmidt, J. W. 2005. Hegemonic Masculinity: Rethinking the Concept. *Gender and Society*, 19(6): 829-859.

[8]Donaldson, M. 1993. What is Hegemonic Masculinity? *Theory and Society*, 22(5): 643-657.

[9]Connell, R. W. 1982. Class, patriarchy, and Sartre's theory of practice. *Theory and Society* 11: 305-320.

[10]Connell, R. W. 1983. *Which way is up? Essays on sex, class, and culture*. Sydney: Allen and Unwin.

[11]Carrigan, T., Connell, R. W., & Lee, J. 1985. Toward a new sociology of masculinity. *Theory and Society*, 14(5): 551-604.

[12]Connell, R. W. 1987. *Gender and Power: Society, the Person, and Sexual Politics*. Malden: Polity Press.

[13]Aldersy, H., Turnbull, A., & Turnbull, H. R. 2016. Family support in Kinshasa, Democratic Republic of the Congo. *Journal of Policy and Practice in the Intellectual Disabilities*, 13(1): 23-32.

[14]Beasley, C. 2008. Rethinking Hegemonic Masculinity in a Globalising World. *Men and Masculinities*, 11(1): 86-103.

[15]Bourdieu, P. 2001. *Jargon and symbolic power*. Paris: Fayard.

[16]Zeleza, P. T. 2009. What happened to the African Renaissance? The challenges of development in the twenty-first Century. *Comparative Studies of South Asia, Africa and the Middle East*, 29(2): 155-170.

[17]Diop, A. C. 2002. Towards the African Renaissance: Essays in Culture and Development, 1946-1960. *New African Journal of Culture, Politics and Consciousness*, 1(1). Retrieved from: http://www.africaspeaks.com/reasoning/index.php?topic=5993.0;wap2. [Date accessed: February 20, 2017.]

[18]Oelofse, J. 2013. *African Renaissance: African rebirth or African enslavement? Global Reboot*. Retrieved from: https://lorenzofioramonti.org/2013/09/03/african-renaissance-african-rebirth-or-african-enslavement/. [Date accessed: February 20, 2017.]

[19]Ndlovu-Gatsheni, S. 2008. Global coloniality and the challenges of creating African futures. *Strategic Review of South Africa*, 36(2): 181-202.

[20]Berry, M. 2015. When "Bright Futures" Fade: Paradoxes of Women's Empowerment in Rwanda. *Signs: Journal of Women in Culture and Society*, 41(1): 1–27.

[21]Cuvelier, J., & Bashwira, M. R. 2016. *Women, conflict and public authority in the Congo*. Rift Valley Institute, PSRP. Briefing Paper. 13 June 2016.

[22]Hodges, M. J., & Budig, M. J. 2010. Who Gets the Daddy Bonus? Organisational Hegemonic Masculinity and the Impact of Fatherhood on Earnings. *Gender & Society*, 24(6): 717-745.

[23]Addis, M.E., & Mahalik, J. R. 2003. Men, masculinity, and the contexts of help seeking. *American Psychologist*, 58(1): 5–14.

[24]Scott-Samuel, A., Stanistreet, D., & Crawshaw, P. 2009. Hegemonic masculinity, structural violence and health inequalities. *Critical Public Health*, 19: 287-292.

[25]Wood, A. E. 2016. Hypermasculinity as a scenario of power: Vladimir Putin's iconic rule 1999-2008. *International Feminist Journal of Politics*, 18(3):2-22.

[26]Kisangani, E. F. 2000. The Massacre of Refugees in Congo. *Journal of Modern African Studies*, 38(2): 162–174.

[27]Scott-Samuel, A., Stanistreet, D., & Crawshaw, P. 2009. Hegemonic masculinity, structural violence and health inequalities. *Critical Public Health*, 19: 287-292.

[28]Hollander, T. 2014. Men, masculinity and the demise of a State. Examining masculinities in the context of economic, political, and social crisis in a small town in the Democratic Republic of Congo. *Sociology*, 17(4): 417-439.

[29]Bard, C., Baudele, T. C., & Mossuz-Lavau, J. 2004. *When women get involved, gender and power.* Paris: Martiniere Editions.

[30]Labda, A. 2011. *Joint Evaluation of Conflict Prevention and Peace Building in the Democratic Republic of Congo. A Synthesis Report June 2011.* Retrieved from: www.diplomatie.belgium.be/en/policy/development_cooperation/ evaluation. [Date accessed: February 20, 2017.]

[31]Ibid.

[32]Ewans, M. 2003. Belgium and the Colonial Experience. *Journal of Contemporary European Studies,* 11(2): 167–180.

[33]Cuvelier, J., & Bashwira, M. R. 2016. *Women, conflict and public authority in the Congo.* Rift Valley Institute, PSRP. Briefing Paper. 13 June 2016.

[34]Austesserre, S. 2016. The responsible to protect in Congo: the failure of grassroots prevention. *International Peacekeeping,* 23(1): 29-51.

[35]Clark, N. J. 2011. UN Peacekeeping in the Democratic Republic of Congo: Reflection on MONUSCO and its contradictory mandate. *Journal of Conflict and Security Law.* Retrieved from: http://resourcelists.stir.ac.uk/lists/1E6D72FC-59CC-9A92-BE79-FE70E3F2B75A/bibliography.html. [Date accessed: October 12, 2016.]

[36]Moix, B. 2016. Turning Atrocity Prevention Inside-Out: Community-Based Approaches to Preventing, Protecting, and Recovering from Mass Violence. *Genocide Studies and Prevention: An International Journal,* 9(3): 59-69.

[37]Lwambo. D. 2013. Before the war, I was a man: Men and masculinities in the Eastern Democratic Republic of Congo. *Gender & Development,* 21(1): 47-66.

[38]Baaz, E. M., & Stern, M. 2011. Whores, Men and Other Misfits: Undoing the "Feminization" of the Armed Forces in the DR Congo. *African Affairs,* 110 (441): 563-585.

[39]Heritier, F. 2012. *Male/female. Knocking down the hierarchy.* Paris: Odile Jacob.

[40]Mitchell, R. 2013. Domestic violence prevention through the Constructing Violence-free Masculinities programme: an experience from Peru. *Gender and Development,* 21(1): 97-109.

[41]Skelton, A. 1993. On becoming a male physical education teacher: The informal culture of students and the construction of hegemonic masculinity. *Gender and Education,* 5(3): 289-303.

[42]Cossa, J. 2009. African Renaissance and globalisation: A conceptual analysis. *Ufahamu: A Journal of African Studies,* 36(1): 1-25.

[43]Ibid.

[44]Collis, M. 1999. Marital conflict and men's leisure; how women negotiate male power in a small mining community. *Journal of Sociology,* 35(60): 63-75.

[45]Connell, R. W. 1987. *Gender and Power: Society, the Person, and Sexual Politics.* Malden: Polity Press.

[46]Le Billon, P. 2001. The Political Ecology of War: Natural Resources and Armed Conflicts. *Political Geography,* 20:562-66.

[47]Burnley, C. 2011. Natural Resources Conflict in the Democratic Republic of the Congo: A Question of Governance? *Sustainable Development Law and Policy,* 12(1): 7-11.

[48]Rose, M. L. 2004. What do we know about natural resources and civil war? *Journal of Peace Research,* 41(3): 337-356.

[49]Beresford, A. 2016. Africa rising? *Review of African Political Economy,* 43(147): 1-7.

[50]Maystadt, J. F., De Luca, G., Sekeris, P. G., & Ulimwengu, J. 2014. Mineral resources and conflicts in DRC: A case of ecological fallacy? *Oxford Economic Papers,* 66(3): 721-749.

[51]Rose, M. L. 2004. What do we know about natural resources and civil war? *Journal of Peace Research,* 41(3): 337-356.

[52]Baaz, E. M., & Stern, M. 2011. Whores, Men and Other Misfits: Undoing the "Feminization" of the Armed Forces in the DR Congo. *African Affairs,* 110(441): 563-585.

[53]Meger, S. 2015. Toward a feminist political economy of wartime sexual violence: the case of the Democratic Republic of Congo. *International Feminist Journal of Politics,* 17(3): 416-434.

[54]Ibid.

[55]Barker, G., & Verma, R. 2008. IMAGES: *International Men and Gender Equality Survey. Men's Survey.* Institudo Promundo, international Centre for Research on Women (ICRW).

[56]Hollander, T. 2014. Men, masculinity and the demise of a State. Examining masculinities in the context of economic, political, and social crisis in a small town in the Democratic Republic of Congo. *Sociology,* 17(4), pp. 417-439.

[57]Connell, R. W. 1982. Class, patriarchy, and Sartre's theory of practice. *Theory and Society,* 11(3): 305-320.

[58]Clattenbaugh, K. 1998. What is problematic about masculinities? *Men and Masculinities,* 1(1): 24–45.

[59]Jefferson, T. 2002. Subordinating hegemonic masculinity. *Theoretical Criminology,* 6(1): 63–88.

[60]Shyaka, A. 2008. Understanding the Conflicts in the Great Lakes Region: An Overview, *Journal of African Conflicts and Peace Studies,* 1(1): 5-12.

[61]Kueleers, F. 2013. Civil wars in the Democratic Republic of Congo: 1960-2010. *African Affairs,* 112 (448): 520-521.

[62]Mail and Guardian Africa. 2016. *DR Congo moves to build $ 100 billion grand Inga dam, to pick phase 1 contractor by August 2016.* Retrieved from: http://mgafrica.com/article/2016-05-07-dr-congo-moves-to-build-100-billion-grand-inga-dam-to-pick-phase-1-contractor-by-august. [Date accessed: February 20, 2017.]

[63]Ram, U., Strohschein, L., & Gaur, K. 2014. Gender socialization: Differences between male and female youth in India and Associations with mental health. *International Journal of Population Research*, Volume 2014, ID 357145. Retrieved from: http://dx.doi.org/10.1155/2014/357145. [Date accessed: February 20, 2017.]

[64]Hollander, T. 2014. Men, masculinity and the demise of a State. Examining masculinities in the context of economic, Political, and Social crisis in a small town in the Democratic Republic of Congo. *Sociology,* 17(4): 417-439.

[65]Lwambo, D. 2013. Before the war, I was a man: men and masculinities in the Eastern Democratic Republic of Congo. *Gender & Development*, 21(1): 47-66.

[66]Hollander, T. 2014. Men, masculinity and the demise of a State. Examining masculinities in the context of economic, political, and social crisis in a small town in the Democratic Republic of Congo. *Sociology,* 17(4): 417-439.

[67]Wood, E. J. 2009. Armed Groups and Sexual Violence: When Is Wartime Rape Rare? *Politics Society*, 37(1): 131–62.

[68]Baaz, E. M., & Stern, M. 2009. Why do Soldiers Rape? Masculinity, Violence and Sexuality in the Armed Forces in the Congo. *International Studies Quarterly*, 53: 495–518.

[69]Ibid.

[70]Rutigalia, L., Gary, B., Contreras, M., Heilman, B., & Ravi, V. 2014. Pathways to Gender equitable men: Findings from the international Men and Gender Equality survey in eight countries.' *Men and Masculinities*, 17(5): 467-501.

[71]Bourdier, P. 2002. *The masculine domination*. Paris: Seuil.

[72]Petersen, A. 2003. Research on men and masculinities: Some implications of recent theory for future work. *Men and Masculinities*, 6(1): 54-69.

[73]Martin, P. Y. 1998. Why can't a man be more like a woman? Reflections on Connell's masculinities. *Gender and Society*, 12(4): 472-474.

[74]Holter, O. G. 2003. *Can men do it? Men and gender equality-The Nordic experience*. Copenhagen: Nordic Council of Ministers.

[75]Laurie, T. 2015. Masculinity studies and the jargon of strategy: hegemony, tautology, sense. *Angelaki: Journal of the Theoretical Humanities*, 20(1): 1-17.

[76]Mbeki, M. 2000. Issues in South Africa foreign policy: The African Renaissance. *Souls* (Spring 2000): 76-81.

[77]Carter, J. M. 2014. Gender socialization and identity theory. *Journal of Social Sciences*, 3: 242-263.

[78]Elkin, F., & Handel, G. 1989. *The Child and Society: The Process of Socialization*. New York: Random House.

[79]Carter, J. M. 2014. Gender socialization and identity theory. *Journal of Social Sciences*, 3:242-263.

[80]Ickes, W. 1993. Traditional gender roles; do they make and then break, our relationships? *Journal of Gender Issues*, 49(3): 71-85.

[81]Henry, S., Gary, B., Maimouna, T., Aliou, B., & Mamadou, K. 2013. *Men and gender equity and gender relations in Mali: Findings from International Men and Gender equity survey*. Summary Report, CARE, UN-Women, Instituto Promundo, Instat, Norad.

[82]Eccles, J. S., & Jacobs, J. E. 1986. Social forces shape math attitudes and performance. *Signs: Journal of Women in Culture and Society*, 11(2): 367–380.

[83]Badinter, E. 1992. *XY: The masculine identity*, Paris: Odile Jacob.

[84]Thompson, E. H. Jr., & Bennett, K. M. 2015. Measurement of Masculinity Ideologies: A (Critical) Review. *Psychology of Men & Masculinity*. Retrieved from: http://psycnet.apa.org/index.cfm?fa=buy.optionToBuy&id=2015-04649-001. [Date accessed: February 20, 2017]

[85]Ickes, W. 1993. Traditional gender roles; do they make and then break, our relationships? *Journal of Gender Issues*, 49(3): 71-85.

[86]Trujillo, N. 1991. Hegemonic Masculinity on the Mound: Media Representations of Nolan Ryan and American Sports Culture. *Critical Studies in Mass Communication*, 8: 290-308.

[87]Ibid.

[88]Mathews, C. R. 2014. The appropriation of hegemonic masculinity within selected research on men's health. *International Journal for Masculinity Studies*, 11(1): 3-18.

[89]Connell, R. W. 2003. Masculinities, change and conflict in global society: Thinking about the future of men's studies. *Journal of Men's Studies*, 11(3): 249-66.

[90]Messerschmidt, J. W. 2012. Engendering gendered knowledge assessing the academic appropriation of hegemonic masculinity. *Men and Masculinities*, 15(1): 56–76.

[91]Brod, H. 1994. Some thoughts on some histories of some masculinities: Jews and other others. In D. S. David and R. Brannon (Eds.). *Theorizing Masculinities*. Thousand Oaks: Sage.

[92]Ibid.

[93]Thompson, E. H., & Bennett, K. M. 2015. Measurement of Masculinity Ideologies: A (Critical) Review. *Psychology of Men & Masculinity*. Retrieved from: http://dx.doi.org/10.1037/a0038609. [Date accessed: February 20, 2017.]

[94]Wong, Y. J., Shea, M., La Follette, J. R., Hickman, S. J., Cruz, N., & Boghokian, T. 2011. The Inventory of Subjective Masculinity Experiences: Development and psychometric properties. *Journal of Men's Studies*, 19: 236–255.

[95]Mbeki, M. 1998. *The African Renaissance*. South African Yearbook of International Affairs. Johannesburg: South African Institute of International Affairs.

[96]Cuvelier, J., & Bashwira, M. R. 2016. *Women, conflict and public authority in the Congo*. Rift Valley Institute, PSRP. Briefing Paper. June 13, 2016.

[97]Kennedy-Kollar, D., & Charles, C. A. D. 2013. Hegemonic masculinity and mass murderers in the United States. *The Southwest Journal of Criminal Justice*, 8(2): 62-74.

[98]Collinson, D., & Hearn, J. 1994. Naming men as men: Implications for work, organization and management. *Gender, Work and Organization*, 1(1): 2-22.

[99]Hearn, J. 2004. From hegemonic masculinity to the hegemony of men. *Feminist Theory*, 5(1): 49-72.

[100]Petersen, A. 2003. Research on men and masculinities: Some implications of recent theory for future work. *Men and Masculinities*, 6(1), pp. 54-69.

[101]Whitehead, S. M. 2002. *Men and masculinities: Key themes and new directions*. Cambridge, UK: Polity.

[102]Bourdieu, P. 1984. *Distinction: A Social Critique of the Judgement of Taste*. Cambridge, MA: Harvard University Press.

[103]Katz, J. 2011. Advertising and the Construction of Violent White Masculinity: From BMWs to Bud Light. In G. Dines and J. M. Humez (Eds.). *Gender, Race and Class in Media*. Thousand Oaks: Sage Publications.

[104]Ibid.

[105]Gardiner, J. K. 2003. Gender and masculinity texts: Consensus and concerns for feminist classrooms. *NWSA Journal*, 14(3): 147-157.

[106]Freedman, E. B. 2002. *No turning back: The history of feminism and the future of women*. New York: Ballantine Books.

[107]Steinem, G. 1992. Foreword. In K. L. Hagan (Ed.). *Women respond to the men's movement: A feminist collection*. New York: Pandora, pp. v-ix.

[108]Segal, L. 2000. *Why feminism?* New York: Columbia University Press.

[109]Gardiner, J. K. 2003. Gender and masculinity texts: Consensus and concerns for feminist classrooms. *NWSA Journal*, 14(3): 147-157.

[110]Connell, R.W. 2002. *Gender*. Cambridge: Polity Press.

[111]Pinsky, D. 2015. *Gendered Identities: Criticizing Patriarchy in Turkey*. Lanham: Lexington Books.

[112]Eccles, J., Jacobs, J. E., & Harold, R. D. 1990. Gender roles stereotypes, expectancy effects and parents' socialization of gender differences. *Journal of Social Issues*, 46(2): 183-201.

[113]Eccles, S. J. 2014. Gendered socialization of STEM interests in the family. *International Journal of Gender, Science and Technology*, 7(2): 117-132.

[114]Freedman, E. B. 2002. *No turning back: The history of feminism and the future of women*. New York: Ballantine Books.

[115]Eccles, S. J. 2014. Gendered socialization of STEM interests in the family. *International Journal of Gender, Science and Technology*, 7(2): 117-132.

[116]Macrae, C. N., Hewstone, M., & Griffiths, R. J. 1993. Processing load and memory for stereotype-based information. *European Journal of Social Psychology*, 23: 77-87.

[117]Connell, R. W. 1982. Class, patriarchy, and Sartre's theory of practice. *Theory and Society*, 11: 305-320.

[118]Demetriou, D. Z. 2001. Connell's Concept of Hegemonic Masculinity: A Critique. *Theory and Society*, 30(3): 337-361.

[119]Whaley, B. R. 2001. The paradoxical relationship between gender inequalities and rape: Towards a refined theory. *Gender and Society*, 15(4): 531-555.

[120]Collier, R. 1998. *Masculinities, crime, and criminology: Men, heterosexuality and the criminal(ised) other*. London: Sage.

[121]Mbeki, M. 1998. *The African Renaissance*. South African Yearbook of International Affairs. Johannesburg: South African Institute of International Affairs.

[122]Lakens, D. 2014. Grounding social embodiment. *Social Cognition*, 32: 168-183.

[123] O'Çonnor, C. 2016. Embodiment and the construction of social knowledge; towards an integration of embodiment and social representation theory. *Journal for the Theory of Social Behaviour* 47 (1), 2-24. Retrieved from: https://scholar.google.co.uk/citations?view_op=view_citation&hl=en&user=3t4SbZUAAAAJ&citation_for_view=3t4SbZUAAAAJ:qxL8FJ1GzNcC. [Date accessed: February 20, 2017.]

[124]Wadesango, N. 2011. Is gender equality still an issue? Tensions and contradictions embedding the work of feminists today. *Journal of Social Science*, 26(3): 163-169.

[125]Ickes, W. 1993. Traditional gender roles; do they make and then break, our relationships? *Journal of Gender Issues*, 49(3):71-85.

[126]Baaz, E. M., & Stern, M. 2009. Why do Soldiers Rape? Masculinity, Violence and Sexuality in the Armed Forces in the Congo. *International Studies Quarterly*, 53: 495–518.

[127]Ibid.

[128]Witworth, S. 2004. *Men, Militarism, and UN Peacekeeping: A Gendered Analysis*. Boulder: Lynne Rienner.

[129]Enloe, C. 2000. *Maneuvers: The International Politics of Militarizing Women's Lives*. Berkeley: University of California Press.

[130]Braudy, L. 2003. *From Chivalry to Terrorism: War and the Changing Nature of Masculinity*. New York: Albert A. Knopf.

[131]Nadelson, T. 2005. *Trained to Kill: Soldiers at War*. Baltimore: Johns Hopkins University.

[132]MacDonald, L., Jones, L., Thomas, P., Le Thi, T., FitzGerald, S., & Efroymson, D. 2013. Promoting male involvement in family planning in Vietnam and India: Health Bridge experience. *Gender and Development*, 21(1): 31-45.

[133]Lakens, D. 2014. Grounding social embiment. *Social Cognition*, 32: 168-183.

[134]Bhalla, M., & Proffitt, D. R. 1999. Visual-motor recalibration in geographical slant perception. *Journal of Experimental Psychology: Human Perception and Performance*, 25, 1076–1096.

[135]Connell, R. W. 2005. Change among the gatekeepers; Men, masculinities and gender equality in the global arena. *Chicago Journals,* 30(3): 1801-1825.

[136]Edwards, K. E., & Jones, S. R. 2009. Putting my man face on: a grounded theory of college men's gender identity development. *Journal of College Student Development,* 50(2): 210-228.

[137]Hoang, T., Quach, T. T., & Tran, T. T. 2013. Because I am a man, I should be gentle to my wife and my children: positive masculinity to stop gender based violence in a coastal district in Vietnam. *Gender & Development,* 21(1):81-96.

[138]Lwambo. D. 2013. Before the war, I was a man: men and masculinities in the Eastern Democratic Republic of Congo. *Gender & Development,* 21(1): 47-66.

[139]Ibid.

[140]Rajan-Rankin, S. 2013. Self-identity, embodiment and the development of emotional resilience. *British Journal of Social Work,* 44(8), 2426-2442. Retrieved from: https://scholar.google.com/citations?view_op=view_citation&hl=en&user=RuTzl4QAAAAJ&citation_for_view=RuTzl4QAAAAJ:u5HHmVD_uO8C. [Date accessed: February 21, 2017.]

[141]Aymer, C., & Patni, R. 2011. Identity, emotion work and reflective practice: Dealing with sexuality, race and religion in the classroom. In P. Dunk-West and T. Hafford-Letchfield (Eds.). *Sexual Identities and Sexualities in Social Work.* Farnham: Ashgate, pp. 163–76.

[142]Hooper, C. 2001. *Manly States: Masculinities, International Relations, and Gender Politics.* New York: Columbia University Press.

[143]Rubin, H. 2003. *Self-Made Men: Identity and Embodiment among Transsexual Men.* Nashville, TN: Vanderbilt University Press.

[144]Connell, R. W. 1982. Class, patriarchy, and Sartre's theory of practice. *Theory and Society* 11: 305-320.

[145]Wadesango, N. 2011. Is gender equality still an issue? Tensions and contradictions embedding the work of feminists today. *Journal of Social Science,* 26(3): 163-169.

[146]Dollar, D., & Gatti, R. 2001. Are women really the fairer sex? *Journal of Economic Behavior and Organisation,* 46: 423-429.

[147]Hanzi, R. 2006. *Sexual Abuse and Exploitation of the Girl Child through Cultural Practices in Zimbabwe: A Human Rights Perspective.* Unpublished Master's Thesis. Pretoria: University of Pretoria.

[148]Cantillon, B. 2001. Female employment differences. *Journal of European Societies,* 3: 447-469.

[149]Jepson, M. 2004. Some reflections on a gender analysis of flexicurity. *Journal of Transfer,* 2: 321-325.

[150]Lewis, L. 1998. Masculinity and the Dance of the Dragon: Reading Lovelace Discursively. *Feminist Review,* 59: 164-185.

[151]Lewis, L. 2007. Man talk, masculinity and a changing social environment. *A Journal of Caribbean Perspectives on Gender and Feminism,* 1: 2-20.

[152]Cossa, J. 2009. African Renaissance and globalization; A conceptual analysis. *Ufahamu: A Journal of African Studies,* 36(1): 1-25.

Chapter 7

Decolonisation and the struggling urban woman: Gendered identities (re)defined and (re)interpreted in ways of surviving social crises in a new social environment

Vuyisile Msila
Institute for African Renaissance Studies, University of South Africa

7.1   Introduction: Women and change

Pozarny[1] wrote about how urban environments tend to change and perpetuate gender roles in cities. Furthermore, he[2] contended that "there is a prevailing conception and some literature suggesting that living in urban areas in lower-income countries brings great benefit, opportunities and independence for women (e.g. employment, access to healthcare, family planning and other services, and relaxed social norms". Women coming from South Africa's rural areas find their roles redefined in urban spaces where they end up moving towards economic empowerment as they (amongst others) struggle to fend for themselves and their families. In cities women confront barriers and inequities when compared to men, although they may be better off than rural women[3]. In the previous chapter by Onditi and Bah, we saw how society reinforces male stereotypes of superiority in a case study conducted in DRC. Without addressing this anomaly, Africa will never achieve a true African Renaissance. In this chapter, the focus is on ways in which women challenge the male dominance and societal stereotypes, even in the face of continuous opposition.

In South Africa, there has been a gradual shift as women leave the agrarian life in rural areas to seek work opportunities in urban areas. Some go to urban areas to join their spouses, but end up joining the work force after a while to supplement their spouses' wages. Others leave the rural areas as single or widowed women to search for a better life. Yet the migration of women from rural to urban areas is not without complexities. Tacoli and Sattethwaite[4] posited that:

> Urbanisation is often associated with greater independence for women. This is the result of better opportunities than in rural areas to engage in paid employment outside the family, better access to services, lower fertility rates, and some relaxation of the rigid social values and norms that define women as subordinated to their husbands and fathers and to men generally. Yet, most urban women experience profound disadvantages compared to men in their daily lives.

Women are not a homogeneous group, as some may seem to imply. Various elements determine their experience in urban areas. Their experiences will never be the same because these factors are determined by aspects such as poverty levels, marital status, health status, and level of education.

The South African government has prioritised the empowerment of rural women because life is not easy for them. In 2012, the then Minister of Women, Children and people with Disabilities, Lulu Xingwana, was quoted as saying; "South Africa has prioritised the empowerment of rural women through the mainstreaming of gender as part of a Comprehensive Rural Development Programme"[5]. However, despite these initiatives, it has not been easy for rural women in South Africa, thus they continue to leave the rural areas for the cities. Arguably however, there are many who may see women in South Africa as potential agents of change in society.

Grown *et al.*[6] contended that inequalities based on gender can be reduced if positive actions are taken to empower women. These researchers added that gender inequality is rooted in internalised attitudes, societal institutions and market forces. "The biggest international and national levels are essential to institute the policies that can trigger social change and to allocate the resources necessary to achieve gender equality and women's empowerment"[7]. Furthermore, these researchers point out that gender inequalities tend to be greater among the poor, especially inequalities in capabilities and opportunities. This case study explores the experiences of women who migrated from rural areas to urban areas. It sought to establish how women try to cope in urban environments as they alter the prejudiced feminine roles in the city. The primary question asked was: 'What elements determine the survival of rural women who have moved to urban spaces?', while the secondary questions were: 'Which factors do women find to be hindrances as they try to survive in the city?' and 'How can women overcome some of the hindrances utilising the African Renaissance paradigm?'

The study was conducted in the province of the Eastern Cape in South Africa. The women mainly came from three areas: Libode, Middledrift and villages outside East London. They had all moved to Port Elizabeth, a city, looking for opportunities. The research explored various questions posed by feminists who focus on the African Renaissance and women. An African Renaissance would be incomplete without the empowerment of African women. In 2006, Africa had high hopes when people saw the first African woman head of state being inaugurated, Ellen Johnson Sirleaf. Sirleaf became the president of Liberia and generally, many progressive Africans hope to see more women leaders on the continent. While women have been leaders in African households in various ways, Amadiume[8] argued that education and access to capital are critical solutions to the marginalisation of women. Women's involvement in society was thwarted by the colonial experience that led to women's marginalisation as well as economic and political disempowerment[9].

Today in African cities and rural areas, many women fight poverty as they struggle for themselves and their children. Today there are numerous debates on the African Renaissance, and as these grow gradually, the society requires the fighting spirit that many women may have in their struggle for social justice. True Pan-Africanism acknowledges that women empowerment is necessary for the total overhaul of colonialism in all its forms. The UNESCO Africa Department publication[10] lists areas that are pertinent when women rise in Africa. Women's rise in Africa means the following:

- Women in prominent positions (government, parliament, etc.) need to help other women rise to prominent positions through initiatives such as positive discrimination;
- Women are often the ones who suffer the most from poverty, exclusion and violence and yet they are also the ones who can end these injustices if they are given the means; and
- Women should be [part of the core of development and in leadership positions; practise has also shown that the most equitable societies are those where women are active participants in the decision-making processes and where they occupy leadership positions.

There is an assumption that when women are involved in their communities, the communities are more successful. Many theories on feminism have explored the women roles in society; below we focus on African feminism.

7.2   African Feminism and Womanhood

The identities of African women have been getting much attention in recent decades. In South Africa there have been several drives to protect women and children, including the annual 16 days of activism against violence on women. In some African states, ministries of women in government have been established to support programmes that promote women achievement and the general protection of women in society, yet the need for African feminism has been necessary to reflect its origins from African cultures. Unlike Western feminists such as Simone de Beauvoir, African feminism does not emanate from essentialists' arguments. In her seminal work, *The Second Sex*, de Beauvoir[11] argued that one is not born a woman but becomes one. Men, de Beauvoir contended, made women *The Other* as they oppressed and stereotyped women, thus appropriating the society into a patriarchy. Furthermore, de Beauvoir[12] demonstrated how society has viewed women as imperfect men, or abnormal deviants. De Beauvoir, an existentialist, maintained that existence comes before essence. She argued that society treats women as *The Other*; they are not men "who are the norm". De Beauvoir did not believe in natural or set roles for woman in society. Society pushes women towards a certain direction of expectations, channelling them into "appropriate" feminine roles. The man always occupies the roles of the self; he is a subject whilst the woman remains an object. However women are capable of liberating themselves; de Beauvoir pointed out that it is through work that a woman can attain autonomy.

Yet Mikell[13] averred that the debates in Western feminism about essentialism and the female body are far from being characteristic of African feminism. Mikell also argued that African feminism is heterosexual, pro-natal and concerned with bread, culture and power issues. There are emerging and established African feminists who argue for the appropriation of African feminism, i.e. feminism that is different from Western forms of feminism (Nnaemeka[14]; Ahikire[15]; Okome[16]). The NGO Pulse[17] noted that:

> Nnaemeka suggests that feminism does not acknowledge the agency and potential of African women. Would a credible African feminism portray women as 'powerless'? Okome notes that in most feminist writings, African women are portrayed as "confused, powerless and unable to

determine for themselves both the changes in their lives and the means to construct these changes." Okome notes that Western feminists usually act as superiors who seek to help and enlighten African women…Western feminists have dominated the discourse on feminist and women's agenda, at the expense of African women.

Unfortunately, many fervent feminists in Africa have also used the Western viewpoint to analyse feminist issues in Africa; many may not even be aware of the spectacles they wear as they analyse African feminist issues. As a result, there is much need to decolonise feminism in Africa. Furthermore, there is a tendency to focus on women oppression (which de Beauvoir emphasises for example) and not the strengths and abilities of women. Jenn Jagire[18] wrote about the need for African feminists to regain agency and to 'de-Europeanise' African feminism, "avoiding perpetuating neo-colonial mentalities and development models that see Africa's women as victims rather than drivers of their own destiny". The decolonisation of African feminism is necessary to understand African women's positions as well as their African contexts. Western models of feminism regard women as helpless, dependent, without vision, perpetually oppressed and continuously oppressable. Several aspects from colonial culture have reflected the helplessness and the dependency syndrome of women. The Bible is one form of literature that has perpetuated this over epochs.

Jagire[19] argued that African women are not commodities or slaves. Several people over the years have assumed the Western feminists' positions and perceived customs such as *ilobola* (the paying of the bride price by the groom's family) as buying the woman or as some form of bartering. Nothing can be further from the truth, however, because *ilobola* in Southern Africa was used as a form of bringing the two families together as one big family by matrimony. "Europeanised Africans deny their African identity. If we do not deEuropeanise our minds, we remain mentally colonised; enslaved to serve foreign masters or foreign cultural interests"[20]. African feminism has been necessitated by a need to address cultural issues faced by women in Africa. The struggle for African feminism is an inclusive one; it needs to be taken by the entire village of males and females. Regarding this, Aidoo[21] claimed that:

> … every man and woman should be a feminist – especially if they believe that Africans should take charge of African land, African wealth, African lives and the burden of African development. It is not possible to advocate independence of African development without also believing that African women must have the best that the environment can offer. For some of us this is the crucial element of feminism.

African societies today have been influenced by the West in a number of ways. Wherever they are, African women will continue to seek to find an identity that will define them as mothers, women, heads of households, and various other roles and identities. African feminism explores the contexts of the black woman in Africa and focuses on being a woman and being black. African feminism is not anti-male, anti-culture or anti-religion, but is a movement whose goal is to empower women, thus ensuring their equality to men[22]; it seeks to confront the system of patriarchy. In this struggle men cannot be marginalised, but African feminism is a relatively a new wave that demonstrates that women are fighters for their spaces and their destinies. The

African woman is not the victim portrayed by Western feminism who is docile and helpless. It is only regrettable that colonialism and its principles have been internalised by African people, thus disregarding history, for example in Africa we spoke of Mother Earth with various goddesses that ruled the earth.

Anker et al.[23] wrote about the changes in women's roles over the past few decades. These authors pointed out that women are tending to marry later, and are moving away from rural areas to the cities. This migration from rural areas and rising education levels have had much impact on women's roles. Anker et al. also pointed out that it is difficult to generalise women's actions across different groups; aspects such as culture, family structure and social class affect women's roles in society. When many women move to the cities or urban areas, they seek to better their lives. Yet, Satterthwaite[24] averred that although urbanisation is linked to independence and opportunity, it also brings risks of violence and constraints of employment "mobility and leadership that reflect deep gender-based inequalities. When women migrate from rural areas to cities, they have to renegotiate their identities and roles in society."

GENDERNET[25] contended that women's economic empowerment matters for pro-poor growth. Furthermore, GENDERNET[26] (2012) pointed out that there are various specific challenges when working with the poorest women. These include:

- lower levels of literacy;
- lower levels of access to and control over resources;
- lower levels of access to networks and people who can assist and support; and
- greater vulnerability to sexual exploitation and abuse at the community level if not the household level.

No society can afford to live with these challenges. Clarke et al.[27] argued that women and girls make up three fifths of the world's poor, hence attempts to defeat poverty have to address gendered norms and practices. "Several studies suggest that the benefits of promoting gender equality never berate widely, as women's empowerment yields economic, health, and educational benefits for families and communities"[28] Wise societies will concentrate on addressing gender inequality by emphasising and enhancing girls' and women's educational, political and employment access. Some authors such as Nickanor[29] argued that women who move from rural to urban settings become vulnerable to food insecurity. Hove, Ngweruma and Muchemwa[30] supported this when they stated that survival is the major concern for the urban poor, and women and children are often the most vulnerable. Furthermore, Hove et al.[31] wrote about how in urban settings children roam the streets, while some women join the ranks of the informal economy especially when there are no prospects of employment. It is usually a disadvantage to the children when women lack education, especially when it comes to health practices[32].

Poor women in urban settings usually lack the resources that can address various aspects such as energy poverty. Balmer[33] also argued that South Africa needs pro-poor policies that can address the challenges that women experience, noting that South African energy policies continue to fail poor women in South Africa.

7.3   Research Methodology

Opportunistic sampling was used to select the participants for this study. Opportunistic sampling refers to when a researcher who is observing a group of people may decide on the spur of the moment to observe certain activities that appear to be interesting, but were not considered important before the study began[34]. The researcher was conducting a study on the correlation between schooling and the socio-economic status of families living in a squatter area, when he discovered that poor women have various challenges concerning the roles that they play when they get to cities, whether they are married or not. Eight participants became part of a qualitative case study. Table 1 below shows the characteristics of the participants:

Table 1 *Characteristics of participants*

Name and Age	Level of Education	Years in City	Children	Marital Status
Anna, 33	Grade 9	05	03	Widowed
Boniwe, 56	Grade 10	08	05	Widowed
Dina, 39	Grade 7	09	02	Single
Ivy, 50	Grade 6	11	03	Single
Liza, 26	Grade 11	03	01	Single
Sasa, 41	Grade 6	07	03	Married
Sonto, 38	Grade 12	09	04	Single
Violet, 40	Grade 5	04	04	Married

The researcher and two assistants shadowed the women for a period of three months, and also interviewed them. The two research assistants were female postgraduate students who were well trained in shadowing and observation skills, however only the chief researcher conducted the structured interviews with the participants. Shadowing schedules were negotiated with the participants before the researchers shadowed the women in their homes, and they also followed them to a few places. The latter included visits to the marketplace as well as when they went to gather wood. Shadowing took four days for each of the participants. Five of the interviews were recorded with the participants' consent. Three participants objected to being audio-recorded. All the interviews were recorded in isiXhosa, which is a dominant indigenous language in the Eastern Cape. These were then translated by the researcher who is a first language speaker of that language.

7.4   The Findings

The participants in the study encountered a number of challenges during the collection of data. Although all of them found that the city offered more opportunities for women, there were also several new challenges, for example employment was not as easy to find as many thought it would be. Furthermore, poverty, poor health, joblessness and difficulty accessing better education for their children were highlighted as critical areas by the women. What was common to all of them was that they did not rely on males for support, hence some tried to be entrepreneurs to support their households by being informal traders. Furthermore, although the participants maintained that much has changed for the better since apartheid days, "the struggle for women is still there". They reiterated that it was a huge challenge to get employment, apart from being a domestic worker. The males were more likely to get working opportunities that their female counterparts cannot access. The women discovered that as they tried to assert themselves in the society they found environments that were hostile to their advancement. Women abuse, societal discrimination and oppressive stereotypes were among the factors that women highlighted as challenges in society. It was also clear from the responses of the women that even human rights traditions favoured males, and usually left women disempowered and more oppressed. The women were also aware, although not in a sophisticated fashion, that they needed to push a feminist agenda; a kind of a programme that would further the fight for women rights and emancipation.

What was critical with the participants was their refusal to be victims of a discriminating society. They tried various ways to confront poverty and helplessness, including attempts to enhance food security, however several factors determined the survival of rural women in cities, amongst which were social capital and level of education. In post-colonial societies, formal education has become one of the major determinants of survival. The research assistants recollected how difficult it was to shadow the participants at times. Among the most challenging aspects experienced by the assistants was the collection of firewood, collecting water from houses close by, as well as queuing for raw sheep intestines in long queues. Sometimes after standing in the queue for a long time, the meat would be finished before the participants bought theirs. One research assistant was distraught after a visit to a municipal clinic where she felt that the service needed much improvement. She cited long queues and said that many patients went back home without being helped with the necessary medication.

The participants talked about a number of factors during the interviews, including their hardships of living in a poverty-stricken environment. Their lives were similar as they all struggled together in their neighbourhood. Many survived through small temporary jobs. Six of the women had children and were helped by the monthly child grants to sustain themselves. Each child receives a government grant of R200 a month (about 20 US dollars). Only Ivy and Boniwe did not receive child grants because their children were older than 18. The menial jobs that all these women did from time to time included domestic duties such as child-minding, ironing, cooking and general cleaning. Two of them had been temporary workers for three months in a local factory, but that job had since ended. The women struggled to survive in the city, and the scarcity of water, electricity and job opportunities were among the most frustrating aspects of living in an urban area. Almost all mentioned how difficult it was to educate their children. The discussion of the findings is set out under three headings below, namely:

i.   General needs in urban settings.
ii.   Women and change: what are the major obstacles?
iii.   Standing their ground: women and sustainable development.

7.5   General Needs In Urban Settings

As highlighted above, the women in the sample shared a number of the challenges that they experienced as migrants in the city. Nene Informal Settlement, the area they resided in, is a new (illegally occupied) area that does not have the necessary infrastructure such as running water and toilets. The women struggled to sustain themselves and their families in such an environment; they struggled to cook and collected wood near a farm that had a bushy area. Three of them used paraffin (kerosene) stoves as well for cooking. Although all of them frequently paid a visit to their rural homes they wanted to make it in the city, where they ironically declared, "it is where the bright lights are". Sasa, who had been in the city for seven years, stated:

> I have been in the city for seven years now. My name is somewhere in the list of those who might get houses. It is tough though, for sometimes you wait forever whilst others get on the list after you do, but they get houses long before you do. Look at this place, no water, no toilets, no electricity. It is a scary place to have your children travel after dusk. But we have no choice, we call this place home.

All the participants concurred that the land their shacks are built on is not good land, as it is hard clay which floods water when it rains. All the women said that they worry when the rain comes as their area has no drainage system. Diseases and health problems frequently irk the community, which usually find themselves defenceless to the health hazards. Ivy lived in a zinc iron shack with no big windows for ventilation. She said:

> Living is difficult. We become sick with our children. When it is cold you find you do not have paraffin to heat your shack. When it is too hot – there is no fresh water. I wish that our government can address our needs. I've been in PE for more than ten years. I have no house still.

The participants belaboured the point that they did not have the means to own anything. The women tried hard to attain self-efficiency but with no jobs, no support and no money, they found this difficult. All had no access to necessary amenities, with the nearest clinic about 25 kilometres away. The participants maintained that their lives had not changed for the better, although the government had implemented many changes in some communities. Annecke (no date) argued that the struggle for democracy in South Africa has put women's rights in the public arena; "the need to include women in the quest for sustainable development is being recognised as regards both their knowledge and use of biomass, and their role as caretakers of household consumption patterns"[35]. Annecke added that women suffer from not having access to electricity and commercial fuels. Oyedego[36] also contended that energy and poverty reduction are connected to socio-economic development, which includes productivity, income growth, education and health. In Nene, poverty is rife and poor health is exacerbated by the conditions created by squalor.

In all these endeavours, many women seek to find the feminist voice as they look for opportunities. As they strive to live in the hurly-burly of the city, the women have started to transform their environment, thus preparing themselves for a renaissance. Mihindou[37] contended:

> …a new millennium is a critical opportunity for transformative change in women's advancement towards equality. Women are key partners for development and their capabilities and leadership skills must be used if there is to be qualitative change for women empowerment and equality and the achievement of an African Renaissance in this continent. The full participation of women in decision-making will bring about an equitable sharing of resources and sustainable human development to the African Renaissance.

The paradox in this study was that the conditions made women proactive, as they sought to live in the city. Generally, some women may think that they need not fend for themselves as this is the function of men – to provide, but the truth is that wherever they are, women should be part of development. Mihondou[38] added that when women are not made part of development strategies, their countries will be operating at half capacity. "The African Renaissance will not reach its full potential for it will lack a solid foundation in the lives of the majority of African people which is constituted by women"[39]. The women in the study demonstrated the will to use the communal *Ubuntu* principle to build and sustain the rebuilding of communities sustained by an African Renaissance. This is not easy, however, as poverty can debilitate the lives of the communities. Yet this may be where the African Renaissance starts – where people realise the need to fight for light that signifies new values and norms. It is the fear of poverty, security and well-being that may delay the women's attainment of certain goals, including the achievement of some African Renaissance goals. Women are bound to lead the renaissance if one considers their numbers and their strength, which is evident as many fend for their families.

7.6 Women and change: What are the major obstacles?

The women in the study showed how they are defined by their femaleness and always dominated by the values of a male-dominated society. They cited a number of obstacles that hinder them from being strong and successful in the society. Annecke[40] argued that men have been dominant in society. Like De Beauvoir[41], Annecke contended that gender is understood as the social construction of biological differences. This means that being born defines one's gender (being male or female) and does not only explain whether one is capable of being pregnant or not. It also explains that certain qualities and patterns of behaviour are socially constructed as acceptable for a particular gender whilst others are not. Amongst others, the participants iterated how difficult it was to find better paying jobs because of their gender. When they left the rural areas to live in the urban area, they did not have the same authority as men.

The African Union found it necessary to declare the year 2015 as the Year of Women's Empowerment and Development towards Africa Agenda 2063. This call was necessitated by the acknowledgement of women's role in African societies. Otas[42] declared that while African women have in some way made strides in political, economic and social development, they are still marginalised within the corridors of power. This was attested to in the study, where women experienced joblessness, social exclusion and an inability to own property. The African post-colonial societies have presented African women with a number of challenges, which have shown the great divide between males and females. Women empowerment is thwarted by a number of factors, including stereotypes, prejudices, history and socialisation. Women's voices have not subsided in their search for human rights for all women. In a January 2016 summit in Addis Ababa, seven challenges were listed as obstacles to African women's progress: economic exclusion; a financial system that perpetuates their discrimination; limited participation in public and political life; a lack of access to education and the poor retention of girls in schools; gender-based violence; harmful cultural practices and the exclusion of women from peace initiatives are major barriers to achieving gender equality in Africa[43]. The African Development Bank Group[44] also mentioned other challenges, including discrimination in formal laws and customary laws; limited access to financial services; and lagging behind in human development. All these demonstrate the need for society to embrace a vision that would empower African women so that they can have access to various opportunities in society.

Poverty also appears to be a key factor in households where women are heads. Seven of the women in this study stated that they are the heads in their families. The University of Western Cape Gender Equity Unit (UWC Gender Equity Unit)[45] pointed out that women-headed families are common among the black population. Furthermore, the unit proclaims that female-headed households are poorer than the average household. The women in this study averred that poverty was the main obstacle to their endeavours to propel their families to success. Another huge obstacle, as mentioned above, is the challenge of the women not to being able to gain from the economy. Adeleye-Fayemi[46] wrote about the context of African feminism and the challenges women face. She also pointed out that globalisation has not helped the cause of women when it comes to the economy. Furthermore, Adeleye-Fayemi[47] argued that globalisation and the implementation of economic policies have compounded the feminisation of poverty. "Global economic trends take local form in terms of loss of livelihoods, unemployment, trafficking in women, street children and a total rupturing of the social fabric that binds communities together"[48].

Adeleye-Fayemi was supported by Kerr[49], who called for feminists to seek alternative economic models for the future. Kerr contended that globalisation can only be truly achieved if progressive male colleagues can show that another world is possible. This world is a world of economic justice, where women are empowered to tackle the causes of poverty and disempowerment. Women are not better off today, as is evident in this study. The UWC publication[50] stated that women still hold a disadvantaged position, although they have gradually been moving into non-traditional careers. "South African women and black women in particular are affected by high levels of unemployment, a situation which is compounded by their reduced access to education and job training"[51]. Economy is linked to education. The women in the study pointed out that they struggle mainly because they do not have the necessary education that would enable them "to be aware of the world around" them.

Improving women's education is crucial for the advancement of families in society. When women have the necessary information, they will be able to withstand other challenges such as health problems. Rural and poor women need education to transform their lives. Leeson[52] cited Msimang, who has declared that like healthcare, housing and employment, education is a service that is necessary for a world that must be struggled for. There are a number of factors that require education for women to survive - economic stability, ways of conserving energy, improving healthcare, as well as understanding of various societal dynamics. Tax[53] affirmed that there are pressures in some societies to deny women of any kind of education. As a result of this, women are illiterate and thus languish in poverty. We find this kind of illiteracy in rural areas and townships in South Africa. Women without education hardly have a voice, i.e. for women to be politically and socially aware, they need education. Usually programmes for women's economic development, education and political equality bow to patriarchal culture. Tax[54] highlighted this when he stated:

> Their education programmes see women as an economic resource - in the World Bank's phrase, 'women are the best investment' – rather than as full human beings. They thus promote narrow vocational training that stops at functional literacy and low level functional literacy and low-level technical skills. Women need a broad humanistic and scientific education for the same reasons men do - so they can understand and appreciate life…

Some experts have argued that there is a need for adult education that would change the social conditions of the people in training and move away from formalised academic training[55]. This implies that adults should get more practical training experience rather than accumulating specific academic qualifications. Yet there are challenges even with those women who qualify with a formal education. Littig[56] contended that few women/girls are interested in technical education, as many women tend to choose "female careers". This sustains the gender differences entrenched by education. The paradox here is that education ends up supporting gender segregation in employment.

The other major obstacle highlighted by the participants was ill health. Women in the study complained about ill health, which makes it necessary for them to visit the clinic frequently. High blood pressure, diabetes and tuberculosis (TB) are among the illnesses that are rife in Nene Informal Settlement. Five participants were suffering from high blood pressure and two of the participants once had TB. Ill health is a major obstacle to migrant women wanting to survive in the city. The UWC publication underscores that poor black African children's ill health has a direct bearing on the health standard of their mothers. "With women making up more than half the population there is an increasing realisation that an improvement to women's health is an improvement to the health of all"[57]. Ill health creates new pockets of poverty among poor women. Dhanraj, Misra and Batliwala[58] postulated that:

Poverty also affects women's health and educational opportunities in both direct and indirect ways: long treks for basic needs deplete women's already low nutrition reserve and increase the opportunity costs of education, healthcare and participation in community life. Inadequate food and water, and cultures that enforce silent suffering, mean women develop a range of chronic diseases such as TB, anaemia and reproductive tract infections that go untreated.

Poor health is a limitation to the poor who would like to try and escape poverty. The situation of poor health also affects children, as research has shown that it is difficult to teach a hungry and unhealthy child. Nene Informal Settlement does not have the necessary infrastructure to support good health.

7.7   Standing their ground: women and sustainable development

The women in Nene Informal Settlement also attempt to sustain themselves by trying to use the environment in the best way they can. Five of the participants had recently joined a group of other women who try to use the management of resources through the creation of an organised women's group. They named this informal initiative Zenzele, an isiXhosa word meaning 'do it for yourself'. Led by a retired nursing sister, the women attended a few participatory classes where they planned to equip one another through the sharing of ideas. This was a good network that has a potential to grow into a powerful women's movement. This group might not have a direct impact on national debates on feminism issues, but has a potential to be strong locally. In fact, these women wanted to build ideas regarding how they could sustain themselves in a tough environment. One of the programmes they introduced was a big tank to receive rainwater, to help curb the travelling to collect water. This was sponsored by one company, together with three mobile toilets. At the time of the study's conclusion, the women were also in the process of organising more toilets that would be able to serve a small Nene Informal Settlement community of about 350 people. With the help of the retired volunteer nurse, the women were also trying to plead with the municipality to introduce a mobile clinic in the area, even if it could only be run for two or three days in a week, as this would be effective in curbing the ecological risks and health hazards. There were, for example, three women in the area who were using old paraffin cans to collect rain water, but this was open and rusty and it was easy for the water to be contaminated. The women were also planning to use a piece of land to plant vegetables that could be used by their families, with the hope of selling some of these.

Griffen[59] argued for the need for women to mobilise and organise themselves in some kind of movement. Griffen also pointed out that the struggle for women's rights has led to the formation of women's groups, which are vital in spreading information that other women in the settlement need. Many ideas cropped up as another group decided to combine and sell fruit bought from the market. Another group decided to bake fat cakes as well as muffins using their paraffin stoves. This informal way of joining the economy should go a long way in helping to sustain families.

In all African societies, women's roles are critical in the production of food and sustainable development. James and James[60] referred to women as the most "overlooked natural resource and hidden treasure". The women usually work the land which has the potential to bring wealth and economic freedom. Without women in Africa living close to the land, we can hardly experience a renaissance. It is for this reason that African nations cannot leave women and girls outside development in education. Women need to be emancipated by society so that they are able to sustain their communities. Louw[61] argued that Africa needs the continuous improvement of standards of living and the quality of life of the masses of people. Furthermore, he cited Barell, who contended that "also included are ensuring the emancipation of women, successfully dealing with the HIV/AIDS pandemic, rediscovering the "African past", recovering cultures… as well as environmental protection"[62]. These are ideas shared with Zeleza, who pointed out that the agenda for African Renaissance is to promote democratisation, peace, stability and sustainable economic development. Furthermore, the African Renaissance sought to resolve the scourge of HIV/AIDS and ensure the emancipation of women. Strong women will enhance the African Renaissance agenda as they find solutions to their plight, thus opposing victimhood. Chentu[63] showed how the poor in Africa can find solutions to problems themselves, pointing out:

> The problem of homelessness and poverty in urban Africa may seem unmanageable, yet solutions are incubating in the very environment where the problem exists. Up to now, the bulk of investment in shelter has come from the poor themselves, outside the realm of local and national government planning systems (Bryant, 1980: 78-85). This needs to be recognised by governments, who treat slum-dwellers as undesirable and a burden to local and national authorities.

7.8   Conclusion

The migrant women in the study demonstrate numerous challenges in the city. As highlighted above, among these are a lack of education, a lack of economic participation, being landless, and poor health. Many left their villages in rural areas hoping to make it in the urban area, only to find new challenges coming up. None of the women in the study felt that the urban area was better than the rural areas, however they appeared to live in the hope that someday there would be light. Yet nothing is going well for these women, as their children are victims of ill health and they have numerous illnesses. The women are aware that their families will never escape the poverty cycle because many older children in Nene have not finished school and are struggling to get jobs like their mothers. The only way of survival for these women is to have a plan of how they can cope in the arid environment. The plan for the formation of Zenzele Group was a good initiative. Although it was unstable in its early stages, with the necessary unity, the group could go far in helping the women cope. The group's ethos of ensuring that the women become proactive will help them in their survival. The African Renaissance that is topical in today's discourse will require the involvement of women in various aspects of life. From the discussions above it is clear that for women's empowerment to happen, first the poor should not be denied effective education. The participants in this study needed education that would empower them for daily living, such as living a healthy life and to conserving energy. Poor women, especially those in rural and impoverished areas, are usually far away from education that would help them cope with life.

Secondly, and linked to the need for education, is the need for entrepreneurship skills. Many women who are landless and poor think that they need to seek a job and work for someone else. This is a fallacy however, as many poor women can generate income for their families by employing entrepreneurship skills where they hire themselves. In reality however, numerous poor women feel helpless when they cannot find employment. When women are empowered through education, they are able to devise a means of starting their own businesses to sustain themselves. Traditionally women are excluded from the mainstream economy, but it is through their endeavours that they can learn basic business skills.

Finally, an African Renaissance will need communal approaches, an element that was evident to a certain extent in this study. There is nothing that leads to despondency as much as when one suffers alone with no prospects of finding any solutions. People learn much from one another as to how they can manage the environment and fight poverty. In a group of people there can be discussions that would bring about solutions. Poor women do not have to suffer alone with no help at hand; women's concerns can be attended to in a gender sensitive environment and realistic fashion. Women's informal groups can act as part of support services to assist in many ways. This includes teaching women who have been assaulted or who live in a violent environment how to access education and health services. Support services can also help to suggest how the poor women can support their children in school. Women need one another for the meaningful transformation of their lives, as well as their society.

References

[1]Pozarny, P. F. 2016. *Gender roles and opportunities for women in urban environments*. Applied Knowledge Services: GSDRC. Retrieved from: https://assets.publishing.service.gov.uk/media/57a0895440f0b652dd000190/HDQ1337. pdf. [Date accessed: November 18, 2016.]

[2]Ibid.

[3]Ibid.

[4]Tacoli, C., & Satterthwaite, D. 2013. Editorial: Gender and Urban Change. *Environment and Urbanisation*, 25(1): 3-8.

[5]SANews. 2015. *Empowering the rural woman*. Retrieved from: www.sanews.gov.za/south-africa/empowering-rural-woman. [Date accessed: November 18, 2016.]

[6]Grown, C., Gupta, G. R., & Kes, A. 2005. *Taking action: achieving gender equality and empowering women*. London: Earthscan.

[7]Ibid.

[8]Amadiume, I. 2005. *Women and Development in Africa*. Retrieved from: http://www.sgiquaterly.org/feature2005Jan-3. [Date accessed: January 20, 2017.]

[9]Ibid.

[10]UNESCO. 2015. *African women, Pan-Africanism and African Renaissance*. Paris: UNESCO Publishing.

[11]De Beauvoir, S. 2009. *The Second Sex*. (Translation by Constance Borde and Sheila Malovany-Chevallier). London: Random House.

[12]Ibid.

[13]Mikell, G. 1997. Introduction. In G. Mikell (Ed.). *African Feminism: The Politics of Survival in Sub-Saharan Africa*. Philadelphia: University of Pennsylvania, pp. 1-52.

[14]Sangonet Pulse. 2010. *African feminism driven by women*. Retrieved from: http://www.ngopulse.org/article/african-feminism-driven-african-women. [Date accessed: September 12, 2016.]

[15]Ahikire, J. 2014. *African Feminism in Context: Reflections on the legitimation battles, victories and reversals*. Retrieved from: http://agi.ac.za/sites/agi.ac.za/files/features_-_african_feminism_in_the_21st_century-_a_reflection_on_ugandagcos_victories_battles_and_reversals.pdf. [Date accessed: September 12, 2016.]

[16]Sangonet Pulse. 2010. *African feminism driven by women*. Retrieved from: http://www.ngopulse.org/article/african-feminism-driven-african-women. [Date accessed: September 12, 2016].

[17]Ibid

[18]Jagire, J. 2010. *Decolonising African Feminism*. Retrieved from: http:www.pambazuka.org/gender-minorities/decolonising-african-feminism. [Date accessed: December 13, 2016.]

[19]Ibid.

[20]Ibid.

[21]Aidoo, A. A. 1998. African women today. In O. Nnaemeka (Ed.). *Sisterhood Feminisms & Power: From Africa to the Diaspora*. New Jersey: Africa Wide Press.

[22]Nkealah, N. 2006. Conceptualising Feminism(s) in Africa. The challenges facing African women writers and critics. *English Academy Review*, 23(1): 133-141.

[23]Anker, R., Buvinic, M., & Youssef, N.H. 1984. *Women's roles and population trends in the third world*. London: Croom Helm.

[24]Tacoli, C., & Satterthwaite, D. 2013. Editorial: Gender and Urban Change. *Environment and Urbanisation*, 25(1): 3-8.

[25]GENDERNET. 2012. *Women's economic empowerment: The OECD DAC network on Gender Equality*. Retrieved from: https://www.oecd.org/dac/povertyreduction/50157530.pdf. [Date accessed: January 12, 2017.]

[26]Ibid.

[27]Clarke, S., Wylie, G., & Zomer, H. 2013. ICT 4 the MDGs? A perspective on ICT's role in addressing urban poverty in the context of the Millennium Development Goals. *Information Technologies & International Development*, 9(4): 55-70.

[28]Ibid.

[29]Nickanor, N. M. 2013. Women and urban food insecurity in Southern Africa. *Backgrounder*, 55(3): 1-8.

[30]Hove, M., Ngwerume E. T, & Muchemwa, C. 2013. The urban crisis in sub-Saharan Africa: A threat to human security and sustainable development. *Stability*, 2(1): 1-14.

[31]Ibid.

[32]Luchuo, E. B., Paschal, K. A., Ngia, G., Njem, P. K., Yelena, S., Nsah, B., & Ajame, N. 2013. Malnutrition in Sub-Saharan Africa: burdens, causes and prospects. *Pan-African Medical Journal*. Retrieved from: http:www.panafrican-med-journal.com/content/article/15/120/full. [Date accessed: March 07, 2014.]

[33]Balmer, M. 2007. Energy poverty and cooking energy requirements: the forgotten issue in South African energy policy? *Journal of Energy in Southern Africa*, 18(3): 4-9.

[34]Struwig, F. W., & Stead, G. B. 2004. *Planning, designing and reporting research*. Cape Town: Pearson Education.

[35]Annecke, W. J. n.d. *Women and energy in South Africa*. Retrieved from: http://www.energia.Org/fileadmin/files/media/reports. [Date accessed: March 11, 2014.]

[36]Oyedego, S. O. 2012. Energy and sustainable development in Nigeria: the way forward. *Energy Sustainability and Society*. 2(1)-17.

[37]Mihindou, P. E. T. 2006. *The African Renaissance and Gender: Finding the Feminist Voice*. Unpublished Masters Dissertation. Stellenbosch: University of Stellenbosch.

[38]Ibid.

[39]Ibid.

[40]Annecke, W. J. n.d. *Women and energy in South Africa*. Retrieved from: http://www.energia.Org/fileadmin/files/media/reports. [Date accessed: March 11, 2014.]

[41]De Beauvoir, S. 2009. *The Second Sex*. (Translation by Constance Borde and Sheila Malovany-Chevallier). London: Random House.

[42]Otas, B. 2015. Empowering African Women: Gender is the Agenda. *New Agenda*, 137 (July/August 2015).

[43]Kamal, B. 2016. *Seven top challenges facing African women*. Retrieved from: htto://www.ipsnews.net/2016/01seven-top-challenges-facing-african-women/. [Date accessed: February 07, 2017.]

[44]Africa Development Bank Group. 2015. *Empowering African Women: An Agenda for Action*. Abidjan: ADBG

[45]UWC Gender Equity Unit. 1997. *Beyond Inequalities: Women in South Africa*. Bellville: UWC/SARDC.

[46]Adeleye-Fayemi, B. 2004. Creating a new world with new visions: African feminism and trends in the global women's movement. In J. Kerr, E. Sprenger, and A. Symington (Eds.). *The future of women's rights: Global visions and strategies*. London: Zed Books, pp. 38-55.

[47]Ibid.

[48]Ibid.

[49]J. Kerr, E. Sprenger, & A. Symington. (Eds.). *The future of women's rights: Global visions and strategies*. London: Zed Books, pp. 152-169.

[50]UWC Gender Equity Unit. 1997. *Beyond Inequalities: Women in South Africa*. Bellville: UWC/SARDC.

[51]Ibid.

[52]Leeson, R. 2004. Gender equality advocates speak: Feminist issues and strategies in the future. In J. Kerr, E. Sprenger, and A. Symington (Eds.). *The future of women's rights: Global visions and strategies*. London: Zed Books, pp. 197-212.

[53]Tax, M. 1999. Power of the word: Culture, censorship, and voice. In J. Silliman, & Y. King (Eds.). *Dangerous intersections: Feminists perspectives on population, environment, and development*. Cambridge: South End Press.

[54]Ibid.

[55]UWC Gender Equity Unit. 1997. *Beyond Inequalities: Women in South Africa*. Bellville: UWC/SARDC.

[56]Littig, B. 2001. *Feminist Perspectives on Environment and Society*. Harlow: Pearson Education.

[57]UWC Gender Equity Unit. 1997. *Beyond Inequalities: Women in South Africa*. Bellville: UWC/SARDC.

[58]Dhanraj, D., Misra, G., & Batliwala, S. 2004. An action framework for South Asia. In J. Kerr, E. Sprenger, and A. Symington (Eds.). *The future of women's rights: Global visions and strategies*. London: Zed Books, pp. 80-96.

[59]Griffin, V. 2004. Globalisation and reinventing the politics of a women's movement. In J. Kerr (Ed.). 2004. From 'opposing' to 'proposing': finding proactive global strategies for feminist futures. In J. Kerr, E. Sprenger, and A. Symington (Eds.). *The future of women's rights: Global visions and strategies*. London: Zed Books, pp. 14-37.

[60]James, V., & James, M. M. 1995. The current and future directions for African women farmers. In V. U. James (Ed.). *Women and Sustainable Development in Africa*. London: Praeger, pp. 15.

[61]Louw, C. A. H. 2000. *The concept of African Renaissance as a force multiplier to enhance lasting peace and stability in sub-Saharan Africa*. Retrieved from: http://www.africavenir.org/fileadmin/_migrated/content_uploads/ LouwAfricanRenaissanceForceMultiplier_03.pdf. [Date accessed: January 12, 2017.]

[62]Ibid.

[63]Chentu, F. 2002. *African Renaissance: Roadmaps to the Challenge of Globalisation*. London: Zed Books.

Chapter 8

Inventing mythologies, rationalising conflict in a state formative African Polity: KMT 3150-3200 BCE

Amon Saba Saakana
Author, Poet, Critic, Karnak House, Trinidad

8.1   Background to the Wsir-Hor–Setekh Conflict

The Contending of Hor and Setekh was discovered on a papyrus dating back to the New Kingdom (1550-1069 BCE), preserved by a lady – as William Kelly Simpson facetiously said – as a source of 'entertainment', although the narrative not only is epic but also a moral tone drama in which might equals right, established tradition is turned on its head, and the pursuit of justice and sustained belief boldly underlines the determination of a single mother, Isata, in defence of her son and the legacy of her dead husband. Wsir, Isata and Setekh (Greek Osiris, Isis and Horus) are repeatedly mentioned in Old Kingdom texts (2780-2081 BCE) and are prominently featured in several contexts, and it has been established that the story itself was first written in the early Middle Kingdom (2025-1700 BCE). That the conflict was related in several texts, although not as a complete drama, attests to the fact that it has its roots from the predynastic or Dynasty Zero to the Old Kingdom, in which all three canonised divinities are attested.

Firstly, one must establish the objective of the story before excavating the monumental role of Isata in it. The sacerdotal colleges encapsulated in the temple-university were clearly the places where academic standards were not only taught, but which were the incubator for the training of young people equipped with indestructible moral fibre so that they could not be persuaded away from the pursuit of defending truth and justice. This is as much the case among the initiated class of the Dogon on the cliffs of Bandiagara in Mali as it is among the Yoruba in South-West Nigeria, and several other classes of peoples who have preserved their religio-university structures on the African continent.

Wsir was murdered by his "brother" Setekh, and his body dismembered into 14 pieces, in order to usurp the throne from him. What is the significance of the 14 pieces of Wsir? Could they represent the 14 *hepsu* (nomes) of Kmt where there were shrinal dedications to Wsir? Bodies of hierarchical figures dying away from home are usually buried in the place of death, but minor body parts, such as a toe or finger nails, are retrieved for ritual burial in the place of birth. This idea is survived by the device of the 14 dismembered parts: what is the purpose and meaning behind Setekh executing this act of murder? The act thus appears not to be derived from Setekh's mind, but from those authorities whose benefit it was to legendarise Wsir within the survival strategy of the state, reeling from a real event of war.

Wsir is searched for and resuscitated by Isata, and impregnated by her brother/husband she bears a son, Hor. She then becomes a single mother but has the support of the goddess Huthor, who acts as surrogate mother to the child (implied but not developed). But the writer of the play focuses the reader's and audience's attention to the singular heroic efforts of Isata so that she resonates with the population as archetypal mother, a paradigmatic figure highly respected from the inception of dynastic Kmt. Isata undertakes to fulfill not only the wishes of her dead husband, but that of a questionable tradition itself which supposedly codifies and sanctifies the model of succession from father to son in a monarchial context. This tradition, upon contextual examination, will be shown to have meaning in the domestic context, when clan/lineage social organisations dominated local and provincial polities, but not the monarchial one. The rest of the play provides contextual understanding of the workings of the divinities. Interestingly, it canonises Isata to the extent where magic and perfidy and/or deceit characterise her moral obligation to fulfill her son's crowning. In contrast, Setekh is ramificationally characterised as strong-headed, unbalanced, vengeful and a homosexual, an assignation guaranteed to generate hostility from the divine judges and certain to create consternation and condemnation by the population (as it was a prohibition in the judgment of the decease's soul in the Hall of Judgment).

This project, therefore, is an attempt to unravel truth from myth, fact from propaganda, and, through comparisons with various African polities, the similarity of cultural experience and the social model of succession and inheritance. This obviously leads to sociological investigation, and the structures of existing models which provide living proof from which to draw a better and more profound understanding, although the events dealt with here are probably older than 5,000 years.

8.2   What is the motive behind the writing of this drama?

This drama was written to perpetuate the myth that the possible in-migrating Wsir/Hor clan had no transparent legitimacy to the kingship and derived its power from being victorious in war against the Setekh clan, whose attestation goes back to at least 4000 BCE, while Wsir/Hor is prominently attested from Naqada III, established in Nekhen but claiming rights to traditional rulership by being buried in the traditionally established seat of monarchial power and revered shrine in Abydju. The state had to institute a mythological narrative and paradigm in which Oneness/Unity is the primary theme.

Writing of the various contending clans/lineage groups in Igbo (Nigerian) society, Mordi observed that, "The *full dynamism of oneness* seen in ritual values in Nigerian communities is borne out of *commitment to the concept of common ancestor or even when two settlements from different ancestors out of a confederation* such as Igbouzo via Isuama Igbo and Ogboli-Nri Igbo movement become one town, *via ritual ideology*... [It is important to] reconstruct Igbouzo-Ogboli migration in order to highlight the importance of ritual ideology..."[1] (emphasis added).

Thus the conflicting Setekh–Wsir/Hor clans are supposed to be reconciled by the manipulation of an imposed mythological paradigm in which both clans are portrayed as descended from one set of parents, Geb and Nut, and an ultimate ancestor, four generations removed, Atum.

Written in the New Kingdom but going back in written form to the Old, though having its foundations in the events at the time of unitising a disparate land mass c. 3150–3200 BCE, this moral drama has enormous implications for the political theatre of modern Africa in which fraud, power, lust and immorality distinctly mark regime after regime. It is a monumental document which, written over 3500 years ago, remains a timeless code of moral conduct lessons for modern African leaders and those in distant, formerly enslaved and colonised lands. It demonstrates the enormous capacity of the state to resolve complex problems of conflict and dissention, by unitising survival devices, among which are rituals and drama, to foster incorporation, peace and order. But the hegemonising of the victor does not resonate with that of the loser, who repeatedly attempts to be reintegrated into his prehistorical role as ruler, and does succeed intermittently during the life of specific indigenous Kmtan nsws (rulers).

8.3   Who Is Wsir/Osiris?

Wsir is represented as the first mortal king of a united Kemet or Tawi (the Double Country). On the surface, his suited clothes are represented by a tight-fitting all-in-one which resembled the performance costume of the late Fela Anikulapo Kuti (whose band was called Egypt 80), which demonstrates the contemporaneity of Kemetan textile designs. Apart from the usually white or green skin-tight costumes that Wsir wears, Budge[2] put forward a more potent and comprehensible interpretation, that in one example of the "suit" it is in fact body decoration or tattoos. And we can compare the body decoration of Wsir with that of Narmer (the nsw who was one of the first to unite south and north into a single state, Kmt), in which the lower part of his body is decorated, already connecting a unique link between the two, as this is not shown as lavishly on other nsws.

Wsir is the senior brother to Setekh, and sisters Isata and Nebethut, who is murdered by his brother in the latter's attempt to wrest the throne from him. Rescued by his sister-wife, Isata, he is resuscitated, symbolically delivers his sperm to her, and receives divine resurrection where he becomes the sole King of the Dead. Wsir is represented by corn stalks from where his body is supposedly at rest in Lower Kemet and from which the fertility of the land is generated. He is also represented as a cosmological god, Ra, taking his place in the daily cycle of the universe. Wsir's authentication as both a solar and earth netjer is confirmed by the characteristic features associated with his parents: Nut as sky and Geb as literally the earth. Corn was a staple diet of Kmt, thus Wsir would be associated with all the plenitudes and sustenance derived from the earth, an inheritance from his father. His mysterious existence would be shrouded in heavenly recitations, emerging from the very beginning of the universe, thus obfuscating any antecedent history of Kmt, particularly that of kings. In this context, one can compare the experiences of Nigerian traditional, precolonial polities to unravel and illuminate some of the goals of the state through its various apparatuses, which involve: "... a special [kind] of power via *ritual ideology – the power to frame alternative, to win and shape consent, that the granting of legitimacy to traditional rulers appears not only 'spontaneous' but natural and normal*"[3].

In this context, the perspective of Castillos[4] confirms the predilection for the expansion of regional chiefdoms to authenticate themselves, through various strategic approaches, as legitimate rulers in the eyes of the population who were not biological kinsmen. Expansion and incorporation or military conquest go hand in glove with ideological constructs in the armoury of the nascent state.

The sources of information on Wsir are transmitted from the last rites ritual performed on the dead, as contained in the *Pyramid Texts*, the *Coffin Texts* and *The Book of Coming Forth by Day*, commonly called *The Egyptian Book of the Dead*. They are not literary tracts but ones of funerary literature. The fact that the ritual was intimately connected to and plausibly the creation of high court officials at the behest of the nsw or the nsw's royal emissary/official cast some doubt as to the authenticity of the motive that brought Wsir into national, and later international, prominence. We should also note that although these books are constructed around final rites, they inevitably take their references from earthly environmental and social details, a feature common to all cultures in the projection of other, unexperienced worlds. These books also have direct allusions to solar and stellar references for the immortal soul of the dead nsw, as well as documentations of a monumental conflict, the mediation of which was fundamental to the ordered administration of the state.

It is plausible too, to hypothesise that the mythological construction of Narmer (one of the first kings to unite Kmt as an historical state) as Wsir at the beginnings of the Old Kingdom (c. 2800–2900 BCE) would have existed historically as oral text, but committed to writing only in the Old Kingdom. (One can compare Homer's *The Odyssey*, which was transmitted orally from tradition and was only committed to writing c. 850 BCE.) Many reasons can be imagined for permanenising the myth: the growth of a social class that was quickly becoming literate or continuous tensions between the Hor and Setekh clans that had to be resolved politically through the medium of invented myth. Extrapolating further along the latter lines, there would have to be a hegemonic state structure to modalise the new dispensation in a manner that could be viewed as everyday:

> "... ritual institutions as one of the apparatuses of the [state] provides in the horizon of thought and action within which conflicts are fought through experienced, obscured and concealed as the [state's] interest which should unite all conflicting parties..."[5] (I have substituted 'communities' with state).

The basis of both *The Contending of Horus and Seth and The Triumph of Horus* is precisely to disguise the origins of the deep-seated conflict between the indigenous clan of Setekh and the perceived outside migrants, later fused with the southern population, of the Wsir-Hor clan. Thus state propaganda is central to the fostering of unity, either through measures of reconciliation or through the demonisation and expulsion of Setekh as a state authority.

8.4   Continuity of Wsir in Narmer at State Formation

The established facts about the process of Kmt's unification are expressed through the Narmer tablet, reproduced below, and various constant, interwoven references to Wsir as the one who first unified Kmt detailed in the several final rites manuals. From a purely historical standpoint we know that Narmer/Menes brought Tawi/the Double Country into a united polity c. 3150 BCE. Mythologically, Wsir is decreed to be the one who formed Kmt into a united state. It is thus difficult, if not almost impossible, to reconcile the two explanations. However, when we do subject the historical and the mythological explanations to detailed scrutiny, established facts and historical reconstruction verify the historical persona and figure of Narmer to be the logical candidate. We are still faced, however, with explaining who Wsir really is and what was the purpose for not only his creation but the entire mythological visioning of the bringing into being of the world, from Nun and Atum to Wsir and his siblings.

Since Wsir was the first earthly king of Kmt, reading from the cosmology of Iunu (Heliopolis), Wsir's name is represented by a throne or seat followed by an eye (which may be interpreted as protection of the throne or seat). With several extant interpretations, Budge comes closest to my understanding: "he who makes a seat" or "seat maker"[6]; I would interpret his name as "throne-maker", since this was accomplished through war and secondly, at death he bequeathed his throne to his only son, Hor. In another context, Budge asserted that Wsir is ordered to humiliate the dethroned Setekh: "Make thy seat upon him. Come forth. Sit thou upon him..."[7]. This injunction appears to confirm the royal status of Setekh, for it is directed to authenticating Wsir's usurping his throne, thus incorporating his traditionally recognised status as nsw. Linguistically, Anselin has shown that Wsir is connected to old or ancient in West Chadic and in East Cushitic. This confirms my hypothesis of a hybrid history of the falcon clan, which may have migrated from South Arabia, a land of falcon master trainers, and intermarried with Nubian nationals (of any ethnic antecedents), a not too impossible idea when considering the range of Upper Kmtan trade relations with the Red Sea, Palestine and the Near East.

Frankfort, in his intuitive, prescient interpretation of Ikher-nofret's rendering of the Great Procession, was able to deconstruct the ritual not as a godly one, but one for a king[8]. Continuing this deconstruction, he wrote: "For in mythology, and hence in the cult of Osiris as a god, Horus alone appears. This very fact suggests that *the Great Procession is concerned not with the myth of Osiris in its late form but with the myth of royalty and the rites of royalty* and which the figures of Horus and Osiris had originally their appointed places...We find Upwaut as the main avenger of Osiris in the text of Ikhernofret, and *Upwaut may... stand for Pharaoh, the earthly embodiment of Horus*. The opening inscription becomes understandable if we assume that it referred originally to a royal rite. If Upwaut [Wepwawet] represents Pharaoh in his aspect of eldest son, *it makes sense to say that the wolf-god "went to champion his father"*[9] (emphasis added).

Frankfort interpreted this text correctly, except he unqualifiedly misunderstood the representation of Upwaut (Wepwawet) as the wolf-god son of Wsir. The invented mythology of Wsir/Hor-Setekh had already become normalised in popular lore, thus he could be represented as part of an elaborate state process of incorporation and assimilation, in which Upwaut, a canine deity, representative of the authentic royal lineage at Abydju, is abducted and represented as an avenger. By so doing, the state incorporates the canine clan as an intrinsic component of the victorious Wsir-Hor. But Frankfort's discerning eye did detect a ruse in the state's passing off Wsir as a divinity rather than as a king.

8.5   Recurring Motif of Conquest and Incorporation in Africa

Traditional Africa is replete with examples of those who have the power to enthrone a king by not only hereditary rights, but by selection or by force of arms. Budge alluded to this well-established tradition in the Sudan[10], but in fact it is a characteristic feature of all of traditional Africa: the chief or king, as dead ancestor, was canonised within the realm of divinity, such as Shango, who ruled on earth as the mortal fourth king of Oyo[11]. Posthumously he was revered for his generosity, his strength of arm, his sense of justice and, above all, he represented protection and patronage, but in life was also ruthlessly in pursuit of war and conquest which his generals contested. These are the qualities that Wsir would have been known for: rewards and giving of alms are characteristics of African monarchial structures, and on death elaborate funerals would be a normative tradition.

8.6   Mythology as Political Rationale

Turning to the mythological or philosophical perspective of the formation of Kmt as a divine state, one has to look at the wider context. The Kmtu conceptualised the beginning of the universe through the existence of abyssal or chaotic waters, Nun, out of which Atum, the self-created, the perfect or complete one, like the one cell amoeba or algae, emerges by himself.

Using the word 'perfect' to describe Atum may be questionable to some, as the word's etymology, according to James and others, is more linked to Lord of Totality (nb tm), and to completeness, finish[12]. I connect tm to Egyptian Arabic, tmm (tamam, which is interestingly attested to in Kmt as "the completed one") which, variegated, could be rendered as perfect. The reason for this connection is that Arab descendants in Egypt inhabit a land that still has everyday recurrences of some Kmtu words resonant in the language, which may well have a contextual connection to its original meaning. And in relation to a question of state of being, the answer is either "Inshallah" or "tamam" (perfect/good).

This movement of Atum out of the chaotic waters here recalls, temptingly, the image of the sun as it rises from the horizon, the juncture of sea and sky as the prelude to this philosophical imaging of creation. Atum then begins the process of creation by sneezing out Shu and spitting out Tefnut, representative of atmosphere/air and order/moisture. It is instructive here to see the mythological mind possessed of scientific principle: sneezing releases air and coughing/spitting produces moisture, and the process of creation is mythologically represented in perfect imagistic and scientific terms, both spitting and sneezing reflect an explosive energy, uncontainable, irrepressible, inevitable. This divine couple in turn parented the first procreated twin of Geb, earth, and Nut, sky. It is apparent that this envisioning of the universe already takes on deep intellectual speculation about origins, and the succeeding quartet of siblings, Wsir, Isata, Setekh, and Nebethut, who acquire the status of the first royal family, provides the basis for the future constitutional governance of dynastic Kmt, embracing maat as a fundamental principle.

When we examine the timescale of this myth it becomes apparent that Wsir's grandparents are Shu and Tefnut, and his great-grandparent is God Atum himself! There is no narrative construct of "after thousands of years a wise king arose...". Wsir is directly genetically connected to forces that predetermine not only his destiny, but provide a paradigm of good governance and the bequeathal of personal characteristics that cast him, a mortal, into the realm of a revered god-king on earth and a judgmental one of the dead.

This myth represents an attempt to memorialise the mortal struggles and triumphs of the first uniter at the sep tepy, the first time in Kmt's history. This canonisation is at the expense of the portrayal of Wsir's "brother", Setekh, as being emblematic of greed, violence, and unmediated power (see discussion below on the role of succession). It was, however, the spiritually intuitive work of Henri Frankfort who first hypothesised that Wsir, of the same falcon clan that brought Hor to the throne, could have been a representative king who preceded Menes[13]. Yet Budge placed the textual reference to Wsir's origins in the first dynasty but did not tie this in with Narmer/Menes[14]. I speculate further that the uniter of a separated, double country was not in fact the historical Narmer, although he incorporated the features of Wosir's couture. The battle for supremacy in enforcing unity over Kmt was resisted by the tjesm/hunting hound clan that Setekh not only clearly represented, but appears antecedent to the hawk/falcon clan in the iconographic records c. 40000 BCE.

In a pioneering essay in *Ancient Egypt*, Newberry[15] provided a detailed representation of hepsu/nomes' emblems and speculative thought as to their interpretation prior to the unification of Kmt: that of the harpoon of the Delta adjacent to which is the falcon, the feathered headdress of the Western Libyan hepsu, the oryx (a canine) and the mountain glyph of the Delta, all representing conquest and incorporation when paired with the falcon emblem have the same semantic meaning.

In theorising around the concept of early conflict, Campagno asserted that the state can emerge "by means of the subjection of one social group by another one"[16]. An elaboration of subjection is now extended to the role of ritual to validate political change, using the Yoruba experience: "Commemorative rituals are re-enactment of major historical events connected with the historical vicissitudes of the dynastic ancestors, some of them validated (or legitimized) the resultant political change... The historical significance are [sic] sometimes forgotten or pushed into the backgound while the ritualized behaviour become[s] emphasized"[17]. But the underlining ideological thrust, as stressed by Andelkovic[18], is that "...the social setting was dominated by *the ideology of sacred power, fully blended with the concentration of economic, political and military power*" (emphasis added).

The Contending of Hor and Setekh was precisely so named because of the raging battles in pursuit of unification, and more than that, control of the state. The Setekh clan, therefore, because of the ferocity and persistence of its resistance, was markedly embalmed with all the negatives that cast it in a role as usurper. The falcon clan, once triumphant, was subsequently couched in the language of netjer/netjeru, in which a divine connection is inherited through four generations. An additional factor that the rationalist scholar would seek to explain is the length of time that elapsed before Wsir's canonisation. We have seen that Setekh, according to the Philae play, was separated by being given rulership of the north, then dually incorporated with Hor and subsequently reduced. It is logical to assume that although the Wsir-Hor clan was victorious, the Setekh clan was sporadically involved in revolt and/or particular nsws who came to the throne may have belonged or affiliated or been sympathetic to the Setekh clan and resurrected him as state netjer. This is no different from the antagonism that breaks out into open and bloody warfare between the Shia and Sunni factions in Islam, a dispute that is still raging 1400 years after the death of the prophet Muhammad. Consequently, the oralisation of the myth could have been established just after Narmer's death and committed to writing from the Old Kingdom (*The Pyramid Texts*).

8.7   Comparative African Paradigms

Supporting comparative but more recent evidence can be shown in the assumption of the primacy of rulership by Wsir/Hor, when we look at conquered boundaries by one Yoruba group over another. Constant references are made by the defenders of Wsir of his now vanquished contender and opponent, Setekh, whose followers are equally described as 'rebels.' Two contending versions of the origins of *owoni* are extant among the Yoruba. One is that Oranyan, the youngest of Oduduwa's children, the legendary founder of Oyo, seeking revenge for his father's humiliation, could not reach his destination and terminated his advancing army near Oyo. He had left behind one Adimu, a priest appointed to officiate at the royal shrine and to control the treasury. Adimu's fame was widespread and surrounding chiefs, kings and princes wanted to know who this Adimu was. The reply given was: *Omo Oluwu ni*, the son of a sacrificial victim, contracted to *owoni*[19]. The veracity of this story is contested and is assumed to be invented because it derives the concept of royal power (*owoni*) in the person of a priest whose origin began in seeking refuge, from committed malfeasances, in the shrine.

But, comparatively, it is interesting to note that in Ottoman Turkey, the sultan's most trusted and exalted official was a formerly enslaved Ethiopian eunuch who controlled the entire treasury and the sultan's harem. Law, however, logically surmises: "It is clear that legends specifically concerned with the origins are especially liable to distortion, or even to pure fabrication. While they preserve a genuine tradition of how the present state of affairs arose, they may equally be merely ingenious speculations or rationalizations. Moreover, origin myths are frequently tendentious, and suffer distortion for ulterior purposes, *seeking to validate claims to superiority or suzerainty...*"[20] (emphasis added).

On the question of priestly incorporation, there is a supporting view of the Adimu narrative. Olomola[21] believed that new dynasties maintained the incumbent priest-kings or priest-chiefs of the now defeated polity of "'autochthonous' societies" to serve "the fertility gods and goddesses while they themselves assumed power." This judicious choice was motivated by the knowledge of these priests of the deities they served and how best to propitiate them. Thus the Adimu myth can be viewed from two angular perspectives, depending on the side of the lens the viewer is looking through.

The couching of the play in unambiguously clear moral tones and appealing to a higher moral authority, the psdjt/Divine Group of Nine, reacts to the demands for moral justification of its actions. We should note that all the netjeru (divinities) who played a formative role at the beginning of creation and in the body of knowing in Kmt, themselves constituted the tribunal and the judges who adjudicate this groundbreaking historic case. The political solution was the incorporation of Setekh as first ruler of Lower Kmt, then rejecting this in favour of symbolically joint rulership, then being removed altogether. This rejection is what creates a void and necessity for justifying the canonisation of the falcon clan, after the fact of its triumph and subjugation of Setekh. As Agrawal persuasively argued, moral justification arises when there is dispute, contestation and resolution sought through a higher authority. This sanctioning of a moral authority becomes moral justification of ultimate value[22]: Wsir as king, Hor as successor, Setekh as enemy, Isata as deeply committed moralist and seeker of justice. However, from a contemporary humanitarian perspective, Isata is projected as using tricks and magic to advance her case.

We need to recapture the political atmosphere at the immediate predynastic and post-dynastic stages in order to better understand the representative meanings attached to the standards of Setekh, the tjesm hound, and Hor, the falcon. Immediately preceding Narmer's reign, Scorpion, the nsw, held several standards, among which was the macehead, including two that iconographically and interpretively represented Setekh (tjesm hound)[23], which confirms the precedence of the Setekh clan as royal bearer. I am here establishing the reconstructive lead taken by Michael Rice, who, like Frankfort and Kemp before him, has profoundly interrogated representations of nascent dynastic contestations of power in the pre- and then current dynastic stages around the standards of Hor and Setekh. Rice has shown that Setekh raised his royal, never-to-be-forgotten head in spasmodic but succeeding generations of royalty. Hotepsekhemwy, the first nsw of the second dynasty, carried Setekh's name in his titulary[24]; Khasekhemwy in the second dynasty displayed both the Setekh and Hor standards[25]; the seventh nsw of the second dynasty, Sekhemib (the heart of Setekh), utilised the Hor falcon until his later name-change to Peribsen, surmounting his serekh (cartouche) with the Setekh tjesm hound[26] and two kingly figures wearing the white crown profiled with the long bovid of the tjesm hound, Setekh, holding not the crook and flail characteristic of Wsir but the was and ankh, clearly Peribsen himself (it is not until the New Kingdom – 16 dynasties later – that Wsir is portrayed in the papyrus of Ani holding the was and ankh)[27]; during the 19th and 20th dynasties the Ramessides resurrected Setekh as a standard and the second nsw of the 19th dynasty, Seti I, the son of Rameses I, ascended the throne to display the tjesm hound prominently and, according to Rice, to honour Setekh "virtually as the equal once more of the greatest gods of Egypt"[28].

These attestations to Setekh's sporadic prominence as kinghead in Kmt confirm varying stages of contestation, unrest and incorporation. Setekh, therefore, is seen as representing a clannic interest that at one stage was prominent in Upper Kmt and was defeated by the clan of Hor (thus of Wsir), but was resurrected as contestation and unrest raised their heads. Since nsw Scorpion is represented as a pre-unification uniter-king of the South, through the use of war-like engagement, followed by Narmer/Menes in his eventual unification of South and North one hundred years later, it appears from the appearance of two major royal and funerary centres in this era, Abydju and Nekhen, that the Setekh and Hor clans may have emerged from these respective bases and contested/rivalled each other over control of trade routes from Nubia and further south[29]. Bard[30] solidified this perspective by stating that, "Geography – and access to trade routes and raw materials – may have played a part in the rise of the centers at Hierakonpolis, Naqada and Abydos. From Abydos [the domain of Khentiamenti, a canine deity] there are important desert routes leading into the Western Desert and from there south into Nubia... Regional polities with increasing control over their economies (agriculture, craft production, regional and long distance trade of goods and materials, and human labour) were undoubtedly developing at Abydos, Naqada and Hierakonpolis in later Naqada II times...". Although she recognises an elemental competition among polities, Bard does not emphasise that these conditions led to war. My perspective is strengthened by one writer who says that state formation can proceed from "factional competition" or "socio-economic troubles as the formation of antagonistic groups as a result of a process of social stratification" or that competition for prestige goods could have led to conflict[31]. These conditions were evident at Naqada II and constituted the basis of the unfolding drama under review, in which competing clans profoundly clashed over control of access to all trade and the southern perimeters, which constituted the three major power centres.

Interestingly, despite the evidence of her research, Bard[32] rejected the notion of "proto-states", leading to Southern unification on the basis of "little archaeological evidence". The confusion generated by this rejection is neutralised by the following paragraph, in which she agrees with John Baines' notion of a "proto-kingship" from Naqada II, which crystalises in "the later unification of southern and northern Egypt [and which] was a creation of this kingship" and its institutionalisation. What signifies her lack of rounded vision or perspective is the fact that she has not made an aggregate of the evidence, and significantly does not examine the prominent myth of the clans of Wsir/Hor narrating an important event, mythologically, which tells of profound conflict over existing conditions which inevitably led to defeat of the opposition and control by the Wsir/Hor victorious faction at Naqada III. Yet Bard is able to say, almost intuitively, that, "Warfare may have played a significant role in the final stages of unification...", although the author is still looking for physical archaeological evidence[33]. Bard went on to investigate the true meaning of the Narmer palette, which demonstrates the conquest of a bearded figure and compares this with Gunter Dreyer's excavated clay labels from tomb U-j, in which a crowned figure is smiting a presumed enemy, and finally admits the importance of warfare in the "consolidation of the early state"[34].

Comparatively, we can look at the origins and development of communities in Africa in which the machinations of the proto-state were played out. Shaka the Zulu emerged from a small clan/village, but was successfully able to impose his might upon the land of Azania through warfare and conquest. For centuries Ethiopia was a basin of frequent clashes between proto-states, until one emperor was successful in imposing his will upon the entire population, uniting the state under one ruler and government. Even under the reign of Haile Selassie, who publicly advocated the shooting of soldiers for robbing farmers of their produce, "Predatory appropriation continued well into the Italian occupation of 1936"[35]. This history of predatory oppression appears to be a direct outgrowth of warring proto-states in which the victor feeds his army through despotic appropriating practices.

In Egyptology, Wsir has sometimes been described as representing one part of Kmt, the Lower, while Setekh was supposedly representative of Upper Kmt and the desert, which points to his authentic southern origins as it is the white crown which is ritualised as the conference of monarchial power. However, we do have the records of the final rites funerary books to confirm the earliest attestations of place of origin of the three primary contenders.

> Worship of Osiris Wennefer, the Great God who dwells in the Thinite [Abydos] nome... first-born son of Nut, begotten of Geb... whose White Crown is tall, Sovereign of gods and men. He has taken the crook and flail and office of his forefathers...

> ...you have appeared as Lord of Busiris [Lower Kmt], as the Ruler who is in Abydos [Abydju/Upper Kmt]. Lord of Lords, Ruler of Rulers, who took possession of the Two Lands even in the womb of Nut...[36].

The above confirms Wsir's predestiny, as it was willed, through procreation and the fact that he was the eldest son, to rule as earthly king. It also states that Wsir had replicated the tradition of his forefathers in his rule as king, but as we know, Geb and Nut are divine and celestial representations and their existence cannot be accepted as royal and earthly, although contradictorily, Geb is an earth netjer. Thus, this lends credence to my hypothesis that the invention of Wsir as descendant of a divine couple and the great-grandson of Netjer Atum gives tremendous validating weight to him as predestined ruler of all of Kmt. There are no earthly ancestors before his appearance, which confirm his mysterious persona in Kmt. But it is interesting, nevertheless, that he is irresistibly portrayed as wearing the white crown of Upper Kmt and not the dual red and white crowns. Again, elsewhere[37] he is represented by the scribe Ani as "Then I will recite glorifications of the White Crown..." This omission shows both his origin in the south and his rulership as emerging from the south, and its authentication of the birthplace of southern hegemony before unifying a divided Kmt. He is also portrayed as "he who is in Nekhen"[38]. Compare this with Wsir's location in the desert which now appears to be a place of peace and silence (BCFD Chapter 175); the harshness of Wsir's death is mediated by apportioning him the peace of the desert, a conceptual tautology as it appeared to be politically defined as a place of *isfet* and of the uncivilised: "the Egyptian pictorially grouped the foreigner with the beast of the desert and pictorially denied the foreigner the blessings of fertility and uniformity"[39]. Yet, in the early predynastic era, the deserts of Nubia and those of the South-East and the West contained abundant evidence of the principles of scientific quest, ordered settlement, organised societies, and high level artistic pursuits which provided the platform/paradigm and impetus for the emergence of the Kmtan state. The apparent contradiction of the Kmtu has to be understood in the periodic necessity of rationalisation and justification, a commonality in all states with different classes, contestation and conflict.

But if Wsir were the great-grandson of God, why would he be granted one part of a country that is unmistakably geographically connected, except this may represent a component, in the initial stages of negotiation, between the two clans; a division of the land to create equity. This is where the propaganda of the state is brought to bear on Wsir's authentication. Note that there is no such record of state for Setekh's inclusion as dual king. He is merely defined as a disorderly brother who utilises brute force to enforce his claim and is momentarily pacified. We should also note that the BD, otherwise *The Book of Coming Forth by Day* (BCFD), quite clearly states that Wsir "took possession of the Two Lands", which implies the use of force - the same unreasoned force that Setekh is tarred with and portrayed as wicked! It is therefore open to interpretation that the Wsir/Hor clan was not satisfied with control of one part of Kmt, but wanted the entirety of the geographical land mass.

We should not miss the point that Wsir is portrayed as dying in Buto (Busiris) but resurrecting in Abydju (Abydos), the latter a feat that could not be assigned to him if his supposed roots were not embedded there. Since the Hor standard has been found in abundance in Nekhen, not Abydju, it is curious that his family did not bury him there. The reasoned deduction would therefore be that Abydju is the historic predynastic centre for royal authority, not just for burial, and the state premeditatedly buried him there to authenticate Hor, his successor. Abydju was royal-focused as a place of origin of the first predynastic kings and became a funerary cult-centre for the monarchy. This consideration permitted Wsir's body to be seen to be buried there for authentication and for the purpose of state propaganda.

 Here we can make a more recent connection with death and burial to historically explain Wsir's own death and burial. Budge stated that Wsir's head and hair were buried in Abydju[40], though dying in Buto, and comparatively, according to Johnson, Oranyan, the legendary first Yoruba oba (king) of Oyo may have died at Oko, "... but his grave with an obelisk over it is certainly shown at Ile-Ife to this day". (Law refuted this by saying archaeological excavations found no grave[41].) It is a custom among the Yorubas – a custom observed to this day – to pare the nails and *shave the head of any one who dies at a considerable distance from the place where they would have him buried. These relics are taken to the place of internment, and there decently buried, the funeral obsequies being scrupulously observed as if the corpse itself were buried there*"[42] (emphasis added). This would place ritual meaning on the assertion that Wsir died in Buto but was permanently interred in the place of his authentication, Abydju.

One can understand better now why there were several significant burial places associated with his death throughout Kmt: mock funerals were consecrated in his memory in all the hespu (nomes) of his kingdom. To strengthen this notion, there is a further example of a Bini (of Benin City) king commandeering his grandson Esikpa to pacify the inhabitants of Lagos. After accomplishing his task, Esikpa died and his remains were returned to and interred in Benin

City[43]. This tradition should not be viewed as unique, as it is still resonant and practiced today in many parts of the world.

Elsewhere, Wsir's enemies, perpetually expressed in all of the funerary literature, are acted upon in the BCFD, by one "...who slew the foes of Osiris and imprisoned those who rebelled against him"[44]. During Ptolemaic domination, Wsir-Sarapis (Wsir as sacred bull) stands behind the kneeling figure of Setekh with knives stuck in his stomach before the standing figures of the four sons of Hor, each with an upraised knife[45]. Compare this perspective with Chapter 175 of the BCDF, where reason prevails in Ra in restraining the soul of Setekh while in his barque[46]. Wsir is thus rightly characterised by Ani (in this book which became a standard for those who could afford it in the New Kingdom, undoubtedly well-paid palace officials like Ani) as "... Him who pacified the Two Lands"[47]. Politically, pacification can only be obtained by diplomatic or violent means; the former has to be dismissed as we have already seen the enemies of Wsir being imprisoned and later sacrificed as goats, i.e. just as goats are offered as sacrifice to the divinities, so are the enemies of Wsir[48].

8.8   Concluding comments

The state, in its continuous attempt to validate the falcon clan in the eyes of the population, incorporates Khentiamenti into the persona of Wsir. Khentiamenti is represented, according to Frankfort, as a dog or jackal, and is referred to as "Chief of the Westerners"[49], a title which demonstrated power over the dead that was later conferred upon Wsir by his state-controlling handlers in the Middle Kingdom. Since Khentiamenti is portrayed as a dog or jackal it is obvious that the selectivity and intentionality of this divinity by the state was no accident; it was designed to authenticate Wsir in the eyes of the unsettled, perhaps unpacified, followers of Setekh, although Khentiamenti supposedly represented the canine Inkpu (Anubis). The fact is that the canine is inalterably associated with the city of Abdyju, regardless of the ephemeral reigning deity. Ultimately, because of the holy, mysterious and heavenly origins and connections of Wsir, he became inevitably permanenised as an all-embracing entity: one who resurrects one who generates fertility; one who exists forever like Ra and Sopdet. This connection can also be better understood if we look at his parents: Geb the earth netjer, Nut the sky netjeret. Thus, Wsir is portrayed logically as inheriting both his father's and mother's characteristics, features and patrimony.

All of the above overt representation, however, unmistakably alludes to Setekh, subsequently transferred to Wsir. It is the canine family who is incorporated, which was a deliberate royal policy to legitimise the falcon clan in the eyes of the followers of Setekh. Thus the mechanism of the state was as far-reaching, propagandistic, and controlling in the third millennium BCE as it is in the 21st century current period.

Control of the state reflects control of images, literature, authenticity, and most importantly, incorporation. Physical violence was the initial triumphal method, but the psyche of the population had to be conquered or pacified by the use of cultural information as propaganda.

In closing, this chapter has attempted to demonstrate that Kmt, projected as part of the Middle East, is shown culturally and in terms of political systems to be intrinsically part of Africa. The themes of this anthology, which incorporate decolonisation, the Wehemu Mesu (repetition of the birth = Renaissance), and the historically attested longevity of pervasive African philosophy, are componentially and collectively intrinsic to an understanding of this essay, and thus of the first independent state in history, Kmt.

References

[1]Mordi, A. A. 1985. Traditional Rulers and Traditional Institutions. In O. Aborisade (Ed.). *Local Government and the Traditional Rulers in Nigeria, Ife*. Ile-Ife: University of Ife Press, pp. 17-19.
[2]Budge, E. A. 1969. *The Gods of the Egyptians, Studies in Egyptian Mythology*. New York: Dover Books.
[3]Mordi, A. A. 1985. Traditional Rulers and Traditional Institutions. In Aborisade (Ed.). *Local Government and the Traditional Rulers in Nigeria, Ife*. Ile-Ife: University of Ife Press, pp. 17-19.
[4]Castillos, J. J. 2009. The development and nature of inequality in early Egypt. *British Museum Studies in Ancient Egypt and Sudan*. Retrieved from: http://www. britishmuseum.org/research/online_journals/bmsaes/issue_13/castillos. aspx. [Date accessed: February 16, 2016.]
[5]Mordi, A. A. 1985. Traditional Rulers and Traditional Institutions. In Aborisade (Ed.). *Local Government and the Traditional Rulers in Nigeria, Ife*. Ile-Ife: University of Ife Press, pp. 17-19.
[6]Budge, E. A. W. 1973. Preface in *Osiris & The Egyptian Resurrection*, Vol. 1. New York: Dover Publications.
[7]Ibid.
[8]Frankfort, H. 1978. *Kingship and the Gods, A Study of Ancient Near Eastern Religion as the Integration of Society and Nature*. Chicago: The University of Chicago Press.
[9]Ibid.
[10]Budge, E. A. W. 1973. Preface in *Osiris & The Egyptian Resurrection*, Vol. 1. New York: Dover Publications.
[11]Ogunba, O. 1973. Ceremonies. In S. O. Biobaku (Ed.). *Sources of Yoruba History*. Oxford: Oxford University Press, pp. 87-110.
[12]Allen, J. 1988. *Genesis in Egypt: The Philosophy of Ancient Egyptian Creation Accounts*. New Haven: Yale Egyptological Studies.
[13]Frankfort, H. 1978. *Kingship and the Gods, A Study of Ancient Near Eastern Religion as the Integration of Society and Nature*. Chicago: The University of Chicago Press.
[14]Budge, E. A. W. 1973. Preface in *Osiris & The Egyptian Resurrection*, Vol. 1. New York: Dover Publications.
[15]Newberry, P. E. 1914. Notes of some Egyptian Nome Ensigns and their historical significance. *Ancient Egypt*, 1: 5-8.
[16]Campagno, M. 2003. From Kin-Chiefs to God-Kings Emergence and Consolidation of the State in Ancient Egypt (From Badarian to Early Dynastic Period, ca. 4500–2700 B.C.). Alain Anselin. 2000. *Cahiers Caribéens d'Egyptologie*. Martinique: Tyanaba.
[17]Olomola, I. 1985. Rituals and Stability: an examination of rituals and festivals as spectacular instruments of government in pre-colonial Nigeria. In O. Aborisade (Ed.). *Local Government and the Traditional Rulers in Nigeria, Ife*. Ile-Ife: University of Ife Press, pp. 283-304.
[18]Andelkovic, B. 2011. Political Organization in Egypt in the Predynastic Period. In E. Tweeter (Ed.). *Before the Pyramids: The Origins of Egyptian Civilization*. Chicago: The Oriental Institute of the University of Chicago, pp. 25-32.
[19]Johnson, S. 1921. *The History of the Yorubas*. London: Routledge Kegan Paul.
[20]Law, R. C. C. 1973. Traditional History. In S. O. Biobaku (Ed.). *Sources of Yoruba History*. Oxford: Oxford University Press, pp. 9-24.
[21]Olomola, I. 1985. Rituals and Stability: an examination of rituals and festivals as spectacular instruments of government in pre-colonial Nigeria. In O. Aborisade (Ed.). *Local Government and the Traditional Rulers in Nigeria, Ife*: Ile-Ife: University of Ife Press, pp. 283-304.
[22]Agrawal, M. M. 1985. Morals and the Values of Human Life. In P. O. Bodunrin (Ed.). *Philosophy in Africa*. Ile-Ife: University of Ife Press, pp. 146-154.
[23]Rice, M. 2006. *Swifter Than The Arrow, The Golden Hunting Hounds of Ancient Egypt*. London: I.B. Tauris.
[24]Ibid.
[25]Ibid.
[26]Ibid.

[27]Budge, E. A. W. 1973. Preface in *Osiris & The Egyptian Resurrection*. Vol. 1. New York: Dover Publications.

[28]Rice, M. 2006. *Swifter Than The Arrow, The Golden Hunting Hounds of Ancient Egypt*, London: I.B. Tauris.

[29]Bard, K. A. 2000. The Emergence of the Egyptian State. In I. Shaw (Ed.). *The Oxford History of Ancient Egypt*. Oxford: Oxford University Press, pp. 61-88.

[30]Bard, K. 2007. *An Introduction to the Archaeology of Ancient Egypt*. Malden: Wily-Blackwell Publishers.

[30]Campagno, M. 2003. From Kin-Chiefs to God-Kings Emergence and Consolidation of the State in Ancient Egypt (From Badarian to Early Dynastic Period, ca. 4500–2700 B.C.). *Cahiers Caribéens d'Egyptologie*. Martinique: Tyanaba.

[32]Bard, K. 2007. *An Introduction to the Archaeology of Ancient Egypt*. Malden: Wily-Blackwell Publishers.

[33]Ibid.

[34]Ibid.

[35]Tibebu, T. 1995. *The Making of Modern Ethiopia 1896–1974*. New Jersey: The Red Sea Press.

[36]Faulkner, R. 1994. *The Book of the Dead/The Book of Going Forth by Day*. San Francisco: Chronicle Books.

[37]Ibid.

[38]Ibid.

[39]Wilson, J. A. 1977. The Function of the State. In H. Frankfort et al. (Eds.). *The Intellectual Adventure of Ancient Man*. Chicago & London: The University of Chicago Press, pp. 185-201.

[40]Budge, E. A. W. 1969. *The Gods of the Egyptians, Studies in Egyptian Mythology*. New York: Dover Books.

[41]Law, R. C. C. 1973. Traditional History. In S. O. Biobaku (Ed.). *Sources of Yoruba History*, Oxford: OUP, pp. 9-24.

[42]Johnson, S. 1921. *The History of the Yorubas*. Routledge Kegan Paul: London.

[43]Law, R. C. C. 1973. Traditional History. In S. O. Biobaku (Ed.). *Sources of Yoruba History*, Oxford: OUP, pp. 9-24.

[44]Faulkner, R. 1994. *The Book of the Dead/The Book of Going Forth by Day*. San Francisco: Chronicle Books.

[45]Budge, E. A. W. 1973. Preface in *Osiris & The Egyptian Resurrection*, Vol. 1. New York: Dover Publications.

[46]Faulkner, R. 1994. *The Book of the Dead/The Book of Going Forth by Day*. San Francisco: Chronicle Books.

[47]Ibid.

[48]Ibid.

[49]Frankfort, H. 1978, *Kingship and the Gods, A Study of Ancient Near Eastern Religion as the Integration of Society and Nature*. Chicago: The University of Chicago Press.

Part 3

Higher Education, Africanisation and Language

Chapter 9

University Students' Activism on Malawi's new language-in-education policy: Singing the African Renaissance Tune

Gregory Kamwendo
Faculty of Education, University of Zululand

9.1   Introduction

In 2014, a new language-in-education policy was announced in Malawi. The policy came through the Education Act of 2012, which stipulated that "the medium of instruction in schools and colleges shall be English"[1]. This announcement pointed out that from then on, English would be the medium of instruction from the first class of primary school up to tertiary level. The previous language policy had placed Chichewa (the national language) as the medium of instruction from Standard (Grade) 1 up to Standard 4, while English used to take over as the medium of instruction from Standard 5 onwards. Naturally, the new language policy was accepted by some but rejected by others. This was expected since language policy in education is one of the most hotly contested issues in Malawi and elsewhere in other African polities, given the high degree of thirst amongst people to become competent in international languages such as English, French, Portuguese and others. International languages are considered to be passports to upward socio-economic and political mobility. For some time, there have been concerns that Malawian learners' competence in English is not good enough, thus when the government in 1996 issued a directive on mother tongue instruction for the first four years of primary school education, some people feared and argued that the language policy would diminish learners' opportunities to gain competence in English. However, the policy directive was never implemented due to a number of factors, which the current chapter will not address due to space limitations thus readers are directed to Kamwendo[2].

When Malawi released the new language-in-education policy in 2014, advocates of mother tongue instruction were naturally disappointed, whilst on the other hand, proponents of English as a medium of instruction were happy with the new language policy. Among the critics of the new language policy were language scholars (see, for example, Miti[3] and Kamwendo[4]), University of Malawi students (see, for example, Kishindo[5]), and some members of the general public. I pay special attention to students of the University of Malawi in their role as critics of the new language-in-education policy.

The University of Malawi is the oldest university in Malawi. It is a public university that was established through an Act of Parliament. In 2014, students in the Faculty of Education at the Chancellor College campus pursued activities that were aimed at persuading government to reverse the new language policy. It is significant to note that university students, who are prospective teachers, decided to participate in actions and debates that speak to language policy reversal. This should be appreciated within the context that universities are institutions of debate and enlightenment. In addition, students are the leaders of tomorrow, and it is important that they voice their views on matters of national importance. One should also recall that during the one-party dictatorship under the founding president, Dr Hastings Kamuzu Banda, academics and students at the University of Malawi could not openly voice their opinions on matters of national relevance. Despite being knowledge producers, university academics and students in Kamuzu Banda's Malawi were silenced, resulting in severe loss of academic freedom (Africa Watch[6]; Kerr and Mapanje[7]). In contrast, in the current chapter I address the post-Banda era (an era of democracy), in which students are free to petition or question government policies or decisions without attracting detention and other forms of repressive treatment.

It is also important to appreciate the sociolinguistic context within which students at the University of Malawi staged a protest against English as the medium of instruction. In sociolinguistic terms, Malawi is classified as an English-speaking country, however only a small section of the population speaks/uses English as a home language. Going by the 1998 population census report (the most recent population census report that carries language data), less than 1% of the population cited English as the language of household communication[8]. Chichewa and other indigenous languages serve predominantly as languages of household communication. To this end, most of the learners encounter English for the first time at school, which is why the University of Malawi students question the wisdom of expecting such primary school learners to learn through a language that is totally foreign from their first class at the primary school. This amounts to setting up the learners for failure.

The focus of the chapter is on the university students' activism in relation to the new language policy. Which song are the students singing? I argue that the students are singing an African Renaissance song through their activism. The chapter employs the African Renaissance (Magkoba[9]; Kamwendo[10]; Banda Saayman[11]; Ajulu[12]; Mbeki[13]; Moodley[14]) and the decolonisation of the mind (Wa Thiongo[15]; Ndlovu-Gatsheni[16]) as its central theoretical foundations. This student activism constitutes what can be called 'voices from below'[17] or alternatively, 'linguistic citizenship'[18]. The chapter has been structured as follows. In the next section, I provide the theoretical orientation to the chapter, after which I discuss the research methodology employed. Thereafter, I present and discuss the findings. In the final section of the chapter, I provide a summary and conclusion.

9.2   Theoretical orientation

9.2.1 The African Renaissance: A brief overview

The African Renaissance is not a new concept. It has been around for some time but it received a special boost from the then Deputy President (and later President) of post-apartheid South Africa, Thabo Mbeki. The African Renaissance has attracted a lot of debate, leaving the concept lacking a common understanding and agreement, but in no way do I consider this to be a weakness. The

African Renaissance is there for everyone to grapple with, and it should therefore not be seen as a monopoly of academics. Even within the higher education environment, the African Renaissance has not been confined to one discipline, but rather it has been found to be of relevance to a diversity of disciplines, for example, theology and religion[19], language policy and planning (e.g. Kamwendo[20]; Moodley[21]), political science (e.g. Moeletsi Mbeki[22]) and economics (e.g. Ajulu[23]). I also take into consideration the notion of coloniality in the post-colonial times, that is to say that decolonisation has not yet been concluded - it is still a work in progress. As Ndlovu-Gatsheni[24] has argued, the process of decolonisation has been rough, and it remains incomplete. In fact, the over-reliance on former colonial languages (such as English) is one example of the failure to decolonise the African mind and other spheres.

As mentioned previously, it was the post-apartheid South African government, through the efforts of the then Deputy President (and later President), Thabo Mbeki, that gave a new lease on life to the notion of the African Renaissance. Moeletsi Mbeki[25], who also happens to be a brother to Thabo Mbeki, asked whether South Africa was going to be the midwife or even father of the African Renaissance. Were other African countries ready to accept the new South Africa (having emerged out of apartheid) as the leader? Whether South Africa leads or does not lead the African Renaissance agenda is perhaps less important than how individuals, institutions or countries push the African Renaissance agenda forward.

But what does the Renaissance mean and imply? I agree with Moeletsi Mbeki[26] that the African Renaissance "has come to mean many things". For example, Ajulu[27] argued that the African Renaissance can be "broadly interpreted as calling for African political renewal and economic regeneration". The African Renaissance means that after having come out of slavery and colonisation, Africa has to regain its rightful position in the world. This means that Africa has to go through a process of being born again, and it is in that regard that the African Renaissance is described variously as rebirth, reawakening, revival, rejuvenation, renewal, regeneration, or restoration. A renaissance is necessary given that although slavery is no longer alive, that African countries have achieved independence, and that apartheid has been abolished in South Africa, the continent continues to suffer from a heavy dependency on the West (especially the former colonising countries), mental slavery (resulting in self-doubt and glorification of anything Western), and a lack of real political and economic independence. Africa has to wake up from its deep sleep and rejuvenate itself in all aspects of life.

As Ndlovu-Gatsheni[28] has rightly noted, decolonisation is actually a myth since coloniality remains strong in various spheres in Africa. For example, Africa remains linguistically colonised. One finds that African countries continue to be named after the former colonisers' linguistic identities, for example Lusophone Africa, Francophone Africa, and Anglophone Africa. Despite the fact that former colonial languages are minority languages (demographically speaking), they continue to dominate and decide the fate of Africans (the majority of whom have no competence in these languages). In view of this over-dependence on the languages of the former colonial rulers, it is important that Africans seek linguistic freedom (or linguistic decolonisation). This linguistic freedom should not mean abandoning international (and former colonisers') languages, but it should mean placing African languages in favourable positions to perform some of the functions that are currently monopolised by the languages that were implanted by colonialism. In the current chapter, linguistic emancipation or the restoration of linguistic dignity is being championed by the students of the University of Malawi, who question an English-only medium of instruction policy in Malawi.

As pointed out earlier, linguistic colonialism has had an effect (whether positive or negative) on African countries. Through colonialisation, Western languages such as English, French, German, Portuguese and others found their way into Africa. Whilst these languages are generally not spoken by the majority of Africans, they remain key languages since they occupy official language status. The same languages also dominate education systems, where they serve as subjects of study as well as media of teaching and learning. As I have outlined, Africa finds itself being divided into linguistic zones that are named after the languages of the former colonising powers. Such linguistic zones include Lusophone Africa (for example, Mozambique and Angola), Francophone Africa (for example, Senegal and Niger) and Anglophone Africa (for example, Malawi and Swaziland). These labels do not mean much and they are actually less meaningful since the majority of the people speak one or more African languages and not these Western languages. The continued use of these linguistic labels is a reminder that Africa is still linguistically colonised. Just think of Swaziland which is a predominantly siSwati-speaking country, and yet it is strangely classified as an English-speaking country. There is a need to pose serious questions such as: Why should we not call it a siSwati-speaking country? Why must African countries, after many years of independence, continue to be named according to the languages of their former colonial rulers?

There is no denying the need to learn and use Western languages such as English, but what remains unwarranted are language policies and practices that privilege such languages to the detriment of Africans who are not competent speakers of such foreign languages. What is being called for is the elevation of African languages so that they can enter domains that are currently dominated by Western languages. This does not mean throwing away Western languages, but rather ensuring an equal footing for Western and African languages. To this end, the society praises the post-apartheid South African government for raising the status of nine African languages to official status, and thereby having eleven official languages. However, this has unfortunately not diminished the dominance of English.

In higher education, some South African universities have taken the "bold move to have African languages as LoLT, but such bold moves are very limited in magnitude and number not only in South Africa, but also on the African continent as a whole"[29]. The University of KwaZulu-Natal (UKZN) in South Africa is one university that stands out very clearly in terms of its transformation agenda, which has seen the elevation of isiZulu as an additional language of scholarship. This university has a bilingual (isiZulu and English) policy, and isiZulu is used a medium of teaching and learning in some modules. Of course the policy has attracted its supporters as well as its critics, but the point is that UKZN has taken a rare bold move to promote an African language[30]. Elsewhere in other universities in South Africa and other African countries, African languages have limited space in the academic enterprise, thus linguistic decolonisation in all spheres of life in Africa remain a work in progress. It is a business to which university students (who are the main actors of the events discussed in the current chapter) are making a contribution.

9.2.2   Student activism and linguistic citizenship: An overview

This chapter focusses on university students' activism, but what is student activism? In this section of the chapter I attempt to briefly unpack this concept. Student activism refers to activities that are undertaken by students in order to bring about change in society. These activities could be aimed at driving social, economic, political, educational and/or other forms of change. Students at various levels of education have participated and continue to participate in activism. The target of student activism varies from case to case, for example, student activism can be focused on internal matters, such as when a matter lies within an institution, or it can be a society-wide issue. With reference to South Africa, perhaps one unforgettable act of student activism was the 1976 Soweto protests. The protests, staged by black (African) students were a denunciation of the use of Afrikaans as a medium of instruction in schools. Some black students lost their lives as the white regime ruthlessly suppressed the protest with the use of heavily armed power. What the Soweto students did can be called action from below; the students campaigned for the use of English as the medium of instruction, not African indigenous languages. The preference for English was part of the philosophy of the liberation struggle in which English was the language that was used by the liberation movements to communicate with the outer world. English, unlike Afrikaans, was positively valued for its importance in global political and economic spheres.

In post-apartheid South Africa, students (especially university students) have not been idle in the language struggles. For example, 2015 saw a number of protests staged by black students across South African universities, known as the 'Fees Must Fall' campaign. Students staged protests whose goal was to force government to introduce free education. Another bone of contention has been the need to transform universities so that they are in line with the post-apartheid reality. For example, at the University of Stellenbosch, students have voiced concerns about the lack, or slow pace, of transformation. This has led to the establishment of a group called Open Stellenbosch (which is predominantly made up of students), which is concerned with what it calls institutionalised racism and a language policy that favours Afrikaans speakers. Black students have called for a transformation of the language policy, as the language policy and related academic practices make it difficult for non-Afrikaans-speaking students to study successfully at the University. In a related case, students at the University of North West (Potchefstroom campus) also complained about racism, as well as being excluded from academic and campus life, on the grounds of not being able to speak Afrikaans. At the Cape Peninsula University of Technology (CPUT), a special dispensation was granted for students to write examinations and tests in Afrikaans at the Wellington campus. Students who had for three years learnt through Afrikaans in the Agriculture Department refused to write examinations in English and they were eventually allowed to write in Afrikaans. The medium of instruction at CPUT is English and the Wellington campus was the exception to the rule[31]. The South African university students' protest activities can be linked to the notion of linguistic citizenship. According to Stroud[32], linguistic citizenship refers to "the situation where speakers themselves exercise control over their language, deciding what languages are, what they may imply and where language issues (especially in educational sites) are discursively tied to a range of social issues, policy issues and questions of equity".

9.3   Methodology

This chapter took a qualitative approach to research, employing documentary research as the method of data collection[33]. The following documents were found to be helpful in providing relevant information on student activism with a link to the new language policy in Malawi: (i) newspaper reports; (ii) the text of the students' petition to the Minister of Education in Malawi; (iii) the BAAL petition; (iv) students' signatures and declaration in support of the BAAL petition; (iv) email communications; and (v) one scholarly publication that is exclusively focused on the language-in-education policy in Malawi. The use of documentary sources in any study has to be accompanied by the usual quality control mechanisms applicable to other information sources and/or methods of collecting data. To this end, I applied quality control notions of authenticity (evidence being genuine, reliable and of dependable origin) and credibility (evidence being free from error and/or distortion)[34]. All the documents were subjected to an authenticity and credibility test.

9.3.1   Presentation and discussion of findings

As I have argued earlier, what the university students did in 2014 amounts to acts of linguistic citizenship that advance the African Renaissance agenda. I now proceed to discuss the students' activism as follows:

i.   Students presented a petition to government, asking for the reversal of the language policy, i.e. the reinstatement of Chichewa and/or other indigenous languages as media of instruction in the first four classes of primary school.

ii.   Students participated in a radio debate on the language policy issue (see Kishindo[35]).

iii.   The students joined members of the British Association of Applied Linguistics (BAAL) in signing a petition which was to be delivered to the government of Malawi through its embassy in London in the United Kingdom.

9.3.2   Students' petition to government

Students from the Faculty of Education at Chancellor College of the University of Malawi marched to the Zomba district commissioner's office and delivered a petition that expressed their discontent over the policy of exclusive use of the English language as a medium of instruction. The petition, dated 13 March 2014, essentially argued that the new language policy goes against UNESCO's[36; 37] principle of mother tongue instruction:

> We as education students at Chancellor College of the University of Malawi, would like to express our discontent over the Ministry of Education's plan to implement a policy that aims at introducing English, obviously a foreign language, as the language of instruction right from standard one in the country's primary education[38].

The issue raised by the protesting students points to the core of UNESCO's[39; 40] position on the medium of instruction for the early phases of education. The United Nations Educational, Scientific and Cultural Organisation has over the years collected empirical evidence that demonstrates that learners who start their schooling by learning through a familiar language such as a mother tongue perform better than their counterparts who engage with schooling through an unfamiliar language. In the case of Malawi, English is predominantly an unfamiliar language, and as the students rightly called it, a foreign language. English is not the mother tongue or home language of the average Malawian learner[41], thus the learners have to learn the English language and gain reasonable competency in it before they can begin to use the same language for learning other subjects.

The students proceeded to dismiss the motivation behind the new language policy. According to the then Minister of Education, Mr Kanyumba, as cited in Kamwendo[42], Malawian learners are not good at speaking English, so the new language policy was meant to improve proficiency and grammar, yet the students argued that:

> We feel that the desire for coming up with a new breed of good English speakers and grammarians is not enough of a reason to drag the Ministry of Education into preference of the new policy over the current one[43].

The petition raised 12 points[44]:

1. *"Mother tongue instruction supports local culture and parental involvement. The use of a familiar language for instruction validates local culture and knowledge, creating a bridge between the formal school system and children's home and community environment. This is true to a very large extent as mother tongue instruction facilitates parental involvement and strengthens community support for education, since language is not a barrier to participating in children's schooling. Parents are required to check the academic progress of their children who at the early stages struggle to settle in school. It will be difficult for the parents (most of whom are not familiar with English), therefore, to follow up on the academic progress of their children."*

   I wish to stress that the use of a local or familiar language as a medium of teaching and learning ensures that upon stepping into a classroom, the learner does not lose the mother tongue; there is no disconnect between the language of the home and the language of the school[45].

   By using the mother tongue as a medium of teaching and learning, the language is being validated as a worthwhile language. When a learner goes to school and finds that his or her language is not used as the medium of instruction, or when he or she is even banned from speaking the language within the school premises, a clear statement is being made that the learner's mother tongue is worthless. When one's language is rejected as worthless, the speakers of that language are essentially declared as worthless. This is how during the colonial era, learners such as Wa Thiongo[46] were punished and humiliated at school for speaking an African language. Even in the post-colonial times, there are cases of schools that ban the speaking of African languages within the school premises. This practice is inimical to the goals of the African Renaissance, that is, to restore the dignity of African languages in formal domains such as education and others.

2. *"The circular issued by The Ministry of Education, Science and Technology in 1996 recognises that learners achieve better education results if learning is in their language of play. As a matter of fact, the circular encouraged primary school teachers to use a familiar local language to explain English concepts whenever necessary."*

This policy, which was never implemented[47], was meant to reduce linguistic barriers in the teaching and learning process. The unimplemented language policy directive sang the African Renaissance tune in the sense that African languages had been designated to make teaching and learning free of linguistic barriers.

3. *"Experience has shown that no country has developed while using a foreign language as the main means of classroom instruction. The policy appears to equate good English-speaking to development which is one of the goals of education. On the contrary, if one looks at the global chart of countries that have seen all sorts of development come their way, it becomes clear that it is only those that have been using local languages that are progressing, for example,all the developed nations of Europe, America and Asia use their own languages as tools for learning in schools and children. If Malawi is to adopt such type of a language policy, the socio-economic gap between the elite and the majority will continue to broaden."*

On this point, the students stressed the critical importance and need for Malawi to wean itself from the undue linguistic dependence on the former coloniser's language. They proceeded to argue, on the same lines as the forefathers of the Pan-Africanist movement and the African Renaissance, that the continued placement of Malawian indigenous languages on the periphery of the socio-economic, political and development agenda is a recipe for underdevelopment. Dijte[48] clearly demonstrated that whilst there is need to use exoglossic languages such as English, the neglect or abandonment of the use of indigenous languages is one of the causes of Africa's failure to achieve sustainable development. As Alexander[49] asked, 'Is it possible to achieve a true African Renaissance without taking African languages on board?' The answer is NO. The continued over-dependence on the languages of the former colonisers in education is further testimony to what Gatsheni-Ndlovu[50] referred to as coloniality in the post-colonial era.

4. *"It is not mother tongue instruction that lowers education standards. In fact there are lots of interfering factors such as lack of motivation for teachers and lack of resources just to mention but a few. We feel that the issue of language is just coming in as a scapegoat."*

That Malawi has one of the most poorly resourced education systems in the world has been documented by the World Bank[51], thus one cannot expect the miracle of high standards of education.

5. *"The use of foreign language (English) for instruction proved a flop when it was once implemented in Zambia, Kenya and Ghana and it is in the records of the Ministry of Education that once such moves flopped in Zambia, they came to learn in Malawi on how we do using mother tongue at the beginning of the first grades then switch to the foreign language."*

    It is surprising that despite the fact that the English-only as medium of instruction policy has failed to work elsewhere, Malawi has forged ahead with the same failed policy. As mentioned in point 6 below, other African countries have noted the pedagogical inadequacy of the English-only policy, and have thus opted to use mother tongues as media of teaching and learning in the early phases of education.

6. *"Fellow SADC member states such as South Africa, Namibia, Zimbabwe, Mozambique and Zambia have adopted serious advocacy for the use of the child's own language as a language of learning in the early years of primary school."*

    The students recognise that all is not bleak, given that some African countries are taking steps to give African languages their rightful place in education as mentioned in point 5. Whilst some SADC states are walking the path of promoting African languages as media of instruction, other member states such as Botswana are advancing the use of English as a medium of instruction as early as possible (see Republic of Botswana[52]).

7. *"There is a usual misconception that long exposure to a foreign language (e.g. English) at an early age results in proficiency in that language. On the contrary, empirical facts as supported by numerous research results show that children who learn how to read and write first in their own language show better proficiency in the second language than those who start with the foreign language".*

    Starting to learn how to read and write in one's own mother tongue speaks well to two adages: charity begins at home, and education is a journey from the known to the unknown. The known is the mother tongue, while English (or any other foreign language) is the unknown.

8. *"Mother tongue instruction improves children's self-concept and identity and it is through identity that culture and tradition can only be validated and reinforced. And it should be known that one of the goals of education is the preservation of the very same culture."*

    Education can preserve or destroy culture and/or language. When a culture or a language is recognised and included in an education system, it gains positive value in the eyes of people. People whose language has been included in education feel good, and those whose language has not been included feel rejected (see, for example, the case of Botswana in Kamwendo, Jankie and Chebanne[53]).

9. *"When instruction is in the mother tongue, teachers and learners can interact more naturally and negotiate meanings together, which greatly improve the effectiveness of the learning process."*

    This point links very well to point 10 below, and both points 9 and 10 sit at the heart of Unesco's[54; 55] position on the role of the mother tongue as a medium of teaching and learning.

10. *"Presentation of curriculum content in an unfamiliar language requires an enormous amount of time to teach children to understand, speak, read and write, something that is extremely difficult and wastes valuable years in the early grades that would be spent in learning academic concepts in a mother language."*

    The presentation of curriculum in a language that learners are not familiar with means that learners now have to struggle with two issues. First, they have to struggle to learn the language through which they have to access the curriculum, and secondly, they have to learn the concepts being passed onto them through the curriculum. This amounts to a situation I describe as fighting a war on two fronts (the two fronts being language and curriculum).

11. *"Language is a vehicle of culture. Therefore, eliminating the only strongest surviving element of the native culture amongst our learners is a major blow to the much-talked about cultural preservation."*

    This point speaks to the heart of the African Renaissance agenda, that is, to restore the dignity and respect of and for African languages and cultures.

12. *"Learning concepts in a foreign language does not mean the mastery of that language. Thus, learning in English (thus, as language of classroom instruction) is different from learning English as a language, that is why there is English as a subject. Therefore, to claim that teaching pupils in English will result in learners speaking and writing good English is not true."*

    There is a need to make a very clear distinction between English as a subject of study and English as a medium of teaching and learning. The former is what can be used to improve learners' proficiency, and it should not be confused with the use of English as the linguistic medium of curriculum delivery. The students are thus correct when they advanced point 12 in their petition.

By delivering the petition, the students constituted themselves as what Lin[56] would call the voice from below. The student teachers, as prospective implementers of government policy, grabbed the opportunity to use their professional and academic knowledge to point out flaws in the new language policy. The students were arguing from a position of strength, backed by empirical evidence documented in the literature. The students' arguments were scholarly and convincing, but they fell on deaf ears. The government likely simply dismissed the students' petition as one of the many noises that students make. But this was not just one of those empty noises; it was a noise that carried a lot of scholarly and pedagogical wisdom regarding the newly released language-in-education policy.

9.3.3 Students' involvement in radio debates

It is important to note that the voices from below[57] also utilised the radio. To this end, a debate on the new language policy took place, involving the public, the University of Malawi's Centre for Language Studies (CLS), and the Faculty of Education students. The debates were aired by a Catholic Church radio called Radio Maria Malawi on 19th March 2014 and 12th April 2014[58]. It is significant to note that the debates were not covered by the government-funded Malawi

Broadcasting Corporation (MBC). One can easily assume that the public radio station, MBC, is a voice of the government; it has in the past not been known to host voices that are contrary to the government's views.

9.3.4　Students' participation in the BAAL petition

The University of Malawi students' participation in activities aimed at persuading the government of Malawi to re-think the language-in-education policy also involved a second petition, which was not produced by the students this time. The BAAL special interest group on language in Africa resolved to petition the government of Malawi. It was decided that some signatures would be collected for presentation to the Malawian embassy in London in the United Kingdom. Signatures were collected from BAAL members and other people, including staff and students of the University of Malawi. Staff and students of Chancellor College of the University of Malawi appended their signatures, with the following declaration: "I fully endorse the statement produced by the BAAL Language in Africa SIG, and its recommendations. I believe that the Government of Malawi needs to urgently review its decision to adopt a 'straight-for-English' and English only policy in education". Students who signed the petition identified themselves as Linguistics students.

The University of Malawi's students' activism in relation to the new language-in-education policy can be seen from the perspective of the notion of linguistic citizenship. According to this notion, it is language speakers themselves who take the responsibility into their own hands to develop and promote languages, and they do not wait for the state to do the job. As per the linguistics human rights paradigm, the state is expected to play a key role in language promotion. For instance, the state is expected to develop and promote indigenous languages for use in education as subjects of study and/or media of instruction. This is what the 1996 mother tongue instruction directive[59] was expected to achieve, but the state failed to implement the mother tongue policy, confirming what Bamgbose[60] called declaration without implementation. Instead of implementing the mother tongue instruction policy, the state instead changed its tune and opted for English medium instruction, thus confirming what Bamgbose[61] called a fluctuation in language policy. Since the state failed to deliver on mother tongue instruction, the university students decided to try to persuade and pressurise the state to re-think the new language policy and re-consider implementing the abandoned mother tongue instruction policy.

It is significant that university students, some of whom were training to be language teachers, engaged in activities aimed at persuading the state to reverse its position on the language-in-education policy. The students, as people who are well versed in Linguistics and Language Education, have decided to serve as what Lin[62] would call the voice from below. This voice from below is responding to the controversial and problematic voice from above, i.e. the new language-in-education policy. In a democracy, it is expected that the voice from above (pronouncements by the state) will be met by the voices from below, and that the voices from below can bring about change in the content of the voice from above. Much as the students did not eventually succeed in making the government reverse the new language policy it is significant that they chose not to be silent. In a democracy, some campaigns take time to reap results however, so one must not look for immediate outcomes.

With regard to voices from below, I distinguish between what I have called voices of ignorance versus voices of knowledge. The voices of ignorance refer to voices that are made out of emotions, without the support of professional and/or scholarly evidence. This is not uncommon given that language is one aspect of life on which almost everyone thinks they have the authority to comment. In contrast, some areas seem to be so specialised that people are not quick to comment on them. Most people, by virtue of being a speaker of a language, grant themselves the authority to register strong views on that language. On the other hand, the very same people find themselves lacking the authority to comment on issues associated with hard science disciplines. For example, how many people can comment authoritatively about issues such as nuclear physics, industrial chemistry, heart transplanting, test tube babies, the zika virus and others? People would tend to leave these matters to the specialised professionals. But when it comes to language, everyone, even the most uninformed, think that they have the authority to voice their position on a language matter. The second type of voice is the voice of knowledge, which comes from people who possess expert knowledge. For example, researchers, academics, practitioners and university students fall into this category. Of particular interest is that as students of linguistics and/or language education, the students display good knowledge of the field of language teaching. For example, the students' arguments in support of mother tongue instruction show that they are aware of UNESCO's[63; 64] position on medium of instruction, as well as the clear distinction between English as a subject versus English as a medium of instruction.

9.4   Summary and conclusion

It is significant to observe that university students, some of whom are training to become language teachers, engaged in activities aimed at persuading the state to reverse its position on the new language-in-education policy. The students, as people who are well versed in Linguistics and Language Education, have decided to serve as what Lin[65] would call the voice from below. I have argued that students' activism fits neatly into the African Renaissance agenda. It is very clear from the students' arguments that they act from a well-informed position, for example they know the place of indigenous languages as well the place of English in the education system. The students serve as an important voice in the campaign to elevate indigenous languages so that they can play respectable, meaningful and pedagogically sound roles in education. It is important to note that the university students are not linguistically colonised. Their arguments point to the decolonisation of the mind (cf Wa Thiongo[66]) as well as the Africanisation of the curriculum, i.e. Africanising the linguistic medium through which the curriculum has to be delivered (cf. Msila & Gumbo[67]). These students refused to join the choruses that denigrate African languages and glorify English (and other Western languages) at the expense of indigenous African languages (cf Kamwendo[68]). These are students who are well placed to contribute to the liberation of Africans from the bondage of linguistic imperialism. Although these University of Malawi students did not name themselves as agents of the African Renaissance, I maintain that their actions speak volumes about the need for an African linguistic renaissance.

References

[1]Republic of Malawi. 2012. *Education Act of 2012.* Lilongwe: Government of Malawi.

[2]Kamwendo, G. 2008. The bumpy road to mother tongue instruction in Malawi. *Journal of Multilingual and Multicultural Development,* 29(5): 353-363.

[3]Miti, L. M. (Ed.). 2015. *The language of instruction question in Malawi.* Cape Town: Centre for Advanced Studies of African Society.

[4]Kamwendo, G. H. 2016. The new language of instruction policy in Malawi: A house standing on a shaky foundation. *International Review of Education,* 62(2): 221-228.

[5]Kishindo, P. J. 2015. The bird that was not allowed to fly: The case of mother tongue language-in-education policy in Malawi. In L. M. Miti (Ed.). *The language of instruction question in Malawi.* Cape Town: Centre for Advanced Studies of African Society, pp. 9-28.

[6]Africa Watch. 1991. *Academic freedom and human rights abuses in Africa.* London: Human Rights Watch.

[7]Kerr, D., & Mapanje, J. 2002. Academic freedom and the University of Malawi. *African Studies Review,* 45(2): 73-91.

[8]Republic of Malawi. 1998. *Malawi 1998 population census report.* Zomba: National Statistical Office.

[9]Makgoba, M. W. (Ed.). 1999. *African Renaissance: The new struggle.* Cape Town: Mafube Publishers.

[10]Kamwendo, G. H. 2010. Denigrating the local, glorifying the foreign: Language policies in the era of African Renaissance. *International Journal of African Renaissance Studies,* 5(2): 270-282.

[11]Banda, Z., & Saayman, W. 2015. Renaissance and rebirth: A perspective on the African Renaissance from Christian mission praxis. *Missionalia,* 43(2): 131-152.

[12]Ajulu, R. 2001. Thabo Mbeki's African Renaissance in a globalising world economy: The struggle for the soul of the continent. *Review of African Political Economy,* 28(87):27-42.

[13]Mbeki, M. 2000. Issues in South African foreign policy: The African Renaissance. *Souls,* 2(2): 76-81.

[14]Moodley, K. 2000. African Renaissance and language policies in comparative perspective. *Politikon,* 27(1): 103-115.

[15]Wa Thiongo, N. 1986. *Decolonizing the mind: The politics of language in African literature.* London: James Currey.

[16]Ndlovu-Gatsheni, S. 2013. *Coloniality in post-colonial Africa: Myth of decolonization.* Dakar: CODESRIA.

[17]Lin, A. R. 2010. Voices from above – voices from below. Who is talking and who is listening in Norwegian language politics? *Current Issues in Language Planning,* 11(2): 114-129.

[18]Stroud, C. 2001. African mother tongue programmes and the politics of language: Linguistic citizenship vs linguistic human rights. *Journal of Multilingual and Multicultural Development,* 22(4): 339-355.

[19]Banda, Z., & Saayman, W. 2015. Renaissance and rebirth: A perspective on the African Renaissance from Christian mission praxis. *Missionalia,* 43(2): 131-152.

[20]Kamwendo, G. H. 2010. Denigrating the local, glorifying the foreign: Language policies in the era of African Renaissance. *International Journal of African Renaissance Studies,* 5(2): 270-282.

[21]Moodley, K. 2000. African Renaissance and language policies in comparative perspective. *Politikon,* 27(1): 103-115.

[22]Mbeki, M. 2000. Issues in South African foreign policy: The African Renaissance. *Souls,* 2(2): 76-81.

[23]Ajulu, R. 2001. Thabo Mbeki's African Renaissance in a globalising world economy: The struggle for the soul of the continent. *Review of African Political Economy,* 28(87): 27-42.

[24]Ndlovu-Gatsheni, S. 2013. *Coloniality in post-colonial Africa: Myth of decolonization.* Dakar: CODESRIA.

[25]Mbeki, M. 2000. Issues in South African foreign policy: The African Renaissance. *Souls,* 2(2): 76-81.

[26]Ibid.

[27]Ajulu, R. 2001. Thabo Mbeki's African Renaissance in a globalising world economy: The struggle for the soul of the continent. *Review of African Political Economy,* 28(87): 27-42.

[28]Ndlovu-Gatsheni, S. 2013. *Coloniality in post-colonial Africa: Myth of decolonization.* Dakar: CODESRIA.

[29]Kamwendo, G., & Mbatha, T. (2016). Introduction: Language issues in the teaching and learning domain at some South African universities. *Nordic Journal of African Studies,* 25(2): 107-110.

[30]Kamwendo, G., Jankie, D., & Chebanne, A. (Eds.). 2009. *Multilingualism in Southern African Education and Communities.* Gaborone: UBTROMSO.

[31]Jackman, R. 2014. CPUT makes exception for Afrikaans. *Cape Times,* 2 September 2014.

[32]Stroud, C. 2001. African mother tongue programmes and the politics of language: Linguistic citizenship vs linguistic human rights. *Journal of Multilingual and Multicultural Development*, 22(4): 339-355.

[33]Mogalakwe, N. 2006. The use of documentary research methods in social research. *African Sociological Review*, 10(1): 221-230.

[34]Ibid.

[35]Kishindo, P. J. 2015. The bird that was not allowed to fly: The case of mother tongue language-in-education policy in Malawi. In L. M. Miti (Ed.). *The language of instruction question in Malawi*. Cape Town: Centre for Advanced Studies of African Society, pp. 9-28.

[36]Unesco. 1953. *The use of vernacular languages in education*. Paris: UNESCO.

[37]Unesco. 2003. *Education in a multilingual world*. Paris: UNESCO.

[38]Chancellor College Education. 13 March, 2014. Memorandum to the Minister of Education: *"Discontent over the use of English as the medium of instruction right from standard one"*.

[39]Unesco. 1953. *The use of vernacular languages in education*. Paris: UNESCO.

[40]Unesco. 2003. *Education in a multilingual world*. Paris: UNESCO.

[41]Republic of Malawi. 2012. *Education Act of 2012*. Lilongwe: Government of Malawi.

[42]Kamwendo, G. H. 2016. The new language of instruction policy in Malawi: A house standing on a shaky foundation. *International Review of Education*, 62: 221-228.

[43]Chancellor College Education. 13 March 2014. Memorandum to the Minister of Education *"Discontent over the use of English as the medium of instruction right from standard one"*.

[44]Ibid.

45 Babaci-Wilhite, Z. (Ed.). 2014. *Giving space to African voices: Rights in local languages and local curriculum*. Rotterdam: Sense Publishers.

[46]Wa Thiongo, N. 1986. *Decolonizing the mind: The politics of language in African literature*. London: James Currey.

[47]Kamwendo, G. 2008. The bumpy road to mother tongue instruction in Malawi. *Journal of Multilingual and Multicultural Development*, 29(5): 353-363.

[48]Dijte, P. G. 2008. *The sociolinguistics of development in Africa*. Bristol: Multilingual Matters.

[49]Alexander, N. 2003. An African Renaissance without African languages? *Social Dynamics*, 20(1): 1-12.

[50]Ndlovu-Gatsheni, S. 2013. *Coloniality in post-colonial Africa: Myth of decolonization*. Dakar: CODESRIA.

[51]World Bank. 2010. *The education system in Malawi*. Washington DC: World Bank.

[52]Republic of Botswana. 1994. *Government White Paper no. 2 of 1994: The Revised National Policy on Education*. Gaborone: Government Printer.

[53]Kamwendo, G., Jankie, D., & Chebanne, A. (Eds.). 2009. *Multilingualism in Southern African Education and Communities*. Gaborone: UBTROMSO.

[54]Unesco. 1953. *The use of vernacular languages in education*. Paris: UNESCO.

[55]Unesco. 2003. *Education in a multilingual world*. Paris: UNESCO.

[56]Lin, A. R. 2010. Voices from above – voices from below. Who is talking and who is listening in Norwegian language politics? *Current Issues in Language Planning*, 11(2): 114-129.

[57]Ibid.

58 Kishindo, P. J. 2015. The bird that was not allowed to fly: The case of mother tongue language-in-education policy in Malawi. In L. M. Miti (Ed.). *The language of instruction question in Malawi*. Cape Town: Centre for Advanced Studies of African Society, pp. 9-28.

[59]Kamwendo, G. 2008. The bumpy road to mother tongue instruction in Malawi. *Journal of Multilingual and Multicultural Development*, 29(5): 353-363.

[60]Bamgbose, A. 1991. *Language and the nation: The language question in sub-Saharan Africa*. Edinburgh: Edinburgh University Press.

[61]Ibid.

[62]Lin, A. R. 2010. Voices from above – voices from below. Who is talking and who is listening in Norwegian language politics? *Current Issues in Language Planning*, 11(2): 114-129.

[63]Unesco. 1953. *The use of vernacular languages in education*. Paris: UNESCO.

[64]Unesco. 2003. *Education in a multilingual world*. Paris: UNESCO.

[65]Lin, A. R. 2010. Voices from above –voices from below. Who is talking and who is listening in Norwegian language politics? *Current Issues in Language Planning*, 11(2): 114-129.

[66]Wa Thiongo, N. 1986. *Decolonizing the mind: The politics of language in African literature*. London: James Currey.

[67]Msila, V., & Gumbo, M. T. (Eds.). 2016. *Africanising the curriculum: Indigenous perspectives and themes*. Stellenbosch: Sun Press.

Chapter 10

'The double-edged sword': African languages under siege

Berrington X.S. Ntombela
Department of English, University of Zululand

10.1 Introduction

The project of colonisation severely altered the linguistic existence of many colonised states, to the extent that Africa continues to be divided along the lines of European languages[1]. Through colonisation, Dutch, which later developed into Afrikaans, and English, were introduced into the South African linguistic repertoire of already existing African languages. Because, among other things, people assert their identity through a language, the colonisation project would not have been completely successful without linguistic conquer. In South Africa, African languages were relegated in favour of the languages of the coloniser to ensure that the identity of the coloniser was inscribed in the psyche of the colonised, albeit in the terms and conditions of the coloniser. That is, the colonised would never rise into equal status with the coloniser; the language was meant to facilitate subservience that the coloniser required – this would not require the coloniser to learn the languages of the colonised.

This chapter argues that although the previously oppressed majority in South Africa rose and gained their freedom, linguistic emancipation seems to be the hardest battle to win or even to wage. Part of that is caused by the power wielded by English, the colonial language. Here I argue that the power that English wields is mostly psychological. It is not that African languages cannot rise to the same status as that of English, but it is the mindset that says, one cannot participate in the global market through an African language, forgetting that Afrikaans wielded the same power as English but was challenged and dethroned by students in the 1976 uprisings. This not only speaks of the subtleties of English as a global language through which nations tap into the global market, but also of the maintenance of the imperialistic agenda where English is used as a cultural and financial commodity. This partly explains why there is much greater financial investment in the teaching and learning of English than in African languages.

This chapter seeks to first highlight the undermining of multilingual reality by colonialists and imperialists in South Africa. I dismiss the popular notion that English came as a saviour among Africans who were ready to tear each other's throats for not wanting to be linguistically dominated by each other. My argument highlights that the multilingual reality testifies to the symbiotic existence of African languages even before the languages of the coloniser came into the picture.

I also discuss the adoption of English as a language of power, education and commerce by Africans. The long struggle for freedom by black South Africans concentrated largely on political freedom. Issues of linguistic identity were never brought into the conscience of the masses. Instead, educational achievement has been equated with proficiency in the English language.

This has been the case since colonial times, where children, however intelligent, would never gain entry into academic institutions without demonstrating facility in the English language. This could partly explain why students in the Soweto uprisings opted for English as a medium of instruction, rejecting the imposed Afrikaans and implicitly eliminating African languages.

The chapter further interrogates excuses when the issue of promoting African languages is brought into the agenda. Many educationists and applied linguists have cited the bilingual case of Canada and tried to replicate it in South Africa. However, Khalema[2] argued that bilingualism, or multilingualism in the case of French Quebec Canada, was regarded as a disguised promotion of the English language due to the power of English. This situation is bound to happen when official languages, as is the case in South Africa, are unequal.

Most importantly, this chapter seeks to revive the quest for linguistic emancipation. Unless we problematise the dominance of English, we will not go very far in elevating African languages to the same level of function. Part of the problem lies with the custodians of African languages. It is not an exaggeration or scapegoat that colonisation altered for the worst the vernacular appreciation and facility. Therefore, there is an even more urgent need for black African minds to be decolonised. The lethargy that characterises the development of African languages is rooted in the perception of the superiority of European languages and culture. The argument for the elevation of African languages or any language first and foremost speaks to the people whom the language identifies and through which they make sense of the world around them. Without this linguistic identification, the African Renaissance cannot be said to be complete.

Although the problem of the siege of African languages is at continental scale, this chapter largely focuses on the case of South Africa. The South African case is interesting in that the Constitution recognises all nine African languages as official, along with English and Afrikaans, formerly the only official languages. Notwithstanding this interesting case, English continues to dominate at almost the obliteration of African languages, especially in education, commerce, the judiciary and the media. Furthermore, if there is anything we could learn from South Africa on language development, Afrikaans is the best example. One lesson is that where there is a will, there is a way. If Afrikaans could develop into a fully-fledged language with capabilities of replacing languages that have been around for millennia, then there is no excuse for African languages. It is the rhetoric that must change and new discourses, perhaps revolutionary, must be adopted.

10.2 The multilingual reality of South Africa

Two scenes from personal experience are worth noting here:

FIRST: *University English classroom practice*. I had just completed a discussion with my students around the prescribed novel *Coconut*, written by Kopano Matlwa[3]. The recurring theme in the book relates to the binary existence of blacks and whites in South Africa. Such existence is characterised by the perception surrounding the superiority of whites as a people, their culture, languages and history to name a few. The blacks, on the other side, are perceived as inferior in terms of their identity as a people, their languages, their culture etc. One such example is demonstrated in the novel by the manner in which English is viewed as indicative of modernity, education and class superiority, whilst anything African is the direct opposite.

After debating these issues with my students for a while we moved on to a grammar session. The focus of the lesson was concord. One male student raised his hand to ask a question. To everybody's surprise, he blurted out his question in isiZulu ignoring his peers' sneers. Although I felt uneasy in that this was an English class and there is an unwritten rule that everybody must address him or herself in English, I refrained from calling that student into order. Here was a demonstration of power relations between languages. I answered his question in English but indicated my curiosity as to why he did not ask his question in English. He said that he wanted to ask his question accurately which might have not been possible with English.

After thinking a lot about this incidence, I arrived at a conclusion that such things are bound to happen in a bilingual or multilingual environment, especially where the involved languages are officially equal. This was even more so after we had deliberated about the negative perception placed on African languages. In addition to the reason that the student provided for asking a question in isiZulu, there was also a sense of testing whether respect and regard for African languages as intellectual languages capable of handling academic matters existed.

SECOND: *Personal communication.* I had received a collection of poems from one student who was looking for a possible publisher. The poems were written in isiZulu. He had also asked me to review them for their fit to school learners as target readers. I provided him feedback on a few poems. Later I remembered a published author who writes in isiZulu who could be of help to this student. I emailed him the following message under the subject 'Book Publication Enquiry':

> Good morning,
>
> I'm Berrington Ntombela currently working for the University of Zululand in the Department of English. I have received a collection of poems from one fellow who wishes them to be published. The poems are written in isiZulu and since it is the area of your expertise, I felt you could be of great help. I have also copied him this message so that future correspondence would be between the two of you. The poems are herein attached. Confirmation of receipt will be highly appreciated.

This is the reply that I received with English translation in brackets and italics (I have used a pseudonym):

> Mahlobo (*Praise name for Ntombela*)
>
> Ngizomthinta ngimchazele (*I will contact him and explain*). Ngeshwa angisasebenzi kubashicileli; ngashiya eminyakeni eyishumi edlule (*Unfortunately I'm no longer working in publication; I left ten years ago*). Okwami kungaba ngukumyalela nje izinkampani angaphumputhela ngakuzo (*For me would be to direct him to the companies where he could try his luck*).
>
> Akuphilwe nje! (*Let's only be well*)
>
> uNakashela (*Pseudonym of the sender*)

This correspondence is another way of showing peculiar linguistic behaviour in a bilingual or multilingual environment. It is obvious that the recipient of my email knows the English language. By replying strictly in isiZulu, the recipient is asserting his identity, perhaps in a similar way my student did in class. These examples show the co-existence of English, the European colonial language, and isiZulu, the African language. Such co-existence is not new but actually predates the present democratic era in South Africa. In the apartheid era, only English and Afrikaans were recognised as official languages. Malherbe[4], for example, carried out an important study on bilingual education which was very well received internationally, and in fact had an influence on international research and thinking[5]. This study was premised on English and Afrikaans being the only official languages, thus excluding the rest of African languages. What Malherbe[6] rightly argued was the benefit of using two languages in an education system, which obviously benefited whites. Paradoxically, African languages, even though not official languages, were used as media of instruction under the arrangement of Bantu education[7]. Therefore, this meant that Africans were already involved in multilingual education because they used an African language for the first eight years of schooling and then switched to English and Afrikaans as dual media of instruction[8].

This multilingual reality was fully acknowledged in 1994 when the government added nine African languages to English and Afrikaans as official languages. This means that South Africa has eleven official languages: Sepedi, Sesotho, Setswana, siSwati, Tshivenda, Xitsonga, Afrikaans, English, isiNdebele, isiXhosa and isiZulu. Interestingly, researchers such as Makalela[9] credit the demolition of Bantustans that kept language groups apart and the officialisation of African languages as responsible for the translanguaging practices among multilinguals in South Africa. She averred that this demolition has led to the fusion of languages into a hybrid language called kasi-taal. However, this hybrid language predates the democratic era in South Africa. Msimang[10], Slabbert and Myers-Scotton[11], Hurst[12] and Brook[13] referred to the same hybrid language as tsotsitaal, which like kasi-taal intelligently fuses a number of languages. Interestingly, the very terms, 'tsotsitaal' and 'kasi-taal', represent the fusion of indigenous languages with Afrikaans, where 'taal' is an Afrikaans term for language and 'tsotsi' and 'kasi' are indigenous language terms for streetwise and township respectively.

Tsotsitaal flourished due to the conglomeration of multiple languages that speakers could draw from. Most importantly, it is for reasons of identity that speakers use kasi-taal or tsostitaal[14], the same way my student and the recipient of my email did. In other words, this multilingual reality speaks to the identity of South Africa as a nation. Therefore, when eleven languages were made official, it was to assert the real identity of the people. Identity was defined by Norton[15] as "how people understand their relationship to the world, how that relationship is constructed across time and space, and how people understand their possibilities for the future"[16]. Therefore, the answer to the question 'Who am I?' lies in the answer to the question 'What can I do?', which essentially speaks to the material access that an individual has that will allow that individual to relate to the world and in turn understand their possibilities for the future[17]. Furthermore, borrowing from Bourdieu, Norton[18] asserted that an individual's worth is defined by what he speaks, which symbolises a right to speak whilst at the same time imposing reception in the listener. The listener's reception is confirmation of the speaker's worth, but what makes the speaker worth anything if it is not the language that connects him with the listener? In other words, if I had demanded that my student (mentioned earlier) speak English, I would have contravened his identity and would have suggested that he is worthless, but actually referring to the worthlessness of his language.

The question of identity is pervasive within black Africans in tertiary institutions and that is never set outside the boundaries of language. For example, on issues of academic literacy, as argued by Norton[19], black students are labelled as 'disadvantaged' on account of their secondary school education and are prone to accusations of plagiarism when their use of English does not match their disadvantaged status. Norton[20] therefore rightly concluded that "identity constructs and is constructed by language"[22]. This means that the marginalisation of one's language, as was the case with African languages, cuts and dismantles identities. Therefore, the swift move by the democratic government to restore the dignity of African languages and the language-in-education policy, which went beyond a simple recognition of the previously marginalised languages by calling for the promotion of multilingualism and the development of African languages so that they could operate at the same level as English and Afrikaans, is one way of re-crafting the dismantled identities of black South Africans.

10.3 The rise of colonial languages

I have indicated that South Africa and many African states are multilingual. The linguistic landscape was, however, frustrated when European languages were introduced during the colonial and imperial expansion. In South Africa, Dutch was the first colonial language to be introduced in South Africa, which was later followed by English. According to Kamwendo[23], the British followed the principle of direct rule in certain colonies and indirect rule in others. In South Africa, direct rule was practised where colonial administrators were imported from Britain[24], however in order to facilitate colonial rule, locals had to be taught the English language, for which responsibility was carried by missionaries. Yet, as Kamwendo[25] stated, missionaries saw it necessary to teach natives their indigenous languages as a vehicle for evangelisation. As a result, many African languages were developed. This means that the English differed from the French and the Portuguese, who used an assimilationist approach that sought to dismantle local cultures and languages and replace them with the 'superior' culture and language of the coloniser.

However, since literacy in indigenous languages was meant to facilitate an evangelisation mission, education beyond primary level was carried out in the language of the coloniser. This paved the way for the perception that no intellectual pursuit can be achieved through a local language. In fact, any prospect of advancement was heavily dependent on the colonial language. Ngugi[26], for example, referred to an all familiar situation where students displaying low attainment in English would not be admitted for university study, regardless of their performance in other subjects like mathematics. In other words, the colonial language became a gatekeeper.

In all colonies, the colonial language became the official language. Local languages, in cases where they were developed, were nonetheless used as *lingua franca*. It must be mentioned that the project of colonisation undermined not only the native languages, but indigenous knowledge systems as well. This was because the medium of expressing indigenous knowledge systems was the very languages that were bastardised by colonisation. The colonisers came with the notion that native languages and their speakers were never developed into languages of intellect. This notion was not unique to Africa, but existed in all colonised territories.

For example, Pratt[27] demonstrated how Spaniards failed to read the letter written by Guaman Poma, which incorporated "Andean systems of spatial symbolism". Because Guaman Poma sought to 'speak' to King Phillip III of Spain, his letter was written in two languages: Spanish and Quechua. Pratt[28] contended that such bilingual facility is unavoidable in the contact zones, by which she referred to the phenomenon where cultures meet and clash in such contexts as colonialism. What is important to note is that the Spanish colonisers did not bother to learn the Andean systems of spatial symbolism, which was used to "express Andean values and aspirations"[29]. As a result, the language and the writing system of the Inca remained unknown to Spaniards because as colonisers they had concluded on the superiority of their language and culture, which explains their assimilationist approach. This also explains why native languages in the Spanish colonies in South America were completely subdued and undermined by Spanish up to today. Horneberger[30], for instance, observed that the Quechua speaking communities of Puno, Peru, where the policy called for the use of Quechua in school, mounted resistance in the belief that the area was a Spanish domain. This is a result of centuries of vernacular degradation and subordination by colonial languages.

Similarly, colonisers of Africa came with the same notion that African languages were undeveloped and Africans were backward, uncivilised savages. In other words, the colonisers assumed that the writing system was introduced by them. On the contrary, there is compelling evidence that Africans had a civilisation and logical system of governance accomplished through their languages both in oral and written form. For instance, Mutwa[31] contended that the Bantu had a symbol-language, which although was not taught to common people but to witchdoctors, elders and the wise ones, was commonly used by women. This symbol-language was used across the tribes, regardless of the languages spoken by individual tribes. For instance, "a Zulu could read and understand anything recorded by a Lunda from Angola, even though he might not understand the spoken language"[32]. Unfortunately, as Mutwa lamented, when the Bantu learnt the European alphabet, this system of writing died out very fast, although it remained in use up to the 20th century. Such a system of writing differed from the style of Chinese or Japanese where symbols represent single characters[33]. In this system, the symbols represent the whole word or complete ideas, and according to Mutwa, the Bantu used to send elaborate letters to each other using this system of writing[34].

All this proves is that instead of colonial languages such as English being saviours, they corroborated in obfuscating indigenous languages. This was achieved by documenting conquests by colonisers in their own languages, which were read largely by themselves and the outside world. In this way, Africa suffered textual conquer[35]. An example is Joseph Conrad, who as part of his profession as a sailor took a voyage to the Belgian Congo and afterwards wrote a novel, *Heart of Darkness*, based on what he supposedly experienced (Conrad[36]; Pakenham[37]) depicting Africa as a land of savages. Because the readership of such works was the colonisers, these stories created as fact the savagery of African people whose languages were probably labelled as dark. When Africans gained facility with the language of the coloniser, they sought to correct many wrongs that colonial writers had made. For instance, writers such as Chinua Achebe responded to Joseph Conrad's *Heart of Darkness* by writing *Things Fall Apart*, a novel in which he demonstrates how the colonial system destabilised and frustrated the indigenous way of life[38]. Unfortunately, although these writers sought to speak back to the 'empire' by using colonial languages, their messages bypassed the locals. This tendency to rely heavily on the colonial language in order to speak to the wider world has continued to elevate colonial languages such as English to the detriment of indigenous languages. Afrikaans, however, demonstrated that such dominance need not be the order of the day.

After the South African War of 1899 to 1902 in South Africa[39], the Afrikaners gained more power until they eventually took over the government. Because they were already detached from the Dutch, they sought to establish themselves as a nation. Part of the instruments of nation building, and actually the most important, was the establishment of the language that would bind them as a nation. At that time, it was already seen that the language spoken by Afrikaners no longer resembled the Dutch in such aspects as grammar and vocabulary due to contact with African languages, thus Afrikaans was born. What made the Afrikaans language project a success was a combination of nationalism and religious ideology that sought to legitimise Afrikaners as a nation united under one language[40]. Therefore, the government spearheaded the development of Afrikaans by setting up a language board that oversaw the development of vocabulary, systematising grammar and compiling dictionaries. After the project of setting up Afrikaans as a fully-fledged language, the language board acted as a watchdog where usage of Afrikaans outside the parameters of the established grammar was discouraged and stigmatised in order not to dilute the language[41]. At that stage, Afrikaans was fully utilised as a medium of instruction and the language of the government, commerce and all government functionaries. Afrikaans children had the privilege of being taught in their mother tongue from the first year at school up to doctoral level at university, a privilege that continues to evade the African child[42].

It was against this backdrop that Malherbe[43] proposed bilingual education, which meant that Afrikaner children would be better educated when they not only used Afrikaans but also English, a language of global influence. Meantime, as mentioned previously, Africans' education was multilingual, with the first eight years in mother tongue instruction after which English and Afrikaans were introduced as dual media of instruction; a system, which if it was not deliberately crafted to be inferior, would have placed Africans at an advantage. Unfortunately, mother tongue instruction with an inferior curriculum was not meant to advance Africans, and English and Afrikaans were only meant to make them better servants. This legacy of the dominance of colonial languages continues to this day. That is, English and Afrikaans are the only languages that are being used as media of instruction in South Africa, and are the visible languages dominating commerce, the judiciary and other sectors.

10.4 South African linguistic resistance

The uprisings of 1976 were a watershed in the struggle against the imposition of Afrikaans as the only medium of instruction. The rejection of Afrikaans was a result of a combination of distasteful experiences by Africans. The apartheid government, through its enforcement of inferior Bantu education, had made Afrikaans synonymous with apartheid. As part of resisting the government repression of the majority, it was incumbent upon the masses to reject the programmes of the government, especially those who sought to promote the values and aspirations of the oppressors. The Afrikaans language was therefore seen as the embodiment of the Afrikaner repressive regime and therefore had to be rejected by all means. As I have argued above about how language expresses the identity of the speaker, it must have felt an insult to be forced to embrace the identity and to identify with the oppressor through his language. Moreover, it had become clear in the sight and psyche of Africans that Afrikaans was only meant to hold them back as subservient and subordinated to the Afrikaner – however proficient they might be in Afrikaans, they would only be good enough as hewers of wood and drawers of water.

The other reason for rejecting the imposed Afrikaans was that it would essentially cut Africans from the wider world. Afrikaans was only South African and since it had proved to be oppressive machinery, it would stamp out chances of appealing to the outside world through English. It must be highlighted at this stage that since Afrikaans and English were dual media of instruction at secondary and post-secondary level, the default medium of instruction fell on English. In other words, the game of Afrikaans resistance was played through the card of English, a formidable competitor.

Canagarajah[44] asserted that resistance provides the oppressed the opportunity to "negotiate, alter, and oppose political structures, and reconstruct their languages, cultures, and identities to their advantage". Furthermore, Canagarajah[45] conceived of resistance as "displaying ideological clarity and commitment to collective action for social transformation". Therefore, we can conclude that the actions of students in 1976 fit this definition of resistance, as it was not a simple uninformed action that did not have social transformation in their educational aspirations. However, the fact that in this linguistic resistance there was no place for African languages, means there was no revolution.

For linguistic revolution to take place, the masses would have to come to the realisation that their languages are as viable as the European ones. For example, political revolutions such as the French Revolution and the dethronement of monarchies in many European nations and other parts of the world were accomplished by the masses' realisation of the viability of alternative forms of government that favoured them. Revolution is not a matter of choosing from the given options, such as either English or Afrikaans in the case of South Africa. On the contrary, a revolution would question the very dominance of these colonial languages, because linguistically, there is no language that is superior to another. Perhaps the answer to the question of why the South African youth of 1976 and the post-apartheid South Africans have not revolutionised against the dominance of English and Afrikaans is two-fold: neo-colonialism ensures that although there is an outside feel of freedom, the colonial master still holds the power, in this case through the languages. Also, colonialism deeply affected the minds, which successfully rendered inferior the languages of the natives.

This affectation of the mind is clearly demonstrated by a second wave of resistance against the Afrikaans language. Ntombela[46] asserted that when apartheid crumbled and the schools that were formerly closed to the blacks (especially Afrikaans medium schools) were opened, parents demanded that an English medium class be opened in order to cater for their children. This was done even against the resistance of many school governing bodies in such schools that also had the right to choose the language that would be the medium of instruction. Further, because the language-in-education policy favoured the promotion of multilingualism, with eleven official languages to choose from, many black schools dropped Afrikaans from their curriculum. English remained the favourite option as it was in 1976.

10.5 The rise of English and decline of African languages

It is not possible to understand and contextualise the rise of English against African languages without looking at the influence of English in the global arena. This means we will have to consider how English has placed itself in other parts of Africa and the world, as this will give us a perspective of the plight of African languages.

Those who normally propose the adoption of mother tongue instruction cite such examples as Germany and France, where education is exclusively in a non-English language. However, the spread of English as a global language means that countries like Germany have had to offer many university courses in English in order to remain competitive. But that has not come without a price. Germans lament the vanishing incentive to develop scholarly vocabulary due to the onslaught of English[47]. This cannot be more relevant than in South Africa, where the development of African languages is stalled by the power of English. It goes without saying, therefore, that the dominance of English as a scientific language reduces scientific knowledge into "an Anglo-Saxon scientific discourse"[48]. This is evidenced in many academic publications that are dominated by English under the argument by many academics that it is futile to publish in a language rarely read by anyone.

However, when looking at it from the students' perspective, as Salomone[49] conceded, it is frustrating that the intellectual perspective is lost in the native language to be replaced by English. But even that replacement denigrates them into second class scholars, as they first have to gain fluency in the target language before they can intellectually operate in it. This phenomenon of the imposition of English is dubbed linguistic dictatorship, which has unfortunately lost all its relevance in the South African context[50]. In other words, if language embodies cultural values and identities, we need to ask what kind of values and identities are represented by English? That is, how possible is it that African values and identities could be genuinely expressed through the medium of English? Nevertheless, we cannot brush aside the global phenomenon of English.

Global English can be mostly conceived in terms of economic imperatives in the global arena. It is that economic cache that English brings that makes it the only linguistic global player. Even the global understanding and implementation of multilingualism has mostly been dominated by English. That is, multilingualism has been equated with the addition of English to a mother tongue and perhaps to another official or national language, especially in Europe[51]. Furthermore, as English dominates higher education, students who come from an ESL or EFL context are expected to abandon their vernacular notions of literacy practices and adopt an English monolingual literacy and discursive reasoning[52]. This means that their construction of world knowledge will inevitably lean on the Anglo-Saxon pattern of thought.

Additionally, the dominance of English in higher education is linked to internationalisation, the global labour market, and institutional profiling[53]. In other words, most institutions justify the adoption of English on the basis that international students favour English medium education, those who seek employment outside their countries can easily find placement if they speak English, and institutions that offer courses in English and also publish in English increase their visibility in academic circles. Even global rankings of universities depend on their language policies, which in many cases must implicitly include English as a medium of instruction. In other words, those institutions that use any other language as a medium of instruction are unlikely to catch up with English medium of instruction institutions[54]. For instance, the main driving force behind France's relaxation of the Toubon Law, which restricted the use of foreign languages (particularly English), was English's ability to lure international students into French universities, which speaks of the dominance of English above all other languages[55].

Such dominance can be partly explained by Lo Bianco's argument that "modernity in the west has developed in such a way that a notion of economics lies at the core of citizens' self-understanding", which explains why language choice is influenced largely by the economic status of that language[56]. Interestingly, although English could be treated like any other foreign language, e.g. Spanish, French, Germany etc. in China, the Chinese do not categorise it as such, arguing that English is for everybody. In fact, as Lo Bianco[57] asserted, others predict that the proliferation of English will eventually relegate its status as a foreign language, becoming part of basic educational skill. Perhaps this is one reason why resistance against English is increasingly becoming irrelevant whilst its dominance is out-explained as part being literate, i.e. English is largely considered as part of academic literacy.

Given the dominant status of English, it may seem that African languages are fighting a losing battle. In fact, the resuscitation and development of a language lies in its educational utility as a medium of instruction (the case of the Basque in Spain is a good example)[58]. Nevertheless, as Mufanechiya and Mufanechiya[59] asserted, whilst there seems to be valid arguments pedagogically and socially to promote indigenous languages in the classroom, that does not seem to be in sync with reality in the world of work and examinations, which continue to be dominated by English. As a result, parents are forced to enrol their children in their earliest years into English medium schools so that they are not left behind, which inversely alienates them from their linguistic world[60].

Furthermore, as Mufanechiya and Mufanechiya rightly argue, the drive towards indigenisation of the economy cannot be set outside the recognition of indigenous languages as viable instruments, both in education and in the society[61]. That is, the continued reliance on English can only mean that the custodians of the English language stand to benefit more economically than natives. Similarly, the educational sector will continue to be controlled by English both in the conception and creation of knowledge.

Mufanechiya and Mufanechiya further observed that there is a lot of talk by academics and politicians about the need to implement mother tongue instruction, which unfortunately lacks realisation, perhaps due to the unstoppable force of the English language[62]. Ntombela[63] similarly argued that such lethargy is a result of a lack of political will. It may also be the case that even politicians and academics have resigned themselves to the power of the English language, and see the interrogation of such dominance as a waste of time.

Moreover, even though Canagarajah[64] argued convincingly on the merits of *lingua franca* English (LFE) on a communicative scale, such success collapses in higher education, as students must suspend their multiple discourses that can be easily accommodated in LFE and must adopt academic discourses which embody the cultural thought patterns of native speakers particularly from the centre, i.e. Britain, North America, Australia etc. Similarly, Canagarajah's proposal of a pedagogical shift, where teachers develop students to engage in a repertoire of codes rather than focusing on a single code language, is defeated by the hegemony of English language in higher education as expressed in academic discourse[65]. Academic discourse favours singularity of code and strictness of conventions, as dictated by disciplinary expectations. Suffice it to highlight that academic discourse has grown to be synonymous with academic English, which is in turn associated with an advanced level of English proficiency.

10.6 Language and decolonisation

The project of decolonisation has never been more urgent. Whilst it should have been natural that after liberation Africans would be at ease with themselves, their cultures and languages, reality seems to point to the fact that they are actually drifting further away as they seek to immerse themselves in the western culture and the English language. This is evidenced by a reported tendency for parents to seek enrolment for their children in English only schools, even though there are provisions for the development of African languages (Kamwendo[66]; Chetty & Mwepu[67]).

Sadly, African intellectuals fail to realise that their promotion of English as the superior code on issues of national, political, and economic importance, mean they are essentially alienating the native speakers of African languages, as they are bound to feel spoken about rather than spoken to and with. In other words, it is through a native language that one can directly address a person without needing a translation. The Afrikaners realised that in order to speak to each other and with each other they could not rely on English, which necessitated that they develop Afrikaans into a language with the same level of facility as English. Also, because the Nationalist Government had the political will, it saw to it that "resources such as terminology banks, a wide range of dictionaries, and a significant literary output" were provided[68].

Therefore, if we are committed to the project of decolonisation, it is imperative to ask the critical question about the audience of our speech or writing. This is imperative because decolonisation must speak to the masses rather than remaining an academic debate handled by academics through the colonial linguistic instrument, which will inevitably hit a brick wall with the masses. However, when such debates begin to be handled in the languages of the masses, which are capable of projecting the African worldview, the fetters of linguistic bondage will soon be undone. Unfortunately, the lack of linguistic representation in such initiatives as Mbeki's African Renaissance is indicative of over-reliance on the western linguistic apparatus and intellectual tradition embodied in the English language[69].

In fact, the hegemony of English language is to the extent that many Africans do not believe that their languages have the capacity to achieve such abstract subjects as mathematics, astronomy and medicine, even though history points to the contrary[70]. For this reason, the project of decolonisation needs to be community driven, for it is at this level that the damage of colonisation is most visible. This is seen by parents in such countries as Uganda, who corroborate with policy makers in discarding the use of local languages in favour of a foreign language, i.e. English (Heugh[71]; Maalim[72]).

However, it is easy to see such attitudes of parents and policy makers as reflecting the historical experiences, where those who grew proficient in English could operate relatively better everywhere than those who only had local languages. Besides, English was the language of the master who controlled the resources that could only be accessed through that language. Unfortunately this is increasingly becoming a status quo, as Chetty and Mwepu (2008) think the use of English as the only medium of instruction is not problematic provided children are taught to be critical thinkers, forgetting that the same children must first learn the foreign language and must also learn new content in the same language, which does not give them space to be critical as they would with their languages[73]. In fact, Maalim posited that children who are taught through a foreign language become passive recipients of knowledge, but are active and able to participate and ask questions when taught in their own language[74].

Furthermore, Maalim cited the case of Zanzibar, where teachers confessed to be spending more time preparing for lessons because of their lack of proficiency in English, rather than concentrating on the content[75]. This reduced the teaching practice into a mechanical process, where the focus was placed on correctness at the expense of content, which arguably compromised quality. Sadly, learners in countries where learning does not take place in their mother tongue such as in Botswana, Tanzania, South Africa, the Democratic Republic of Congo, Brunei, etc. have been easily categorised as though they were naturally passive learners[76]. Given such a situation, it is not easy to train children in such contexts to be critical thinkers.

Additionally, Chetty and Mwepu's conclusion that South Africa cannot afford the costly exercise of promoting nine of the eleven official languages[77], and Ntombela's implication that the diversity of languages in South Africa is hampering the development of indigenous languages, seem to be premised on the ideology of linguistic diversity as a problem[78]. It was against this backdrop that many nation states, especially in the first world, adopted an assimilationist approach in language planning so as to unite the nation under one language[79]. However, Hornberger asserted that there has been an ideological shift where plurality of languages has come to be recognised as an asset, especially in the emancipation of marginalised language communities[80]. Notwithstanding this progress, globalisation seems to be shifting the commitment of developing local languages to the development of the English language. As a result, as English continues to be the official language in many parts of the world, locals seem prepared to sacrifice their indigenous languages in order to secure their children a better future.

For example, although Swahili has been cited as a success story in Africa, its replacement by English in Zanzibar, which has been extended to Grade 5, is tragic and retrogressive to say the least[81]. It is unfortunate and fallacious that the English language has been viewed as synonymous with quality education. On the contrary, research confirms that quality education is achieved through mother tongue instruction[82].

Nonetheless, within educational circles, English continues to be regarded as a panacea capable of emancipating previously economically disadvantaged black students. Such rhetoric continues to peg English as an economic vehicle whilst downgrading African languages as uneconomical, which development is implicitly shunned as an economic waste[83]. Another unfounded rhetoric propagated by Chetty and Mwepu is that the tendency for liberation stalwarts to address the masses in the medium of English could "be seen as an attempt to unify a people susceptible to be divided along ethno-linguistic lines", which paints Africans as anarchists perpetually in need of a coloniser mediator.

Chetty and Mwepu further attempted to defend English as a 'killer' language (the one responsible for the decline and endangerment of other languages), arguing that the dominance of isiZulu in KwaZulu Natal has played a similar role of marginalising other African indigenous dialects of the province[84]. They however fall short of mentioning those dialects marginalised by isiZulu. Besides, the issue at hand is not about dialects as English has dialects of its own, but about languages. In other words, such a defence is indicative of the indirect legitimisation of the hegemony of the English language, further instilling the erroneous notion of linguistic intolerance among Africans. Furthermore, Chetty and Mwepu's continued reference to the use of English by South African black liberation stalwarts as evidence of the liberating force of English, does not take into account the wider audience on a global scale who needed to be addressed in the global language[85]. What is problematic about Chetty and Mwepu is that they remain uncritical of the continued use of the colonial language long after liberation.

Chetty and Mwepu further consider the cost of multilingualism to be beyond the reach of South Africa, which is not true. We must bear in mind that prior to democracy, black South Africans were already involved in some form of multilingual education, that is, for the first eight years the medium of instruction was an African language, which was replaced by English and Afrikaans – a dual media of instruction. What this essentially says is that African languages had already undergone enough development to have them as media of instruction, i.e. developing African languages would not mean starting from scratch. The problem is therefore not with cost, but with the ideology that essentialises English to the point of erasing African languages. This over-glorification of English can be traced back to the damage of colonialism, where European languages were by default placed as superior to African languages[86]. Unless Africans wake up to that fact and commit to dealing head-on with the effects of colonialism, the project of decolonisation will remain a mirage.

10.7 The way to a linguistic African Renaissance

Restoring African languages to their rightful place requires not only commitment, but a drastic change in the minds of Africans. In the preceding discussion, I referred to some excuses that are cited for not promoting multilingualism involving African languages. One such excuse is that more parents are actually calling for more English, which makes it unnecessary to pursue the development of African languages. However, it turns out that this excuse is mythical. Heugh[87], for example, argued that those who spread this perception deliberately ignore research that suggests the opposite. For instance, in 1992, the Department of Education and Training (DET), in preparation for education post-apartheid, conducted a survey, where contrary to the DET's expectation that parents would call for English medium of instruction from the word go, the results indicated that only 22% would support English medium of instruction from the word go, while 54% preferred a gradual transfer to English, 13.4% opted for a sudden transfer to English, and 7.5% would rather retain the status quo[88]. In fact, the availability of educational resources after school hours in languages other than English dispels the belief that English is equated with education; a perception that is growing in other sectors globally[89].

In other words, a linguistic renaissance calls for a renewed commitment to the development of African languages and the understanding of the forces that militate against it. It needs to be understood that the education system is unfortunately skewed in favour of the aspirations of a few elite, who by choice of English only are interpreted as representative of the wishes of the underclass majority[90]. As Bamgbose rightly argued, this minority would rather maintain the status quo because they are the only ones who stand to benefit[91].

Furthermore, research abounds that supports mother tongue instruction. Without a doubt, the apartheid system, along with Bantu education – especially the inferiority of the curriculum – did a disservice to the black populace. Paradoxically, one aspect that seems to have worked, according to Heugh, is the switch from mother tongue instruction after eight years to English and Afrikaans, because it gave learners enough time to be grounded in the mother tongue and had enough time to learn the second language before it became the medium of instruction[92]. Nevertheless, the reason why mother tongue instruction has not been supported politically is because it has been equated with Bantu Education in its perception as inferior to English and Afrikaans. That is why there is an urgent need to resuscitate the status of African languages because it was the system that rendered them inferior. What needs to be realised is that the apartheid regime did not promote equality between black African students and their white peers. This means that they could not have given the same curriculum and even if they had, the regime would still have blocked black Africans from accessing the same jobs and services. For example, it was common during the Comrades marathon in the apartheid era that the black Africans who won would not be recognised. The same would have been the case for black Africans in the education sector. Therefore, the rejection of mother tongue instruction on account of Bantu Education is tantamount to having thrown the baby away with the bath water.

An African linguistic renaissance must also take into cognisance that those who are set to benefit from the status quo are those who care less about the interests and aspirations of being African. Johnson, for instance, who incidentally is a Rhodes University scholar who studied at Oxford University (like Cecil Rhodes the imperialist capitalist who studied at Oxford after whom Rhodes University is named), in a scathing attack of Makgoba's Africanisation project at UKZN, warned UCT that its proposed language policy that includes isiXhosa will relegate the university to the status of a bush university[93]. He argued that isiXhosa, not being the dominant language of the Western Cape, should not even be considered at a university of the calibre of UCT, suggesting rather the use of English, French, Arabic, and Swahili, which he considered the dominant languages in Africa. In other words, none of the nine official languages – minus English and Afrikaans – should be promoted at university level if the drive is to Africanise the institution. That is, international students will never come for any of their native languages or South African languages; they want English[94].

Furthermore, Johnson suggested that UCT, like any other reputable university, should strive to maintain the same level as the US Ivy League universities and Oxford and Cambridge. These universities, he argued, will never dream of transformation, which in the case of South Africa is compromising standards. In fact he is downright against transformation, bemoaning the decamping of white students (who were UKZN's historical clients) and the "better Indian students", *inter alia*, on account of the promotion of isiZulu in the university's language policy. This decamping to other institutions, particularly UCT, led to the influx of African students, whom Johnson (2016) described as semi-literate, lacking the habit of study, and reliant on the regurgitation of lecture notes. Notably, the whites and 'better' Indians that decamped were relative beneficiaries of the apartheid system. These stereotypes about African students and their languages are products of the colonial mindset. It is apparent that if Africans do not take the initiative of resuscitating their languages, there will be no meaning to an African Renaissance, as Alexander emphasised that the two are inseparable[94].

10.8 Conclusion

In this chapter I have argued about the multilingual reality in South Africa. The recognition of eleven official languages is a step forward in the linguistic emancipation of formerly marginalised languages. Such recognition has normalised the facility of African languages in educational settings and general communication, as demonstrated by my student in class and the recipient of my email message. In fact, despite being given an inferior curriculum, black South Africans were already operating in a multilingual education system. Unfortunately, the scourge of Bantu education stigmatised the use of African languages in education. There seems to be failure in separating the goodness of mother tongue instruction from the inferiority of Bantu education.

I have also discussed how colonial languages, particularly English, rose to the detriment of local languages. Through the project of colonialism, European languages were introduced as the embodiment of civilisation and modernity. This meant that any prospect of participating in the economic structures of the colonised states could only be accomplished through the languages of the coloniser. This unfortunately did not end when the colonised states secured independence. The dominance of European languages, especially English, continues now through globalisation. The South African case is even more worrisome because we have a Constitution that supports the promotion of indigenous languages, yet there is a notable absence of commitment – a move that seems to be taking us back to unilingualism, with English reaping all the benefits.

This lack of commitment in developing African languages is at the same time promoting English as the only viable language based largely on its international standing. Sacrificing the local on account of the global does not seem problematic at all (especially to beneficiaries of the English language) sadly. Instead of insisting on the development of local languages, there is now an emerging rhetoric of preservation, as if African languages belong to a museum. For instance, the MEC for Culture, Sport and Recreation, in a National Book Week (NBW) campaign, echoed the words of the NBW ambassador who bemoaned the scarcity of books in African languages in places such as airports, making such places look like they are in the US and not in Africa. She encouraged people not only to take pride in their home languages, but to preserve them as well (SABDC, 2016).

The linguistic resistance against the imposition of Afrikaans in the 1976 uprisings and the demand for English classes in predominantly Afrikaans schools post 1994 shows that it is possible to make a linguistic shift. Unfortunately, this resistance has not done African languages any good, because instead of promoting the prestige of local languages, English got promoted. The solution lies in a linguistic revolution which will catalyse decolonisation. It is my opinion that the lethargy in promoting indigenous languages is a result of neo-colonialism, which necessitates a decolonisation of the mind. Furthermore, the commitment to bring to the agenda an African Renaissance cannot be meaningful without linguistic emancipation.

References

[1]Kamwendo, G. H. 2010. Denigrating the local glorifying the foreign: Malawian language policies in the era of African Renaissance. *International Journal of African Renaissance Studies*, 5(2): 270 – 282.

[2]Khalema, N. E. 2016. Linguicism and nationalism: A post-colonial gaze on the promotion of Afrikaans as a national language in apartheid South Africa. *International Journal of Language Studies*, 10(1): 91 – 110.

[3]Matlwa, K. 2007. *Coconut*. Auckland Park: Jacana.

[4]Malherbe, E. L. 1946. *The bilingual school*. London: Longmans Green and Company.

[5]Heugh, K. 2000. *The case against bilingual and multilingual education in South Africa*. PRAESA occasional papers No. 6. Cape Town: PRAESA.

[6]Ibid.

[7]Ibid.

[8]Ibid.

[9]Makalela, L. 2015. Translanguaging practice in complex multilingual spaces: A discontinuous continuity in post-independent South Africa, *International Journal of the Sociology of Language*, 2015(234): 115 – 132.

[10]Msimang, C. T. 1987. Impact of Zulu on Tsotsitaal. *South African Journal of African Languages*, 7(3): 82 – 86.

[11]Slabbert, S., & Myers-Scotton, C. 1996. The structure of Tsotsitaal and Iscamtho: Code switching and in-group identity in South African townships. *Linguistics*, 34: 317 – 342.

[12]Hurst, E. 2008. *Style, structure and function in Cape Town Tsotsitaal.* Unpublished Doctoral Dissertation. Cape Town: University of Cape Town.

[13]Brook, K. 2010. *Interactions of South African languages: Case study of Tsotsitaal.* Paper presented at Global Wordnet Conference, Mumbai, India. Retrieved from: http://www.globalwordnet-iitt2010.in/proceedings.php. [Date accessed: August 23, 2010.]

[14]Hurst, E., & Mesthrie, R. 2013. When you hang out with the guys they keep you in style: The case for considering style in descriptions of South African tsotsitaals. *Language Matters*, 44(1): 3-20.

[15]Norton, B. 1997. Language, identity and the ownership of English. *TESOL Quarterly*, 31(3):409 – 429.

[16]Ibid.

[17]Ibid.

[18]Ibid.

[19]Ibid.

[20]Ibid.

[21]Ibid.

[22]Ibid.

[23]Kamwendo, G. H. 2006. No easy walk to linguistic freedom: A critique of language planning during South Africa's first decade of democracy. *Nordic Journal of African Studies*, 15(1): 53 – 70.

[24]Pakenham, T. 2014. *The scramble for Africa.* London: Abacus.

[25]Kamwendo, G. H. 2006. No easy walk to linguistic freedom: A critique of language planning during South Africa's first decade of democracy. *Nordic Journal of African Studies*, 15(1): 53 – 70.

[26]Ngugi, W. T. 1996. *Decolonising the mind: The politics of language in African literature.* Nairobi: East African Educational Publishers.

[27]Pratt, M. L. 1993. Arts of the contact zone. In D. Bartholomae & A. Petrosky (Eds.). *Ways of reading: An anthology for writers.* Boston: Bedford St. Martins, pp. 326 - 348.

[28]Ibid.

[29]Ibid.

[30]Hornberger, N. H. 2002. Multilingual language policies and the continua of biliteracy: An ecological approach. *Language Policy*, 1: 27 – 51.

[31]Mutwa, V. C. 1998. *Indaba, my children.* Edinburgh: Canongate.

[32]Ibid.

[33]Ibid.

[34]Ibid.

[35]Ntombela, B. 2012. Literature and culture: Literature and identity building. In A. Roscoe and R. Al Mohrooqi (Eds.). *Literacy, Literature and Identity.* Newcastle upon Tyne: Cambridge Scholars, pp. 136 - 151.

[36]Conrad, J. 1961. *Youth. Heart of darkness. The end of the tether.* London: Dent.

[37]Pakenham, T. 2014. *The scramble for Africa.* London: Abacus.

[38]Ntombela, B. 2012. Literature and culture: Literature and identity building. In A. Roscoe and R. Al Mohrooqi (Eds.), *Literacy, Literature and Identity.* Newcastle upon Tyne: Cambridge Scholars, pp. 136 - 151.

[39] Pakenham, T. 2014. *The scramble for Africa.* London: Abacus.

[40]Khalema, N. E. 2016. Linguicism and nationalism: A post-colonial gaze on the promotion of Afrikaans as a national language in apartheid South Africa. *International Journal of Language Studies*, 10(1):91 – 110.

[41]Ibid.

[42]Ntombela, B. X. S. 2016. The burden of diversity: The sociolinguistic problems of English in South Africa. *English Language Teaching*, 9(5): 77 – 84.

[43]Malherbe, E. L. 1946. *The bilingual school.* London: Longmans Green and Company.

[44]Canagarajah, S. 2007. Lingua franca English, multilingual communities, and language acquisition. *The Modern Language Journal*, 91: 923 – 939

[45]Ibid.

[46]Ntombela, B. X. S. 2016. The burden of diversity: The sociolinguistic problems of English in South Africa. *English Language Teaching*, 9(5): 77 – 84.

[47]Salomone, R. 2015. The rise of global English-medium of instruction and language rights. *Language Problems & Language Planning*, 39(3):245 – 268.

[48]Ibid.

[49]Ibid.

[50]Ibid.

[51]Doiz, A., Lasagabaster, D., & Siera, J. M. 2011. Internationalization, multilingualism and English-medium of instruction. *World Englishes*, 30(3): 345 – 359.

[52]Ibid.

[53]Ibid.

[54]Lo Bianca, J. 2014. Domesticating the foreign: Globalisation's effects on the place/s of languages. *The Modern Language Journal*, 98(1): 312 – 325.

[55]Ibid.

[56]Ibid.

[57]Ibid.

[58]Doiz, A., Lasagabaster, D., & Siera, J. M. 2011. Internationalization, multilingualism and English-medium of instruction. *World Englishes*, 30(3): 345 – 359

[59]Mufanechiya, T. & Mufanechiya, A. 2011. The use of English language as the medium of instruction in the Zimbabwean Junior Primary schools. *Nawa: Journal of Language & Communication*, 5(1): 115 – 127.

[60]Ibid.

[61]Ibid.

[62]Ibid.

[63]Ntombela, B. X. S. 2016. 'The burden of diversity': The sociolinguistic problems of English in South Africa. *English Language Teaching*, 9(5):77 – 84.

[64]Canagarajah, S. 2007. Lingua franca English, multilingual communities, and language acquisition. *The Modern Language Journal*, 91: 923 – 939.

[65]Ibid.

[66]Kamwendo, G. H. 2010. Denigrating the local glorifying the foreign: Malawian language policies in the era of African Renaissance. *International Journal of African Renaissance Studies*, 5(2): 270 – 282.

[67]Chetty, R., & Mwepu, D. 2008. Language policy and education in South Africa: An alternative view of the position of English and African languages. *Alternation*, 15(2): 329 – 345.

[68]Kamwendo, G. H. 2006. No easy walk to linguistic freedom: A critique of language planning during South Africa's first decade of democracy. *Nordic Journal of African Studies*, 15(1): 53 – 70.

[69]Ibid.

[70]Mgqwashu, E. M. 2008. Literate English for epistemological access: The role of English studies. *Alternation*, 15(2): 301 – 328.

[71]Heugh, K. 2000. *The case against bilingual and multilingual education in South Africa*. PRAESA occasional papers, No. 6. Cape Town: PRAESA

[72]Maalim, H. A. 2015. The replacement of Swahili medium of instruction by English from Grades 5 in Zanzibar: From complementary to contradictory. *Nordic Journal of South African Studies*, 24(1):45 – 62.

[73]Chetty, R., & Mwepu, D. 2008. Language policy and education in South Africa: An alternative view of the position of English and African languages. *Alternation*, 15(2) :329 – 345

[74]Maalim, H. A. 2015. The replacement of Swahili medium of instruction by English from Grades 5 in Zanzibar: From complementary to contradictory. *Nordic Journal of South African Studies*, 24(1):45 – 62.

[75]Ibid.

[76]Ibid.

[77]Chetty, R., & Mwepu, D. 2008. Language policy and education in South Africa: An alternative view of the position of English and African languages. *Alternation*, 15(2): 329 – 345

[78]Hornberger, N. H. 2002. Multilingual language policies and the continua of biliteracy: An ecological approach. *Language Policy*, 1: 27 – 51.

[79]Ibid.

[80]Ibid.

[81]Maalim, H. A. 2015. The replacement of Swahili medium of instruction by English from Grade 5 in Zanzibar: From complementary to contradictory. *Nordic Journal of South African Studies*, 24(1): 45 – 62.

[82]UNESCO. 2016. *If you don't understand how can you learn?* Global education monitoring report. Policy paper 24. UNESCO.

[83]Chetty, R., & Mwepu, D. 2008. Language policy and education in South Africa: An alternative view of the position of English and African languages. *Alternation*, 15(2): 329 – 345.

[84]Ibid.

[85]Ibid.

[86]Kamwendo, G. H. 2010. Denigrating the local glorifying the foreign: Malawian language policies in the era of African Renaissance. *International Journal of African Renaissance Studies*, 5(2): 270 – 282.

[87]Heugh, K. 2000. The case against bilingual and multilingual education in South Africa. *PRAESA occasional papers No. 6.* Cape Town: PRAESA.

[88]Ibid.

[89]Lo Bianca, J. 2014. Domesticating the foreign: Globalisation's effects on the place/s of languages. *The Modern Language Journal*, 98(1): 312 – 325.

[90]Heugh, K. 2000. *The case against bilingual and multilingual education in South Africa.* PRAESA occasional papers, No. 6. Cape Town: PRAESA

[91]Bamgbose, A. 2000. *Language and exclusion: The consequence of language policies in Africa.* Hamburg: Lit Verlag.

[92]Heugh, K. 2000. *The case against bilingual and multilingual education in South Africa.* PRAESA occasional papers, No. 6. Cape Town: PRAESA.

[93]Johnson, R. W. 2016. UCT's critical choice: Go private or become another Turfloop. *Biznews.com.* Retrieved from: http://www.biznews.com/thought-leaders/2016/05/04/rw-johnson-uct-critical-choice-go-private-or-become-another-turfloop [Date accessed: March 12, 2016.]

[94]Ibid.

Chapter 11

Internationalisation and Africanisation of Master of Public Health Curricula in South Africa: Implications for Curriculum Transformation

Jackie Witthuhn
School of Health Sciences, Monash South Africa

Our people who were once enjoined to look to Europe and America for creative sustenance, turned their eyes to Africa - Nelson Mandela (1997).

11.1 Introduction and Background

An unprecedented transformation has been taking place in higher education in the past century. This change is of significant scope and diversity and has ensured that higher education institutions are able to prepare students globally to become a labour force fit to function in the interconnected world[1]. These substantive changes have been necessary and continue to be needed in higher education to prepare students for global perspectives and international experiences as they enter the globalised workforce of the current and future era[2]. Changes in higher education and the presence of a more diverse student population have also led to, and necessitated, changes in and differentiation within curricula[3].

The impact of the trend towards globalisation and internationalisation in higher education has also been felt in Africa, including South Africa[4]. Initially it was only evident in a small way, but its considerable growth is now evident in the increasing number of foreign students and academic staff from other countries who study and teach at South African higher education institutions. Considering the impact of globalisation and internationalisation on higher education in Africa and South Africa, we also cannot ignore the influence of 'Africanisation' in the higher education context. For Knight[5], as a concept, Africanisation can be understood to encompass all the dimensions of the process whereby a university endeavours to establish, and maintain, an African character to achieve certain academic, economic, political and cultural aims. Given the context thus outlined, the call for the Africanisation of the curricula in higher education institutions in South Africa has become inescapable. Recent protest action on university campuses nationwide has drawn attention to critical issues affecting the higher education arena, including the need for the transformation and Africanisation of the curricula. Horsthemke[6] highlighted that to encourage and promote Africanisation, higher education should look at changing the administrative bodies, the syllabi and their content, the curricula, and the criteria that determine what constitutes excellence in teaching and in research. Louw[7] also suggested that during the process of the Africanisation of curricula, the African reality should be earnestly considered when designing programmes and curricula. Louw[8] further explained that indigenous knowledge should be the point of departure for developing study material to meet the African framework. The need for an African approach to the internationalisation of higher education is illustrated in what Kotecha, as cited in Botha[9], referred to as the responsible approach, which "aligns the international dimension of the sector to the enhancement of the national, regional and continental development imperatives". It is therefore important for higher education institutions on the African continent, and consequently also in South Africa, to find a balance between the processes of internationalisation and Africanisation within their own organisations[10].

This chapter aims to clarify concepts in relation to internationalisation and Africanisation in the context of higher education and the associated curricula. The urgent need for curricula transformation in general, but also in relation to the Master of Public Health Curriculum (MPHC) in South Africa, is discussed. A brief synopsis is provided of the current status of MPHC, which is based on a recent study at South African higher education institutions. The synopsis is based on the views and understanding of the concept's internationalisation and Africanisation in relation to MPHC, but also takes account of the principles, rationales and processes for internationalisation and Africanisation of the curriculum, as reported by Master of Public Health (MPH) course coordinators, lecturers and students. The chapter concludes with recommendations towards the role of higher education institutions in curricula transformation as part of the African Renaissance movement in South Africa.

11.2 Explicating the concepts *Africanisation, Internationalisation* and *Curriculum*

To contextualise this chapter, it is necessary to explore the meaning of the concepts that underpin it. These concepts, which are also inherent to the transformation of higher education institutions, include internationalisation and Africanisation. It is also deemed necessary to include a discussion of these concepts as they pertain to higher education both in an African and a South African context, and their relevance more importantly to curricula developed in higher education institutions.

11.2.1 Internationalisation in relation to higher education and curricula in Africa and South Africa

According to Caruana as cited by Jones[11], there is little common understanding of the term 'internationalisation' in academic circles. The concept's meaning ranges from being associated with international rankings, to student recruitment, partnerships, research and teaching collaboration, mobility programmes and delivery in other languages. This has come about through curriculum internationalisation and the development of 'global perspectives' for all students and disciplines. The conceptualisation of internationalisation is sometimes also related to a university's mission so this breadth of interpretation is hardly surprising, however certain commonalities exist.

Knight[12] defined the internationalisation of higher education as the process of integrating an international/intercultural dimension into the teaching, research and service of the institution.

Similar definitions also describe internationalisation as a process, but focus on developing programmes and policies. Altbach[13] declared that internationalisation has more to do with the "specific policies and programmes undertaken by governments, academic systems and institutions, and even individual departments to deal with globalisation". All things considered, the concept 'internationalisation' is interpreted and used differently across countries and by different stakeholders[14]. Internationalisation is thus often seen as a process in higher education, as their institutions incorporate both international and intercultural dimensions in their main service functions, i.e. teaching and research.

With a widespread global increase in the number of international students, the internationalisation of higher education has become a catchphrase and is one of the major forces affecting and shaping higher education as it changes to meet the challenges of the 21st century[1] (Knight[15]; De Haan & Sherry[16]). It is forecast that by 2025 the demand for international education will grow to 7.2 million students – a quantum leap from 1.2 million students in 2000[17]. The internationalisation of higher education is a strategic theme in current research and is stated to be an educational goal at both national and institutional levels[18]. This trend is evident in educational policies that mention the need for international relevance in higher education and the mission statements of institutions that refer to preparing students for a global community.

Leask[19], amongst others, commented that the internationalisation of higher education has changed shape and purpose over the decades, which has consequently changed the meaning attached to the concept. In the last two decades, a number of definitions have been put forward by various researchers such as Knight[20], Knight and de Wit[21], and Van der Wende[22]. A common element of the definitions is the linking of the internationalisation of universities to 'globalisation' and the 'intercultural' dimensions integrated into the teaching, research and service functions of an institution. Knight's understanding of the internationalisation of higher education has been evident in the literature since the mid-1990s, and her work and definitions have influenced thinking on internationalisation and globalisation.

Mthembu[23] examined and clarified the meaning of the internationalisation of higher education for universities in Africa and in an African context, specifying three types of reaction to internationalisation processes. The first type is the "Embedding of an External Space onto an Internal Space". This type of internationalisation is discernible when a university in Africa adopts the identity and nature of another identity or culture, and at the same time embeds itself in the values, beliefs, conceptual system, philosophy and epistemology of the other. This can be compared to the colonisation process where the French came to Africa to render the African French, and where curricula and content foreign to African thinking and culture were embedded.

The second type is "Embedding of an Internal Space onto an External Space", which happens when a university external to Africa encompasses the values, beliefs, conceptual system, philosophy and epistemology of the African institution into its own. Thus, the internal space that Africa represents embeds itself within the external space that the rest of the world external to Africa represents. Mthembu[24] saw this as a challenge for universities in Africa to contribute to uniquely changing the other.

The third type is the "Isomorphism of the Two Spheres". Isomorphism between spheres happens when a university in Africa and a university in Europe or elsewhere external to Africa have 'equivalent', but not necessarily the same or similar, values, beliefs, conceptual systems, philosophies and epistemologies. In this case there are equal partners, and Africa has an equitable contribution to make to the world because there is some uniformity and equity among universities, all of which contribute towards making the modern university what it is.

In relation to the types of processes, Mthembu[25] further claimed that it would not be unreasonable to hypothesise that until recently, internationalisation for universities in Africa have been Type 1 embedding. Modern universities in Africa have been subservient in nature, form, and aspiration to universities in the West, which were established during the post-colonial period as imperfect clones of the universities of the West. Mthembu's[26] final analysis of the situation is that African universities cannot progress from a Type 1 to a Type 3 level without proving themselves at a Type 2 level, through establishing a united and unique contribution to the rest of the world.

For South Africa to take its place in the wider world and to ensure South Africa's role in the national development of the country, Kishun[27] reasoned that the question to ask is whether internationalisation is significant to South African universities as part of the post-apartheid transformation of higher education in South Africa. Botha[28] responded to this by stating that the internationalisation of higher education across the world has become the norm, claiming that it is also true for South African universities. The internationalisation activities of all local universities have increased dramatically in volume, scope and complexity over the past two decades. Rouhani[29] explained this further by saying that the increasing flow of international students to South Africa has brought new challenges and opportunities for its higher education institutions, which are caught between two countervailing necessities. On the one hand, there is the need to address the demands of institutional and systemic transformation resulting from an international student profile and student demands; while on the other hand, there is the attempt to come to terms with the pressures of internationalisation. Yet most of the institutions were, and maybe still are, unprepared for the rapid influx of international students that took place in the 1990s after the birth of the new democratic South Africa.

Kwaramba[30] maintained that South Africa is emerging as a major exporter of HE in the region as it has a large number of public universities - far more than any other country in Africa. Comparing South Africa with other countries across the world as a destination for higher education students from sub-Saharan African countries, especially Ghana, Nigeria and Kenya, South Africa is the second most popular country after the United States of America. South Africa has been rated one of the top ten destinations for foreign students waiting to pursue HE away from their home countries (UNESCO, 2009 as cited by Kwaramba[31]). By 2009, approximately 60 000 of the 2.8 million international students worldwide were enrolled in one of South Africa's 23 public universities (*Sunday Times*, 11 August, 2009 as cited by Kwaramba[32]).

In addition, with regard to policy and the institutionalisation of internationalisation of higher education, McLellan[33] drew attention to the fact that internationalisation is not listed by name as a policy objective of higher education in South Africa. However, the importance of internationalisation is implicit in and relevant to many of the priorities outlined in at least three of the country's key policy documents that influence higher education and its implementation. These are the 1996 White Paper on Science and Technology; the 1997 Education White Paper 3: A Programme for the Transformation of Higher Education; and the 2001 National Plan for Higher Education (NPHE). One of the key features of the two White Papers and the NPHE is that they relate to internationalisation and express the realisation that South Africa must address national needs within a global context as an imperative. Allowing the transformation process and curricula restructuring to work towards relevance and flexibility is suggested. All three South African policy documents recognise the global context as the background against which the country's thinking, institutions and individuals should operate, even when simultaneously considering national priorities.

'Internationalisation of the curriculum' is frequently cited in the literature as a strategy to engage with a diverse student population. Crosling, Edwards and Schroder[34] argued that the internationalisation of curricula is a response to the challenge to prepare graduates for employment in the global economy where they may work internationally. The introduction of international elements into the curricula is one of the most essential aspects of the internationalisation of higher education[35]. The internationalisation of curricula provides the most solid guarantee for the consolidation and institutionalisation of the international dimension in higher education.

Welikala[36] highlighted the complex landscape of research with regard to the internationalisation of curricula in higher education. The notion is multi-faceted and meanings and practices are vague due to a lack of clarity regarding the concept, thus he stated that further research is needed if clarity regarding the internationalisation of curricula is to be obtained. Knight[37] agreed that conceptual confusion and great diversity of the interpretation of the concept exists and that the concept is not clearly understood, however the importance of offering multi-dimensional curricula cannot be denied. Multi-dimensionality implies that both an international and intercultural dimension are included in a curriculum. In the African and South African contexts, it would be feasible to assume that the intercultural refers to an African or 'Africanised' approach. In general, HE throughout the world is under pressure to adapt to a global model, but at the same time is obliged to respond to national and local forces if it is to be relevant within its own context.

The conclusion that Mestenhauser and Ellingboe[38] drew almost two decades ago still stands, that the literature about international education "is generally silent about the nature of the internationalised curriculum and yet every field and discipline in international education makes assumptions about what to teach, how to teach it, when and to whom, in what sequence, and what quality and quantity". This clearly remains relevant for the present. Humphrey[39] agreed that the internationalisation of curricula is definitely not characterised by a clearly defined set of ideals or best practices, and that this concept needs further exploration and research. In their work, not one of these authors cited any research findings on which this internationalised form of curricula is based. This means that the concept of the internationalisation of curricula is still unclear and strategies for the process need to be sought, defined and refined.

11.2.2 Africanisation in relation to higher education and curricula in the contexts of Africa and South Africa

The need for an African approach to the internationalisation of higher education in South Africa cannot be overlooked. The democratisation of South Africa has necessitated the transformation of its education system. Naledi Pandor, Minister of Education for the period 2004-2009, was of the opinion that it is necessary to ensure that our commitment to Africa and to African solutions is reflected in the culture, organisational ethos and curricula framework and content of our higher education institutions[40]. South African universities are thus not only faced with the imperative of internationalisation, but also with that of Africanising the purposes, functions and curricula of universities (Moja, as cited by Kishun[41]). Moreover, Moja alluded to South African higher education institutions being faced with a double-edged sword. On the one hand, Africa has to redress the crippling legacies of the past, such as the policies of international development agencies including the World Bank that neglected African universities, while on the other hand, the globalising world brings new challenges. Moja (in Kishun[42]) thus proposed that a balance be struck between responding to inherited problems and new demands. These reflections seem to suggest that conflict between the idea of being African and the need to adapt to aspects of Western culture should be addressed and resolved.

Moreover, while some scholars have argued for a balanced knowledge creation approach between the global and local, Mbeki[43] contended that to address the critical needs of the continent, a distinctively African knowledge system with an objective of meeting the goal of recovering the humanistic and ethical principles embedded in African philosophy is necessary. According to Mbeki[44], such knowledge systems have to include an African identity and vision in higher education; a colonial-Western identity is neither suitable nor compatible with this identity. The critical point of departure should be an emphasis on an African identity and vision that encompasses African conditions, knowledge, experiences, values, worldviews and mindsets, centred on scholarship adopting a knowledge-seeking approach.

According to Nkoane[45], the Africanisation of African universities means at least redefining African-ness; collecting the roots of knowledge production; adapting curricula to meet African needs and aspirations; fostering indigenous languages as media of instruction; and the responsiveness of education to African cultures. Ramose[46] also wrote that:

> Africanisation holds that the African experience in its totality is simultaneously the foundation and the source for the construction of all forms of knowledge. ...Africanisation holds that different foundations exist for the construction of pyramids of knowledge. It disclaims the view that any pyramid is by its very nature eminently superior to all others. It is a serious question for a radical and vertical change of paradigm so that the African may enter into genuine and critical dialogical

encounter with other pyramids of knowledge. Africanisation is a conscious and deliberate assertion of nothing more or less than the right to be African.

In the same vein, Makgoba[47] also defended the Africanisation of higher education in South Africa, emphasising in his argument the importance of relevance and contextualisation in all HE functions. It can be assumed that relevance refers to a specific context and making sure that developed competencies relate to the contexts where Public Health Practitioners will work or practice. Husen, as cited by Van Wyk and Higgs[48], stated that the challenges of the African universities are similar to those of any other postmodern university, in that they have to fulfil the role of training professionals, promoting access, extending the frontiers of knowledge and serving the national economy. In doing all this, they must provide a service to the African continent and its people. Horsthemke[49] concurred when he explicated that higher education in Africa has to focus on the rebirth of the African voice and identity, and that Africanisation should be taken seriously by governments and higher education institutions.

Horsthemke[49] distinguished between positive and negative connotations in terms of the notion of Africanisation. Makgoba, Ramose and other authors as cited by Botha[51] embraced affirmation, whereas Grill (as cited by Botha[52]) described some negative conceptualisations of the term. De Beer[53], in her submission to the Centre for Education Policy Development, confirmed that Africanisation does not mean that Africa should isolate itself from the rest of the world, but neither does it mean that inferior or lower standards should be adopted. One important aspect that was raised by scholars in the field was that African higher education institutions can be both internationally competitive and uniquely African at the same time.

Taylor[54] pointed to the fact that the South African Minister of Higher Education and Training, Blade Nzimande, specifically called for the transformation of higher education institutions in March 2010. The *Soudien Report* also addressed the need for the Africanisation of curricula, and recommended that a body be established to specifically coordinate, oversee and guide the process and character of this[55]. However, progress in this regard seems slow and requires further investigation, as little appears to have emerged thus far regarding this matter. There seems to be two schools of thought about this. A minority of scholars argue for an 'exclusive' African approach to curriculum development, while the majority of scholars suggest a balanced or 'hybrid' approach that includes both the global and local dimensions of knowledge[56]. Ultimately, from the many reflections on Africanisation, the deduction that can be made is that the evident conflict can be resolved by being African and adapting to acceptable aspects of Western culture.

In a recent presentation at a prominent South African open distance learning higher education institution, Odora Hoppers[57] referred to the topic of the Africanisation of curricula as a tricky subject where nobody exactly knows what it should be. The risk that the Africanisation of curricula can become a 'cut and paste' job without academic understanding and not realising that people's lives and futures are at stake was further highlighted. Odora Hoppers[58] explained that Africanisation is essentially about African people being given the space to become themselves without duress. Both Taylor[59] and Louw[60], like Odora Hoppers, stressed the importance of restructuring curricula and the fact that the Africanisation of curricula is an imperative.

Moreover, it was suggested that it is time to rethink local content with a renewed focus on indigenous knowledge. Seepe, as cited by Louw[61], argued that indigenous knowledge systems would encourage learners to draw on their cultural practices and daily experiences as they negotiate and grapple with new situations and unfamiliar terrain. Le Grange[62] was also of the opinion that the inclusion of indigenous knowledge in South African curricula policy statements is a positive step and could provide opportunities for debate and interaction between Western and indigenous worldviews.

Botha[63] agreed with the majority of scholars who have recommended a balanced approach to the Africanisation of curricula, and wrote about the importance of compatibility between the global and local knowledge paradigms. Louw[64] similarly described Africanisation as an attempt to suggest ways to create a rich environment for active learning for the students who choose to study in Africa and have to still compete with the rest of the world. The balance between the local and global content matter is thus important. Those advocating for the Africanisation of higher education institutions have to be reminded to keep their eyes on the bigger picture, as what is happening in the global community inevitably dominates their teaching[65]. Academics should not forget to acknowledge that local villages have their 'place in the sun' that is part and parcel of their own indigenous knowledge, which can easily fit newly created study material that will be on a par with that offered globally. Louw[66] argued strongly for the inclusion of indigenous knowledge in the transformative curriculum design that envisages long-term curricula reform. Knowledge, skills and competencies, and values should be taught holistically from this perspective while taking the African reality seriously. Other thoughts include the fact that the internet has brought the global community into the local village, and although knowledge systems should be contextual, they should not be context-bound[67].

Fourie[68] explained that, as far as curricula are concerned, Africanisation means:

> ...an attempt to move away from course syllabi received from colonial or the apartheid system. It goes far beyond a simple adaptation to include transformation and innovation in the sense that the curricula should respond to the needs of our people and help them in their fight against underdevelopment, poverty, wars, diseases, unemployment and illiteracy.

This quotation consolidates what other writers have been saying, i.e. Africanisation implies that African academics should concentrate on the needs of African people[69]. The design of new curricula which are Africanised should help students to overcome the multi-faceted challenges of nation-building; national reconstruction; economic, technological, and scientific development; national, sub-regional and African integration; democratisation and globalisation. Africanisation does not imply that the entire curricula should be changed, but suggests that some of it will definitely need to be redesigned to focus on African philosophy and context. The Africanisation of curricula would demand that more research be done on African-related issues, and that current expertise in relation to African affairs be enhanced, whether from a South African or a continental perspective. However, Mangu, as cited by Fourie[70], stated that Africanisation does not mean compromising quality or lowering standards, as conservatives and radicals from the left and right who oppose Africanisation often fear. Nevertheless, as Louw[71] reminded us, the majority of African students come from educationally disadvantaged backgrounds and are thus often inadequately prepared for tertiary education. Needless to say, the assumption that this will have a negative and time-consuming impact on teaching staff at higher education institutions is justifiable. Nonetheless, attempting to address the challenges around the Africanisation of curricula is essential.

11.3 Master of Public Health training, curriculum developments and the need for change

There is limited capacity for training in public health in most higher education institutions in Africa. For the more than 900 million people living in Africa, there are only about 500 full-time Public Health Professionals, and half the countries in Africa do not even provide for postgraduate public health training[72]. The need for public health programmes, degrees and more trained Public Health Professionals is therefore clear. It is interesting to note that Zwanikken *et al.*[73] found that the number of Master of Public Health Practitioners in low- and middle-income countries is increasing. However, questions are being raised about the relevance of the outcomes of the programmes and the extent of the positive impact on their immediate locales. Admittedly, this development is a response to the crises in human resources for health provision and the need for a well-established public health workforce. A Master of Public Health Practitioner programme prepares medically and non-medically trained professionals for leadership roles in the evaluation of the health of populations. This is done through the planning, implementation and evaluation of interventions within the framework of a health care system. These programmes should concentrate on promoting well-being so that ill health is prevented. The fact that contexts within the low- and middle-income countries differ significantly from those of high income countries leads to questioning whether the existing MPHPs in the low- and middle-income countries are effective, and whether the taught competencies from these programmes are relevant to the contexts where they are practised[74].

Since the 1990s, internationally, higher education institutions have used detailed descriptions of expected performance or competencies as drivers of curriculum development. Programme evaluation, job function delineation and continuous professional assessments too have followed this global trend. Over the past decade, public health competencies have received considerable attention and have been developed and refined in a range of countries. In the north, the United States of America revised existing documents in 2010; the Public Health Agency in Canada published their Association of Schools of Public Health in the European Region (ASPHER) list in 2007; in Europe a list was drafted in 2008 and redefined in 2011; and in 2008, the United Kingdom endorsed the Public Health Skills and Career Framework. In the south in Australia, the Foundation Competencies for MPH alumni was published in 2009[75].

Frenk *et al.*[76] referred to the Global Independent Commission reviewing *Education for Health Professionals* for the 21st century, which recognises the transformation of education, as key to strengthening health care systems that promote health equity within and between countries. In addition, it is recognised that all health professionals in all countries should be educated to mobilise knowledge, to engage in critical reasoning and ethical conduct, and to competently participate in patient and population-centred health systems as members of locally responsive and globally connected teams. Providing more detail about competencies, Fleming *et al.*[77] referred to the fact that the majority of public health courses throughout the world have been at postgraduate level, referring to the 'Core Competencies for Public Health Professionals' that help to strengthen public health workforce development.

In the United States of America, a consensus set of competencies were listed as analytic assessment, policy development and programme planning, communication, cultural competency, community dimension of practice, basic public health services, financial management, leadership and systems thinking. In the United Kingdom, meanwhile, the Faculty of Public Health, a standard setting body, identifies the curriculum areas by outlining the competencies or learning outcomes that trainees in public health need to attain in order to complete training. Nine key areas relate to the three domains of public health practice, namely health protection, health improvement and service quality. Key areas include surveillance and assessment of a population's health and well-being; assessing the evidence of the effectiveness of health and health care interventions, programmes and services; policy and strategy development and implementation; strategic leadership and collaborative working for health; health intelligence; and academic public health.

The fact that restructuring the curriculum in terms of competencies constitutes a statement of intent on behalf of the provider neither demonstrates whether these competencies were acquired, nor whether the selected competencies had any effect either in the workplace or on society[78]. Very few Masters Programmes in health and health care define their intended impact on the workplace and in society as outcomes. Likewise, impact indicators are not specified[79]. In response to this gap, six low- and middle-income countries' higher education institutions, including the University of Western Cape and higher education institutions in Vietnam, China, Mexico, Sudan and The Netherlands, came together in December 2011 to design comparative impact evaluations across programmes. What is interesting and worthwhile noting is that the specific issues lacking were added to a new set of competencies as gender issues and 'pro-poor' and equity-based approaches. Competencies added to the existing list related to the social determinants of health, cultural and context-sensitive competencies, as well as context sensitivity to policies. Furthermore, inter-sectoral engagement was noted as a critical principle. The final set of seven core Public Health Competencies developed comprise policy development; planning and management; leadership and systems thinking; communication; analytical assessment; context-sensitive competencies; as well as community and inter-sectoral competencies[80].

Particularly relevant was the formation of the Association of Schools of Public Health in Africa (ASPHA) in November 2010, which provides a strategic opportunity for Schools of Public Health to jointly foster the practice and quality of public health training in Africa. This body has been working towards standardising the training for the Master of Public Health Degree (MPHD). One of the measures taken was to define the core competencies. Fonn[81] reminds us of the international trend to review curricula and core competencies for health professionals. The Association of Schools of Public Health in Africa, in collaboration with a number of international organisations, also defined core public health competencies for their African institutions by exploring the public health competencies appropriate for Africa. Moreover, the Association of Schools of Public Health in Africa put this framework forward as an initial discussion document with the aim to work towards benchmarking public health training in Africa. This document is currently only in a first draft stage and needs to be finalised, however some international and South African higher education institutions are consulting and including some of these 'African' competencies during their current curricula contextualisation reviews.

The need for change is apparent in the working environment of the public health workforce, which has changed dramatically in recent years due to rapid social, technological, political and economic changes[82]. Frenk *et al.*[83] asserted that the scope of responsibility for Public Health Professionals is broad and ever-increasing, and that many have had insufficient education and training on how to address the increasingly diverse and emergent public health challenges. The need for transformation in public health practice as well as the necessity for education providers to keep pace is recognised by local and global practitioners. Health care workers of the future must be equipped to listen, understand, support and collaborate with those in need, as well as being fit for purpose in the global employment market. McKimm and McLean[84] substantiated the above by saying that health care professionals must be prepared to 'think globally and act locally', and that the global health workforce needs to be culturally competent and socially acceptable. Global practitioners' advocacy role extends beyond the national boundaries and needs to work within disparate health care systems amidst shifting populations and changing disease patterns[85].

Suggestions towards change were explained by Fonn[86], who noted that Schools of Public Health in Africa (including South Africa) should respond to the many universal or global health issues that confound improvements in population level health through reviewing approaches to public health training. The author recommended a public health approach, focusing on research, collaboration, advocacy and networking, and strengthening health systems management. Fonn[87] referred to the problem of current programme specific interventions and a 'one-size-fits-all' approach as not being locally relevant. To overcome this problem, her suggestions included public health training focusing on local content and the local disease burden, so that graduates have the appropriate knowledge and skills for the environments in which they will work.

Furthermore, in order to develop the much needed globally competent public health graduates, careful consideration of an appropriate curricular approach is required. Public health curricula should train graduates to be change agents, who are equipped to think critically, make decisions, work as a team and provide leadership. It is important for graduates to understand the social determinants of health and disease to enable them to identify inter-sectoral partners with whom to work[88]. McFarlane *et al.*[89] agreed by stating that health professionals and students are demanding education programmes and curricula to prepare them for work in global health environments and academic institutions. Fleming *et al.*[90] verified this by stating that thoughtful mapping of curricula and levels of competencies is needed to address the future needs, skills and attributes of graduates. Attributes of global citizenship as well as specific global health content should be included. Frenk *et al.*[91] proposed transformative learning and suggested that in order to develop global health practitioners, education needs to consider the local context but global resources should be harnessed so that local challenges can be addressed using global knowledge, experience and shared resources. Frenk *et al.*[92] elaborated further by saying that preparing students for the dynamic changing global health care workforce requires an even more encompassing approach. Exposure to an international curriculum can challenge students, staff and institutions to think more broadly about how their skills might be utilised to serve communities in the most effective way.

It is clear that the MPHD in Africa should include universal core competencies common to any MPH graduate programme, but should also take account of the factors that have affected public health in Africa and address the needs particular to the continent. This approach should reverse the declining trends in health in many countries, including those in Africa. This will also enable any Public Health Professional to function successfully in both a global and a local setting.

11.4 The current status of the Master of Public Health curriculum in higher education institutions in South Africa

Academics who design and teach Master of Public Health Programmes (MPHPs) and students who follow the MPHP provided some insight into the current status of MPHPs in higher education in South Africa.

11.4.1 Understanding and views regarding the concepts 'internationalisation' and 'Africanisation' in relation to higher education

Evidence from the relevant literature suggests that HE has entered a new and challenging phase. A prevailing concern of these current challenges, which is undisputedly global, is the internationalisation of curricula and programmes. It can be argued that the unique circumstances that exist in higher education institutions in South Africa, which include a diverse African student profile, demand both an internationalised and Africanised approach to curricula development. The reason behind this is to ensure that students are equipped with the necessary knowledge and skills to perform and succeed in an African and globalised world. The internationalisation of curricula is imperative to providing relevant tuition to diverse student populations, and in the African context, the Africanisation of curricula is also especially important. Unfortunately, it would seem that because the concepts 'internationalisation' and 'Africanisation' are poorly defined, and perhaps even unsuccessfully implemented in higher education, the understanding of these concepts and processes is vague. This observation is not unexpected in light of evidence in the literature[93] that the concept of internationalisation is interpreted and used differently across countries and by various stakeholders.

Two possible reasons can account for this observation. Firstly, exposure to the process of internationalisation is limited since information on this process is not readily available and therefore the implications of the process are unknown. Secondly, the research landscape surrounding the internationalisation of curricula in higher education is simultaneously vague and complex, as Welikala[94] highlighted. It is furthermore multi-faceted; the meanings of the concept and its practices are vague due to a lack of clarity regarding what it is and what it entails. For the concepts to be better understood, they will undoubtedly need to be better defined and clarified. The processes of internationalisation and Africanisation seem to be interpreted and understood according to experience rather than formal definition. Furthermore, an understanding of the principles and rationales for the process of internationalisation and Africanisation need to be outlined for them to be better understood.

11.4.2 The extent to which Master of Public Health curricula presented at Higher Education Institutions in South Africa are viewed as being internationalised

It is generally believed that programmes are internationalised because institutions review curricula on an ad hoc basis and it is presumed that the purpose of these reviews is to determine their relevance and applicability to an international audience. Motivation for confirming that curricula are internationalised includes the fact that many international students are enrolled for courses; that the Master of Public Health Degree (MPHD) is recognised internationally; that there is international collaboration within the Schools and Departments of Health Science; that international benchmarking of the curricula occurs; that content and activities focus on global health issues; that international staff are employed in the higher education institutions to teach modules in the MPHD; and that student exchange programmes are followed.

11.4.3 The extent to which the Master of Public Health curricula presented at Higher Education Institutions are viewed as being Africanised

It is claimed that the curricula are informally adapted to ensure that ideas and principles of Africanisation are incorporated, but since formal directives regarding the inclusion of Africanisation processes are not in place, it cannot be unequivocally stated that the curricula are Africanised. In reality, the Africanisation of curricula is effected by lecturers who have taken the initiative to make their curriculum relevant to the African context. Certain fields of study are more Africanised than others, which points to the fact that there is no consistent approach or guiding principles regarding the Africanisation of MPHC as a whole. Justification for arguing that the MPHC is Africanised is based on the observations that the higher education institutions belong to the African Association of Public Health; that African textbooks in Public Health are used in teaching the programme; and that there is a diverse student profile – most of whom originate from a diversity of African countries – requiring Africanisation to ensure relevance.

11.4.4 Principles and rationales guiding the process of the internationalisation and Africanisation of the Master of Public Health curriculum

The rationale for the internationalisation of curricula is emphasised in order to produce global citizens and graduates who are able to work in any part of the world. Zimitat, as cited by Jones[95], as well as Webb[96], argued that graduates will be obliged to compete in international or multinational work environments and they need to be prepared for this eventuality. Botha[97] and Neale-Shuttee and Fourie[98] pointed out that students should have a secure place in the job market; should be exposed to the best and most up-to-date and relevant training; ought to acquire and develop multiple skills; and should be able to cope with the ever-increasing changes and skills that are transferable across cultures, climates and contexts. Leask[99] agreed and specified that 21st century university campuses and universities have a responsibility to prepare all graduates to live and work in a global society.

Rationales for the internationalisation and Africanisation of the curriculum include the diverse student profile, the global relevance of the MPHD, as well as the importance of recognising the African culture and identity. The literature specifically categorises rationales for the internationalisation and Africanisation of higher education as being economic, political, cultural and academic in practice (Knight[100]; De Wit[101]). Research in these areas has indicated that reference made to the rationales for internationalisation has an economic, cultural or academic connotation, although it was not specifically verbalised in this way. The rationales were global competitiveness; global acceptance of Public Health Professionals; and global accreditation and international recognition of the MPHC. The diversity of the general student profile was highlighted as another justification for the internationalisation and Africanisation of the MPHC. The only economic rationale highlighted was global competitiveness. Rationales with a political orientation were not mentioned. The respondents clearly recognised cultural rationales by referring to intercultural recognition and inclusion. Rationales relating to an academic significance were mentioned as international exposure in academe and the development of an international profile and the status of the institution.

With regard to the principles of the internationalisation and Africanisation of curricula, the literature referred to the ten 'Global Perspectives' of an internationalised curriculum, cited as the principles developed and presented by McKinnon[102]. The focus of these principles was on learning outcomes, content, teaching activities, feedback, training and support, and assessment tasks that respond to and enhance the international context and relevance. The only responses from my research participants that could be categorised as principles were the importance of having a balance between local and global contexts, as well as ensuring that the MPHC content is relevant to the geographical context of students.

11.5 Processes followed by higher education institutions in promoting internationalisation and Africanisation

Formal education-related activities, processes or minimum standards to facilitate the internationalisation and Africanisation of the MPHC are not in place at the higher education institutions that participated in the research. However, institutional and faculty strategies and approaches, including the appointment of international experts as well as strategic collaboration with other institutions from international and African countries, are facilitated and monitored. The higher education institutions' mission and vision statements that reflect both an international and African perspective are seen as strategies to ensure the internationalisation and Africanisation of the curricula. It is generally believed, however, that the formalisation of the processes to facilitate internationalisation and Africanisation would infringe on academic freedom.

In this chapter I have outlined the importance of curricula transformation in current times, as well as the principles that currently direct transformation processes. There are a number of recommendations that can be posited to promote and support the changes, which are briefly presented below.

All institutions in Africa should strive to embrace and incorporate the relevant processes associated with internationalisation and Africanisation, as these concepts are inextricably connected to curriculum development and transformation in the current age and higher education institutional climate. Internationalisation is a prevailing global reality in higher education institutions and Africanisation is a fundamental process in African higher education contexts. Both concepts need to be unequivocally elucidated to ensure clarity of meaning, and that those who use and apply these concepts have an accurate understanding of the essence of the concepts and are able to understand the requirements posed by implementing these processes. Internationalisation and Africanisation practices implemented in higher education institutions should be aligned with the concomitant agreed upon and accepted policies on these processes with a full understanding of the concepts. In the absence of a formal review process to establish whether the MPHD is indeed internationalised, a formal review process to establish this should be instituted. A framework that outlines the criteria to be used to establish the extent to which a curriculum is internationalised needs to be developed. In addition, a formal in-depth review of the MPHD needs to be conducted. Due to uncertainty regarding the precise meaning of the concept, guidance regarding its meaning and how Africanisation can be effected in practice should be addressed at the institutional level by the relevant higher education institutions and Schools of Public Health. Academics should understand the essence of the process of Africanisation and should be supported in Africanising the curricula and programmes offered at the institutions. All higher education institutions need to raise awareness regarding the principles and rationales that govern the internationalisation and Africanisation of curricula among staff and students, to ensure that the MPHC is adequately internationalised and Africanised according to established principles and rationales. The higher education institutions should further address the processes that facilitate the internationalisation and Africanisation of the curricula in a formalised and structured manner.

11.6 The role of higher education institutions in curricula transformation

An enabling higher education institutional environment with a supportive management structure will assist in addressing the insecurities, uncertainties and lack of support hampering the planning and implementation of the internationalisation and Africanisation of the curricula in higher education institutions. The development and communication of institutional policy for the internationalisation and Africanisation of the curricula needs to be prioritised, as must the development of clear definitions and guidelines in a South African and African context, including communication on processes to clarify the 'what' and 'how' to all staff and students, as part of existing institutional policies on internationalisation. Equity, redress and diversity should be taken into consideration when planning and implementing the internationalisation and Africanisation of curricula at higher education institutions. With regard to teaching and learning practices across schools and faculties, coherency and systematic practices need to embed both international and African perspectives. Ongoing training and curriculum transformation workshops in collaboration with all relevant stakeholders, including staff, students, alumni, employers, and subject experts, need to be prioritised. With reference to ongoing curricula review processes as well as interdisciplinary curricula planning, funding, resources and skills need to be ensured to enable curricula contextualisation. The Africanisation of curricula demands that more research be conducted on African-related issues and that current expertise in relation to African affairs needs to be enhanced, whether from a South African or continental perspective, or both. A niche area should be instituted for this purpose. More research in Africa by Africans should be prioritised, and publication in appropriate accredited international journals should be promoted. Ongoing consultation with relevant stakeholders in the process towards implementing and developing an internationalised and Africanised curricula, including students, alumni, academics, professional bodies and both private and public employers, should receive attention. The inclusion of both global and local content should be highlighted and an appropriate balance must be ensured between the two in the curricula as part of the suggested implementation strategy, including the strengthening of local and relevant teaching. In addition, research towards the development and writing of African-based modules and textbooks should receive attention. By expanding opportunities and the availability of international exchange programmes for staff and students, they will be able to reflect on their experiences in relation to those of others from whom they could possibly learn. The attendance of international and local conferences and training sessions should also be promoted to ensure that stakeholders remain informed and are able to share global and local initiatives and developments. Lastly, the increase of financial and human resources for the internationalisation and Africanisation of curricula should be prioritised.

The process and road forward to effect the internationalisation and Africanisation of the curricula regarding the MPHC is expected to be a long and challenging one. To realise this goal, the recommendations offered will have to be taken seriously at national, institutional and school levels.

11.7 Concluding comments

To conclude, both concepts – internationalisation and Africanisation – need further exploration, clarification and research. The implementation of internationalised curricula is still unclear however, and strategies for the process need to be sought, defined and refined. Existing frameworks and processes for doing so should be consulted and adapted to ensure contextual relevance when implemented and evaluated. Regarding Africanisation, acceptance of the notion and concept is needed before progress can be made. It is important to realise that Africanisation is not about lowering standards or excluding or isolating Africa from the rest of the world, but rather to instil pride and confidence in its ability to be successfully represented in a global knowledge society. Africanisation is seen as one of the imperatives of the transformation of higher education in South Africa. The need for an African approach to the international dimension of curricula, as well as the importance of striking a balance between the global and local content, is clear. However, to give Africa its rightful 'place in the sun', there is a need to focus on the inclusion of indigenous knowledge systems in our curricula to ensure redress, equity, social justice and inclusion as part of the African Renaissance movement.

In closing, a quote to capture the essence of the issue at hand:

> *In our curricula lies the very identity of our society. If we therefore want to change our society, address inequalities and develop ourselves into a just and healthy society, we need to change the very content of the vehicle through which we teach and develop our young people.* Dr Blade Nzimande

References

[1] Altbach, P. G., Reisberg, L., & Rumbley, L. 2009. *Trends in global higher education: tracking an academic revolution.* A report prepared for the UNESCO 2009 World Conference on Higher Education. Paris: UNESCO.

[2] Kishun, R. 2007. The Internationalisation of Higher Education in South Africa: Progress and Challenges. *Journal of Studies in International Education,* 11(3-4): 455-469.

[3] Altbach, P. G., Reisberg, L., & Rumbley, L. 2009. *Trends in global higher education: tracking an academic revolution.* A report prepared for the UNESCO 2009 World Conference on Higher Education. Paris: UNESCO.

[4] Botha, M. M. 2007. Africanising the curriculum: An exploratory study. *South African Journal for Higher Education,* 21(2): 202-216.

[5] Knight, J. 1994. *Internationalization Elements and Checkpoints. Canadian Bureau for International Education.* Research Monograph No. 7. Ottawa: Canadian Bureau for International Education.

[6] Horsthemke, K. 2004. Knowledge, Education and the Limits of Africanisation. *Journal of Philosophy of Education,* 38(4): 571-587.

[7] Louw, W. 2010. Africanisation: A rich environment for active learning on a global platform. *Progressio,* 32(1): 42-53.

[8] Ibid.

[9] Botha, M. M. 2007. Africanising the curriculum: An exploratory study. *South African Journal for Higher Education,* 21(2): 202-216.

[10] Ibid.

[11] Jones, E. 2011. Internationalisation, multiculturalism, a global outlook and employability. *Assessment, Teaching and Learning Journal,* 11: 21-49.

[12] Knight, J. 2008. *Higher education in turmoil: The changing world of internationalization.* Rotterdam: Sense Publishers.

[13] Altbach, P. G., Reisberg, L., & Rumbley, L. 2009. *Trends in global higher education: tracking an academic revolution.* A report prepared for the UNESCO 2009 World Conference on Higher Education. Paris: UNESCO.

[14] Knight, J. 2004. Internationalization Remodelled: definition, approaches, and rationales. *Journal of Studies in International Education,* 8(1): 5-31.

[15] Ibid.

[16]De Haan, D., & Sherry, E. 2012. Internationalisation of the Sport Management Curriculum Academic and Student Reflections. *Journal of Studies in International Education,* 6(1): 24-39.

[17]Knight, J. 2010. Internationalisation and the Competitiveness Agenda. In L.M. Portnoi., V.D. Rust and S.S. Bagley (Eds.). *Higher Education, Policy, and the Global Competition Phenomenon,* New York: Palgrave Macmillan, pp. 205-218.

[18]Svensson, L., & Wihlborg, M. 2010. Internationalising the content of higher education: The need for a curriculum perspective. *Higher Education,* 60: 595–613.

[19]Leask, B. 2011. Assessment, learning, teaching and internationalization – engaging for the future. *Assessment, Teaching and Learning Journal,* 11(Summer): 5-20.

[20]Knight, J. 2004. Internationalization Remodelled: definition, approaches, and rationales. *Journal of Studies in International Education,* 8(1): 5-31.

[21]Knight, J., & de Wit, H. 1995. Strategies for Internationalisation of Higher Education: Historical and Conceptual perspectives. In H. de Wit (Ed.). *Strategies for internationalisation of higher education: A comparative study of Australia.* Amsterdam: European Association for International Education, pp. 5-32.

[22]Van Der Wende, M. 2007. Internationalization of Higher Education in the OECD Countries: Challenges and Opportunities for the Coming Decade. *Journal of Studies in International Education,* 11(3-4): 274-289.

[23]Mthembu, T. 2004. Creating a Niche in Internationalization for (South) African Higher Education Institutions. *Journal of Studies in International Education,* 8: 282.

[24]Ibid.

[25]Ibid.

[26]Ibid.

[27]Kishun, R. 2007. The Internationalisation of Higher Education in South Africa: Progress and Challenges. *Journal of Studies in International Education,* 11:455.

[28]Botha, M. M. 2010. Compatibility between Internationalizing and Africanising Higher Education in South Africa. *Journal of International Education,* 14(2): 200-213.

[29]Rouhani, S. 2007. Internationalisation of South African higher education in the era. *Journal of Studies in International Education,* 11(3-4): 470-485.

[30]Kwaramba, M. 2012. Internationalisation of higher education in Southern Africa with South Africa as a major exporter. *Journal of International Education and Leadership,* 2(1):1-23.

[31]Ibid.

[32]Ibid.

[33]McLellan, C. E. 2008. Speaking of Internationalisation: An Analysis Policy of Discourses on Internationalisation of Higher Education in Post-Apartheid South Africa. *Journal of Studies in International Education,* 12(2): 131-147.

[34]Crosling, G., Edwards, R., & Schroder, B. 2008. Internationalizing the curriculum: the implementation experience in a Faculty of Business and Economics. *Journal of Higher Education Policy and Management,* 30(2): 107.

[35]Van Der Wende, M. 2007. Internationalization of Higher Education in the OECD Countries: Challenges and Opportunities for the Coming Decade. *Journal of Studies in International Education,* 11(3-4): 274-289.

[36]Welikala, T. 2011. *Rethinking International Higher Education Curriculum: Mapping the research landscape. Teaching & Learning Position Paper.* Nottingham: Nottingham University.

[37]Knight, J. 2004. Internationalization Remodelled: definition, approaches, and rationales. *Journal of Studies in International Education,* 8(1): 5-31.

[38]Mestenhauser, J. 1998. Portraits of an international curriculum: An uncommon multidimensional perspective. In J. A. Mestenhauser and B. J. Ellingboe (Eds.). *Reforming the higher education curriculum: Internationalizing the campus.* Phoenix: Oryx Press, pp. 3-39.

[39]Humphrey, D. 2008. *Internationalising the curriculum – Approaches, methods and techniques.* Paper presented at the Annual Learning and Teaching Conference, United Kingdom.

[40]Botha, M. M. 2007. Africanising the curriculum: An exploratory study. *South African Journal for Higher Education,* 21(2): 202-216.

[41]Kishun, R. 2007. The Internationalisation of Higher Education in South Africa: Progress and Challenges. *Journal of Studies in International Education,* 11: 455.

[42]Ibid.

[43]Mbeki, T. 2005. *Opening Address.* Cape Town: Conference of the Association of African Universities.

[44]Ibid.

[45]Nkoane, M. M. 2006. The Africanisation of the University in Africa. *Alternation,* 13(1): 49-69

[46]Ramose, M.B. 1998. Foreword in S. Seepe (Ed.). *Black Perspectives on Tertiary Institutional Transformation.* Johannesburg: Vivlia, pp. iv-viii.

[47]Makgoba, M. W. 1997. *Mokoko: the Makgoba Affair: A reflection on transformation.* Florida: Vivlia.

[48]Van Wyk, B., & Higgs, P. 2004. Towards an African philosophy of higher education. *South African Journal of Higher Education,* 18(3): 196-210.

[49]Horsthemke, K. 2004. Knowledge, Education and the Limits of Africanisation. *Journal of Philosophy of Education,* 38(4): 571-587.

[50]Ibid.

[51]Botha, M. M. 2007. Africanising the curriculum: An exploratory study. *South African Journal for Higher Education,* 21(2): 202-216.

[52]Ibid.

[53]De Beer, M. 2010. *Collaboration Recommendations for Culturally Relevant Teaching and Learning in Higher Education.* University of the Free State. Abstracts and Summaries for the NQF Research Conference; 2-4 June 2010.

[54]Taylor, S. 2010. *The performance of South African schools: implications for economic development.* Unpublished doctoral dissertation. Stellenbosch: Stellenbosch University.

[55]Ibid.

[56]Ibid.

[57]Odora Hoppers, C. A. O. 2012. *Africanisation of the Curriculum. A presentation at UNISA College of Education Tuition Committee.* Retrieved from: www.unisa.ac.za/news/index.php/2012/09/africanising-the-curriculum. [Date accessed: March 1, 2014.]

[58]Ibid.

[59]Taylor, S. 2010. *The performance of South African schools: implications for economic development.* Unpublished doctoral dissertation. Stellenbosch: Stellenbosch University.

[60]Louw, W. 2010. Africanisation: A rich environment for active learning on a global platform. *Progressio,* 32(1): 42-53.

[61]Ibid.

[62]Le Grange, L. 2007. Integrating Western and Indigenous Knowledge Systems: The Basis for Effective Science Education in South Africa? *International Review of Education,* 53(5/6): 577-591.

[63]Botha, M. M. 2010. Compatibility between Internationalizing and Africanising Higher Education in South Africa. *Journal of International Education,* 14(2): 200-213.

[64]Louw, W. 2010. Africanisation: A rich environment for active learning on a global platform. *Progressio,* 32(1): 42-53.

[65]Ibid.

[66]Ibid.

[67]Horsthemke, K. 2004. Knowledge, Education and the Limits of Africanisation. *Journal of Philosophy of Education,* 38(4): 571-587.

[68]Fourie, P. J. 2005. The last word. The "Africanisation" of communication studies. Where do we stand with the "Africanisation" of communication studies? *Communicar,* 24(1): 171-176.

[69]Ibid.

[70]Ibid.

[71]Louw, W. 2010. Africanisation: A rich environment for active learning on a global platform. *Progressio,* 32(1): 42-53.

[72]Fonn, S. 2011. Linking public health training and health systems development in sub-Saharan Africa: opportunities for improvement and collaboration. *Journal of Public Health Policy,* 32: 44–51.

[73]Zwanikken, P. A. C., Huong, N. T., Ying, X. H., Alexander, L., Wadidi, M. S. E. A, Magaña-Valladares, L. *et al.* 2014. Validation of public health competencies and impact variables for low- and middle-income countries. *BMC Public Health,* 14: 55. DOI: 10.1186/1471-2458-14-55.

[74]Ibid.

[75]Ibid.

[76]Frenk, J., Chen, L., Bhutta, Z. A., Cohen, J., Evans, T., *et al.* 2010. Health Professionals for a new century: transforming education and strengthen health systems in an interdependent world. *The Lancet,* 376(9750): 1923-1958.

[77]Fleming, M. L., & Parker, E. 2009. *Introduction to Public Health.* Sydney: Elsevier.

[78]Zwanikken, P. A. C., Huong, N. T., Ying, X. H., Alexander, L., Wadidi, M. S. E. A, Magaña-Valladares, L. *et al.* 2014. Validation of public health competencies and impact variables for low- and middle-income countries. *BMC Public Health,* 14: 55. DOI: 10.1186/1471-2458-14-55.

[79]Ibid.

[80]Ibid.

[81]Fonn, S. 2011. Linking public health training and health systems development in sub-Saharan Africa: opportunities for improvement and collaboration. *Journal of Public Health Policy,* 32: 44–51.

[82]Kuiper, T., Meijer, A., & Moust, A. 2011. Innovation in Public Health Teaching: The Maastricht Experience. *Public Health Reviews,* 33: 300-14.

[83]Frenk, J., Chen, L., Bhutta, Z. A., Cohen, J., Evans, T., *et al.* 2010. Health Professionals for a new century: transforming education and strengthen health systems in an interdependent world. *The Lancet,* 376(9750): 1923-1958.

[84]McKimm, J., & McLean, M. 2011. Developing a global health practitioner. *Medical Teacher,* 33: 626-631.

[85]Ibid.

[86]Fonn, S. 2011. Linking public health training and health systems development in sub-Saharan Africa: opportunities for improvement and collaboration. *Journal of Public Health Policy,* 32: 44–51.

[87]Ibid.

[88]Ibid.

[89]Macfarlane, S. B., Jacobs, M., & Kaaya, E. E. 2008. In the name of global health: trends in academic institutions. *Journal of Public Health Policy,* 29(4): 383-401.

[90]Fleming, M. L., & Parker, E. 2009. *Introduction to Public Health.* Sydney: Elsevier.

[91]Frenk, J., Chen, L., Bhutta, Z. A., Cohen, J., Evans, T., *et al.* 2010. Health Professionals for a new century: transforming education and strengthen health systems in an interdependent world. *The Lancet,* 376(9750): 1923-1958.

[92]Ibid.

[93]Knight, J. 2004. Internationalization Remodelled: definition, approaches, and rationales. *Journal of Studies in International Education,* 8(1): 5-31.

[94]Welikala, T. 2011. *Rethinking International Higher Education Curriculum: Mapping the research landscape. Teaching & Learning Position Paper.* Nottingham: Nottingham University.

[95]Jones, E. 2011. Internationalisation, multiculturalism, a global outlook and employability. *Assessment, Teaching and Learning Journal,* 11: 21-49.

[96]Webb, G. 2005. Internationalisation of the curriculum, an institutional approach. In J. Caroll and J. Ryan (Eds.). *Teaching International Students: Improving Learning for All.* Abington: Routledge, pp. 109-118.

[97]Botha, M. M. 2007. Africanising the curriculum: An exploratory study. *South African Journal for Higher Education,* 21(2): 202-216.

[98]Neale-Shutte, M., & Fourie, J. 2006. Challenges to Internationalisation in African Higher Education: A Case Study. *South African Journal of Higher Education,* 20(1): 41-54.

[99]Leask, B. 2011. Assessment, learning, teaching and internationalization – engaging for the future. *Assessment, Teaching and Learning Journal,* 11(Summer): 5-20.

[100]Knight, J. 2004. Internationalization Remodelled: definition, approaches, and rationales. *Journal of Studies in International Education,* 8(1): 5-31.

[101]De Wit, H. 2010. *Internationalisation of Higher Education in Europe and its Assessment, Trends and Issues.* NVAO Nederlands-Vlaamse Accreditatie organisatie. Retrieved from: http://www.nvao.net/page/downloads/Internationlization_of_Higher_Education_in Europe_DEF_december_2010.pdf. [Date accessed: November 30, 2012.]

[102]McKinnon, S. 2013. What does it mean for us? Academics' perceptions of internationalising the curriculum: The Global Perspectives Project at Glasgow Caledonian University, *International Enhancement Themes Conference: Enhancement and Innovation in Higher Education.* Glasgow, 11-13 June 2013.

Chapter 12

A critique of Africanised Curricula in Higher Education: Possibilities for the African Renaissance

Mago W. Mndawe
College of Education, University of South Africa

12.1 Introduction and Overview

Education researchers seem to agree that education is a complex and challenging enterprise. Its implementation is seen as guided by well thought-out design and development plans, that depend on well trained educators, involved parents, and learners who are fully taking learning into their own hands. We also know the importance and effectiveness of well-resourced learning institutions. This observation about education points to the current changing role of education and educators. Calderhead[1] argued that there are two visions for teaching which are frequently presented by national education policies. Vision one is the challenge of teaching in the present time, including perceived problems and difficulties encountered in the process. Vision two is the question of how teaching ought to be or how it is expected to be in future (as guided by the 'future context of human life'). Critiquing these visions, Calderhead[2] pointed out that visions of teaching will always be embedded within a particular cultural and ideological context, attaching importance to particular values or practices, and in the process of teaching, identifying any other aspects or processes of teaching that do not undergird the cultural and ideological contexts is problematic. In South Africa, for example, the concern in education after 1994 has been to change the notion of perceiving learners as empty vessels that are ready to be 'filled in' with knowledge, and educators as the possessors of all that is to know, making education the most sought-after commodity in the world. Or should one say, in some parts of the world?

The commodification of education is a direct result of a market ideology in which education is seen as a commodity to be produced and delivered at the best price. Needless to say, this is fodder for globalisation[3]. There has been little research focused on "understanding the processes of teaching and learning as they occur in classrooms and to the factors that influence and support the quality and effectiveness of those experiences"[4]. "There is a need for policymakers to appreciate much more fully the complexity of teachers' work, the contribution of appropriate training and support, and the importance of maintaining a work environment that elicits and fosters teachers' enthusiasm, energy, commitment and expertise"[5]. Goodland[6], commenting on the change reforms needed in education in the United States of America (USA), pointed out the complexity of the process of educators rethinking their ideas about teaching and their own practice, and went on to emphasise the importance of learning institutions working within the context of their community support. This observation by Goodland cannot be confined to the USA only, however, as education is a global humanity programme.

Weimer[7] pointed out five assumptions that devalue university (higher education) teaching or education (note that the words 'teacher' and 'educator' are used interchangeably in this chapter), namely that teaching excellence is nothing more than a matter of technique; teaching requires no training or ongoing professional development; pedagogical practice and scholarship can exist without standards; the wisdom of practice contains no real knowledge of importance; and content (not students or learning) should drive instructional decision making). Without critiquing the five assumptions that devalue higher education teaching, I want to single out content and argue that in the South African higher education landscape, curriculum content should be Africanised as explored in this chapter. The intention is not to suggest in any way that content, and not students and learning, should drive instructional decision-making, and that such an endeavour should deliberately create opportunities for the development of the African Renaissance. The focus of this chapter is therefore that content is but one aspect of the success of higher education; what is taught, by whom, and for whom is critical for the African Renaissance.

It is for the above reason that the issue of Africanising curricula in higher education learning institutions has become central to education discourse in South Africa and beyond. This thinking seems to suggest that higher education will be able to account to relevant content, and why it is taught. Before addressing these questions however, I want to focus on the so-called elusive and nebulous concept, *Africanised* or *Africanisation*. Although numerous scholars have ventured to clarify what they see as an Africanised curriculum (Makgoba[8]; Nkoane[9]), some are critical of the Africanisation of education in teaching and learning (Horsthemke[10]; Mangu[11]). Some scholars claim that Africanisation has been 'hijacked' by politicians for their own political advancement. Of course, such a notion is not far from the truth since education is always perceived as an instrument for advancement; advancement in getting out of poverty, advancement in getting ahead in life, advancement in being prosperous. Besides, scholars like Freire[12] and many others are convinced that education is political by its nature, and therefore needs to advance Africanised curricula derived from African thought and African ways of knowing.

Makgoba[13] averred that key features of Africanisation suggest that it is a way of life for Africans, and that it incorporates, adapts and integrates other cultures into and through African visions, and in the process, provides the dynamism, evolution and flexibility so essential in the global village. He further claimed that "Africanisation is the process of defining or interpreting African identity and culture". Ramose[14] argued that Africanisation claims that the African experience in its totality is simultaneously the foundation and the source for the construction of all forms of knowledge, and could be used for enriching or providing useful insights into its own content or the content of what an African curriculum ought to be. Of note from the two observations is that Africanisation emanates from an African identity; it is a way of life of the African people, it is their experience in totality, and it is dynamic and flexible. These are useful observations that portray Africanisation as "being at the heart of a people" and also portray a non-conclusive knowledge creation process, but it is an incomplete one (see a later discussion regarding the open-endedness of an Africanised curriculum). A clarification not so different from the one pointed out by Makgoba is that of Louw[15], who claimed that Africanisation:

...reflects our common legacy, history and postcolonial experience. Through this legacy, we have to connect with the broader African experience and establish a curriculum that binds us together. We then confront our own sense of Africanness, transcend our individual identity, seek our commonality, and recognise and embrace our otherness.

Furthermore, Louw[16] pointed out that, "Africanisation seems to be about shared beliefs, values and assumptions that can be found in the language practices and beliefs of all African cultures, and it seems to be more of a communal activity than an individual thing". This is an emergence of Africans' pride in their identity as a people, and its curriculum should be underscored by a local indigenous knowledge programme, geared to foster Africans' competitiveness in the global space.

This chapter is therefore premised on the understanding and acknowledgement that Africanising curricula in higher education is non-negotiable and imperative if Africa is to legitimise its African knowledge systems, which are pillars of the African Renaissance. Of note is the content of the African Renaissance as perceived by what Mangu[17] argued for; a call to all African academics to concentrate on the needs of African people and design curricula, which intends to:

...improve the life conditions of their people and help them overcome the multifaceted challenges of nation-building, nation reconstruction, economic, technological, and scientific development, national, sub-regional and African integration, democratisation, globalisation, and so on.

In addition, Mangu declared that Africanised curricula would demand that we research more on African-related issues and enhance our expertise on African affairs. There are numerous socio-economic, bio-physical, environmental, political and health problems and crises that the world is faced with, and Africa in particular. A more relevant and appropriate curriculum is thus a necessity.

12.2 Conceptualising an Africanised Curricula in Higher Education

Intrinsic value of cultural practices can be acknowledged by different African peoples, but they also acknowledge the cultural evolution of such values. This view is key to knowledge creation since knowledge is not static but dynamic. Within this frame of thought there is also the understanding that the Africanisation of education and knowledge are two projects that are usually discussed together. Do they mean different things? Horsthemke[18] perceived them as two distinct projects that warrant a separate discussion for conceptual clarity, and for the sake of Africanisation of knowledge which is a difficult and problematic idea.

Quoting Matos, Secretary General of the Association of African Universities, Horsthemke[19] stated that the process of Africanising universities has proved to be a difficult one that is still far from being complete. This is just where the problem lies. How can Africanisation be complete? Can the production of any kind of knowledge be complete? As alluded to above, certainly not.

As cultures evolve and traditions change, so the way of doing and perceiving things change, sometimes for the better and sometimes for the worse.

It is for this reason that this discussion is grounded in constructivism and social-culturism approaches to knowledge construction, and that these approaches are of course underscored by Derrida's[20] perspective of education. Note also that constructivism approaches are underscored by the notion that understanding and learning are active, constructive, generative processes (e.g. assimilation, augmentation, adaptation, etc.), and self-reorganising (e.g. a teacher's words do not simply become directly engraved in a student's mind after passing through the ear, but rather, those words are acted upon and interpreted by the student)[21]. These scholars further pointed out that socio-culturism's central notion is that learning is enculturation; the process by which learners become collaborative meaning makers among a group defined by common practices, language, the use of tools, values, beliefs, and so on, with a goal to enable practices and meaning making that are appropriate in the professional culture of the domain under study. For example, scientists understand science as those ideas that are embodied in their everyday practices[22].

In the same line of thought, Vygotsky's Social-Cultural Theory seems to concur with the above, and adds that social-culturalism eliminates social interactions that occur in learning communities or in social learning environments. Vygotsky[23] further contended that learning is an active process in which learners construct new ideas or concepts based upon their current and past knowledge. This scholar argues that learners choose and permute knowledge, construct hypotheses and make decisions, and while performing these learning activities, they rely on their cognitive structuring of knowledge, however Freire[24] put this idea differently when he declared that educators' mediation of learning should be much more effective, as educators lucidly and objectively make clear to the learners that changing one's position in what one knows is legitimate, and that there should be reasons for positions made for change. However, Freire[25] cautioned that the relationship between educators and learners is complex, fundamental and difficult, and that it is a relationship which should be thought of constantly. What is critical in this view is that meaning is made in social interactive relationships, and that the learning relationship, although complex, is not linear. It must enable learning to thrive, and to enable change to take place between those engaged in learning. This line of thinking also points to the fact that learners are not empty when they enter the learning relationship; they are endowed with cultural and traditional ways of knowing which are essential for learning.

Beside the fact that both the theory and practice of Africanisation are critical in higher education curricula, it is crucial that some of the key concepts of Africanised curricula are illuminated. This will further ground the exposition of different sections of this chapter for emphasis and understanding. The concepts below are not necessarily the focus of exploration themselves, however they are key concepts in this study that give guidance to what Africanised curricula in higher education should engage with if the African Renaissance programme is to be advanced.

12.3 Curricula appropriate for the World Citizenry

There is agreement amongst people of the world that the world is not just one big whole, but it is many parts; there is one world, with many parts called countries. This points to the view that the world is plural in nature, and because it incorporates everything that is common to humanity, it does not discriminate – it accommodates, it does not single out - it embraces all. However, each country seems to be more concerned with what is common to the country itself and not to other countries, i.e. it discriminates itself, sets itself apart and sees itself as different from the rest. By so doing it fosters that which is different in each country and not that which is common in all the countries. These two dialectical sides of the same coin, based on the notion of similar countries versus different countries, can be perceived as a strength and a weakness when one wants to understand singularity and plurality. Higher Education curricula that ignore the complementary and supplementary nature of the two opposite approaches to knowledge use and appreciation stand to hegemonise either singularity or plurality. For example, although the peoples of Africa are different in their languages spoken and their cultural ways of life, they are all common to each other because they all love peace, prosperity and good health, and all of them are on the African continent. Therefore, diversity should be acknowledged, celebrated and used to strengthen commonality: humanness that loves peace, good health and prosperity and a better life for all. There are, therefore, common things in Africa, and they need to bind Africans to a diversified perspective; a perspective that allows them to appreciate difference but also appreciate commonality. Teffo [26] concurred that this is an enabling African educational philosophy.

Such an African educational philosophy is premised on African peoples' deliberate advancement - educationally, economically, politically and so forth - and therefore African peoples' ways of knowing become pertinent to such an African philosophy. Scholars like Gutto[27] also acknowledged the necessity of African indigenous knowledge systems in enhancing knowledge deficits in society. Mbeki[28] and Makgoba[29] called for an African Renaissance, perceived by many scholars as a pillar for African thought and way of life, and Ntuli[30] reaffirmed what he calls *African civilisation*, which he perceives as the African way of knowing and day-to-day living. All these notions of knowledge systems are African perspectives – African ways of looking at their own world (Africa) and the world at large. Of note is that what underscores African knowledge systems is an African educational philosophy that does not view the world as belonging to just individuals, but that starts with the common (community/many) and ends with the particular (individuals/differences). This philosophy seems to be missing in Higher Education learning. This discussion thus deliberately seeks to embed Africanised curricula in Higher Education in African Renaissance programmes as mandatory, and as an integral exercise for individual countries of Africa, Africa as a whole, countries of the world and the world. This means that the curricula reforms of teaching and learning at higher education institutions ought to transform to African ways of knowing if they seek to be inclusive and enhanced. However, my word of caution is that higher education curricula are not immune to curricula in higher education designed and implemented elsewhere in Africa and the world.

12.3.1 African educators (and scholars) accorded the opportunity to contribute with 'indigenised' approaches

It is a known fact that there are numerous factors that affect educational outcomes beyond the schooling institution, for example support within the family and support among peers, however the educator seems to be the most influential person in the lives of learners[31]. Of note is that in many reforms initiated globally, instead of galvanising sufficient support for educators, reforms seem geared towards taking control "out of the hands of teachers and teacher educators, and training and support are being replaced by prescription and regulation"[32]. This situation needs to change. In the African context, the educator needs to be accorded the opportunity to not only facilitate learning, but to be a creative and innovative planner of learning experiences grounded in the knowings of the institutional community, the community within the area of the institution, and the world at large. This does not in any way diminish the role of the external community, however Calderhead[33] cautioned:

> Within the rapid educational reforms that have occurred over the past decade, the processes involved have not generally changed from the textbook ideals. More typically, teachers have been viewed as production workers, mechanically implementing the plans of others. Or, where they are involved in the development and management of reform, their involvement has been viewed as either motivational strategy, winning teachers round to the new ideas, or as a perfunctory acknowledgement or token act of respect for the profession that carries the responsibility for making the new ideas work in practice.

Reiterating the notion of an indigenised teaching and learning enterprise, Atal[34] contended that during the 1970s, "indigenous scholars from the Third World raised their voice against the implantation of social sciences perpetuating 'captivity' of mind", and that "they were joined by a number of social scientists from Western countries sharing this concern". This is a clear indication that indigenous people felt that teaching and learning did not address their needs since it was a mere implantation of the social sciences 'captivity of the mind' agenda. This fact does not need more clarification; when education stops being seen as emancipatory and enabling, and is seen as sending the mind to captivity, it simply means that it is an education not grounded on the knowings and needs of the people it aspires to educate. Clarifying what the characteristics of a 'captive mind' are, Alatas[35] explained that "a captive mind is the product of higher institutions of learning, either at home or abroad, whose way of thinking is dominated by Western thought in an imitative and uncritical manner" and that "it is alienated from the major issues of society".

It is hoped that Africanising the curricula in higher education will enable students to realise that learning should be in harmony with their own cultural traditions and the dictates of their local situations. Of note is the reiteration by Alatas[36] that educators needed for courses in Africanisation need to be carefully selected from a pool of emancipated scholars in Africa and the diaspora; these should be scholars who understand universal knowledge and cultural grounded knowledge, and in the interest of Africa, these should be educators who are schooled in the African Renaissance programme.

12.3.2 African students accorded the opportunity to contribute with 'indigenised' knowledge

Students are perceived as creators of knowledge during their participation in their learning; they are not empty vessels "ready to be filled with knowledge"[37] through transmission teaching strategies. The teaching and learning environment acknowledges the fact that students come into the internal learning environment with a knowing of their own, which is informed by the African context by and large, and to a lesser degree by the global capital, thus they have a rich external learning institutional context in African knowing. Hence, this knowing needs to be explored using different strategies in the internal teaching and learning environment. It is for that reason that Higher Education Summit Forum/Academic Experience[38] cautioned that if students are denied:

> ...from bringing their own reference points to the study ...surely this must affect the ability of the students to perform at their best? A whole module on family law is about western legal concepts: learning and debate takes place in that context, interrogation of indigenous family law is left to a small part of one module on indigenous law. How will the indigenous knowledge about indigenous family law and the thinking behind it be recognised in the students' performance? How will it be allowed to develop and adapt to modern cultural changes? How will it contribute to the advancement of our western based legal concepts?

Attesting to this view of students being active participants in the process of making meaning of what they are learning and bringing their varied ways of knowing into the learning environment, Nkoane[39] reiterated that "Africanisation of universities is about turning the globe over so that we see all the possibilities of the world, where Africa assumes a role of a subject rather than an object that is positioned at the margins".

12.3.3 An opportunity to legitimise universal 'humanness'

One extremely dangerous approach to the sovereignty of countries and communities has been the division of people into separate states. Although this view enables each country to manage its own affairs (as argued above), it has created the thinking that each country is "bigger" than the other and led to the birth of the so-called 'super powers' notion. Needless to say, social, political, human, religious, environmental and health injustices all came to the fore due to the fact that the sovereignty status of countries superseded the primary goal of the humanness of states, i.e. ensuring good governance and human development. It is for this reason that Africanised curricula should aspire to develop people who are grounded in their indigenous ways of knowing, but who also possess world citizenry capital.

12.3.4 An opportunity to acknowledge the interconnectedness of disciplinary knowledge

To be able to explore environmental issues, political solutions, health responses and economic problems that have become too complex and fluid to contemplate, there is a need for a sound understanding of the interconnectedness of disciplinary knowledges. Maila (2012: 1159-1160)[40] reiterated the fact that higher education learning should be geared towards understanding the current local and global challenges. This scholar further indicated that social constructivist epistemology denotes:

> ...organisations/situations as complex, dynamic contradictory entities, constantly (and actively) transformed by human beings. This means that education systems across the globe should make it their business to educate for local living and international living. Furthermore, higher education should design and plan open learning curricular; curricular that acknowledges that there is no single reality or truth; that contexts play a pivotal role in shaping meaning making, and that contexts exist because of meanings shaping them.

Plurality in knowledge construction allows for multi-faceted approaches to be at play. Africanised curricula are fundamentally seen as pillars of new ways of approaching teaching and learning for both local and international settings, underpinned by a deliberate undertaking that the interconnectedness of knowledge, approaches or strategies to teaching and learning is not only crucial for humanity, but also for the African Renaissance agenda.

12.3.5 An opportunity to acknowledge Africanisation as an open-ended knowledge creation approach

According to Atal[41], "the Westernisation/modernisation package has a much wider clientele". Why? Because "academic colonisation ... went beyond the boundaries of political colonies; countries that managed to retain their political autonomy could not prevent the vicarious colonisation of their academia".

It is in the academic space that colonisation sank its teeth into the matters of indigenous people and their education, and promoted the implantation of social sciences perpetuating captivity of mind. This occurred in both the colonised countries and the non-colonised ones. The status of education as a service to the community was gradually changed to a status of class and individual benefit to oneself. UNESCO[42] seems to bemoan this situation when saying:

> [The] number of indigenous social scientists have undoubtedly increased but they are more in contact with their Western colleagues than with their counterparts in the Third World or, for that matter, even within their own region; the question these social scientists ask, the paradigms and research techniques they employ, the vision they have of the future of their countries-all these are for the most part imported from the West, or at best adapted from the work of the Western thinkers including social scientists. No wonder then, that social sciences in the Third World are often judged to be irrelevant and the social scientists accused of being alienated from their societies.

Nkoane[43] argued that this state of things should change. He noted that the Africanisation of higher education should be about turning the globe over so that all the possibilities the world can offer can be noted, and Africa may assume her role of a subject rather than an object positioned at the margins. Needless to say, now, more than before, Africanised curricula are needed for Africa in particular, as well as for the world in general.

12.4 Why are Africanised curricula in higher education needed more than before?

Often people regard formal education as a way of accessing a variety of things including finances or wealth. This notion is not only short-sighted, but is also irresponsible on the part of those who perceive education as a necessary fulfilling act and not just for "accumulation of opulence". Nussbaum[44], critiquing the education system of some of the schools in India, relates this story:

> I visited the literacy program for girls, housed in a shed next door (to the Patnacentered NGO Adithi). The girls of the village, goat-herds by day, were beginning their school day around 4 p.m. about 15 girls in all, age 6-15, and come to this single classroom for three hours of after-work learning. There are no desks, no chairs, no blackboard, and only a few slates and bits of chalk. Nonetheless, it all seemed to work, through the resourcefulness and passion of the teachers, themselves poor rural women who have been assisted by Adithi's programs. Proudly the girls brought in the goats that they had been able to buy from the savings account they have jointly established in their group. Mathematics is taught in part by focusing on such practical issues. After that, the girls performed for us a play that they had recently performed for the village. It was about dowry, and the way this institution makes female lives seem to be of lower value to parents than male lives.

From this narrative, Nussbaum drew the following conclusions: 1) the close linkage between education and critical thinking about one's social environment; 2) the emphasis on the arts as central aspects of the educational experience; and 3) the intense passion and investment of the teachers, their delight in the progress and also of the individuality of their students. Other themes that emerged from this scene are: 4) a deliberate effort to educate the girl child; 5) a deliberate effort to teach multiple disciplinary, instead of hegemonising certain fields of study; 6) teaching how to outsmart poverty right from an early age; and 7) how socio-cultural learning cannot be extricated from the development and economics of the day. I therefore intend using these observations by Nussbaum[45] and those proposed by myself to guide the discussion. In other words, I see these themes as pivotal to broad-based and plural Africanised curricula that offer learning opportunities that are both particular, but also diverse.

Attesting to the skewed and uncritical enterprise of education worldwide, Alatas[46] strongly believed that to date, interest in universities (higher education institutions of learning) and development has primarily been focused on growth problems and structural educational planning. The content of university courses has received less attention, i.e. what actually transpires in classes, not just the name of the course printed in the syllabus. The content of courses can be a serious problem if it is insufficient[47]. This means that attention should be given to it, because it can breed a dysfunctional generation of graduates, especially in the social sciences and humanities. If courses are not closely related to the problems and mentality of the surrounding society, the role of the university degenerates to that of a status factory. This allegation was supported by Nkoane[48], who also claimed that if higher education does not produce knowledge capable of addressing local people's needs, it tends to be status focused.

It should, therefore, be noted that Africanised education should maintain African awareness of the social order and rules by which culture evolves[49]. Nkoane further indicated that Africanised curricula should foster an understanding of African consciousness; should facilitate a critical emancipatory approach to solving the problems of people's lives; and should produce the material and capacities for Africans to determine their own future(s). He further related that key to this view is the deliberate effort to cultivate people's ability to first love themselves; to maintain affectionate relations and positive regard among themselves; to cultivate the achievement of a collective, cooperative, unifying consciousness and behavioural orientation; and to encourage the ability to engage in productive, pro-social and proactive, rather than counterproductive, self-defeating and reactionary, activities[50]. Taking this thought further, Ntuli[51] argued that Africans need to decolonise their minds, as they have been "interpolated into the Western ideological machinery".

It is a relief to note from the copious volume of literature on this subject that most scholars argue that to Africanise curricula in higher education will need a mind-shift from the 'used-to do' syndrome. Nkoane[52] was of the opinion that Africans themselves need to develop a new mind-set towards the Africanisation of the education enterprise. He further emphasised the need for Africans to:

> ...call for the re-invigoration of Africa's intellectuals, and the production of knowledge which is relevant, effective and empowering for the people of the African continent, and more particularly, the immediate African societies the university serves.

Written differently, this means that "The African University needs to be relevant and responsive to the needs of the African people from which it draws its identity. It needs to show respect and acknowledge the culture of the people it is serving". Summing up his views on this subject, Nkoane[53] averred that:

> Afrocentric education seeks to foster in its learners an African consciousness and behavioural orientation which will optimize the positive expression of African learners' fundamental humanity and ability to contribute significantly to the total growth and development of the African community of which an African learner is a member.

This observation concurs with all views that perceive the Africanisation agenda as being key to the advancement and production of appropriate knowledge for the African Renaissance programme. In order to achieve this goal, Leifer[54] alleged that Eurocentric social power, among other subjects, should be analysed, as this impacts on educational institutions in Africa and continues to influence the lives of individuals and societies in Africa. Nkoane[55] was convinced that African Higher Education should "imbue or permeate its clients and African communities with an African conscious science which will maximise the positive expression of fundamental humanity and ability to contribute to the growth and development of African communities", of which Higher Education is an integral part.

Affirming this notion, Kebede[56] suggested that a serious attempt should be made to decolonise the African mind, by radically transforming the curricula of schools and Higher Education. In order to achieve this, he suggested that Higher Education should change curricula in accordance with societal needs, which will lead to a changing of the way in which teaching and learning are constructed. Kebede[57] argued that Africans need broader approaches to effective transformation in learning, based on a solid understanding of the context-specific socio-political causes of learning.

12.5 Avoiding the hegemonisation of the Africanisation of higher education curricula

This approach to Africanisation is grounded on a broad-based framework of knowledge construction – both in its epistemology(-ies) and pedagogy(-ies). It is perhaps known that narrow approaches to knowledge creation are based on hegemonic approaches, which focus only on who creates knowledge, for whom, and why. It is also known that there are numerous factors that drive people or societies to view their ways of knowing as superior to other ways of knowing. In this critique, I argue that knowledge is constructed for particular environments, not negating the fact that knowledge is applicable to other environments through adaptation or non-adaption. This notion means that all knowledges are important to society, making it unjust to impose knowledge in any environment instead of negotiating common ground meaning for all participating in learning or the use of knowledge therein.

12.5.1 The world needs different types of knowledges for advancement

According to Walkerstein[58], complexity studies reject the notion advanced by the Newtonian thought that "science assumed that there were simple underlying formulae that explained everything". The 21st century has definitely disproved this assumption. The notion of varied contexts seeking varied solutions has taken centre stage in scholarship. Epistemologies and methodologies that advance alternatives to solutions and the acknowledgment of the multi-faceted nature of knowledge seem to offer humanity better ways of resolving crises and mitigating risks in different environments (Ward[59]; Giroux[60]; Maila[61]).

12.5.2 Different problems, risks and vulnerabilities need interconnected and multi-faceted ways of knowing

Walkerstein[62] further argued that "truth is complex for the simple reason that reality is complex. And reality is complex for one essential reason: the arrow of time. Everything affects everything and as time goes on, everything expands inexorably". The explanation of this is that reality is socially constructed. Block[63] reiterated the notion that education helps us, together, to solve the pressing problems of the day, from economic to political and social crises, from global warming to ecological disaster and war. This scholar further asserted that:

> Education is about how we live together. What do we know of our fellow South Africans or any other people: about their cultures, their need and aspirations? Do we understand the constitutional imperatives that bind us together? Are our children to be citizens of the world, building peace and solidarity wherever they go?

In order for learners in Africa to understand their continent and its diverse cultural groupings, they must understand and know themselves as Africans; they must understand that the Africa they live in is complex and the same time vulnerable to all the other challenges that are experienced in other parts of Africa and the world. If they are to be able to mitigate, adapt or adopt ways that can address these challenges, they need to be provided with learning experiences that allow them to bring their traditional ways of knowing into the classrooms so that they enrich teaching and learning with varied possibilities to understand reality.

12.5.3 Different countries need different ways of knowing to address the problems and challenges experienced at various times and in various contexts

In order for any country to advance economically, politically, environmentally and otherwise, all injustices to humanity (all peoples of the world) must be declared crimes against humanity. In other words, this would mean:

- **All human rights are deliberately advanced**: political, environmental, religious, health, and genocides crises need culturally embedded human values and principles. This means that all human rights genocide should be seen as universal crimes which transcend cultural boundaries and religious divides. They can be understood by all religions and human beliefs worldwide.

- **"Motho ke motho ka batho" (You are because I am).** This is a powerful statement in African communities. It breaks down the barrier of seeing difference as intolerable, as seeing the unfamiliar as evil, the seeing of what I do not like as game to be destroyed. It points to the fact that "I cannot exist without you"; if I destroy you I am actually destroying myself. This is a fact engrained in the African psyche of humanness. This fact cause one to be humble and know that one is not better than another, and therefore one cannot desire to be alone in this planet/world.

- *The content paradigm enterprise assumes knowledge is static*[64]. Given the mere fact that this chapter is about a particular curriculum for Higher Education, some scholars might immediately think that I am advancing Africanisation as a particular "bounded body of knowledge". Perhaps yes, a particular field of knowing, but certainly not bounded. Since African knowings are embedded within certain African milieus they cannot be context-fixed, but should be context-dynamic. This means that as society or communities change in how they view reality and how they use their knowings in new changing contexts, their knowings are also informed by these changing contexts. I agree with Weimer that the "the legitimacy of goals unrelated to content must be recognised, and the continued failure to do so devalues the whole education enterprise". This means that a blend of content and learning objectives is a solution.

- *Courses designed to teach 'selective assimilation'.* This means that students should be deliberately taught how to selectively choose a subject matter that is universally used from the one which is based on the cultural background of the West. The line of argument here is that when students know their own and acknowledge their own knowings, it will be easy to critically understand other knowledge types. These courses, according to Alatas[65], "should not just busy themselves with the simple adaptation of techniques and methodologies but should be busy with the conceptual apparatus, systems of analysis, and selection of problems". Of note is that there is a need to continue developing concepts and methods that are suitable for the challenges, risks and vulnerabilities experienced by various societies worldwide. These will be proper and meaningful to the objective situation. Alatas[66] lamented the follies of the 'captive mind', saying that "another great problem of the captive mind is that it is not able to differentiate the universal from the particular; it subsumes both under the universal. When a captive mind studies the sciences from the West, phenomena which are distinctly Western are often considered to be universal... It assumes that what is good in one place is good in another also and what is valid in one is valid in another"[67].

- *Materials suitable for the course of Africanisation should be prepared.* Journals should be published solely on Africanisation in Higher Education curricula, and the works of proponents of Africanisation and the African Renaissance programme should be promoted in Higher Education libraries and courses. These should be materials that encourage dialogue and participation in community life. Although the website, Higher Education Summit Forum: Academic Experience, Indigenisation and Africanisation, decried that "there are insufficient resources allocated to address the problem adequately"[68], this in essence means that the curricula of Higher Education fails to address the needs of present South Africa, focusing instead on addressing European and American issues.

The issue of the design and development of study materials for Africanisation seems to be key to Maluleke[69]. He posited that staff need to be reoriented before initiating this process and suggested that (i) a brief manual should be supplied to all staff who are engaged in the writing of course materials on how to ensure that the study materials are specifically orientated towards African contexts and realities; (ii) a check-list should be completed by course writers either at the beginning or at the end of each lesson/chapter; and (iii) strategies should be put in place to ensure that the demographics of staff reflect the realities of our contexts.

Coupled with the above suggestions, Maluleke[70] pointed out that at the heart of the Africanisation of tuition is the creation of space for African ideas and African intellectual traditions alongside other ideas and traditions. He cautioned, however, that:

> In doing this we must be careful not to merely fall into the usual clichés and stereotypes so that Africa is only represented by reference to poverty, disease and underdevelopment... Africanisation of Tuition will mean the production of materials whose content takes Africa seriously. This means that the materials will take seriously the good news, the bad news as well as the potential of Africa tuition.

Africa must advance herself, whilst partnering with all countries, who want to assist her advance.

What we note here is that designing learning curricula for Africanisation is a deliberate and critical reflective design plan. It cannot be done otherwise. Staff must be knowledgeable about what needs to be achieved through Africanised curricula; they must know how to design and develop materials for open-ended and multi-dimensional perspectives on knowledge construction, where all learners' indigenous knowledge systems count.

Medium of instruction should also be the vernaculars. Aikara[71] argued that Higher Education institutions seem to prefer English as the medium of instruction instead of the vernaculars. My argument for the vernaculars is that English was used by the colonisers precisely to ensure that they maintained power over the indigenous people. They used English as a medium of instruction to ensure that they maintained the 'commercial status' of their subjects, and promoted middle class 'elites' who could serve their administrations. This education enterprise during the colonialist period was purely geared to subjugate and control the indigenous people. We all know that the knowledge capital and 'soul' of any people is in the language they speak. You are who you are because of the language you speak. I concur with Aikara[72] that:

> Education through the English medium continues to be an important factor determining one's access to higher occupational placement and career mobility ...hence; the elite and the rising middle class sections seek education through the English medium. Thus, while there is increasing pressure from the vernacular on the one hand, the demand for English education is ever increasing on the other. Perhaps, policymakers should intervene with relevant policies that will ensure that the vernaculars are used in Higher Education whilst ensuring that English is also used for 'business purposes'.

Attesting to the harm that English as a language of instructions causes to indigenous languages, Kwesi Prah[73] argued that:

> The use of French or English in the elementary school is but a destruction of the African mind because these fragile minds are impressionable ... when you impose a foreign language as a language of culture, you systematically destroying them ... the use of a given language leads you to assimilate

at the same time the culture and the vision of life of those whose language you have borrowed ... the problem we face here is that through the colonial encounter Africans in most areas of human activity have acquired a syndrome of inferiority. The language problem and dependency on colonial languages is a reflection of this.

The author called for a dedicated move to eradicate and demystify the thinking that being educated in a language other than English retards one's intellectual development[74]. He reiterated the known fact that the language of a people embraces their capital knowings. As per Ntuli[75], one may say that the language of a people contains their civilisation and their identity – who they are as a people. For that reason, I also concur with Vilakazi[76], who emphasised that:

It is through language that people understand culture, produce knowledge and interact with the world. The mastery of language in which any discipline is taught is the prerequisite to the mastery of subject matter. The problem for non-English speakers, in institutions of learning in which English is the language of instructions, seems to be that such teaching and learning does not build upon the linguistic and conceptual resources derived from one's lived experiences or home environment, but seeks ... to implant linguistic and conceptual apparatuses from somewhere else, and as such cultivating a learner who is alienated from his or her home environment and the challenges the local context faces.

Nkoane[77] and Diop[78] concurred when they argued that the promotion of indigenous languages as media of instruction (teaching in and not about) appears to be an absolute necessity for the recovery and revalorisation of African knowledge and culture. Their conviction was based on the understanding that learners learn better in their mother tongue because of an indisputable accord between the spirit of a language and the mentality of the people who speak it. Using an indigenous language as language of instruction is, however, perceived by many scholars, especially scholars from the West, as taking steps backward instead of moving forward. However, if one considers the importance of broadening not just the knowledge base in Africa, but also ensuring that the knowledge constructed is relevant and useful to Africa in resolving the plethora of political, economic, health, and environmental problems the continent and the world faces, surely providing learners with the space to learn indigenous languages and interact better with the world cannot be seen as taking a step backward; it must be viewed as progressive and democratically informed.

Closely related to this concern is the argument by some scholars that there has been resistance to implementing Africanised curricula for various reasons, including compromising quality by lowering of standards and increasing black academics in all levels of academia[79]. In this chapter, the argument advanced is that broadening the knowledge base of what we know or want to know cannot be perceived as compromising quality, unless the very nature of what quality is to Africans is at the centre of the debate about Africanisation.

12.5.4 Curriculum as open-ended inquiry

According to Msila[80], indigenous knowledge systems have an opportunity to bring forth an inclusive approach to education. This means that indigenous knowledge systems have the potential to develop learners in an 'African way', which is much different from the Western forms of education. Attesting to this claim, Bitzer and Menkveld[81] argued that indigenous knowledge systems should be conserved and respected as they are a culmination of the accumulated wisdom of generations of people living in a particular context; they are an embodiment of a different distinctly African mode of thought and they serve as a conduit for the articulation of what local people know while involving them in the collection of knowledge required for development. This observation by Bitzer and Menkveld is important in this discussion as it points to the fact that indigenous knowledge systems are endowed with local people's ways of knowing, and thus are underscored by varied African ways of knowing, which are contextually informed and also inform their contexts. Kincheloe[82] concurred with this claim regarding dialogical teaching and learning, "Learn with and learn from". It is for these reasons that I argue that Africanised curricula should encourage possibilities and hope, which are better taught within open-ended and plural ways of learning.

Lamenting the narrow approaches to knowledge construction in Higher Education as a result of "closed" learning approaches to teaching and learning, Beck[83] further pointed out that the focus on a non-linear theory of knowledge creation process seems to shift from one that is clear, cooperative and similar to the process of communities of learning, to one that is unclear, uncooperative and polarised networks of people and coalitions acting on knowledge. As pointed to earlier, the world we live in today fails to address critical life threatening political conflicts, economic meltdowns, environmental crises, and many more life problems, simply because of these educationally engrained linear approaches to learning, instead of adopting new ways of knowledge constructions that are non-linear.

Songca[84] concurred with the observation made above, claiming that there are a number of factors that indicate that the traditional methods of acquiring knowledge and solving problems are inadequate, and that the problems such as poverty, violence, exploitation and oppression that confront us in this century force us to deal with the realisation that humanity in the 21st century needs to do things differently, besides trying to think creatively and innovatively to solve problems. This means that in order for Higher Education to produce knowledge that is capable of understanding the present world and provide appropriate knowledge for the future world, education should be embedded in diverse ways of knowledge creation and ways of knowing. Needless to say then, Africanised designed and implemented curricula cannot be marginalised in Higher Education if the African Renaissance programme is to be progressively advanced.

12.6 Designing Africanised Curricula

The document cited from the following website is a clear indication that dialogue around Africanisation is long overdue (Indigenisation and Africanisation, CEPD. Higher Education Summit Forum: Academic Experiences[85]). Africa and the rest of the world should take this agenda seriously, hence initiatives like this book are commendable and must be encouraged. Rightfully Africans must start (if they had not started) or continue (if they already started) to speak with their own voices from their own knowledge base, and continue to seek ways and strategies to open up the previously marginalised knowledge systems. No Higher Education institution should see itself as inadequate when it comes to the design and implementation of Africanised curricula.

In this chapter, the understanding is that learners learn better in a setting which allows them to be part of the learning; they must be responsible for their own learning; they must participate in their learning; they must be understood as bringing valuable knowings into the learning environment; and they must construct their own meanings of what is learned. Mergel[86] concurred with this view when pointing out that "constructivism promotes a more open-ended learning experience where the methods and results of learning are not easily measured and may not be the same for each learner". In other words, if learning is to be designed to be meaningful to learners, it must allow them to bring different views and knowings into the learning environment. Jonassen[87] listed the following advantages that emanate from the use of constructivism in instructional design, namely that it:

- provides a multiple representation of reality;
- presents authentic tasks which are contextualised;
- provides real-world case-based learning environments;
- fosters reflective practice;
- enables context- and content-dependent knowledge construction; and
- supports the collaborative construction of knowledge through social negotiation, but does not compete among learners for recognition.

According to Dunlop and Grabinger[88], Butterfield, Wambold and Belmont[89], and Bostock [90], the literature on constructivist theory and Africanisation points to the fact that study material designers should incorporate the following key elements into Africanised curricula design:

- Student-owned study materials, where the student's voice is heard and where the student takes responsibility and initiative for his or her learning.
- Active students busy with a learning process based on active learning theories.
- Authentic learning concepts with authentic assessments based on real-life or simulated situations.
- Students and academics negotiating meaning.

Louw[91] indicated that The Directorate: Curriculum and Learning Development (DCLD) at the University of South Africa offers the following pointers for the design of study materials in order to ensure Africanised course materials for active learning:

- Promote study and investigation within authentic contexts.
- Encourage the growth of student responsibility, initiative, decision making and intentional learning.
- Cultivate collaboration between students and academics, where possible.
- Utilise dynamic, interdisciplinary, generative learning activities that promote higher-order thinking processes to help students develop rich and complex knowledge structures.
- Assess the student's progress in content and learning-to-learning within authentic contexts using realistic tasks and performances within the constraints of the African technological environment.

It should be noted that although the above elements point to what the University of South Africa has decided to consider as critical elements in the design of Africanised curricula materials, other universities may find these elements useful in their endeavours to Africanise learning curricula. Although the above elements geared to opening up Africanisation in learning are critical and desirable to Higher Education designers, I must caution that there are numerous questions that some educators might want answered regarding the implementation of an Africanised curriculum. According to Louw[92], some of these questions are:

- How do curriculum designers construct teaching and learning according to the social aspects of constructivism?
- What can we adopt and adapt from the West?
- What has the West adopted from Africa?
- What must we reject as detrimental?
- How can we integrate constructivism?
- How can we integrate what we borrow into our own continuities?

My thinking tells me that these questions are pertinent for this discussion, especially because they force us to critically think and reflect on how we want to design and implement Africanisation. What counts as legitimate knowledge in African indigenous knowledge systems? As Odora Hoppers[93] put it, "politicians and educators have too easily forgotten that in a context of hegemony, creativity and attempts to regain 'one's mind' are often immediately constituted as subjects for therapy, a pathology positing demonic possession"[94]. This means that Africanised curricula are neither devoid of epistemology nor of pedagogy, and should be studied within such a framework.

I propose that in order to design and implement a holistic, Africa-centred curriculum within a learning environment that supports the values of all learners, where all learners belong and are able to contribute their opinions to an open learning environment, in an environment that derives its knowledge capital from African indigenous ways of knowing, without peripherising Western ways of knowing of course, it should be collectively created. I also concur with Appiah[95] that there is an urgent need for an ethical universal agenda where learners from two worlds can accommodate the differences between them to transcend social fragmentation. Such an agenda will not continue to ignore what Africanised curricula can contribute to African problems and solutions. Coupled with this agenda it is worth noting that "Afrocentric education cannot exist without recognising its counter discursive challenges. Since education systems in Africa are by definition influenced by their colonial past(s), they need to engage this reality head-on"[96].

12.7 Conclusion

Most scholars agree that learners taught within open-ended and plural ways of learning and knowledge construction call for educators to dare and have the predisposition to fight for justice and to be lucid in defence of the need to create conditions that are conducive to pedagogy in schools[97], while also allowing own home language learning. I also concur with almost all of the scholars who argue that higher education in Africa should be Africanised in order to enable Africanised curricula to prosper and promote the African cultural lifestyles of learners. Reiterating this view, Ankomah[98] affirmed that Africans must Africanise curricula in order to allow themselves the time and space to deal with some of the inadequacies of the current curricula in institutions of higher learning. Caution is made, however, that the Africanised curricula must be implemented consciously, purposefully and systematically, without resorting to failing strategies.

It is for the above reasons that Ankomah[99], quoting Steve Biko that the greatest weapon in the hands of the oppressor is the mind of the oppressed, commented that "we must liberate our minds, (and the) Africanised curricula will assist all Africans to be taught in this enterprise". Of course it must be noted that Africanising curricula is not for Africans and Africa only, but for humanity worldwide. Various scholars in this chapter have espoused the view that African higher education is key to the agenda of Africanising learning, and also of representing the African experience and ideas within African culture and the broader African Renaissance agenda; it has to play a pivotal humanising role both locally and internationally, and needs to help liberate African people as well as the international community from inhuman and dehumanising ideas and practices, from resolutions of complex environmental problems and political crises, and other social problems.

Summing up this chapter is not an easy thing to do as the exploration can always be perceived as being biased towards African persons, given that the author is an educator in an African Higher Education institution. However I want to emphasise what Kebede[100] said, i.e. that African reality should be taken seriously in curriculum design; that knowledge, skills/competencies and values should be taught holistically, from this perspective; and that indigenous knowledge should be the point of departure when designing Africanised curricula and study materials. It is envisaged that such Africanised curricula will play a progressive role in advancing the African Renaissance programme, not only in South Africa, but also beyond her borders.

References

[1]Calderhead, J. 2001. International Experiences of Teaching Reform, In V. Richardson (Ed.). *Handbook of Research on Teaching*. Washington, DC: American Educational Research Association, pp. 777-800.

[2]Ibid.

[3]Ibid.

[4]Ibid.

[5]Ibid.

[6]Ibid.

[7]Weimer, M. 2006. Assumptions that devalue university teaching. *International Journal for Academic Development*. Retrieved from: www.tandfonline.com/doi/full/10.10.1080/1360.144X.2013.805693?mobileUi. [Date accessed: July 6, 2016.]

[8]Makgoba, M. W. 1997. *Mokoko: The Makgoba affair – a reflection on transformation*. Florida: Vivlia.

[9]Nkoane, M. M. 2006. The Africanisation of the University in Africa. *Alternation*, 13 (1): 49-69.

[10]Hortshemke, K. 2004. Knowledge, Education and the Limits of Africanisation. *Journal of Philosophy of Education*, 38(4): 571-587.

[11]Mangu, A. M. B. 2005. *Towards the African University in the Service of Humanity: Challenges and prospects for Africanisation at the University of South Africa*. Seminar on Africanisation organised at the University of South Africa, 3 March 2005, Pretoria.

[12]Freire, P. 1985. *The Politics of Education*. Westport: Bergen and Garvey Publishers.

[13]Makgoba, M. W. (Ed.). 1999. *African Renaissance: The New Struggle*. Johannesburg: Mafube.

[14]Ramose, M. B. 1998. Foreword. In S. Seepe (Ed.). *Black perspective(s) on tertiary institutional transformation*. Johannesburg: Vivlia.

[15]Louw, W. 2010. Africanisation: A rich environment for active learning on a global platform. *Progressio*, 32(1): 42-54.

[16]Ibid.

[17]Mangu, A. M. B. 2005. *Towards the African University in the Service of Humanity: Challenges and prospects for Africanisation at the University of South Africa*. Seminar on Africanisation organised at the University of South Africa, March 3, 2005, Pretoria.

[18]Hortshemke, K. 2004. Knowledge, Education and the Limits of Africanisation. *Journal of Philosophy of Education*, 38(4): 571-587.

[19]Ibid.

[20]Deconstructing Jacques Derrida. *Los Angeles Times Magazine*. July 21, 1991. Retrieved from http://articles.latimes.com/keyword/jacques-derrida. [Date accessed: October 19, 2016].

[21]Soloway, E., Jackson, S. L., Klein, J., Quintana, C., Reed, J., Spiltulnik, J., Stratford, S. J., Studer, S., Jul, S., Eng, J., & Scala, N. 1996. *Learning Theory in Practice: Case Studies of Learner-Centered Design*. New York: ACM.

[22]Ibid.

[23]Vygotsky, L. 1978. *Mind in society: The development of higher psychological processes*. M. Cole, V. John-Steiner, S. Scribner, E. Souberman (Eds.). Cambridge: Harvard University Press.

[24]Freire, P. 2005. *Teachers as cultural workers: Letters to those who dare teach*. Colorado: Westview Press.

[25]Ibid.

[26]Teffo, L. 2011. Epistemic pluralism for knowledge transformation. *International Journal for African Renaissance*, 6(1): 24-34.

[27]Gutto, S. B. O. 2006. Towards a new paradigm for Pan-African knowledge production and application in the context of the African Renaissance. *International Journal for African Renaissance*, 1(2): 306-323.

[28]Mbeki, T. 1998. *Public Affairs Section*. Tokyo: United Nations University.

[29]Makgoba, M. W. (Ed.). 1999. *African Renaissance: The New Struggle*. Johannesburg: Mafube.

[30]Ntuli, P. P. 1999. The missing link between culture and education: Are we still chasing gods that are not our own? In M. W. Makgoba (Ed.). *African Renaissance*. Cape Town: Mafube, pp. 184-199.

[31]Scheerens, J. 1992. *Effective Schooling: Research, Theory and Practice*. London: Cassell.

[32]Calderhead, J. 2001. International Experiences of Teaching Reform. In V. Richardson (Ed.). *Handbook of Research on Teaching*. Washington, DC: American Educational Research Association, pp. 777-800.

[33]Ibid.

[34]Atal, Y. 2004. The call for Indigenisation. In P. N. Mukherji and C. Sengupta (Eds.). *Indigeneity and Universality in Social Sciences: A South Asian response*. New Delhi: Sage Publications, pp. 99-113.

[35]Alatas, S. H. 2004. The Captive Mind and Creative Development. In P. N. Mukherji and C. Sengupta (Eds.). *Indigeneity and Universality in Social Sciences: A South Asian response*. New Delhi: Sage Publications, pp. 83-98.

[36]Ibid.

[37]Freire, P. 2005. *Teachers as cultural workers: Letters to those who dare teach*. Colorado: Westview Press.

[38]The Centre for Education Policy Development (CEPD). 2010. Higher Education Summit Forum: Academic experience, Indigenisation and Africanisation. Retrieved from http://www.cepd.org.za/?q=node/143. [Date accessed: November 13, 2016.]

[39]Nkoane, M. M. 2006. The Africanisation of the University in Africa. *Alternation*, 13(1): 49-69.

[40]Maila, M. W. 2012. Re-thinking complex, fluid and contradictory knowledge(s) in higher education. *South African Journal of Higher Education*, 26(6): 1159-1169.

[41]Atal, Y. 2004. The call for Indigenisation. In P. N. Mukherji and C. Sengupta (Eds.). *Indigeneity and Universality in Social Sciences: A South Asian response*. New Delhi: Sage Publications, pp. 99-113.

[42]UNESCO. 2004. *Interregional Cooperation in the field of Social Sciences*, pp. 226.

[43]Nkoane, M. M. 2002. *Constructing Knowledge through learner-centred approaches*. Unpublished paper. Presented at the University of Witwatersrand, Johannesburg, South Africa.

[44]Nussbaum, M. 2006. Education and Democratic Citizenship: Capabilities and Quality Education. *Journal of Human Development*, 7(3): 385-395.

[45]Ibid.

[46]Alatas, S. H. 2004. The Captive Mind and Creative Development. In P. N. Mukherji and C. Sengupta (Eds.). *Indigeneity and Universality in Social Sciences: A South Asian response*. New Delhi: Sage Publications, pp. 83-98.

[47]Ibid.

[48]Nkoane, M. M. 2002. *Constructing Knowledge through learner-centred approaches*. Unpublished paper. Presented at the University of Witwatersrand, Johannesburg, South Africa.

[49]Ibid.

[50]Ibid.

[51]Ntuli, P. P. 1999. The missing link between culture and education: Are we still chasing gods that are not our own? In M. W. Makgoba (Ed.). *African Renaissance*. Cape Town: Tafelberg, pp. 184-199.

[52]Nkoane, M. M. 2002. *Constructing Knowledge through learner-centred approaches*. Unpublished paper. Presented at the University of Witwatersrand, Johannesburg, South Africa.

[53]Ibid.

[54]Leifer, P. 1969. *The Falsification of Afrikan Consciousness*. Chicago: University of Chicago Press.

[55]Nkoane, M. M. 2002. *Constructing Knowledge through learner-centred approaches*. Unpublished paper. Presented at the University of Witwatersrand, Johannesburg, South Africa.

[56]Kebede, M. 2004. African development and the primacy of mental decolonisation. *Africa Development*, XXIX(1).

[57]Ibid.

[58]Walkerstein, I. 2004. Social Science and the Quest for a Just Society. In P. N. Mukherji and C. Sengupta (Eds.). *Indigeneity and Universality in Social Sciences: A South Asian response*. New Delhi: Sage Publications, pp. 66-82.

[59]Ward, M. 2002. Environmental Management: Expertise, uncertainty, responsibility. In J. Hatingh, H. Lotz-Sisitka and R. O'Donoghue (Eds.). *EEASA Monograph*, Pretoria: Human Science Research Council.

[60]Giroux, H. A. 2007. Introduction: Democracy, education and the politics of critical pedagogy. In P. McLaren and G. L. Kincheloe (Eds.). *Critical pedagogy: Where are we now?* New York: Peter Lang, pp. 1-5.

[61]Maila, M. W. 2012. Re-thinking complex, fluid and contradictory knowledge(s) in higher education. *South African Journal of Higher Education*, 26(6): 1159-1169.

[62]Walkerstein, I. 2004. Social Science and the Quest for a Just Society. In P. N. Mukherji and C. Sengupta (Eds.). *Indigeneity and Universality in Social Sciences: A South Asian response*. New Delhi: Sage Publications, pp. 66-82.

[63]Block, P. 2009. *Community: The Structure of Belonging*. Cincinnati: Berrett-Kohler.

[64]Weimer, M. 2006. Assumptions that devalue university teaching. *International Journal for Academic Development*. Retrieved from: www.tandfonline.com/doi/full/10.10.1080/1360.144X.2013.805693?mobileUi=). [Date accessed: July 6, 2016.]

[65]Alatas, S. H. 2004. The Captive Mind and Creative Development. In P. N. Mukherji and C. Sengupta (Eds.). *Indigeneity and Universality in Social Sciences: A South Asian response*. New Delhi: Sage Publications, pp. 83-98.

[66]Ibid.

[67]Ibid.

[68]The Centre for Education Policy Development (CEPD). 2010. Higher Education Summit Forum: Academic experience, Indigenisation and Africanisation. Retrieved from http://www.cepd.org.za/?q=node/143. [Date accessed: November 13, 2016.]

[69]Maluleke, T. S. 2005. *Africanisation of tuition at Unisa: A perspective from the College of Human Sciences*. Seminar on Africanisation, March 3, 2005. University of South Africa, Pretoria.

[70]Ibid.

[71]Aikara, J. 2004. The Indigenous and the Modern: Education in South Asia. In P. N. Mukherji and C. Sengupta (Eds.). *Indigeneity and Universality in Social Sciences: A South Asian response.* New Delhi: Sage Publications, pp. 331-361.

[72]Ibid.

[73]Prah, K. 1999. African Renaissance or Warlordism. In M.W. Makgoba (Ed.). *African Renaissance: The New Struggle.* Cape Town: Mafube, pp. 37-61.

[74]Ibid.

[75]Ntuli, P. P. 1999. The missing link between culture and education: Are we still chasing gods that are not our own? In M. W. Makgoba (Ed.). *African Renaissance: The New Struggle.* Cape Town: Tafelberg, pp. 184-199.

[76]Vilakazi, H. W. 1998. Education Policy for Democratic Society. In S. Seepe (Ed.). *Black Perspectives on Tertiary Institutional Transformation.* Johannesburg: Vivlia.

[77]Nkoane, M. M. 2006. The Africanisation of the University in Africa. *Alternation,* 13(1): 49-69.

[78]Diop, B. 2000. African Education: Mirror of Humanity. In P. Higgs., N. C. G. Vakalisa, T. V. Mda and N. T. Assie-Lumumba (Eds.). *African Voices in Education.* Cape Town: Juta, pp. 84-102.

[79]Sonnekus, I.P., Louw, W. & Wilson, H. 2006. *Emergent learner support at University of South Africa: An informal report.* Pretoria: Unisa.

[80]Msila, V. 2009. Africanisation of education and the search for relevance and context. *Educational Research and Reviews,* 4(6): 310-315.

[81]Ibid.

[82]Kincheloe. J. L. 2005. *Critical Pedagogy Primer.* New York City: Peter Lang Publishing.

[83]Beck, U. 1999. *What is Globalization?* Cambridge: Polity Press.

[84]Songca, R. 2006. Transdisciplinarity: The dawn of an emerging approach to acquiring knowledge. *International Journal for African Renaissance Studies.* 1(2): 221 – 232.

[85]Centre for Education Policy Development (CEPD). 2010. Indigenisation and Africanisation - Higher Education Summit Forum: Academic Experiences. Retrieved from: http://www.cepd.org.za/?q=node/143. [Date accessed: January 23, 2016.]

[86]Mergel, B. 1998. Instructional Design & Learning Theory-Study Guide. Saskatoon: University of Saskatchewan. Retrieved from http://etadusask.ca/802papers/mergel/brenda.htm. [Date accessed: November 12, 2016.]

[87]Louw, W. 2010. Africanisation: A rich environment for active learning on a global platform. *Progressio,* 32(1): 42-54.

[88]Ibid.

[89]Ibid.

[90]Ibid.

[91]Ibid.

[92]Ibid.

[93]Odora Hoppers, C. A. 2000. African Voices in Education: Retrieving the Past, Engaging the Present, and Shaping the Future\. In P. Higgs, N. C. G. Vakalisa., T. V. Mda and N. T. Assie-Lumumba (Eds.). *African Voices in Education.* Landsdowne: Juta, pp. 1-11.

[94]Ibid.

[95]Appiah, K. A. 1992. *In my father's house: Africa in the Philosophy of Culture.* Oxford: Oxford University Press.

[96]Nkoane, M. M. 2006. The Africanisation of the University in Africa. *Alternation,* 13(1): 49-69.

[97]McLaren, P. 2003. *Life in schools: an introduction to critical pedagogy in the Foundations of Education.* Boston: Pearson Education.

[98]Ankomah, B. 2008. Why should journalism curriculum be Africanised? *Global Media Journal African Edition,* 2(2): 154-163.

[99]Ibid.

[100]Kebede, M. 2004. African development and the primacy of mental decolonisation. *Africa Development,* XXIX(1).

Part 4

Ideology, Youth, Music and Leadership

Chapter 13

Towards Africa's renewal: Decolonisation, Black Consciousness and the youth

Vuyisile Msila
Institute for African Renaissance Studies
University of South Africa

13.1 Renaissance: Youth seizing the future

Rodney[1] contended that society has a role to play in isolating the youth from insults that perpetrate Africa's underdevelopment. African youth need to be conscientised against the continuing exclusive westernisation of the continent as well as its denigration. Young people in Africa today have a critical role to play in extracting the continent out of the colonisation, both economically and mentally. Oppressive regimes always attempt to have a grip on the future so that they are able to have full control over young people. Fanon[2] declared:

> And the youth of a colonised country, growing up in an atmosphere of shot and fire, may well make a mock of, and does not hesitate to pour scorn upon the zombies of his ancestors, the horses with two heads, the dead who rise again, and the djinns who rush into your body while you yawn. The native discovers reality and transforms it into the pattern of his customs, into the practice of violence and into his plan for freedom.

The decolonisation process has an immense role to play in the transformation of youth and the restoration of their dignity as citizens. An African Renaissance would need an emancipated youth who have been decolonised and prepared for a national renaissance. In South Africa today, young people are affected by social ills in a number of ways; homelessness, poverty and joblessness are among the major societal challenges that affect the youth. These challenges affect their self-esteem as they struggle for other battles such as economic freedom and the general decolonisation of society. In *Toward the African Revolution*[3], Fanon called for the youth of Africa to come together and "dig the grave in which Colonialism will finally be entombed!" Fanon perceived decolonisation as a violent encounter, hence colonialism can only be met with force. Some critics have demonstrated why Fanon continues to be relevant today and the need to revisit his work in the contemporary Africa[4]. This chapter briefly focuses on "new" themes that seem to have arisen in the students' battles as they search for decolonisation in South Africa. It looks at Black Consciousness tenets that imbue their struggle for a free education, a free society and relevant philosophies. These include the need for self-reliance, the conscientisation of youth, the role of Black Consciousness, and using revolutionary thinking to prepare for an emancipatory life.

In South Africa, 2015 and 2016 will be marked in history as years in which the youth stood up for social justice, decolonisation, and the search for relevant higher education. Amongst others, the youth called for an education system that would free them from the challenges of society. There are several aspects that still marginalise the youth from actively participating in transforming society. Quality and affordable education continue to be among the major struggles for young people, especially those coming from indigent families. It is within this context that the student upheavals in 2015 clearly demonstrated the hunger of students to be part of social change. Incidentally, the youth's role in the total liberation of the society has never been so crucial in our complex society. It is committed and patriotic but critical youth who will build a productive society. In 1962, the then prime minister of Tanganyika (now known as Tanzania) spelt out the role that youth needed to play in Africa's progress. He said that the youth had a responsibility of "effecting the transformation of colonial, poverty-stricken Africa into a free continent in every sense of the word"[5]. Nyerere also highlighted the pressure that young people had in leading nation building and forging unity among African states[6]. These ideals were shared by Bantu Biko (who led the Black Consciousness Movement in the 1970s), as he magnified the role of young people of his time.

The youthful Biko was only 31 years old when he died after an extended brutal torture in police cells; a young person ahead of his time in philosophical thought. His philosophy of Black Consciousness (BC) organised many other young people who were able to take the struggles of the oppressed black people forward. The national unrest by students in 1976 to 1978 was mainly due to the growth of the Black Consciousness Movement.

Biko perceived the black youth in his time to be responsive to the suffering of the society's oppressed and destitute; the young people were intent on changing their world, thus leading South Africa to a future they were aspiring to. But what does BC mean today for the African Renaissance? And how can BC influence the current debates and struggles in African societies? This chapter builds upon themes that have been explored already in this book, using BC as a lens. African philosophy, African Renaissance, Pan-African identity and decolonisation are some of the themes explored. The use of the BC lens has been necessitated by the widespread use of BC principles by black youth, in particular in the struggles for social justice and decolonisation. Biko resonated with young people in 2015 as he did in 1976, as they fight for free quality education. The youth's calls for relevant philosophy are appeals for the renaissance that several authors have discussed in this volume.

13.2 In search of a Philosophy: Blacks back to a Renaissance

Arguably, Black Consciousness can be referred to as a renaissance of black values, culture and a redefinition of black history. In the 1920s Harlem in the United States, when they spoke of a black renascence or renaissance in the arts, they referred to the reawakening of black identity in cultural and social forms. Yet others argued that this black revolution was more than mere aesthetics, for art was "wedded to politics, black literature to black power"[7]. Black Consciousness reclaims black civilisations obfuscated by colonialism in the years of domination. It cannot be said to be the ultimate goal of blackness, but any ideal life for black people can only be attained in earnest through self-knowledge, and all forms of this are contained by a renaissance embraced by Black Consciousness. The Pan-African struggles have always sought to vividly define the African in Africa as well as in the diaspora. Whether defined or implied, there has been propinquity between Black Consciousness and the movement towards the attainment of an African Renaissance. Over the years, the ideals of Black Consciousness have been expatiated through the operations of the American Black Power movement. Ngugi[8] has demonstrated how consciousness and renaissance have been personalised through the lives of Bantu Biko, Mangaliso Sobukwe and Nelson Mandela in South Africa. Ngugi posited that:

> One associates Sobukwe and Biko with consciousness, Mandela with the renaissance. But it is significant that these three lives, while inextricably linked to Black and social imagination everywhere, are South African and the concepts of consciousness and renaissance have found new life in South Africa today.

Black Consciousness is a naissance of the mind; a philosophy that constantly reminds black people of their ancestry and their belonging to an African heritage. Sometimes flippantly misinterpreted as black racialism, in building a history, black people need unity and the awareness of self. When colonial domination confronted black people alone, they wrongly believed that they had no right to be proud of their blackness and no liberty for a renaissance. Yet there are scholars who question the African Renaissance and its existence. Mzamane[9] stated that the concept of African Renaissance might be more constraining than liberatory, especially when seen as an attempt to enforce a homogeneous culture and identity. Furthermore, Mzamane noted that the use of the concept should be more illuminating than confining. In this regard, this is why I think that without acknowledgement of history all would be hollow. An African Renaissance should address the cultural dominance of Africans by Western influence, and prepare the indigenes to govern their world with independence, efficacy and pride.

Black people need to revive their sense of identities of cultural heritages, histories and renascence. From the time of the contact with the colonialists or oppressors in Africa, black people lost these. The loss was gradual in certain aspects, but in others it was sudden. The colonialists' agenda remodeled what Biko referred to as the "empty shell" of the black person's being. When we talk of a renaissance, it is not only a way to reinvent Africa in black people, but it is a need to enhance the black identity as black people's empty shell images are discarded. Van Grasdorff[10] contended that:

> The first methodological and philosophical pillar of the African Renaissance endeavour was expressed by Amilcar Cabral when he maintained that an African Renaissance is unthinkable outside of the culture, language and history of the masses-outside the institutions which the people build according to their own needs and which they control internally. This is not in the least a call for an uncritical return to a mythical past, but rather a return to the sources meaning the critical appropriation of the vigour, vitality (life) and the ebullience of African existence by the assimilated African elites who had been alienated from their source by colonial culture and history...

For the black person, the call to embrace an African Renaissance is a reclamation of the core of existence. It is central to understanding and addressing the emotional and intellectual ravages given birth to by colonialism and oppression. Biko's Black Consciousness was also a call for black reinvention; a form of unapologetic black renaissance and resistance. This chapter explores the various facets of Black Consciousness and the African Renaissance.

13.3 Whose renaissance?

The more we talk of a renaissance in South Africa, the more black Africa should think of Black Consciousness as a harbinger thereof. Going back to understanding blackness and culture is the first step on the path of being a receptacle to the African Renaissance that we aspire to. It will be difficult and almost impossible for black people to embrace a renaissance without first coming to grips with a Black Consciousness that will shed all the negative factors that culminate in what Biko referred to as "an empty shell". The lack of self-worth and doubting oneself in a white world are some of the elements of this empty shell syndrome. A new Africa that is not intimidated by whiteness will need to challenge fear as people assume Black Consciousness, so as to understand themselves and their world. Black Consciousness encapsulates the black imagination that aspires for a free world. It is a boundless imagination that captures not only a renaissance of the mind, but freedom, democracy and the will to live for the betterment of others and the self. African Renaissance cannot be attained by black Africans until they understand that they need to own their heritage, their history, their memory, their pride and their dignity. Without understanding the self as a proud individual in society, there can be no freedom.

Apartheid and colonialism were violent towards black people. As a result, in many places such as hostels in Johannesburg and townships in Umlazi and New Brighton, many witnessed what was termed *black on black* violence. Black people detested each other based on political affiliation, but the ugliest was when tribal lines were used to segregate one black from another. Now, as we speak of a renaissance, we need to ensure that justice and peace prevail among all people in society, especially black groups. A divided nation cannot be ready for any rebirth. Black Consciousness comes in handy enhancing justice and solidarity after years of strife, hatred and suspicion. People need to be free mentally if they are to be able to know and understand the renaissance. Black people may today be politically free, but it is a deeper psychological freedom that many need to realise a new world; a rebirth; the realisation of a true emancipation. There are still many black people who may think that it is not natural to be at the same level as, or in a better position than, white people. Unfortunately, this is not limited to a certain class or category of black. At one university where I worked I had a black colleague, a senior professor, who refused to supervise white postgraduate students. He did not say it in as many words, but he felt inadequate supervising white students. There were several like him who just could not defeat their fear. These were highly qualified colleagues, but their colour disqualified them from leading white students. Black Consciousness has a huge didactic role to play in all sectors of society. The strength to reclaim their dignity and pride needs to come from within the black people who in many ways are oppressed – by their whims. Gibson[11] contended:

In short, Black Consciousness is a philosophy of self-emancipation. Like Fanon, Biko understands that there is no demiurge, that freedom cannot be given. There is no use in simply waiting for men with guns to come and liberate them. They must stand up to oppression together and move forward together. Surely this was what we the Soweto student rebellion of 1976 heralded. And, for Biko, this idea of autonomy was not only necessary but practical.

Black people in particular, due to their unique history, must realise the need to seize freedom and embrace it jealously. They need an understanding to know that political oppression will persist as long as they do not free their psychological selves and shirk the myth of the white superiority that many may have internalised. In various ways, our media continues to perpetuate this in a number of ways, including the idea of beauty. In 2013, a controversial poll held in Cape Town created a racial uproar where the main question was which was the most attractive race. The poll was conducted by *Varsity News*, a University of Cape Town (UCT) student newspaper. The results were represented in a pie chart with the following statistics:

- 38% of students thought the Whites were the most attractive.
- 8% thought Africans were attractive.
- 19% thought Coloureds were attractive.
- 14% thought Indians were attractive.
- 11% thought Asians were attractive[12].

Many people perceived this as gobbledygook, and even more disconcerting was that it was conducted and promoted by young intellectuals. These are some myths that black people need to dispel instead of internalising them. In a quest for rebirth there should be efforts to clarify what society is all about. Language and culture are factors that can be used to dispel myths, starting at primary schools where children need to know the issues of blackness. Understanding blackness is crucial to realising black personhood; it is ensuring that black thoughts lead the process of redeeming the soul and making right choices for the children who grow up in a segregating society. Below the focus is mainly on pan-Africanism, as well as how black people can move towards a renaissance by casting off the colonial shackles.

13.4 Pan-Africanism, Black Renaissance and the casting off of shackles

The debates on renaissance cannot be complete without acknowledging the role of Pan-Africanism in liberating the colonised. The Azanian People's Organisation's (AZAPO) website[13] explicates the role of BC and Pan-Africanism, exposing the inevitable link between the two philosophies. The website points out that BC in South Africa has always been established on the country's reality, but also includes the black people's struggles throughout; "it is this genealogy that gives BC a strong internationalist and Pan-African orientation and sensibility" (AZAPO). Snail[17] also argued that it was in Pan-Africanism that the ideas of consciousness, self-actualisation and black consciousness were born. Furthermore, Snail argued that:

...the Black Consciousness Movement was given impetus by African nationalism and how that nationalism was later moulded and shaped by African thinkers of the 1950s and 1960s into Pan-Africanism.

Similarly, Omotoso and Layode[15] declared that:

Pan-Africanism can be described as a socinternationalisation of curriculumultural movement for Black Consciousness. It is a philosophy that represents the aggregation of the historical, cultural, artistic, scientific, and ethical legacies of Africans from the past to the present with the aims of unifying Africans and protecting them as a people of collective identity struggling to evolve a more positive image of themselves...This presupposes the general acceptance and use of Pan-Africanism as a social psyche, which emphasises the rights and aspirations of Africans to self-determination and self-government...

Asheekwe[16] also wrote about how Africans can understand Pan-Africanism by looking to the life and works of Biko. Asheekwe contended that back people could find inspiration from one another in a struggle against white oppression. This writer cited Booker T Washington, who maintained that black people needed to organise themselves instead of lobbying whites to apologise for slavery. "By doing this blacks could uplift themselves from their financial destitution and equality would follow. WEB du Bois, the founding father of Pan-Africanism, and Steve Biko shared a belief that a multi-racial and multi-cultural society could be created in their respective countries"[17].

The Guyanese scholar Walter Rodney wrote about how power politics, domination and economic exploitation lead to a dilapidated state of political and economic development. Africa may never again rise, some have said, but others argue that it is the Africans themselves who will determine that. There is sometimes a disconnect between what our leaders aspire to and what our people would like to achieve. Rodney[18] argued that Europe did much bad for Africa, and there was nothing else but bad. "Colonialism had only one hand – it was a one-armed bandit... What did colonial governments do in the interest of Africans? Supposedly, they built railroads, schools, hospitals and the like. The sum total of these services was amazingly small"[19]. William Easterly[20] also argued that even currently, the West's efforts to help Africa have done so much ill and so little good. Colonialism and exploitation long delayed the African Renaissance agenda on the continent. Tanzania's Julius Nyerere sought to achieve a society based on *Ujaama*, a socialist system of village co-operatives in which citizens would be able to live off their land, bolstered by familyhood and communalism. The system sought to instil a sense of self-reliance among Tanzanians to work their land and thereby move towards prosperity. Yet Westernisation made people move away from the land and settle in cities for better opportunities. *Ujaama* floundered as people pushed their children to succeed in formal education and move away from tilling the land. This shows that people need to understand the philosophies that have the potential to uplift their lives; even the best philosophies will fail in the absence of true understanding and ownership.

We are now at a time when some of us need to go back to the land. Africa can only rise when Africans begin realising the wealth in their soil. But we also need conscientious intellectuals to lead the renaissance. Africans need to understand and believe in this revival and reclaim the renaissance we aspire to, yet the battle for land ownership continues. The rebirth of Africa should also translate into an extended philosophy of *Ujaama* among African states, where leaders strive to attain similar goals through collaboration. Corruption will always be inimical to good governance and an enhanced African Renaissance. In South Africa, we have seen how corruption, perceived and real, makes people doubt where they are being led, seeking light in a seemingly doomed environment.

Many African governments have not entrenched the need for a rebirth after their countries were freed from colonial governments. Frequently, a *laager* has been created by intellectuals that excludes the masses. We should believe in the notion of trying to find African solutions for African challenges. I refuse to believe in some Afro-pessimists' view that the Africans will devour one another. Arguably there is still hope, as professed by great Africans who walked before us: Kwame Nkrumah, Patrice Lumumba, Robert Sobukwe and a hundred others. But we need to work hard to build our institutions to reflect the African essence. Universities and government departments are among the institutions that should uphold African ways. Of course they should always do this in conjunction with the communities: grass-roots "organic" intellectuals still carry the ways of being African. Africa needs to be reborn, time is running out and we cannot blame colonialism for eternity.

Over the years, Africans have tended to forget about traditional culture. There have been two extremes. On the one hand are those who do not care and do not even look back at where Africa was in precolonial times, while on the other are those who believe we need to go back to the Africa of yore as we make sense of the present. Yet as Mphahlele, cited by Msila in Chapter 2, pointed out, we should not forget that Africa is not as pristine as is sometimes portrayed. Mphahlele stated that he would like to also think of Africa as a violent and morbid society[21].

Chinua Achebe[22], in his classic novel *Things Fall Apart*, wrote about a precolonial Africa that had strengths and weaknesses. He showed the gap found by the colonialists, which they used to annihilate the African mind and the land. When intellectuals in Africa reflect on Africa, they need to remember our weaknesses as well. It is true, though, that colonialism did destroy some of the values that the African was known for. Fear was introduced with the capture of slaves, for example. Yet Africans should drag themselves out of slavery by discarding the shackles of the mind that Steve Biko talked about so loudly. It is when the Africans reinvent themselves that they will find the new Africa. Rebirth is the strongest way to the future; it is the answer to the challenges of globalisation. We need to begin with our cultures, our languages and our identities. The battle for rebirth needs courage to seize the new day. Disempowered people cannot reclaim the African Renaissance. In several chapters in this book I have shown how Africans need a well-grounded education system to better their society. We need an education that reflects an African identity that Biko talked about.

13.5 Education, identity and renaissance

Mbulelo Mzamane once spoke of the necessity to see the African in education. In the Can Themba inaugural lecture in 2013, Mzamane lamented, "There is nothing African in South Africa's system of education"[23]. He was echoing the sentiments of an earlier South African scholar,

Ezekiel Mphahlele, who in his lifetime emphasised the need to focus on the African identity in various spheres of life, albeit refusing to romanticise Africa as his negritude contemporaries did at the time. For several years the question in African universities has been, *To Africanise or not to Africanise?* Detractors have been dismissive, almost to the brink of boorishness; they are so disparaging that they do not see any obligation to change the current higher education institutions. Questions have been *What will that bring us?* and *Won't that drop the standards?* The most popular, perhaps, has been *What do you mean by that?* These questions highlight the fear of the unknown. The image of Africa conjures that which is mysterious and inimical to modernity.

One colleague was once so flippant that she asked whether those who espouse this will come to class barefooted, brandishing their spears in one hand and chalk and books in the other. I found this very woeful that an important academic debate can be relegated to such frivolous argument. Yet it is crucial to respond to this question constructively to determine exactly what is meant when we talk about an Africanised institution.

Several South African academics, such as Mzamane, Mphahlele and Makgoba, who spoke about the African university, were speaking of capturing an African identity in African institutions. In the past two decades, I have attended various conferences where intellectuals never moved beyond definitions in their quest. I have found this to be a form of derision; a farce or escapism that deliberately delays the process of Africanising institutions. Policy windows have been opening for us to push the African agenda into higher education institutions, yet institutions of higher learning still barely reflect the continent on which they are situated.

One should also acknowledge the grievous mistake made by ebullient Africanists who label Africanisation as merely an antithesis of Westernisation. This should not be the case; scholars such as Wiredu have shown the need for the West and Africa to coexist for real advancement. The major injustice and paradox in our institutions is their disregard of that which is African and indigenous. An important component of this injustice is the reluctance to open programmes where African languages are used.

In many universities in Africa no African languages are spoken, and there do not seem to be any intentions of using them. It is a commonplace to find a Department of French or German where these languages are taught by native speakers. Yet usually a disservice is done to African languages that are commonly taught in English, as if to acknowledge that they are vanquished and cannot continue to proliferate without the colonial languages. So patronising have the English language and other languages used to teach these African languages been, that their teachers will say that these institutions are assisting the development of the indigenous languages. The African agenda in institutions has failed as long as the African languages are still marginalised and offered as appendages of other languages. I have yet to see postgraduate theses written in African languages. This is an anomaly considering that Afrikaans speakers can still write their theses in Afrikaans. In fact, they can do all university modules in mother tongue from year one. The Tswana and the Venda students do not have this right; they need to learn content in a language that is not black and indigenous. It is for this reason that the University of KwaZulu-Natal needs to be applauded for introducing isiZulu as a language of which students need to have a working knowledge. This makes sense for a university situated in a province where isiZulu is the majority language.

Language is a good starting point for African philosophy, yet opponents have long been stating two things: that indigenous languages are not congruent with academic language, and that students who live outside KwaZulu-Natal will be at a disadvantage. Both these are ill-informed positions, because firstly, Afrikaans was also developed over time to be suitable for academia, and secondly, it can never be a disadvantage to learn any new knowledge in a higher education institution.

Universities have a duty of also ensuring that they help to bring back a revitalised society by gleaning from the neglected African values. A number of intellectuals have argued about the dissipating morality in African societies, which are ravaged by war, selfishness, hunger and various other ills. Universities can start working towards solutions by engaging with the communities around them, where they will see how people have lost the values of *Ubuntu*. Again, maybe this can be a starting point of our universities if they undertook to model such principles. Teaching and research needs to reflect these principles, however in search of accolades, academics may forget to lift each other up by learning from one another. In fact, this is also where the Pan-African agenda also has a role to play. African higher education institutions should continue to try and find a common intellectual agenda so as to lead the African continent. Pan-Africanism should move beyond glorifying the African past but should rather see how to address the present challenges in Africa. Linkages among African institutions will be crucial here as the quest for African nationalism is uplifted.

Africa has numerous challenges: poverty, war, disease, corruption and injustice are among them. Whilst universities must not be the only citadels of knowledge production, they can facilitate and take the lead in the advancement of the African life. There is a need to move beyond the colonial framework but, unfortunately, this is where many intellectuals are stuck as they continue to define their intellectualism in high flown exoglossic languages. Africa needs answers to many of her problems and higher education institutions do have some of the keys.

The time is now ripe for the intellectuals to break the deafening silence, because the space where the argument for Africanisation should be taking place remains conspicuously empty and silent. Unfortunately, these debates are confined to huge conference halls where their impact is negligible. Instead, African intellectuals have to come to the fore to push for real transformation in African institutions. Presently the zeal of the strong Africanists is not reflected in their departments or institutions. Pan-Africanism needs to build African nations as we strive for African advancement. We have seen the crumbling of African states and thus the question will haunt intellectuals – *What have we done for the continent?*

South Africa needs to take the lead and build critical intellectuals who will be at the forefront of drawing closer to their communities. We have many questions to answer and our institutions of higher learning cannot be protectionist; there need to be constant interactions between community intellectuals and those from the institutions. Society needs to see the emancipatory role that the higher education institutions can play, but first Africa needs liberated intellectuals who are not shy of the truth. It is time that knowledge is unchained for Africa to prosper.

13.6 Needing to help Africanise institutions (of higher learning)

The #RhodesMustFall Campaign in 2015 ignited many debates that questioned the culture of African institutions. Many role-players also started posing relevant questions and discussing why all African institutions need an African philosophy. Why an African philosophy at a higher education institution?

Aren't these institutions supposed to cover more than this, one colloquium participant asked flippantly three months ago, much to the disdain of many in the audience?

Over decades I have noted that when it comes to African philosophy or related fields, people pose many questions that betray their derision. For many of these folks there is nothing wrong with Greek mythology or German Classics and ancient Western philosophies. These have paradoxically become part of modernity, yet studying anything African stalls civilisation as it takes us back a few centuries.

Numerous institutions of higher learning have been complicit, as they ignored an agenda to include the African philosophy in their curricula. Some may introduce that one course or module that deals with elementary Sesotho or isiNdebele, and will vouch that their curricula are transformed and Africanised. On the one hand, this can be a naïve and sometimes innocent belief that they have indeed Africanised, yet on the other, it is a deliberate malicious intent to exclude the real Africanisation agenda.

The major challenge to many institutions of higher learning has been the need for African universities to respond to the challenges of the continent. There are still a few who try to move beyond theory, but African institutions do not just need one module in African philosophy. The philosophy should cut through their modules across the curricula, otherwise the practice will be a farce.

Yet one cannot ignore the fact that there are still many in academia who disparage African philosophy and question these challenges as oddities that have no place in any institution seeking global diversification. With the challenges that African philosophy encounters, one has to applaud the institutions that have just discovered the existence and the need for this African philosophy.

The realisation that we have to nurture an African university can never be underestimated, yet the quagmire that our universities get into as they attempt to Africanise is threefold. The first involves the community; the second is the research agenda that needs to be followed; and the third is the critical time at which to sensitise our students on Africanisation.

In most cases our higher education is dead as it fails to respond to the needs of the communities living in the African landscape. There is a tendency by academics to believe that the communities are peripheral to what is happening within the higher education institutions. The academics may believe that they are the sole authority who ought to jealously lead the development of curricula, but nothing could be further from the truth. If our institutions of higher learning should embrace Africanisation they need to start with the communities, because understanding what they want is among the best ways of addressing the issues of relevance.

Rural universities in Africa, for example, should know how to connect with the communities by assessing what their needs are. Some rural campuses are far from cities and the communities around them have special needs such as the preservation of water and community health research. These universities should have programmes that address these and similar challenges, but this also needs one to have an understanding of how African communities work, because in many cases people have to negotiate entry into villages through the chiefs.

Second, the idea of relevant research is crucial for all African universities. On a theoretical level, there are still numerous African institutions that would like to reincarnate their systems to lean towards Africanised philosophy, however they still find it hard to define what their African philosophy entails. The paradox of many in African institutions is the need for them to be re-Africanised after years of being enmeshed in exclusive Western values.

More researchers have to take it upon themselves to lead in a curricula reform that would ensure that African models in research form part of the curricula. Where there is no literature, universities need to create these through meticulous research. There should also be practical research to address challenges such as malaria, farming and planting. Other challenges include corrupt governments, running democratic elections and how to merge traditional aspects and Western models, and African universities should lead in these areas.

Moreover, education remains the uppermost important factor that can change countries' economies and futures. Research all over Africa should endeavour to find ways of critically engaging role-players on how to better education. Frequently universities try to introduce African philosophy to students at university; if the students are fortunate, there may be a chapter in a module that deals with African philosophy. Again, if they are lucky, they may get an entire course on this philosophy. However this is where the problem lies, for it may be too late to teach African philosophy for the first time at university. Schools should thus begin the journey of empowering the pupils in African philosophy. By the time the students reach university, they need to have a full understanding of what it means to be an African.

The irony of introducing African philosophy into many African institutions of higher learning is that this will shock the system as it will transform the embedded institutional cultures.

One author spoke of the need to reincarnate institutions of higher learning. Reincarnation may mean the rebirth and revitalisation of an African ethos. Indigenous languages struggle in African universities, yet African institutions of higher learning are supposed to reflect the cultures of the continent rather than exclusive Anglo-Saxon traditions. The late Russel Bot from the University of Stellenbosch once spoke of the need for multilingualism in African institutions, a picture that would portray what Bot called "an Ubuntu of languages".

African higher education institutions are still battling to achieve this. They ought to be a beacon of hope to Africa's rebirth, but unfortunately we still have to achieve this. In the 1940s, Anton Lembede spoke of the need for an African spirit that would be informed by the culture and history of Africa that we all need for a rebirth.

13.7 Conclusion

As Mzamane noted, we are at a time when we need a meaningful and illuminating form of renaissance. There is a need to move away from a renaissance that is usually seen as a passing fad. The reinvention of Africa and the black former colonised will need well-defined black identities and destinies. These identities and reinvention seek to address Western hegemony as they empower the black populace with a light that displays the sense of some wonderful inspirations that can be found in blackness. Marable[24] contended that for great African nationalists such as Pixley kaIsaka Seme, John Dube and various other African intellectuals, the concept of an African or black renaissance was a bid to "renegotiat(e) the relationship between the black world and the European domination, political as well as cultural and ideological"[18]. Black Consciousness resonates with the ideals of a black renaissance. While the concept of a black renaissance emerged in the United States some decades ago, its elements are similar if not identical to black consciousness which seeks to see the total emancipation of black people. The renaissance that imbues this consciousness also seeks to overcome the psychological makeup amassed by oppression. The renaissance needs to consciously oppose the evils of colonialism and its remnants. Black Consciousness and renaissance are indeed the cornerstones of social transformation for the entire black Africa, yet many African countries still wrestle with many of these issues. An understanding of the black destiny is the prerequisite of comprehending the point of a renaissance. The concept 'renaissance' can be so alien to black people who experience poverty; there is nothing to be proud of when people do not have shelter, food or power.

Finally, the debate in this chapter shows that Black Consciousness continues to play an immense role in the freedom of black people, as well as to the former oppressor. Whilst we all know the injury created by colonialism, black people cannot continue reflecting the images of portraying themselves as mere victims in a struggle where they have no say. Black Consciousness means taking charge in the issues of blackness, for the renaissance will never be received by a docile people. When Barney Pityana and Biko pronounced, "Black man you are on your own", it was not a racist cry but a demand for an empowered black people; a call for black people who are hungry for a black renaissance.

References

[1]Rodney, W. 2009. *How Europe underdeveloped Africa*. Abuja: Panaf Publishing.
[2]Fanon, F. 1963. *The Wretched of the Earth*. (Translation by C. Farrington). New York: Grove Press.
[3]Fanon, F. 1964. *Toward and African Revolution*. (Translation by H. Chevalier). New York: Grove Press.
[4]Shawawy, H. 2011. *Frantz Fanon, globalisation and the African Revolution*. Retrieved from: https://www.pambazuka.org/global-south.Frantz-fanon-globalisation-and-african-revolution. [Date accessed: January 30, 2017.]
[5]Nyerere, J. K. 1968. *Education for self-reliance: Freedom and Socialism*. Dar es Salaam: Oxford University Press.
[6]Ibid.
[7]Davis, C. T., & Walden, D. (Eds.). 1970. *On Being Black: Writings by Afro-Americans from Frederick Douglass to the Present*. Connecticut: Fawcett Publications.
[8]Wa Thiong'o, N. 2003. *Consciousness and African Renaissance: South Africa in the Black Imagination*. The Fourth Steve Biko Annual Lecture. University of Cape Town, South Africa, 12 September 2003.

[9]Mzamane, M. V. 2001. Where there is no vision the people perish: Reflections on the African Renaissance. *Hawke Institute Working Paper Series no. 16.* University of South Australia.

[10]Van Grasdorff, E. 2005. *African Renaissance and Discourse ownership in the information age: The internet as a factor of domination.* New Brunswick: Transaction Publications.

[11]Gibson, N. C. 2011. *Fanonian practices in South Africa. From Steve Biko to Abahlali BaseMjondolo.* Scottsville: UKZN Press.

[12]Racist Article tarnishes University of Cape Town. Retrieved from: www.publicnewshub.com/racist-article-tarnishes-university-of-cape-towns-image. [Date accessed: January 16, 2017.]

[13]Azanian People's Organisation Website. Retrieved from: http://azapo.org.za. [Date accessed: November 10, 2016.]

[14]Snail, M. 2008. The Black Consciousness Movement in South Africa: A Product of the entire Black World. *Historia Actual Online*, 15:51-68.

[15]Omotoso, S. A., & Layode, E. A. 2014. Pan-Africanism and the place of Africa in contemporary world of power politics. In T. Falola & K. Essien (Eds.). *Pan-Africanism and the politics of African citizenship and identity.* Routledge: New York.

[16]Asheekwe, T. n.d. *Black Consciousness.* Retrieved from: https://southernafrican.news/2012/05/28/black-consciousness/ [Date accessed: September 23, 2016.]

[17]Ibid.

[18]Rodney, W. 2009. *How Europe underdeveloped Africa.* Abuja: Panaf Publishing.

[19]Ibid.

[20]Easterly, W. 2006. *The white man's burden.* New York: Penguin.

[21]Mphahlele, E. 1980. On Negritude in Literature. The Rand Daily Mail. Johannesburg, June 7, 1968. In A. L McLeod and M.B. McLeod (Eds.). *Powre Above Powres: Representative South African Speeches, the Rhetoric of Race and Religion.* India: University of Mysore.

[22]Achebe, C. 1958. *Things fall apart.* London: Heinemann.

[23]Mzamane, M. 2013. *Inaugural Can Themba Memorial Lecture.* State Theatre, Pretoria. 21 June 2013.

[24]Marable, M. (Ed.). 2005. *The new black renaissance.* New York: Paradigm Publishers.

Chapter 14

Duende in Maskanda Music

Mxolisi Nyezwa
Imbizo Arts of South Africa
Port Elizabeth

14.1   Arts and the African Renaissance

Okumu[1] argued that African societies will need the collaboration of many societal institutions. Among these are cultural organisations and national governments. This chapter focuses on how indigenous music and poetry in maskanda play a role in decolonisation and/or the African Renaissance. The recently established South African Music Awards (SAMA) by the national broadcaster, the South African Broadcasting Corporation (SABC), is among the worthy steps taken in the right direction, as celebrating indigenous art forms is crucial to nation building and recognising all the cultural groups. Okumu also spelled out four specific roles that the national governments should play:

> …establish national awards for achievements in literature, music and visual arts, and for outstanding contributions to the case of the disadvantaged and to the development of inter-ethnic relationships. Fourth, seek to limit the negative cultural impact of the business sector by evaluating the social consequences of the form and content of commercial advertising; the aims must be to ensure adequate controls to preserve traditional African social mores and values.

There are many art forms that are critical for the self-discovery of Africans. In this chapter I explore a South African music form referred to as maskanda, which is described as a Zulu folk kind of music. The singer is usually accompanied by a guitar as he tells a story in his lyrics. Many songs are started with praise poetry or *izibongo*. There have also been a growing number of Xhosa groups that sing maskanda. The language groups isiZulu and isiXhosa are both Nguni languages, which are frequently very difficult to differentiate because they share many words. The maskandi genre has been growing and among the known artists are Bhekumuzi Luthuli, Thokozani Langa, Phuzekhemisi, Izingane Zoma, Mgqumeni, Obhejane, Shwi Nomtekhala and several others. There are several music genres that enable Africans to celebrate their cultures and their identities. Cultural expression is crucial in any renaissance; society demonstrates its beliefs and values through literature, music, art and drama, which contribute to shaping its unique identity[2]. Colonialism destroyed many cultural values in Africa, and music is one aspect in which Africans lost their cultural expression. Bantu Biko[3], like Fanon[4] and many other Afrocentric intellectuals, has written about the loss of culture by Africans. Biko[5] contended that:

The advent of Western culture has changed our outlook almost drastically. No more could we run our own affairs. We were required to fit in as people tolerated with great restraint in a Western type society. We were tolerated simply because our cheap labour is needed. Hence we are judged in terms of standards we are not responsible for. Whenever, colonisation sets in with its dormant culture it devours the native culture and leaves behind a bastardised culture that can only thrive at the rate and pace allowed it by the dominant culture.

Indigenous forms of music today seek to oppose this culture of colonialism and assert the identity of the African. The arts in Africa have not been devoid of racism; Frantz Fanon has demonstrated that "racism bloats and disfigures the face of the culture that practices it". Furthermore, Fanon argued that no social group, no country and no civilisation can be unconsciously racist. Among other battles the arts need to withstand is the fight against racism, as the arts in Africa need to consciously stand for an African Renaissance. The revival that can be brought by art forms such as music, poetry and visual arts is invaluable for society. Many contemporary artists have realised and underscored the need to liberate Africans through the arts (Chinweizu[6]; Ngugi[7]). The maskanda music that is defiantly sung in indigenous languages addresses some of the anomalies created by colonialism.

The arts, like language, play a critical role in African philosophy. In fact, many African philosophers are either artists or people who use the influence of arts to express Africanness. In South Africa, Credo Vusamazulu Mtwa is an *isanuse* or a Zulu Shaman who uses art, among other things, to express life and the history of Africa. His art is based on philosophy that has moved orally from generation to generation. Credo is said to have been able to adapt African traditional motifs and Western religious mythical symbolism to redefine indigenous African religion[8]. In his life time Credo has carved countless sculptures that reflect African life, Shaka the Zulu King, Ngungunyani of the Tsonga, as well as Nomkhubulwane the indigenous female goddess worshipped by mainly the Nguni. Credo's art reflects the communal nature of art in African society; it evokes values of the African village before the usurpation by colonial culture[9]. African philosophy seeks to retain these as societies look forward to embracing the renaissance. It is not art that does not seek to display other influences, but its essence is to show the African values influenced by a Pan-African culture.

The indigenous music of maskanda is a form of music that also wants to uphold certain values in indigenous society. The discussion in this chapter also focuses on how this kind of music seeks to change the society. There have been many movements in the past that sought to define African values through art. Among these was the Negritude Movement, which has always been criticised for the valorisation of African culture. Msiska[10] posited that:

Negritude, begun in the 1930s in France by Leopold Sedar Senghor and Aime Cesaire among others, sought to define and represent the essential core of African values as embodied in African spirituality and experience. In Senghor's case, this took the form of a preoccupation with the representation of the ancestral presence in literature and a positive revalorization of black identity. Additionally for Senghor, African art is conceived as inherently committed because it is intrinsically social and communal, as opposed to the individualism of European art.

Yet, without overemphasising African art as the Negritude Movement is always accused of, the role it plays is immense. The dancing maskandi who believes in his guitar swears by his ancestors and culture[11]. The dance and the drum reflect the African identity and set of values[12].

14.2 Explicating the brief nature of maskanda

Accompanied by less sophisticated instruments such as the guitar, the drum and the concertina, the maskandi tell stories in their songs, which cover a number of themes from social reality. Although the maskanda music may have started in Zulu folk history, today there are several variations from other Nguni groups, including *isibhaca*, *umxhobanyawo* and *isigexe*. Ntaka[13] cited Mathenjwa, who traced the word 'maskandi' from the Afrikaans word, 'musikant', which literally means music maker. According to Mathenjwa[14], maskanda refers to the type of music, and one who sings or performs this kind of music is a maskandi. Maskandis are unique in that they perform in their traditional Zulu garb. With their guitars playing, their songs respond to issues in society. Ntaka[15] argued that all types of music, including maskanda, contribute to the development of culture. "Through music, people are able to express their ways of life. Music, on some occasions informs culture…Music is thus an articulation of objectification of the philosophical and moral systems"[16]. Some experts link the performance of maskanda to the reflection of Africanness. Masilela[17] pointed out that the "African languages are the spiritual music of the African people". It was certainly for similar reasons that BW Vilakazi wrote: "I have an unshaken belief in the possibilities of Bantu languages and their literature, provided the Bantu writers themselves can learn to love their languages and use them as vehicles for thought, feeling and will"[18]. One cannot disavow the importance of the languages in the African Renaissance; these are the similar arguments highlighted by Ntombela in Chapter 10 as well as Kamwendo in Chapter 9 of this book. The decolonisation of culture should indeed start with language; this is an argument that was also raised by Diop[19] in the 1940s when he first talked about the concept *African Renaissance*. Maskandi presents culture in indigenous rhythms, language and narration; few cannot be touched by the sense of belonging shown by the maskandi when they perform with their zeal and vigour.

14.3 Indigenous languages and Poetry in Maskanda

The maskanda is able to address issues of renaissance and decolonisation through its poetry; the lyrics that are laden with several messages. Furthermore, there is always the influence of the oral traditional forms used in maskandi songs, including duende, on writing isiXhosa (a Nguni language) poetry. I am particularly concerned with the influence and use of *ukuzithutha* (invoking of traditional clan names and praises) and the role of *inkenqe* (duende) in the composing and singing of maskanda songs. Tied closely to this is my interest in the methods of creating maskanda music, and how they can be used to modernise poetry in isiXhosa. I then focus on how these can invoke the sense of a renaissance.

Modern written poetry in isiXhosa is still bound by the depleted language and structures of traditional forms, with content that extols the special features of isiXhosa culture - communion with the world of the spirits or ancestors (throbbing drums, flowing rivers, spirit dances, incantations to accompany libations). At their worst, both traditional and modern forms in isiXhosa poetry seek to admonish and to intimidate readers. For all these reasons, when I first started writing poetry in my teens, I chose to write in English rather than isiXhosa. My feelings about this have changed in recent years. At the same time, I have been encouraged by the emergence of confrontational and free-spirited poets who have widened the margins of isiXhosa literature, and emboldened me to write in my mother tongue.

Any language is a living, breathing entity that becomes defiled through bad habits, and needs to be renewed. My suspicion is that the unpopularity of Nguni books (e.g. in isiXhosa and isiZulu) can be addressed through writers employing more innovative styles and forms in their writing of Nguni languages. Contrast this structural default in Nguni poetry writing today to the freedom that is often displayed in the songs of maskandi like Mfaz' omnyama, Phuzekhemisi, Ihash' elimhlophe, Skipa Somntwana and Inkunz' Emnyama. The audiences are confronted in these artists' rendition and performance of their songs with greater introspection and a more sensitive and powerful use of language. In Phuzekhemisi's angry songs of protest against the erstwhile inhumane system of apartheid, there is more desperation and hunger to express a calamitous existence than in any available modern text of isiZulu or isiXhosa poetry. In another maskandi's humorous and yet desperate plea for forgiveness and love, the listener's mind is assailed by conflictual and yet highly emotive expressions of guilt and remorse:

Sisikhwele into endidina apha kuwe	*Your jealousy disturbs me*
Uthi ndinqinile	*You complain that I am not man enough*
Ndizakuhamba nawe	*I will continue to court you*
Ndizokutyeba	*And be stronger as a result*

The artist later in this song heaps praises on his cheated lover and sings with aplomb and loftily:

Uyingwe!	*You are a tigress!*

Ikhanda Lenja uses an inspired language and captures with flair and ingenuity a seemingly contradictory situation, love versus lust:

Qoma ntombi	*Baby girl accept me*
Isoka lakho liyadakwa!	*Your beau does not take care of you!*

I am fascinated by the ability of the lyricists of maskanda to bend the Nguni language with far greater ease than the general speakers of the language, including poets. A maskandi with a lonely four-stringed guitar will unlock the fixed forms in Nguni languages in much the same way as the enigmatic dances and bellowing singing of traditional healers (amagqirha) during their exorcising of invading and evil spirits from a human subject. I believe that maskanda music, a primarily Zulu and secondarily Xhosa traditional musical form, can extend the space for poetry writing and performance in the isiXhosa language, even more so because of the growing popularity of maskanda in the urban centres of South Africa. Apart from searching the role of traditional music as a purveyor of African values, I would also like to explore the relationship between this (maskanda) music and Nguni poetry, to see if and how poets can transpose its rhythmical patterns into the making and singing of their poems.

The maskanda lyricists portray an adventurous and creative spirit that seeks respite and solace in words, in the self-affirming possibilities of music. It is rare to find such scope and depth of expression in recently published isiXhosa poetry. In his introduction to *Umoya Weembongi*, a volume of isiXhosa poems by John Solilo, Opland[20] wrote:

> When he (John Solilo) prepared the poem ("Ntab' elanga") in Izala, he changed the criticism of Britain to a criticism of the commander and added a mollifying concluding stanza in which he adopted a non-partisan stance.

It is debilitating that this failure to speak and write freely as poets, in open conversations with the readers of books and with communities, has continued to dog and bear down heavily on the progress of isiXhosa poetry for so many decades after John Solilo's time, up to this day. The colonial influence continues currently as artists tend to be constrained. One of the styming factors against the progress of isiXhosa poetry is how it is taught by isiXhosa language teachers at secondary and high schools in South Africa. Frequently many isiXhosa writers and poets are excluded from the education system in favour of the circulation of preferred writers whose work often did not challenge the establishment.

> The early newspapers favoured such creative genres as history and dramatic dialogue, and encouraged the submission of Xhosa songs, but initially admitted poetry only in Victorian style. James Stewart, as editor of *Isigidimi*, in 1871 rejected an izibongo for publication because he did not wish to lend an encouragement to the initiation ceremony during which it was produced[21].

IsiXhosa prose has fared no better over the years. Traditionally the isiXhosa novel always focused on family life. One can think of many powerful isiXhosa novels like *UDingezweni*, *Ukuba Ndandazile*, *Buzani kubawo*, *Ingqumbo yeminyanya*, and *Ityala lamawele*. Some of these novels also touched on customary law and matters of governance and chieftainship pertinent to the Nguni tribal life. The dominance of this family theme has unfortunately led many writers to believe that it is the only important topic for writing isiXhosa fiction or poetry. The legacy and influence of the missionaries and their drive to civilise the African through religion and other ways are permanent features in isiXhosa literature to this day.

Oral traditional forms like *ukuzithutha* and *inkenqe* are not incongruent to maskandi compositions. They are integral features in a highly-ordered pattern of creating and performing

Maskandi compositions. Walter Ong's[22] thoughts on orality and literacy in his book, *Orality, Literacy, and Modern Media*, explain some of the intricate connections between mnemonic methods of oral cultures and how these methods were used by oral societies to organise experience intellectually. What Ong's[23] studies also revealed is that in a similar fashion to maskandi and their approach to music compositions, isiXhosa poets and writers can employ oral traditional methods within modern parameters and syntax to unlock the isiXhosa language.

> In an oral culture, to think through something in non-formulaic, non-patterned, non-mnemonic terms, even if it were possible, would be a waste of time, for such thought, once worked through, could never be recovered with any effectiveness, as it could be with the aid of writing. It would not be abiding knowledge but simply a passing thought, however complex. Heavy patterning and communal fixing formulas in oral cultures serve some of the purposes of writing in chirographic cultures, but in doing so they of course determine the kind of thinking that can be done, the way experience is intellectually organised. In an oral culture, experience is intellectualised mnemonically[24].

When the numerous intrusions into isiXhosa cultural thought finally caused isiXhosa poetry to lose its power to organise thought and experience mnemonically, isiXhosa poets and writers lost their ability to be engaging; with thought's suppression, Nguni poetry and creative fiction lost its capacity to formulate new dreams, and IsiXhosa poetry stopped being memorable. I contend that this limitation to be mnemonic has been subverted by maskandi lyricists in their compositions. To be successful in this project to circumvent the suppression of their creativity, maskandi reverted to an earlier mode of oral expression and began to use positive self-praise (*ukuzithutha*) and *inkenqe* (responding to one's spirits), as the inspirational methods and systems to enliven thought and expression, and to "intellectualise" experience mnemonically.

The maskandi carries the souls of social minorities. Its choruses are far from monolithic. Very often the songs praise both young and old, the powerful and powerless. Maskandi straddles the rural and the urban spaces. The maskandi have developed a deceptively simple style of singing that is both highly original and very innovative in execution. The maskandi blend specific and often contrasting attitudes and views about local black cultures, languages and religions, which has made demands on the lyrical and music composition. One will often find deep associations between contrasting abstractions and images in maskanda songs. This unique crafting and bending of the vernacular languages lends the poetry to the music. I needed to teach myself this extraordinary skill to write isiXhosa poems.

Ndiyoyika ukugula   *I fear white sickness*

Ndagula ndiseyadini   *I fell sick in the communal yards*

The sickness that Skipa Somntana sings about is the ancestral calling to divine healing; to be an *igqirha*. The sickness is a transitional place; a place of crossing between the mundane and secular world of men and women, and the unseen, far-flung spiritual home of the ancestors. What is particularly interesting for me is the horror of the next line, 'Ndagula ndiseyadini', whose vehemence lies in the unpredictability of divine calling. IsiXhosa speakers do not ordinarily use these archaic modes of conversing in isiXhosa. These are forms of isiXhosa that have been lost to the professional speakers: writers, journalists, teachers, and the educated men and women in high society who are fundamentally opposed to the new innovations in the writing and speaking of isiXhosa.

It is not true that highly developed languages possess rich terminology pools. Growth in vocabulary often erodes a language's expressive power by depleting its images. A language stammers through a myriad of soulless and barren images like an infant, incapable of articulating its real self. IsiXhosa poets must stop obsessing about the paucity of their language for it is not lacking any value. Languages tend to fall by the wayside, and become forgotten or extinct because of concerted and deliberate efforts not to use them. This deterioration is often expedited by a disregard for poetry. Are maskandi aware that their song-writing is the closest form that we have to modern poetry in isiXhosa? Noluthando Mpola's doctoral thesis, entitled, *An Analysis of Oral Literary Music Texts in isiXhosa*[25], discusses the relationship between songs composed in isiXhosa and *imibongo* (oral literature). In her abstract, she argues that:

> In traditional Xhosa cultural settings, poetry and music are forms of communal activity enjoyed by that society. Music and poetry perform a special social role in African society in general, providing a critique of socio-economic and political issues …. In the same way that izibongo can be analysed in order to appreciate the aesthetic value of an oral literary form, the same can be said of composed isiXhosa music …..

> Composers and writers of izibongo are similar artists and, in the words of Mtuze in Izibongo Zomthonyama (1993) "Bathwase ngethongo elinye" (They are spiritually gifted in the same way) … Song composition is a vehicle for transmitting culture orally in the same way that performers of izibongo transmit cultural knowledge.

Ntuli[26] made clear distinctions between poetry and lyrics in maskanda music:

> Maskandi poetry is a type of self-praise which the musician recites while playing a musical instrument. The main purpose of the recitation is to introduce the performer. The poet uses features such as repetition, linking, parallelism and imagery …. Maskandi poetry has many features found in ordinary izibongo.

Referring to the lyrics of maskandi, Ntuli noted:

> The lyrics which are punctuated by the praising usually focus on the composer's personal experiences or observations about conditions in his environment. Love is the most popular theme.

Ntuli's discussion on maskandi poetry is limited by his failing to look closely at the poetry in the lyrics. A typical example of this omission comes from David Ngcobo's song, 'Njomame', which Ntuli quotes in his article[27]:

> *Nang' uMhlongo uzenz' inkosi,*   *Here is Mhlongo making himself king,*
> *Ukhwela phezu kwendlu …*   *He climbs on top of the house …*

The quick poetic turn in the isiZulu language in these two verses is palpable. The sudden movement from the description of Mhlongo as a 'cheat' to associating his act of cheating with 'climbing on top of the house' is a poetic framing of the language. I see a problem in Ntuli's flat uninspired translation of the two verses into English which fails to capture the mischievous glint, the quirkiness and insightfulness of the original isiZulu verses. 'Ukukhwela emthini', climbing a tree, has alluring and magical associations in African folklore and tradition. The phrase denotes a mystical presence with an oblique reference to mankind's co-habitation with *uQamata*, the African conception of God. This deference to the sanctity and interest of *Qamata* in human affairs is so pervasive in the African view of life, that a child is taught from an early age never to point upwards at the sky with a finger as this is a transgression against God; an affront to *uQamata*. African traditional rites and beliefs are still strongly fixed in the modern forms of vernacular languages which are used by the poets today. We find similar interpretations in the application of traditional concepts like 'ihlathi' - the bush, 'umlambo' - a river, 'ubusuku' - the night; concepts which are so saturated and packed with ancestral and dark meanings that they often inspire the dread of endless voids, of infinity. Such terminologies are not easily translatable to Western linguistic forms. Maskandi lyricists, who come from a strong rural culture, are quite aware of the power of their vernacular languages. They craft their lyrics and use the language fully conscious of this rich tapestry of idiomatic phrases and poetic forms available to them.

Another example of the disingenuous treatment of Maskandi lyrics by commentators comes from another set of lyrics which Ntuli[27] quotes. This time the poet and composer of the lyrics is the artist Thikazisa Manqele in his song, 'Khetha ntombi':

Wonke la masok' ayaziphekela,	*All the young men cook for themselves,*
Ngayithatha bengafuni,	*I took her against their wish,*
Sebeyithwal' abakwaBiyela;	*The Biyelas were carrying her away;*
Besiyeshela sobabili,	*Two of us were courting her,*
Intomb' ikheth' emthandayo"	*The girl chooses the one she loves.*

Again, the beauty of the last two lines in this stanza is marred by the rather lifeless translation of the text.

Besiyishela sobabili,	*Two of us were courting her,*
Intomb' ikheth' emthandayo	*The girl chooses the one she loves*

There's a surge of excitement in the two lines, a deference to the respect for women in African societies. In this context, the noun 'girl' is not appropriate as an equivalent of the adoring term, 'intombi'. As a poet, I also struggled to understand why Ntuli[28] chose to ignore the poetry in maskandi lyrics for the more conventional praises or izibongo. His omission pushes the daring poetry into the background. I found most of Ntuli's remarks about maskandi lyrics reductionist and offensive, as they are full of generalisations and gloss over critical cultural issues in the psycho-sociological reality of most African communities. Taken at face value his conclusions will misinform, or worse still mislead, readers of the sociological role and the psychological framework that imibongo provided for African ritual and customary practice.

Again we see the ability of the maskandi to stretch the limits of the language and to bend it in such a way that speech serves its purpose, which is to transform man from a passive receptive animal to a creator of his world. At odds with the urban environment around him and dislodged from his past, the maskanda flees from himself. He begins to see life not simply as it is, but as he envisions it can become. And he does so with just that much more force; a greater thrust and a compelling outrage against the familiar forms inside our society's prevailing norms. His trusted tool is a sharp knife that he uses with skill to chop the language into tiny fragments and sections in order to expose the lies and sift the truth. What he has learnt, which is a by-product of being a modern citizen, is that being civilised is tantamount to being a cheat. Layers upon layers of half-truths and naked lies have masked the face of the modern man and disfigured his relationships with himself and with the world. Man's language, his one token that distinguishes him from beasts, has been embedded and contaminated with hypocrisy and false sentiments. Man no longer has a voice, and on occasion, when he forcefully manages to make a sound with his tongue and his parched lips, only a gibberish noise escapes from his mouth to confound the world.

Inkathazo	*Trouble*
kufanele ukushiywa ngemva ngabantu	*your own folks will abandon you*
maxhaphetshu uwele imimango	*and overnight you will live alone*
xa kunzima akuncedi ukutyhafa	*in doubt do not despair*
wena sowufanelwe ziintlungu nezinyeliso	*your suffering can be your solace*
ungqongwe kukungcola	*evil will follow you*
ukungavisisani akutyiwa	*in bad company you will not prosper*
zininzi izinto abantu abathi yimpucuko.	*there's so much evil that tastes sweet.*

The language of a maskanda is the language of a frenetic man, a madman. His songs are never settled on any one theme but jump up and about and all over, trying to grasp the invisible. Meaningless images and fierce metaphors incessantly crowd the air and assail the listener's nerves. The maskanda doesn't seek to make peace with the world. He aims for disruption of the senses, for war, as he is a roving character, an unhappy bandit. His songs always begin with squealing guitar sounds that shock the audience. The maskanda doesn't aim to please anyone. He is an artist and not an entertainer, a vituperative poet and a griot whose only task is to judge and condemn the world. His ruse of singing his melodies in staccato and riffs seeks to jar the senses and undress the false language that men and women use to mystify their lives, distorting life in an incredible play. Another trick that the maskanda plays again and again on the audience is that of downplaying his purpose and mission, cajoling his listeners to a false confidence by reminding them of his humble origins. He tells his audience now and again that he comes from a certain rural land by the mountains, and he drank his water from a certain river. This tracing of himself back to a rustic past is juxtaposed with the lyrical harshness and the fatality of his message.

Hadebe[29] wrote about Phuzekhemisi's music as a form of social protest. The maskandi musicians are utilising their genre which was on the margins from the elite for many years. They use this to protest in a way that when one hears these lyrics on radio it is difficult to ignore their message. Phuzekhemisi has a song about his dog Dlayedwa that he needs to pay tax for. The song became popular as the hit was played repeatedly in Nguni radio stations in particular. Phuzekhemisi in the song is disgusted and is against a government that makes him pay a dog tax. Another popular song by Phuzekhemisi made him unpopular to headmen (*Izinduna*) because the hit song was against community meetings (*izimbizo*), while a third song, Izwe Alithuthuki (No improvement in this land), is a protest song as Phuzekhemisi still sees squalor among his people although they live in a free South Africa.

Can we sum up all these elements of language and the various modes of expression that maskandi employ in songwriting and performance as poetry? And if that is the case, is it good poetry?

<table>
<tr><td>

Umaskandi
umaskandi uwelile
ngongcwalazi lwemivundla
ndimvile endiculela
ngentsholokazi enkulu
kamyoli ebusuku

lena yimbongi yakomkhulu
ehlalise phantsi zonke iimbongi
ngesigingci sakhe senkcenkce
uvuthulula uthuli

sakusoloko simangalisiwe
yiloo mbekokazi inkulu
ezakowethu iimbongi zingxathile
zimele kude zixakiwe

sophethuka sigoduke
sihlininiz' iintloko sidangele
sihlaziyek' iintliziyo sibonile
sikhohliwe sothukile.

</td><td>

The maskandi
the maskandi has left us
in the evening
I heard him sing
in the loudest voice
peaceful in the night

he is the paramount poet
who stands tall above others
with a cheap zinc guitar
he prepares the way

he will always confound us
with his grace and humility
other poets wait by the sideline
confounded and confused

we will turn back and return home
shaking our heads in disbelief
our hearts refreshed by what we saw
astonished and full of questions.

</td></tr>
</table>

The two poems 'Inkuthazo' and 'UMaskandi' are my personal responses to the predicament of the maskanda figure in our society; an impenetrable and heroic character who stands precariously on society's margins. The first poem empathises with the lonesome plight of the maskanda to finally admit that, 'zininzi izinto abantu abathi yimpucuko'. 'UMaskandi' is a more direct poem; a ballad that sings passionately of the commendable warlike features of the maskanda. The maskanda is portrayed as a martyr, someone who represents the most laudable features of our humanity. Again there is the allusion to the marginal and incongruous state of the maskanda in the final stanza; an invocation that aims to awaken the missing spirituality in the plastic lives that we have built for ourselves.

In his unpublished essay *Poetics and Narratives,* Nolutshungu[30] aptly refers to this strange force and inexplicable behaviour that he calls *inkenqe*, often demonstrated by the maskanda in performance:

> A power that lives in a person in a form of a spirit that is reflected through a person's actions and communication. If you do not have *inkenqe* you can't make it as a musician or a poet, and duende or inkenqe cannot be avoided or ignored, it must be embraced by the artist, who must let it take charge of his or her creative life.

This is what Garcia Lorca calls duende, although in isiXhosa we have an almost identical concept called *inkenqe* that the maskandi also experiences - flushes and bouts of extreme creative energy.

> The duende – where is the duende? Through the empty arch comes an air of the mind that blows insistently over the heads of the dead, in search of the new landscapes and unsuspected accents; an air smelling of child's saliva, of pounded grass, and medusal veil announcing the constant baptism of newly created things[31].

The maskandi's approach to composition, his abstraction of words and the cold trajectories of his lyrics become instantaneously famous or indifferent. All of a sudden, without any palpable reason whatsoever, he wants to smoke a pipe or to sing horribly. And he dreams he is alone and drunk, dancing deliriously in a strange place. And God is his witness. "God is my friend", Marvin Gaye once told us. I know now God is a female or an ant.

The diabolical obsession with keeping isiXhosa pure and the limits and restraints on making the language sing are at long last being loosened. Buzani[32], Nolutshungu[33] and Billie[34] are three poets who approach the poem as a body of pleasure and anguish, something to be noticed, temporarily experienced and captured for its inventive light, but never permanently detained. Due to this new perception that they bring to writing in isiXhosa, new peculiarities, pleasurable inventions and angles have suddenly opened or are defiantly brought in. We see new "leapings", wild associations in their poetry that surge boundlessly forward, at a staggering pace like wild horses. Robert Bly writes about this feeling as a "kind of elation … associated with dark sounds"[35]. Buzani[36] associates powerfully in a poem about life that he calls 'Ubomi'.

ngumthombo	*it is a river*
umpompoza amanzi abandayo	*of cold water*
kucula amaza	*sea waves sing*
aculela imbewu kulwandlekazi	*a seed trapped in a huge ocean*
isiqalo sobomi bam	*life begins*
kukhala umntwana	*with a baby's cry*
ekhonjiswa ubomi	*my life hobbles*
ubomi bam.	*before my eyes.*

Bly also offers us the concrete critical impulses, and takes us step-by-step through the processes that consume a poet at the moment of creation:

> The poet enters the poem excited, with the emotions alive; he is angry or ecstatic, or disgusted. There are a lot of exclamation marks, visible or invisible …. when the poet brings to the poem emotions from his thought-life and his flight-life, emotions which would be intense whether the poem were written or not, and when he succeeds in uniting them with the associative powers of the unconscious, we have something different … [37].

This again evidences duende or *inkenqe*, "a power that lives in a person in a form of a spirit"[38]. In his poem called 'Ibhayibhile', Nolutshungu asks some disturbing questions about the efficacy of modern day religion, especially Christianity, with its posturing and heretical doctrine of good ethics and exemplary living.

ngumlom' uvuz' igazi	*its mouth drips blood*
ngumphefuml' umhlophe	*its heart is pure*
bubumnyam' ukucac' enkungwini	*its evil contrasts sharply with its purity*
bubunzulu bengqond' ukusinda	*its load heavier than the soul*
khaniphinde zidwesha nisondeze amehlo	*come folks and scrutinise once more*
nani bantu nibeke iindlebe	*folks open your ears once more*
nithi umthetho omdala utheni?	*what did the old law proclaim?*
nithi omtsha wona uze nabani?	*who brought to us this new law?*
gxabhagxabhisani ningekaphum' iingongoma	*hurry up before it is too late*
quphani engeka thi gqi umntu wento	*make haste before the culprit arrives*
hlalani phantsi nizole	*sit down and be calm*
niphulaphule ngemiphefumlo	*listen to him with your hearts*
hayi ngenyama ethwele ukufa kwenu	*not with your poisoned flesh*
celani kumntu wento	*address your requests to the messenger*
nive kuye ukuba uthini na yena	*and hear what he will say*
nants' incwadi yakhe idid' amakholwa	*here is his book confusing the converts*

behla benyuka   *they go forth and come back*

benyuka behla   *go up and come down*

mna ndithe cwaka   *but I remain quiet*

kodwa ndijongile!   *yet my eyes can see!*

The representation of popular music, especially Maskandi, has made a similar impact on my understanding of the role of poetry and how as poets writing in our vernaculars we should approach lyrical composition, and introduce 'leaping' and ingenuity, inventiveness and surprise in our literary compositions. *Ukuzithutha* transmitted culture and served highly oral traditions to know the clan's lineage. The practice of *ukuzithutha* was encouraged among the boys who became the custodians of the culture. *Ukuzithutha* prevented intermarriages between members of the same clan, an act considered an abomination among the Nguni people. Its role in fomenting the space for the wider innovative use of the language by *iimbongi* (praise-singers) was paramount – helping to preserve local histories and culture, preserving the vernacular languages, and focusing the clan on crucial cleansing and appeasing rituals and libations for the ancestors.

Poets often employ 'self-referencing' or 'posting' in their composition of text. The technique is similar to *ukuzithutha*, as both seek to recall the past and to locate an aspect of familiarity with the past. The individual positions himself in the social and cultural world around him to better understand his present and future roles. Posting is used widely by maskandi. In an angry song published in 2000 addressed to an unnamed female companion titled 'Ngisebenzile Mama', Mfaz' Omnyama firmly reprimands a young woman for rejecting his advances:

We mama uyangithuka   *Woman you insult me*

Uthi ngiyivila   *You say I am lazy*

Awubhek' iinkomo zami   *But look at my cows*

Ngisebenzile   *I have done well*

Much as Mfaz' Omnyama exposes his chauvinism in this song by expecting the young woman to accept him because of his material possessions, his cows, the lyrics in the song also betray the insecurity of most traditional African men when proposing love to the confident, independent, modern African woman. It is inconceivable to imagine that Mfaz' Omnyama was indeed "insulted" in this instance, but the maskandi purposefully chooses to accentuate and exaggerate his feelings of hurt and disappointment in his lyrics. He "goes into himself", traces his life paths and points to his achievements to try and instill some confidence and commitment for mutual and reciprocal love. The technique of posting in this song has obviously been used by the artist to create feelings of guilt, and thus to weaken the young woman's defenses. A poem, a dance routine, a sculptural piece, a fictional story, all harness strong feelings and convert these into energy fields to stir readers and admirers of art. This is the primitive and sexual love that overwhelms the poet. At the heart of every poet is the need to know oneself, to locate one's bearings and destiny. The technique of posting or *ukuzithutha* serves to map the paths that the poet walks. It helps to strengthen the writing, affirming inert boundaries, the heart's territories. A small number of poets and artists are able to manipulate this energy field in order to "increase the speed of energy transfer"[39].

The process of creating the text, shaping it into a poem, or arranging the melody into a final song is a paradoxical and disastrous affair. The artist develops practical methods to make the process more manageable, less traumatic for himself. The poet exploits a short pause in the basic rhythm of the music to place himself above others and physically enters the poem. He thinks of himself as a humble man who comes from a rustic village with clean air and a running river. His songs melt with nostalgia and longing. In other words, the artist (who is in reality a grown-up person) assumes the foetal position inside a mother's womb. The earth is the mother, the giver of life.

To the composer alone the timing for posting is very crucial. To post successfully, the music of the poem must in turn be ripe. Spirituality must be invested in the poem to allow for this tangential drift to matters of no particular importance. This is the ascetic world at which the poet arrives, the world of *intwaso*, or "initiation into divinership". His digression becomes a momentary flight; a poor excuse to begin the long process of healing. The same practice is often seen in *amagqirhas'* divination and healing methods, where a highly cantankerous chant is often followed by *ukunuka*, the smelling of the source of the ailment, the diagnosis.

Amagqirha also depend on this fast transfer of psychic energy to reveal the sources of the evil that consumes a community. After writing a number of lines about Maskandi in the poem 'Ingoma', I also went on a tangent. The waning of the impulse after the early stanzas threatened to collapse the poem's energy. Posting was used to revive the poem, i.e.

yiyo ke leyo imbongi	*hear the poet*
ithetha izinto ngezinto ingaphezi	*exclaiming secrets*
yiyo ke leyo imbongi ibhuda	*hear the poet blustering*
yiyo ke leyo imbongi ibhonga	*hear the poet bellowing*
ithetha ngaphandle kwemvume	*speaking in jest in defiance*
ingatshatisi	*creating a havoc*
ishenxisa ingxolo nokufa	*challenging noise and death*
nokumila kwako	*and its foundation*
icikida impilo injalo ingafihl'	*revealing life and its secrets*
ityhiliz' isihelegu	*pushing aside catastrophe*
kunjalo nje ingabhampuli	*unperturbed*
yiyo ke leyo inkunz' endala	*hear the old bull*
isiphathel' ufele	*bringing us a cow's thick skin*

The energy of the poem was turning inward, so I ascended to a higher orbit where fast transfers of energy allowed new heights of experience and ecstasy. Likewise, maskanda is characterised by poets who self-reference text in order to drive their sonorous sounds. Posting in poetry is another manifestation of duende or *inkenqe* in the creative person.

Here are a few examples of poems where posting is used to arrive at surprising places, making huge leaps in their work. The first example is my own poem, 'Amanzi'. The first seven lines of this poem are a linear and simple description of water and its use, but the poem changes abruptly from line eight, "kumhla ndaqal' ukuphila/ndaqal' ukupheph' izifo/ ndancokola ndaneenkani", where the poet suddenly turns his vision inward to speak about his fears, and then later indicts the ubiquitous evil of men and women that is obdurate, anti-spiritual and anti-human:

amnandi amanzi	*water is joy*
anencasa acwengile	*its taste is sweet and calming*
adlamkisa umxhelo	*and revives inside*
ondla umzimba	*water feeds the body*
amnandi amanzi	*water is joy*
abaleka phezu komhlaba	*it runs over the earth*
adlamkisa indalo	*and restores life*
kumhla ndaqal' ukuphila	*once I felt its healing*
ndaqal' ukupheph' izifo	*I avoided diseases*
ndancokola ndaneenkani	*I spoke stubbornly*
ndalusana emandlalweni	*and became a young born in a bed*
ndinovalo ndothukile	*I was afraid and astonished*
ndawasela amanzi	*I drank the cold water*
ndasondela ebuntwini.	*and became a human boy.*

...

... I want to describe myself
like a painting that I saw
a few feet off, and close up,
like a word that I finally understood,
like a pitcher I use every day,
like the face of my mother,
like a ship
that took me safely
through the wildest storm of all[40].

I weave; from having spun, I am weaving.
I search for what follows me and hides from me among archbishops,
under my soul and behind the smoke of my breathing.
such was the sensual desolation
of the maiden goat that ascended
exhaling lethal petroleums,
yesterday sunday on which I lost my saturday.

such is death, with her daring husband[41].

what I want should not be confused
with total inactivity.
life is what it is about;
I want no truck with death.

if we were not so single-minded
about keeping our lives moving,
and for once could do nothing,
perhaps a huge silence
might interrupt this sadness
of never understanding ourselves
and of threatening ourselves with death.
perhaps the earth can teach us
as when everything seems dead
and later proves to be alive[42].

ndiya kuhlala ndinani phina ndingumntu nje   *how long will I stay with you as a human?*
ndingumntu nj' int' ehlal' ihambele?   *a human who visits occasionally?*
ndingumntu nj' int' ehlal' ihlal' ifuduke?   *a human who leaves?*
ndingumntu nj' int' ehlal' ihlal' ihlal'   *and goes back home again?*
igoduke?[43]   *I am not praising you mbona but burdening*
andikubongi mbona ndiyakufomba,   *you,*
noko ndakha ndazek' ityala emlungwini,   *I once made myself unpopular to white people*
ndabong' inkosana yaphum' ufundo,   *and praised a young chief and he abandoned*
    the new ways,

kwathiwa ubumzonda ntoni na umntwan'   *I was asked did I despise the chief's son*
enkosi,   *to praise him till his back broke,*
ukumbong' ade asuke aphuk' umqolo,   *till he abandoned his birth right for chieftaincy?*
ade ashiy' isihlalo sakowabo sobukumkani?

14.4 Conclusion

In conclusion, we need to understand indigenous music, its poetry such as maskandi's, as a way to illuminate the African Renaissance and decolonise the arts. As mentioned above, indigenous music today brings forth the hope of redress in society, as there is a need to eclipse the atrocious apartheid legacy. Vokwana[44] claimed that as the apartheid legacy dwindled, embracing a new sense of Africanness formed part of negating the harm of the apartheid years. There was this need to reclaim heritage; "apartheid, as a direct result of the colonial encounter, was largely instrumental in processes of erasure of the indigenous and by implication, African ways of life". In debates about language that we have read about in Chapters 9 and 10, indigenous music plays a critical role. Art forms such as music, drama and literature are all pivotal to the development and promotion of African philosophy discussed by several authors in this book. Ikuenobe in Chapter 1 and Msila in Chapter 2 wrote about the critical nature of traditional philosophy to support the African Renaissance. The maskandi plays much in this area. Indigenous music's role cannot be underestimated. The maskanda's lyrics are written with a number of objectives in mind; love, social protest, didactic purposes and various others. Music can also be used to create a peaceable community, but it is usually these people who tend to be oppressed by undemocratic governments.

In Mali recently, arts and culture were used to speed up peace and unity after a retracted conflict. The invaders in Mali tried to destroy the Malian culture and this spurred the musician Fademata Walet Oumar to protest; "They want to ban our music...they will have to kill us first[45]." Furthermore, Schneider[46] wrote that:

> The invaders attempted to erase Mali's culture: silence her griots – the musical internet for much of Mali, bearing news and history through their songs; destroy her unique mud-brick shrines and UNESCO World Heritage sites which have weathered the desert over five hundred years; and burn her manuscripts, priceless repositories of knowledge from Timbuktu's Golden Age. They failed … Malians outwitted them, continuing to blend music behind closed doors, and exile in neighbouring countries.

Music played a great role in the resistance against domination in Mali, thus there is still hope that the culture embedded in African Renaissance principles will enable Africans to face certain societal challenges. Indigenous music such as maskanda discussed in this chapter enables artists to use their rich languages to pose questions to society. Singing in African languages, African-styled music is one way of addressing past imbalances as shown above, and this includes affirming black cultures. Indigenous music is also about heritage and indigenous knowledge systems. Music should also help in the digitisation and documentation of black artists such as Mahlathini, Ladysmith Black Mambazo and a host of others. Indigenous music promotes oral history, language, and identity. Mugovhani[47] wrote about the need to promote indigenous cultures in order to help the country achieve total emancipation and recognition of previously marginalised societies. This author adds, "indeed South Africa needs to respond to the changing cultural landscapes and interface with other knowledge systems..." Furthermore, Mugovhani[48] averred that:

> The time has come for all African countries to carry the flag for African civilisation. This challenge includes leading the processes of cultural emancipation within our communities first before globalisation. The concept of African Renaissance in post-colonial South Africa should be pursued vigorously, and as in many other developing countries, national institutions of higher learning should be in the forefront in spearheading the attainment of the ideological objectives.

Afro-jazz, maskanda and other African music forms have long begun to underscore the ideals of the African Renaissance. These artists' songs are not only for mere entertainment, but they form part of social commentary and social protest. Many use social satire to comment in their songs.

References

[1]Okumu, W. A. J. 2005. *The African Renaissance*. Trenton, N.J. and Asmara, Eritrea: Africa World Press.

[2]Ibid.

[3]Biko, S. 1987. *I write what I like*. London: Heinemann.

[4]Fanon, F. 1963. *The Wretched of the Earth*. New York: Grove Weidenfeld.

[5]Biko, S. 1987. *I write what I like*. London: Heinemann.

[6]Chinweizu. 1987. *Decolonising the African Mind*. Lagos: Pero Press.

[7]Wa Thiong'o, N. 1986. *Writing Against Colonialism*. Criticism and Ideology: Second African Writers' Conference, Stockholm, 1986.

[8]NLA Design and Visual Arts. *Credo Vusamazulu Mutwa*. Retrieved from: https://nladesignvisual.wordpress.com/2013/05/22/credo-vusamazulu-mutwa/. [Date accessed: January 12, 2017.]

[9]Ibid.

[10]Msiska, M. n.d. *Africa Realism – Reality in African Aesthetics and Literary Criticism*. Retrieved from: http://science.jrank.org/pages/10995/Realism-Africa-Reality-in-African Aesthetics-Literary-Criticism.html. [Date accessed: January 12, 2017.]

[11]Msila, V. In Preparation. *The Black Griots and Renaissance*.

[12]Ibid.

[13]Ntaka, G. M. 2007. *Music as culture, music in culture: An analytical study of the history and actual context of mbaqanga music in South Africa*. Unpublished Doctoral Thesis. KwaDlangezwa: University of Zululand.

[14]Mathenjwa, L. F. 1995: *An Analysis of Maskandi Poetry as a Genre of Southern African Poetry*. Unpublished M. Ed. Dissertation. Pietermaritzburg, University of Natal.

[15]Ntaka, G. M. 2007. *Music as culture, music in culture: An analytical study of the history and actual context of mbaqanga music in South Africa*. Unpublished Doctoral Thesis. KwaDlangezwa: University of Zululand.

[16]Masilela, N. 2006. *Mazisi Kunene (1930-2006): An Appreciation*. Retrieved from: http://pzacad.Pitzer.edu/NAM/general/essays/mazisi-app. [Date accessed: November 24, 2016.]

[17]Ibid.

[18]Ibid.

[19]Diop, C. A. 2000. *Towards the African Renaissance: Essays in Culture and Development, 1946- 1960*. New Jersey: Red Sea Press.

[20]Opland, J. 2007. The first novel in Xhosa. *Research in African Literatures,* 38(4): 88-110.

[21]Ibid.

[22]Ong, W. 2011. Orality, Literacy, and Modern Media. In D. Crowley and P. Heyer (Eds.). *Communication in history: Technology, Culture, Society*. London: Routledge.

[23]Ibid.

[24]Ibid.

[25]Mpola, M. N. 2007. *An analysis of oral literary music texts in isiXhosa*. Unpublished Doctoral dissertation. Grahamstown, Rhodes University.

[26]Ntuli, D. B. 1990. Remarks on Maskandi Poetry. *South African Journal of African Languages*, 10(4):302 -306.

[27]Ibid.

[28]Ibid.

[29]Hadebe, J. S. 2000. *Izwe alithuthuki by Phuzekhemisi as sung in KwaZulu-Natal: Maskandi song as social protest*. Unpublished Masters dissertation. Durban, University of Natal.

[30]Nolutshungu, S. 2015. *Iingcango zentliziyo*. Unpublished Masters Dissertation. Grahamstown: Rhodes University.

[31]Bly, R. 1975. *Leaping Poetry: An Idea with Poems and Translations*. Boston: Beacon Press.

[32]Buzani, M. W. 2014. *Ndisabhala Imibongo*. Port Elizabeth, Imbizo Arts of South Africa.

[33]Nolutshungu, S. 2015. *Iingcango zentliziyo*. Unpublished Masters Dissertation. Grahamstown: Rhodes University.

[34]Billie, A. 2016. *Umhlaba Umanzi*. Unpublished Masters Dissertation. Grahamstown: Rhodes University.

[35]Bly, R. 1975. *Leaping Poetry: An Idea with Poems and Translations*. Boston: Beacon Press.

[36]Buzani, M.W. 2014. *Ndisabhala Imibongo*. Port Elizabeth, Imbizo Arts of South Africa.

[37]Bly, R. 1975. *Leaping Poetry: An Idea with Poems and Translations*. Boston: Beacon Press

[38]Nolutshungu, S. 2015. *Iingcango zentliziyo*. Unpublished Masters Dissertation. Grahamstown: Rhodes University.

[39]Bly, R. 1975. *Leaping Poetry: An Idea with Poems and Translations*. Boston: Beacon Press.

[40]Ibid.

[41]Eshleman, C. & Buncia, J. R. (Eds.). 1978. *Cesar Vallejo: The Complete Posthumous Poetry*. Barcelona: Editorial Laia.

[42]Neruda, P. 1974. *Extravagaria*. New York: Farrar Straus & Giroux.

[43]Mqhayi, S. E. K. 1988. *Imihobe nemibongo*. Pretoria: De Jager-Haum.

[44]Vokwana, T. 2007. Resurrecting an African identity through popular music in the post-apartheid South Africa. In E. Akrofi, M. Smit and S. Thorsen (Eds.). *Transformation and Negotiation*. Stellenbosch: Sun Press.

[45]Schneider, C. P. 2014. *Upfront-the Timbuktu Renaissance: harnessing Music, Heritage and Culture to Save Mali*. Retrieved from: http://www.brookings.edu/. [Date accessed: February 01, 2017.]

[46]Ibid.

[47]Mugovhani, N. G. 2013. *African Renaissance, Indigenous African music and globalisation: Collusion or collision?* Retrieved from: https://www.researchgate.net/publication/29/757424. [Date accessed: December 12, 2016.]

[48]Ibid.

Chapter 15

African Renaissance: Learning from some African Indigenous leadership practices

Vitallis Chikoko
School of Education
University of KwaZulu-Natal

15.1 Introduction

The concept, *African Renaissance*, is tackled in almost every chapter of this volume. It is about renewing the African continent in several spheres, including culture. This is a renewal that occurs with time, as society evolves and seeks progress. Frequently change is necessitated by societal challenges, and with Africa's many challenges critics will argue that change is continually necessary. It was the Nigerian writer and literary critic, Chinua Achebe, whose classic novel *Things Fall Apart*[1] exposed some of Africa's challenges. Some would, like I do, contend that given Achebe's work, the African Renaissance should not be just another renewal, but must a be self-renewal that responds to the need to take a collective responsibility as Africans take responsibility to resuscitate the continent.

In Chapter 1 of this book Ikuenobe points out that an African Renaissance needs to infuse the positive features of modernity and tradition and shed the negative features. In addition, Msila in Chapter 2 states that the word 'renaissance' conjures hope, progress, resilience and the defeat of colonialism. Finally, Mndawe in Chapter 13 contends that an African Renaissance has to do with rebirth, rejuvenation and restoration. But Khoza[2] argues that Africans must begin the renewal journey by admitting that there is a problem. We have become a sick continent and Africans are largely to blame as they find themselves in the midst of an African crisis. The following ills, as identified by Ngambi[3], characterise this crisis:

- Poverty
- High levels of unemployment and under development
- Poor health
- Poor and inadequate institutional planning
- Abuse of power
- Lack of accountability
- Inadequate education and high levels of illiteracy
- Despondency and apathy
- A high violent-crime rate

Tsedu, quoted by Ngambi[4], had the following to say about Africa:

> African structures are all gone. Those that are still around are being ridiculed each day, from circumcision and cultural practices to religion and the medicines of our forefathers. Yet, Africans were not always like this. The forefathers and mothers who built [Great] Zimbabwe, and the pyramids of Giza, who taught the Greek mathematicians the basics of algebra and trigonometry were great people. The leaders of the kingdom of Monomotapa, Timbuktu, Mapungubwe, etc., were great leaders. They could never have succeeded in doing what they did if they were selfish and lacked work ethic.

Tsedu's argument above shares the challenges that Africa is exposed to, however I present this chapter as an Afro-optimist. This chapter comprises the mainstay of my 'story', which has to do with how Africa can draw from its very rich leadership past towards renewal. I identify and discuss six leadership hallmarks drawn from a study I led, which involved conversations with selected village elders in four Southern African countries, Lesotho, South Africa, Zambia and Zimbabwe, about African indigenous leadership practices. I briefly examine the notion of indigenous knowledge, give an overview of African indigenous knowledge, and juxtapose the terms 'leadership' and 'African indigenous leadership'.

15.2 The notion of Indigenous Knowledge

The term 'indigenous' refers to the root of things; something natural and innate to a specific context. Kolawole[5] defined 'indigenous knowledge' as the technical insight or wisdom gained and developed by people in a particular locality through years of careful observation and experimentation with the natural phenomena around them. Indigenous ways of knowing are based on locally, ecologically, and seasonally contextualised truths of particular natural groups of people. These natural groups of people are characterised by complex kinship systems of relationships among people, animals, earth, the cosmos, and so on, from which all knowing originates[6]. Indigenous Knowledge Systems experts such as Barnhardt[7], Cajete[8], Battiste and Barman[9] have described indigenous knowledge as knowing based on the teachings and experiences passed on from generation to generation. Indigenous knowledge is rooted in the spirit, health, culture and language of a people and therefore cannot be divorced from the people in question. It is a way of life; it has a traditional authority system; it is dynamic, cumulative and stable; it is a way of life where wisdom means using traditional knowledge in 'good' ways; it means using the heart and the head together to make decisions that will benefit the whole community; it survives because it comes from the spirit; it is the relationships and a code of ethics that govern the appropriate use of the environment; it is recognising that this code of ethics includes rules and conventions promoting desirable ecosystem relations, human-animal interactions and even social relationships[10].

15.3 Overview of African Indigenous Leadership

African indigenous leadership is an institution that has developed for centuries. Gebrehiwet[11] rightly argued that this leadership has served the African people through wars, slavery, famine, liberation struggles and during the post-colonial periods. Gebrehiwet further reported that African indigenous leadership is rooted in the ties of the family, clan and community[12]. "It gives freedom to live within your society comfortably without hurting anyone and without being hurt by anyone"[13]. Moral responsibility played an important role in the governance of African societies, thus providing guidance on how people would live together peacefully as part of a larger community. Every member of society partook in determining the political, economic, social and cultural systems, which allowed everyone a sense of belonging. Gebrehiwet argued that given the less complicated nature of pre-colonial political organisation in Africa, colonialists found the Africans very gullible people, and took advantage of this as they plundered the continent in various ways. Thus African leadership structures were influenced by the colonisers - many a post-colonial African leader adopted an imposed system in its entirety.

This changed system manifested itself in two main forms. Firstly, the African political leaders have denied their people opportunities to participate meaningfully in the processes of running their localities by institutionalising "unAfrican" and imposing models, thus caring little for the welfare of their people. Second, the violent military coups that have occurred in several parts of Africa have been more vicious and brutal than colonial regimes, thus eradicating both political stability and democracy. In the process, the fundamental principle that the government belongs to the people and for the people, was violated. Writers such as Mungazi[14] contentiously argued that Africans cannot blame the colonialists for the failure to uphold the fundamental principles of democracy, yet Marker[15] argued that there are several lingering effects of colonialism and these manifest themselves in various ways. Moreover, former South African President Mbeki[16] blamed a lack of leadership for Africa's problems. Mbeki also called for the need to conscientise the youth to continue the struggle for the continent's liberation (the youth debate is raised by Msila in Chapter 14).

15.4 Understanding the terms 'leadership' and 'Indigenous African leadership'

Leadership is a multi-faceted, expansive and forever evolving concept. Bennis and Nanus[17] stated that, "Leadership is a word on everyone's lips. The young attack it, and the old grow wistful for it. Parents have lost it and the police seek it. Experts claim it and artists spurn it, while scholars want it. Philosophers reconcile it (as authority) with liberty and theologians demonstrate its compatibility with conscience. If bureaucrats pretend they have it, politicians wish they did. Everybody agrees that there is less of it than there used to be".

Forde[18] reported that the words 'lead' and 'load', are both derived from the same word: 'loadstone'. The 'loadstone' (or 'lodestone') is the magnetic metal in a compass that points to or finds the way north, thereby enabling travellers to be 'led' to their destination. Forde[19] then argued that from this origin, certain connotations regarding the term 'leadership' persist. These include journey, change, transformation, renewal and movement towards something better. According to Covey[20], "Leadership is communicating to people their worth and potential so clearly that they come to see it in themselves... It is geared towards socially positive outcomes that not only meet the needs of the followers but also elevate them to a 'better place'[21] or to 'higher levels of motivation and morality'"[22]. To Heifitz[23], leadership is "The activity of mobilising people to deal with their tough issues". It is about inspiring, intellectual stimulation and personal consideration[24]. True leadership, however, is concerned with creating an environment in which all people can reach their full potential.

From an African perspective, "Traditional Leadership in the African context emphasises a culture that builds communities"[25]. Indigenous African leadership is rooted in chieftaincy and village community[26]. Ngambi[27] succinctly summarised the features of such indigenous African leadership as follows:

> (African leaders) inspire a shared vision. They have a dream or vision, in which all members find their place and all members of the community are shareholders. They acknowledge that leadership is a dialogue, not a monologue.
>
> Create disciples, not followers, though trust, integrity and reliability.
>
> Communicate through stories and dialogue-sharing wisdom.
>
> Build relationships based on the *Ubuntu* philosophy (for example invitations are informal and inclusive).
>
> Share responsibility and accountability.
>
> Lead by example. They take cognisance of the fact that titles are granted, but it is behaviour that gains you respect and fosters commitment.
>
> Challenge the process and venture out. …There is no one who claims to have achieved his/her personal best by keeping things the same. The leader's primary contribution is in the recognition of good ideas and the support of those ideas so that people in the community or organisation can feel safe to take calculated risks that will lead to success.
>
> Foster collaboration and trust. Leadership is a team effort.
>
> Encourage the heart. They create a culture of celebration…

In the African context, the primary role of leadership is nurturing the spirit and culture of societal institutions and communities. It is believed that indigenous African chiefs are first and foremost the guardians of the spirit and culture of their communities. Above all the other duties they perform, they must first be suitable and competent in discharging their cultural and spiritual roles. Thus the term 'leadership' is understood as the art of developing, expressing and defending stability and values[28]. Therefore, the strength of such leadership lies in service, moral principles and standard of conduct. The qualities of a leader are self-knowledge, integrity, commitment, empathy, cultural sensitivity and competence. Leadership development is advocated as employing participatory strategies, giving voices to those who have not been heard before[29].

15.5 Drawing on some African leadership hallmarks

15.5.1 The spirit of knowing and caring for one another

One of the pillars of leading a community in most traditional African contexts lies in the spirit of knowing one another, as well as what is going on at any given time in the village. Through knowledge of the people, the leaders are able to care for them. In this regard, the following is what a village elder among the Lamba clan of Zambia had to say:

> *Basulutani* (Lamba name for headmen) take care of the people; they know who has a visitor, where they are from and why they have come into the village in detail and when they will go back. They know if they have come to stay and which piece of land to give them. They know who is sick and for how long. They know everybody and everybody knows them too.

In modern society, such behaviour is likely to be viewed as intruding into others' private lives, eavesdropping, and perhaps out of order. While we may no longer be living in such communal contexts, while it has become a security matter for our neighbours to know everything about us, and while we may no longer need a piece of land from the *Basulutani* for our livelihood, I argue that there remains a lot to learn from this African traditional approach. There are many questions that we may need to pose, including:

- How much non-intrusive knowledge do we have about the people around us: our children, siblings, partners, husbands and wives, let alone neighbours?
- How much non-intrusive knowledge do the people around us have about us?
- How much concern do we have for the welfare of those around us and in the wider community?
- Have we become too busy with our own personal issues to the point that the notion of 'community' has become a tired concept?

Among the Shona people of Zimbabwe there is a popular saying that goes: *Zvangu zvaita* (what I wished for has come to fruition). At face value there may not seem to be anything untoward in someone acknowledging the things going right in one's life, however in my experience this term became popular during the hard economic times of the past decade or so - a time where a culture of survival of the fittest prevailed in most situations. The African Renaissance requires that we pay more attention to community interests than we currently see on the African continent today. In his book, *Attuned Leadership,* Khoza[30] stated that the argument throughout that book is that morality is the key to leadership. Khoza[31] expressed concern about the ethics of modern business houses as follows:

> …there is so much evidence of greed and hypocrisy at the highest levels. Yet the principles of ethical leadership apply across the board, whether one is referring to a government, an enterprise, an activist body, a church or a neighbourhood association. There is no true leadership without service to the community and there is no interest greater than the common interest…

Caring for others is not necessarily about providing them with ready-made goods. The most sustainable form of caring is, as we see in the quote above, providing them with 'a piece of land', a means of production, one in which the recipient will have to do the producing. I find this to be quite rich in meaning. In the African context, an equilibrium in the community can only be reached when all work the land by contributing to the economic well-being of the community. In a similar instance, a traditional XiTsonga expression goes: *Mangwa yi pfumale timhondzo hi ku rhumisa* (The zebra lacks horns because it sent for them). This comes from folklore and means that those who rely on others to do work for them will, without doubt, lose out on many valuable things, but they have the potential to become self-reliant if they go for it[32]. However we are not always in good health to be able to 'till the land'. Sometimes we get sick. We are sick when we do not have what it takes to 'till the land' in terms of knowledge and skills. We are sick when the 'playing field' is uneven for us. There can be many more forms of sickness on our part. To what degree do our African societies today adequately know about, care about and address the assorted sicknesses among their own people? There cannot be any African Renaissance without knowing and caring.

One day as I was writing this chapter, an acquaintance sent me a SMS that I found interesting entitled *Sober Reflections*. I do not have the original source from which the friend got it. It read as follows:

> Your BIRTH came through **Others**
> Your NAME was given by **Others**
> You were EDUCATED by **Others**
> Your INCOME indirectly comes from **Others**
> Your RESPECT is given by **Others**
> Your first BATH was given by **Others**
> Your last BATH will be done by **Others**
> Your FUNERAL will be organised by **Others**
> You will be taken to your FINAL RESTING PLACE by **Others** and
> EVERYTHING you owned will be inherited by **Others**

I found this message not only fascinating but also quite startling. It cut across our entire lives. Without others, I would not be seeing the present and obviously would have to forget about any future. The African Renaissance should be about doing things for others; it should be about selflessness. The ills bedeviling Africa I highlighted earlier are perfect examples of African leaders in all spheres of life and work forgetting about others. Because we are interconnected from the village to country, all the way to the continent, EVERYTHING we mess up will be 'inherited' by others.

15.5.2 May I work with you? A deep sense of belonging

Another leadership hallmark is to do with the inculcation of a deep sense of belonging among community members. Commenting about how united the entire Lamba tribe was regardless of where one stayed, an elder therein had the following to say:

> We do not preach unity we live it. You cannot divide us. We know how we are related and we take pride in the unity we uphold as a tribe, whether you are coming from across the border (DRC) or lived elsewhere for many years, if you are a Lamba, it is enough we will track down your genealogy and tell you how you are related to us.

The ability to trace one's genealogy is also linked to the knowing I discussed above, in that the tracing can only succeed if people know one another through the generations. The notions of 'you belong to us' and 'we belong to you' and therefore everyone belongs define the way people live in this context. For every human being it is comforting to belong. That sense of belonging is likely to motivate one to seek to contribute to the welfare of the same community. In this connection the behaviour of an individual and group is shaped by that sense of unity, therefore leadership is not something to be preached or lectured to people - instead it is lived. Arguably, in today's institutions and organisations, there is a lack of a sense of belonging. In school classrooms, for example, learners often do not feel a sense of belonging any more. Absenteeism, lack of interest, bullying, academic failure and violence are some of the ills in institutions.

In his book entitled, *Leading like Madiba: Leadership Lessons from Nelson Mandela*, Kalungu-Banda[33] relates a true story which he entitled, *When are you going to dismiss us Mr President?* He preludes this story by pointing out that when a new head of state takes office it is always taken for granted that it is not just the outgoing leaders who must vacate the office, but also those who worked with them; their team. Kalungu-Banda[34] then reported that a short while after the inauguration of South Africa's President Nelson Mandela, he was invited to a meeting by his staff. The staff representative asked President Mandela why he was torturing them by not informing them of the office reshuffle and who were to lose their jobs. The staff was certain that the new head of state would have his staff appointed thus replacing the old. But Mr Mandela retorted:

> But you are my people. Since I came into this office, everything has been managed extremely well. I am pleased with the way you are all working. Unless you do not want to work with me, all I can say is that I find you very supportive and competent in your role. Maybe you would like me to request formally, 'May I work with you?'

There was total silence in disbelief and the President requested that the meeting end there to allow him to attend to his next appointment. The staff had a very restricted sense of belonging but this was not entirely their fault. The world today sadly comes across like that. It took the wisdom (and wisdom follows later in this chapter) of President Mandela to disrupt the narrow conception of belonging. In South Africa there is a very pleasant saying, which is also a preamble to the Congress of the People's 1956 Freedom Charter[35], which goes: 'South Africa belongs to all those who live in it'. I wish this were true in day-to-day living. Similarly, Africa should belong to all those who live in it. But what does it mean to belong to Africa? In the preceding story, President Mandela told the staff that they all belonged because they were doing what was required of them. If Africans are to renew Africa, they must diligently sacrifice for Africa. It takes sound leadership to help people feel that they belong.

We can also draw from one of King Shaka's practices. The *amabutho* (young army recruits) were drawn from all corners of the kingdom. This was a calculated way of mitigating the formation of ethnic divisions. The result was a strong army of young men who were driven by the 'I belong, you belong, and we all belong' factor. This was enough of a motivation for them to go out there and win battles and wars. Perhaps this is one of the reasons why King Shaka became one of the most revered African leaders. In seeking to advance an African Renaissance we need to build a sense of belonging among African peoples.

15.5.3 Dialogue

In every African traditional context, dialogue among the various stakeholders was a key approach to decision-making and so there was always a structure for that. To illustrate, the Zulu people have an *Imbizo,* the Sotho have a *Lekgotla,* the Lamba have a *Pa Nsaka,* the Shona have a *Dare.* Dialogue took place in both the nuclear and extended family set-ups. There were expert advisors about all aspects of life including courtship, marriage, divorce, conflict and crime; village elders would be consulted on various matters. Before any matter escalated to the headman or chief, there would have been several conversations at various levels. However, the African culture, perhaps like other cultures of the world, is often heavily criticised for being highly patriarchal. But in talking to women village elders, another permutation which is seemingly less written about and even less understood, it emerged that women actually made significant decisions. The following is how one woman elder in Zimbabwe expressed it:

> Even in the midst of patriarchy, men got wisdom from their wives before meetings. If a meeting (*Dare)* were to take place tomorrow or any time soon, men would tap ideas from their wives beforehand. In the *Dare* a man's worth was measured by the amount of his wisdom over the issue at hand. Although the men would not disclose the sources of such wisdom, a lot came from their wives.

While this response cannot absolve men from patriarchy, it seems to advise us that African culture may not be as simplistic as presented by colonial scribes. The role of women in the African society would need to be understood from more nuanced lenses than is often the case, for example, King Shaka is reported to have learnt resilience and wisdom from his aunt. Leadership is not always about being in front, and it is not about being the mouthpiece. It is about having the humility to share one's wisdom without claiming the credit. It is about garnering followers who can then take ownership of the idea and make use of it. We need the wisdom even of the ordinary citizen.

15.5.4 Leadership in the veins

In the preceding section on dialogue, I ended up arguing that in the African context every one of us has a part to play in leading society. That also links up quite well with the section about the sense of belonging. A related leadership hallmark quite evident in most African traditional contexts is the automatic assumption of leadership roles by any member of the community, in response to a situation. To illustrate, the following is what one Zimbabwean village elder had to say:

> Even among the children, there would be one who had to assume a leadership role, the elder son or daughter. For instance, as an older child you cannot ignore the wrong doings of the younger ones, you have to stop them, you cannot say, I am going to wait for my mother or father. No! That would be a disgrace to you, because you are regarded as a leader. In fact on their return the parents would ask why you allowed the younger ones to misbehave.

Writing in the context of the business world, Khoza[36] declared that corporate social responsibility is everybody's business. All those in that 'world' should care about it. For Khoza[37], it is about collectively committing to sustainable progress and building a better world. Similarly, in the African context, leadership is in one way or the other everybody's business. It is about building a better family, village, clan and society. The example of the role of children above tells us that leadership is not only learnt early in one's life, but also practiced at the same time. The nature of life on its own teaches one to lead. The African Renaissance demands that as individuals and groups we should embrace leadership as part of our roles because it is already in our veins by virtue of being African. Just like a child's parent is not always going to be present to provide guidance, but will question him or her for not exercising leadership where it was required, other people are not and do not have to always be there to provide us leadership, and society shall demand explanations from us for not exercising it accordingly. Thus, closely related to the leadership in the veins hallmark, is the issue of collective responsibility. In our conversations with village elders across the four countries, this matter came out very strongly as illustrated below:

> ... children belonged to the entire village. As a parent or adult, you were to guide every child, I mean every child. If children are fighting, insulting each other or anything unacceptable. As an adult, it was a shame to ignore bad behaviour, it was a curse on you to let that happen in your presence. Other people would be worried about you. And you would be called for a special hearing whether you were man or woman.

15.5.5 The spirit of hard work

In all the SADC countries we studied, the spirit of hard work stood out as a hallmark that was cherished and strongly encouraged among all people, young and old. Among the Shona people of Zimbabwe, we learnt that hard work is encouraged in day-to-day conversations. For example, if somebody travels to some far-away place on some mission, on their return the most likely question they are asked is: *Makativigirei?* (What did you bring us?) At face value this question sounds as if people merely like presents, especially those from elsewhere. Of course it is a pleasant thing to receive. To the one who travelled, it is a good feeling to celebrate the journey and to show that one is a 'has been to', by giving. A negative surface meaning to that question is that people are poking their noses into others' affairs. Why should you know what I brought? Why did I have to bring something for you? Why do you not leave me alone? However there is a much deeper meaning to the seemingly simple and intrusive question. It is not about literally bringing everybody a present, after all, it is not practical to do so. It is an in-built question about progress for all of us in the community. It is about pinning down the citizen who travelled to have them reflect on the worth of their journey. It is about encouraging purposeful living, in which everybody must play a part for the good of us all. This is why the question is 'What did you bring us?' and not 'What did you bring me?'

We learnt also that children were not absolved from answering these simple, friendly but deep-rooted questions. For example, on meeting a relative, friend, neighbour or just a member of the community, a school-going child should expect to be asked the following question in one form or another: *Wakaita nhamba ani?* (What was your class position last term?) (How are you doing in school?) To the child who is asked, the teaching is that he/she must do well in order to proudly answer a question which, whether they like it or not, will be asked by several people on different occasions. It also means people other than one's nuclear family are interested and following one's progress. It means that it is a virtue to succeed. To the one who asks it means they feel a sense of responsibility to encourage success among the youth. It is in the veins to do so. It means the children belong to the entire village and their success is the village's success. The African Renaissance is about the success of this big village called the continent. We in that village are responsible for its success.

There are many other scenarios that might explicate the Shona adult world as well. This time it is about an adult engaged in some learning programme such as a degree. On meeting relatives, friends, acquaintances and some such, the issue of studying usually takes centre stage in terms of what the parties discuss because of the high value attached to it. The overarching question however is: *Munopedza riini?* (When are you finishing?) The teaching here is that what one has started by way of advancement or any form of progress must be completed. All community members are with the one studying in spirit, and this explains why they are keen to know when the final product is arriving. In some cases it is also about encouraging one to finish the present task in order to proceed to something else bigger that is waiting. To the one studying, the question says it is doable and people are waiting to celebrate the completion.

The three questions above represent what I would call leadership through friendly questions. For it to stick, the friendly question is asked within the context of some work either being done or having been achieved. Somebody would have travelled. Somebody would be in the formative years growing up and studying. Somebody would be advancing himself as an adult. Linking this 'story' to the African Renaissance, I see a dual role for all of us Afro-optimists. One role, and perhaps the major one, is that we must be engaged in work in our various areas to rebuild and grow Africa. It is about doing real work. If we do that work well, we will attract friendly questions of encouragement and these will propel us to do more. The second is that we must shoulder the responsibility of asking our fellow Africans friendly questions about what they do. We must exercise leadership through constant friendly but intent inquiry.

King Moshoeshoe of the Mountain Kingdom of Lesotho led his people during the challenging 1800s, which are known for the *Mfecane* (1813-1830) tribal invasions that decimated many chiefdoms. During that period, King Moshoeshoe warded off attacks from many enemies including Shaka's Zulus and Mzilikazi's Ndebele[38]. As time went on King Moshoeshoe informed his people that these wars were bad because they robbed them of precious time to engage in worthwhile activities. Instead, he advocated and strived to build peace. In this regard, a *Mosotho* village elder, also a retired teacher, had the following to say:

> King Moshoeshoe insisted on building peace and knew that as long as people fought they would be no peace. People wasted too much time and energy fighting instead of producing food and he was tired of these wars.

Long after King Moshoeshoe, the continent of Africa still suffers from endless worthless wars. Africans are yet to achieve the peace that the King called for, and these wars and other forms of conflict rob the continent of its precious resources, including time for development. Most important of all, its people find themselves wielding guns to fight and kill fellow Africans. If Africans are going to succeed in renewing this continent, they should experience a rebirth in thought processes as well.

There are many examples that we can extract from recent history that demonstrate that hard work does indeed pay dividends. Many African intellectuals, for example, did much to try to improve the lives of fellow Africans, even when colonialism was rampant. Over a century ago a black intellectual, John Dube, initiated a system of education with production among African students. There were many like Dube who, after succeeding in Western education, came back to Africa to introduce an education system for black Africans. Today institutions of higher learning call for the Africanisation of the curricula to ensure that the education of Africans is not exclusively Western. As a continent, Africans find themselves wanting in terms of self-reliance in many spheres of life. For example, they still export raw materials and wait for other nations to refine those materials, after which they then sell the expensive goods back to Africa. If we are to achieve a renaissance, we have to increase our self-reliance. Africans have to ask themselves hard questions about the purpose of education systems on the continent.

15.5.6 Wisdom

I purposely decided to flag the issue of wisdom at the end of this chapter. This is so because what I have been discussing all along boils down to the need for us to draw from the wisdom of African ancestors in terms of how they led society. I still have some wisdom to share in this section, going back to the Kingdom of Lesotho. Many strange things happened during the 1800s as African tribes jostled for power and resources. Such jostling obviously resulted in people dying, thus perpetuating rivalry and animosity between and within tribal groups. A Mosotho village elder reported the following incident to us:

> When King Moshoeshoe's grandfather Peete Peete was killed and eaten by cannibals, his people were so angry and wanted to hunt these people and kill them. The King refused and said 'let us

give them a herd of cattle perhaps they did so because they were hungry.' He continued and said, 'You cannot kill them because after eating my grandfather, their stomachs have now become my grandfather's grave, so you cannot dig-up my grandfather's grave'.

During King Moshoeshoe's time, cattle were the greatest form of wealth among the African people. Moshoeshoe wisely disarmed his people's enemies by what we may call 'going against the grain'. Sometimes leadership requires having to go against the grain. In Moshoeshoe's case, it entailed forfeiting some of his Kingdom's wealth over and above the loss of his grandfather, who of course was a priceless resource, in order to advance an important principle, an example of a position that modern Africa often fails dismally to take. If we are to renew Africa and address the myriad of challenges that I identified at the beginning of this chapter, we will need to go against the grain. For example, African politicians and bureaucrats must get out of their comfort zones and stop government incurring unnecessary expenditures including overstaffing. We should all forfeit some of our luxuries for the benefit of poor communities of Africa. We need to work on how we can shed the past.

15.6 Conclusion

In this chapter, I have not only highlighted how Africa may lose as things fall apart, but I have also exhibited that through intentional leadership Africa can be transformed and the renaissance dream can come to fruition. I have positioned myself as an Afro-optimist as I foresee several ways in which we can eschew the challenges that continuously hinder progress on the continent. My optimism is not unfounded. It is proudly informed by the rich endowment of how our African ancestors used to perform their duties well. It is strongly anchored in the shrewd leadership of our esteemed African forebears. Therefore, my 'story' in the chapter has been that our future lies in looking back to the past and selecting good aspects of leadership hallmarks that made our ancestors great people. The six leadership hallmarks discussed: the spirit of knowing and caring for others; a deep sense of belonging; dialogue; leadership in the veins; the spirit of hard work; and wisdom, are drawn straight from Africa's experience. Finally, during the Zimbabwean war of liberation, one of the most touching slogans was: *Iwe neni tine basa* (Shona language for literally: You and I have our work cut out). In my judgment, that slogan summarises the message behind these leadership hallmarks towards the African Renaissance, but they are by no means exhaustive.

References

[1]Achebe, C. 1958. *Things Fall Apart*. London: Heinemann.
[2]Khoza, R. J. 2011. *Attuned Leadership: African Humanism as Compass*. Johannesburg: Penguin.
[3]Ngambi, H. 2004. African Leadership: Lessons from the Chiefs. In T. N. A. Meyer and I. Boninelli (Eds.). *Conversations in Leadership: South African Perspectives*. Randburg: Knowledge Resources, pp. 107-132.
[4]Ibid.
[5]Kolawole, O. D. 2005. Mainstreaming locals' knowledge and implications for higher education in the South. *South African Journal of Higher Education*, 19:1427-1443.
[6]Hammersmith, J. A. 2007. *Converging Indigenous and Western Knowledge Systems implications for tertiary Education*. Unpublished Doctoral Thesis. Pretoria: University of South Africa.

[7]Barnhardt, R. 1986. *Domestication of the Ivory Tower: Institutional Adaptation to Cultural Distance.* Fairbanks: University of Alaska.

[8]Cajete, G. 1986. *Science, a Native American Perspective: A Culturally Based Science Education Curriculum.* Unpublished Doctoral Dissertation. Los Angeles: International College.

[9]Battiste, M. & Barman, J. (Eds.). 1995. *First Nations Education in Canada: The Circle Unfolds.* Vancouver: University of British Columbia Press.

[10]Nakashima, D., Prott, L. & Bridgewater, P. *Tapping into the world.* Retrieved from: www.unesco.org/education/tlsf/docs/module_11doc. [Date accessed: June 12, 2016.]

[11]Gebrehiwet, R. *Indigenous leadership styles and contemporary governance in Africa: A case of the Ethiopian Gada system.* Retrieved from: www.nai.uu.se/ecas-4/panels/101-120/panel-111/Robiel-Kassa-full. [Date accessed: August 2, 2016.]

[12]Ibid.

[13]Ibid.

[14]Mungazi, A. D. 1996. *The Mind of Black Africa.* Westport: Praeger Publishers.

[15]Marker, S. 2003. Effects of colonisation. Beyond intractability. In C. Burgess and H. Burgess (Eds.). *Conflict Information Consortium.* Boulder: University of Colorado.

[16]SABC News. 2016. *Mbeki blames lack of leadership for Africa's ills.* May 26, 2016.

[17]Bennis, W. & Nanus, B. 1985. *Leaders: The Strategies for Taking Charge.* New York: Harper and Row.

[18]Forde, R. D. 2010. *Minds and Hearts: Exploring the Teacher's Role as a Leader of Pupils in a Class.* Unpublished Doctoral Thesis. Durban: University of KwaZulu-Natal.

[19]Ibid.

[20] Covey, S. 2004. *The 8th Habit.* London: Simon and Schuster.

[21]Forde, R. D. (2010). Minds and Hearts: Exploring the Teacher's Role as a Leader of Pupils in a Class. Unpublished PhD Thesis, University of KwaZulu-Natal: Durban.

[22]Burns, J. 1979. *Leadership.* New York: Harper and Row.

[23]Heifitz, R. 1994. *Leadership without Answers.* Cambridge: Harvard University Press.

[24]Forde, R. D. 2010. *Minds and Hearts: Exploring the Teacher's Role as a Leader of Pupils in a Class.* Unpublished Doctoral Thesis. Durban: University of KwaZulu-Natal.

[25]Ngambi, H. 2004. African Leadership: Lessons from the Chiefs. In T. N. A. Meyer and I. Boninelli (Eds.). *Conversations in Leadership: South African Perspectives.* Randburg: Knowledge Resources Publishing, pp. 107-132.

[26]Ibid.

[27]Ibid.

[28]Preece, J. 2003. Education for transformative leadership in Southern Africa. *Journal of transformative leadership in Southern Africa,* 1(3): 245-263.

[29]Learn/Leadership regional network for Southern Africa. 2002. *Unpublished outline plan for leadership development programme.* Pretoria: South Africa.

[30]Khoza, R. J. 2011. *Attuned Leadership: African Humanism as Compass.* Johannesburg: Penguin.

[31]Ibid.

[32]Ibid.

[33]Kalungu-Banda, M. 2006. *Leading like Madiba: Leadership lessons from Nelson Mandela.* Cape Town: Double Storey.

[34]Ibid.

[35]Freedom Charter. 1955. *Freedom Charter.* Retrieved from: www.anc.org.za. [Date accessed: January 5, 2017.]

[36]Khoza, R. J. 2011. *Attuned Leadership: African Humanism as Compass.* Johannesburg: Penguin.

[37]Ibid.

[38]South African History Online. *King Moshoeshoe 1.* Retrieved from: www.sahistory.org.za/people/king-moshoeshoe-i. [Date accessed: January 22, 2017.]

Chapter 16

Concluding Comments: Towards a new African Society

Vuyisile Msila

The opening chapters of this book spell out as to why we need to rethink the African philosophy as we reaffirm the ideals of an African Renaissance. The debates in the volume also examine how and why Africans need to decolonise knowledge and uphold indigenous knowledge systems, thus creating a sound African philosophy. Furthermore, the reader gets to understand why the African philosophy is pertinent for an African Renaissance. African philosophy has deep implications and unblemished meaning for African ways of life. Indigenous knowledge(s), decoloniality and transformation in African societal institutions all struggle to be realised without a foundation of an African philosophy. We usually overlook the role of the indigenous knowledge systems and how African philosophy talks to the essence of being African and being in Africa. As the African societies speak of an African Renaissance we need to think of this as a prerequisite to revitalise the lost African identity as we erase the vestiges of absolute European domination. The illustrious Africanist, Walter Rodney, spoke about the way Europe underdeveloped Africa[1]. Furthermore, Rodney contended that there is a necessity to decolonise Africa, which was underdeveloped by colonial domination[2]. There was no way that the defeated Africans could assert their philosophy when the threat of colonialism consumed their identity and dignity. Yet Africans have tried over the epochs to affirm themselves, and African philosophy is about the recouping of the strength, assertion and belief in the potency of the African realm.

Africans are now at a crossroads as they seek to define who they are, yet they want to define themselves in a rather complex environment that was muddled by imperialism. They need to establish the preconditions for an African Renaissance and the formulation of an African philosophy. This volume of essays has shown the various ways in which Africans can create development as they jostle for realisation and fulfilment on the continent. Okumu[3] argued that success in Africa is attainable and it can happen through the advancement of science and technology, relevant research, the development of human resources, utilising natural resources and preventing and resolving conflicts. Similarly, various discussions in the collection of chapters here have displayed this. Part 1 focusses on the theory of African philosophy while others look at conflict, gender as well as arts. The authors have raised debates necessary in the resurging African intellectualism that seeks to bring forth solutions to Africa's ills. Although all the authors perceive hope in the African philosophy, it is not without a reflective critical eye. As many look at the African philosophy, they try to find ways of attending to the huge challenges of society. The current African societies battle in finding answers to the colonial plunder, and Africa still struggles with the use of colonial languages, creating relevant Afrocentric curricula in schools, and developing relevant more critical African universities. Yet all these chapters either imply or state directly that the decolonisation of the mind needs to happen for people to be receptive to

African philosophy that would enhance the African societies.

A growing number of African intellectuals are realising that the search for African indigenous knowledge systems should be a simultaneous quest for redeeming our African societies from the ills that thwart or hinder progress. The least that the African indigenous knowledge systems and the African Renaissance should do is to give direction, provide maps of how people can ensure that there is food security, reduce conflict, and hold elections to form the basis of democratic governments free from despotism and domination. Currently universities are seeking answers as to how to help African youths study through relevant pedagogy with affordable tuition fees or free education. Conscientious Africans would want to know how we can do this through the application of African philosophy. Several authors have recommended solutions to some African challenges such as women's self-sustenance, indigenous languages in higher education, and using history to understand the present and the future. What has come out in many of the chapters here is that African philosophies are not flawless; they are not as pure as some would like us to believe. For example, in this volume we saw the need to address male domination and uphold African feminism and womanhood. An African Renaissance will be incomplete without gender equality, social justice and stability in institutions such as higher education establishments.

It is clear from the chapters that people who are not emancipated mentally will not be ready for an African Renaissance. Education can play a crucial role in this regard, and much can be borrowed from the tenets of Pan-Africanists that Isaac-Martins discussed in her chapter. Ayokhai and Naankiel spelt out how Azikiwe brought theory into pan-Africanism, for example it was he who first wrote about renascent Africa, although he never endeavoured to intellectually engage with the concept[4]. The fathers of Pan-Africanism in Africa wanted to achieve a united Africa from Cape to Cairo. It has always been an elusive dream; an ideal that has failed many a good leader. Yet Pan-Africanism is seen as an intellectual movement that can give meaning to African Renaissance and African philosophy, thus emboldening Africa's renewal. Ali Mazrui contended that the intelligentsia is needed to support Pan-Africanism, adding that the origins of modern intellectualism and of Pan-Africanism are intermingled[5]. Mazrui further argued:

> In depth Pan-Africanism as a system of ideas did not aspire to be as 'scientific' as Marxism and modern socialism. But in breadth Pan-Africanism covered a wider agenda – concerned not only with political economy, but also with African culture, aesthetics, poetry and philosophy...More activist in his Pan-Africanism was Kwame Nkrumah of Ghana. He became the champion of the most ambitious form of Pan-Africanism – the quest for regional integration of the whole African continent.

In various ways, the contributors capture the ideas couched by this definition of Pan-Africanism. The call for African philosophy and the demand for an African Renaissance are synonymous with the appeals to emancipate Africa and its people from the shackles of colonialism. This volume's contents display how Africa can be renewed through not only politics and philosophy, but through language and arts as well. Several authors have also in various ways highlighted the importance of democracy for an African Renaissance to happen.

Several chapters imply or explicitly point out that there is a necessity for communities to practice democracy if development is to prevail in Africa. They perceive democracy as a critical aspect; a prerequisite for African renewal. Mangu[6] argued that democracy should precede an African Renaissance, and like Mazrui, noted that African intellectuals have a crucial role to play in ensuring that the African Renaissance is brought to fruition. Contributors to this volume refer to the need to use the constitution in various African states to ensure that equality is observed, be it language rights or a decolonised system of education.

Arguably, democracy remains one of the major challenges to an African Renaissance today, as some African states continue to struggle with embracing democratic principles. Yet the ideal of the African Renaissance is to underscore the critical nature of social role-players in the enhancement of democracy, for without the establishment of a strong democratic tradition, there can be no African rebirth in economic and technological terms[7]. This author wrote about a need for an enlightened civil society if democracy is to be achieved, thus enabling people not only to vote but to be accountable as well. Through democratic processes citizens can move towards the idea of an African Renaissance. Okumu[8] cited Obasanjo who spoke about the potential of democracy to bring forth national unity as well as curb ills such as tyranny and corruption. To this end Obasanjo and Mabongunie are quoted as saying:

> Perhaps the first step would be the need to prevent the constant privatization of the state by our power elites. This must be done in addition to a move to separate the business of governance from the business of economic transactions. One of the anchoring bases of this move is the need to embrace, integrate, imbibe and acculturate the spirit of mutual empowerment between the state and the people[9].

Bringing in democratic living in Africa will require the involvement of various role-players, which may lead to an African Renaissance.

Among the factors that have been linked to democracy is the use of indigenous languages. The language conundrum has never been such a contentious issue in (South) Africa. There is much realisation that people also need to speak their indigenous languages instead of accommodating only the European languages. Kamwendo focused on the Malawian case where there is a motion to accommodate Chichewa as an official language at University instead of English only. Msila in Chapter 2 cited Wiredu, who described the relevance of language in the formulation of African philosophy. The contributors have frequently referred to the position of universities in highlighting some of these issues.

Across the continent, the university has never been perceived as so relevant to the surrounding communities. Witthuhn in Chapter 11, for example, raised crucial arguments regarding how we have to internationalise the higher education curricula as we Africanise knowledge in general.

On the 27th of February 2017, many listened to former South African President Thabo Mbeki at Unisa's ZK Mathews Great Hall as he gave his inaugural speech as the University of South Africa's Chancellor. Some authors have cited Mbeki numerous times in the chapters, and in his speech he echoed many sentiments raised by contributors in this volume. Mbeki's speech underscored the role of intellectuals at universities as people search for relevance and African philosophy. He elicited hope as his inaugural address enhanced the transformation agenda embraced by a few gradually changing African universities. The issue of relevance and the need for an Afrocentric university has never been so distinct, and Mbeki cited Nyerere who pointed out five decades ago that a university was not established for prestige but to develop its communities. This is reminiscent of what Nyerere said earlier as president of a newly liberated Tanganyika in 1961, stating that others may be aiming to reach the moon, but first we need to reach the villages, and all other dreams will follow[10]. This is the essence of relevant African education, and Nyerere's message, like Thabo Mbeki's, has never been so relevant as calls for the decolonisation of higher education are coming from all fronts, as we have seen in the essays in this volume.

Chancellor Mbeki poses questions about expectations of higher education at a time when almost all African universities are discussing their responses to demands for an Afrocentric university. Among these calls are student demands that appeal for sustainable funding as they redress the injustices of the past. He asks a pertinent question as to how society will sustain higher education at a time when there are a myriad challenges that include corrupt practices from certain corners. Despite these challenges, however, Mbeki suggests that we should continue examining the propinquity between society and higher education, posing the crucial question of whether our society is clear enough in its expectations of higher education[11].

There have been several reasons as to why various institutions are still failing to implement decolonised curricula in Afrocentric campuses, and the deliberation in this regard has been unchanging. Among these are fear and panic in confronting the new. Although the most persistent question that has caused this resistance has been concerns about academic standards, some critics contend that quality will plummet after Africanisation because the West will not be used as a yardstick. The latter is an argument that has pervaded since the late 1990s when people such as Professor Malekgapuru Makgoba popularised this concept in higher education.

The former president highlighted the role of universities in opening up people's opportunities, and producing activists for a renaissance rather than obfuscating people. Universities, Mbeki averred, should correct the injustices of the past as they uplift the citizens. Mbeki knows that an African Renaissance is about redressing gender, community involvement and creative thinking. He envisages a system that emancipates, where the students learn to apply new knowledge and are thus able to redeem society of some societal ills. In these chapters these notions are reflected as contributors maintain that stable and socially just universities will be critical in building progressive societies.

Mbeki is unequivocal that we need education that is globally relevant, which would mean building our own intellectuals who will learn from Africa's context as they enhance the local, while the West will also glean from Africa's experiences. In 1998 Mbeki was quoted as saying, "those who have eyes let them see - the African Renaissance is upon us, as we peer through the looking glass darkly, this may not be obvious. But it is upon us." The upheavals in South African universities ignited so many debates that questioned the culture of African institutions this year. Many role-players also started posing relevant questions and discussing why all African institutions need an African philosophy. Why an African philosophy at a higher education institution?

There are numerous institutions of higher learning that have been complicit as they ignored an agenda to include the African philosophy in their curricula. Some may have introduced one course or module that deals with elementary Sesotho or isiNdebele, and will vouch that their curricula are transformed and Africanised. On the one hand this could be a naïve and sometimes innocent belief that they have indeed Africanised. On the other, though, it is a deliberate malicious intent to exclude the real Africanisation agenda. The major challenge to many institutions of higher learning has been the need for African universities to respond to the challenges of the continent that Mbeki mentions above. There are still a few that try to move beyond theory. African institutions do not just need one module in African philosophy; the philosophy should cut through their modules across the curricula, otherwise the practice will be a farce.

The realisation that we have to nurture an African university can never be underestimated, however the quagmire that our universities get into as they attempt to Africanise is threefold. The first one involves the community, the second is the research agenda that needs to be followed, and the third is the critical time at which to sensitise our students on Africanisation. In most cases our higher education is dead as it fails to respond to the needs of the communities living in the African landscape. There is a tendency by academics to believe that the communities are peripheral to what is happening within the higher education institutions. The academics may believe that they are the sole authority who ought to jealously lead the development of curricula, but nothing can be further from the truth. If our institutions of higher learning should embrace Africanisation, they need to start with the communities, because understanding what the communities want is among the best ways to address the issues of relevance.

Rural universities in Africa, for example, should know how to connect with the communities by assessing what their needs are. Some rural campuses are far from cities and the communities around have special needs such as the preservation of water and community health research. The universities should thus have programmes that address these and similar challenges. But this also needs one to have an understanding of how African communities work, because in many cases people have to negotiate entry into villages through the chiefs, which requires an understanding of the African set-up.

Second, the idea of relevant research is crucial for all African universities. On a theoretical level, there are still numerous African institutions that would like to reincarnate their systems to learn towards an Africanised philosophy. However, they still find it hard to define what their African philosophy entails. The paradox of many in African institutions is the need for them to be re-Africanised after years of being enmeshed in exclusively Eurocentric values.

More researchers have to take it upon themselves to lead in curricula reform that would ensure that African models in research form part of the curricula. Where there is no literature, universities need to create these through meticulous research. There should also be practical research to address challenges such as malaria, farming and planting. There are many other challenges which include corrupt governments, running democratic elections and how to merge traditional aspects and Western models. African universities should lead in these areas.

Moreover, education remains the uppermost important factor that can change countries' economies and future. Research all over Africa should endeavour to find ways of critically engaging role-players on to how to improve education. Frequently, universities try to introduce African philosophy to students at university. If the students are fortunate, there may be a chapter in a module that deals with African philosophy. Again, if they are lucky, they may get an entire course on this philosophy. However this is where the problem lies, for it may be too late to teach African philosophy for the first time at university. Schools should begin the journey of empowering the pupils in African philosophy. By the time the students reach university, they need to have a full understanding of what it means to be an African. The irony of introducing African philosophy for many African institutions of higher learning is that this will shock the system as it transforms embedded institutional cultures.

One author spoke of the need to reincarnate institutions of higher learning[12]. Reincarnation may mean the rebirth and revitalisation of an African ethos. Indigenous languages struggle in African universities, yet African institutions of higher learning are supposed to reflect the cultures of the continent rather than exclusive Anglo-Saxon traditions. The late Russel Bot from the University of Stellenbosch once spoke of the need for multilingualism in African institutions, a picture that would portray what Bot called "an Ubuntu of languages". African higher education institutions are still battling to achieve this. They ought to be a beacon of hope to Africa's rebirth and unfortunately, we still have to achieve this.

In the 1940s Anton Lembede spoke of the need for an African spirit that would be informed by the culture and history of Africa that we all need for a rebirth. Some of these notions will be spread by the crucial role of the arts in the quest for an African Renaissance. Art within the context of African Renaissance is very critical; it is as critical as language and culture as discussed in various chapters in this book. Art in Africa is not only for aesthetic purposes, but is a philosophy that also reflects identity and heritage. A song, a sculpture, a poem all could be reflections of numerous aspects of heritage. Arguably, an ultimate African Renaissance will be as strong as its art. People who treasure their music, their poetry and their artefacts will nurture the African Renaissance. During the years of apartheid and colonialism in South Africa, countless artists came out to celebrate being African; they were intent in opposing a colonial culture that sought to eclipse the African cultures. In the 1950s, writers such as Dhlomo, Mqhayi, Jolobe, Rubusana and Mofolo all wrote within the constraints of the time as they reminisced about Africa and what it represented. In their works there was the nostalgia of wanting to move towards a free Africa using the arts medium. Later, when the struggle against apartheid strengthened, there were even younger but intensely conscientised artists who used art to seek freedom; Dumile Feni and Gerard Sekoto (exiled sculptors and painters), Ingoapele Madingoane and Zeke Mphahlele (writers of different generations), as well as Sankomota and Bayete (music groups). All these artists envisaged their art forms as a means to liberate an oppressed people, as they reflected on the African past and the envisaged future. For example, the poet Madingoane wrote in one of his poems (he referred to these as black trials) in the collection, *Africa my beginning*[13]:

> i talk about me
> i am africa
> i am the blazing desert yonder
> egypt my head the nile my oasis
> flow on nile flow on my life blood

These black trials that Madingoane used to recite for gathering crowds rallied the masses under an African dream; a desire to reach Africa. It was a call for a renaissance, and this was evident in various "relevant" artists. Enambe[14], writing about Nigeria, delineated the role of the arts:

> The roles of art to the society are numerous: art promotes our cultural heritage and creates identity. Nigeria is known for her traditional art cultures of Nok, Ife, Benin, Igbo, Ukwu, Owo, Esie, etc. Through artworks the history of Nigeria is documented. Nigerian traditional arts have survived the test of time with recorded history of the oldest art discoveries south of the Sahara.

Effective art will be informed by the society's philosophy or the destination, i.e. where the society should be. The rise in music groups singing indigenous music, for example, may be an indication of a growing cultural consciousness among Africans who seek to free themselves from cultural bondage. Chinweizu[15], the Nigerian critic, has criticised what he calls Europhilia, which he says is an uncritical acceptance of Western ways. When Africans lose their culture, their art suffers from this cultural dependency. Although Chinweizu is frequently criticised by some Africanists such as Mazrui[16] and Hadgor[17] for misusing history, he has pronounced the role of arts and how arts should be in Africa. In Chapter 14 Nyezwa demonstrated why maskanda should be perceived as an emancipatory medium. These are useful artists in developing "black philosophy", as they sing for the community and this community is critical for the development of an African Renaissance. The artists as ambassadors of culture should lead in the fight for an African Renaissance. They should show their people why they need to appreciate their own indigenous cultures. Conscientious artists will play a role in linking the African past with the envisaged future. In the process of decolonisation the Africans will also learn much from others.

In conclusion, this volume hopes to add to a growing body of knowledge on the decolonisation of knowledge. When intellectuals in Africa reflect on the continent, they need to highlight its weaknesses as well. It is true, though, that colonialism did destroy some of the values that the African was known for. Fear was introduced with the capture of slaves, for example. Yet Africans should drag themselves out of slavery by discarding the shackles of the mind that Steve Biko talked about so loudly. It is when the Africans reinvent themselves that they will find the new Africa. Rebirth is the strongest way to the future. Rebirth is the answer to the challenges of globalisation. We need to begin with our cultures, our languages and our identities. Africans need to reclaim the new dawn as an empowered people. This book has reminded us all of the need for Africans to rethink their marred philosophy as they rebuild their renaissance.

References

[1]Rodney, W. 2009. *How Europe underdeveloped Africa*. Abuja: Panaf Publishing.

[2]Ibid.

[3]Okumu, W. A. J. 2002. *African Renaissance: History, significance, and strategy*. Trenton: Africa World Press.

[4]Ibid.

[5]Mazrui, A. A. 2005. Pan-Africanism and the intellectuals: rise, decline and revival. In T. Mkandawire (Ed.). *African intellectuals: Rethinking Politics, Language, Gender and Development*. London: Zed Books.

[6]Mangu, A. M. B. 2006. Democracy, African Intellectuals and African Renaissance. *International Journal of African Renaissance Studies*, 1(1): 147-163.

[7]Okumu, W. A. J. 2002. *African Renaissance: History, significance, and strategy*. Trenton: Africa World Press.

[8]Ibid.

[9]Ibid.

[10]Nyerere, J. K. 2011. *Freedom and Liberation*. Dar es Salaam: Oxford.

[11]Msila, V. 2017. Mbeki: The African Renaissance's drum major. *Pretoria News*, p. 7, 02 March 2017.

[12]Barnett, R. 1997. *Realizing the University, An Inaugural Lecture*. University of London - London: Institute of Education.

[13]Madingoane, I. 1979. *Africa my beginning*. Johannesburg: Ravan.

[14]Enambe, B. B. 2013. The role of arts education in Nigeria. *AJOTE*, 3(1). Retrieved from https://journal.lib.uoguelph.ca/index.php/ajote/article/view/1963/2934. [Date accessed January 14, 2017].

[15]Chinweizu. 1975. *The West and the rest of us: White predators, Black slavers and the African elite*. New York: Vintage.

[16]Mazrui, A. A. 1976. Review: The West and the rest of us: White predators, Black slavers and the African elite. *ASA*, 2: 142-144.

[17]Hadjor, K. B. 1990. *African in an era of crisis*. Trenton: Africa World Press.

Index

A

Activism, 115, 146–147, 150–151, 156–157
African, 2–19, 21–33, 35–42, 54–71, 73–89, 106–117,
    121–131, 146–151, 157–159, 161–179, 181–189,
    191–208, 224–239, 257–262, 271–278
  education, 21–22, 27–33, 145–146, 157–159, 161–165,
    173–176, 178–179, 181–184, 186–187, 191–205,
    210–211, 219–222, 230–235, 267–269, 272–276
  languages, 25, 27–28, 30–31, 146, 148–150, 153–155,
    157, 159, 161–178, 230–232, 234, 238–239,
    253–254, 271–273, 276
  phenomenology, 73, 75, 77, 79, 84–85
  philosophy, 1–5, 9, 17–19, 21–33, 89, 91, 183, 199,
    205, 225–226, 229–230, 232–234, 238, 253,
    271–277
  renaissance, 1–3, 13–16, 27–29, 38–41, 47–50,
    107–114, 125–128, 146–148, 157–159, 219–222,
    224–227, 235–239, 252–255, 271–274, 276–278
  thought, 2–5, 10, 12, 19, 23–26, 29, 32–33, 39, 48–51,
    64, 88, 187, 202–203, 205, 216
  tradition, 2, 4–8, 10–18, 22, 74, 76, 134, 172, 244, 257,
    273
African Union, 64, 69–70, 122
Afrikaans, 28, 82–83, 150, 158, 161–162, 164–165,
    167–169, 171, 173–177, 231–232, 239
Afro-Western, 35–37
Anglophone, 148–149
Anglo-Saxon, 169–170, 234, 276
Anti-colonial, 89
Arab, 64, 134
Atum, 130, 133–135, 139

B

BAAL, 151, 156
Bantu Education, 164, 168, 174–176
Basulutani, 261
Belonging, 64–67, 79, 93, 205, 221, 226, 239, 259,
    262–264, 268
Benin, 36–37, 140, 277
Bilingualism, 162
Black Consciousness, 57, 224–229, 235–236
Black Renaissance, 227–228, 235–236

C

Caring, 7, 13–14, 16, 259–262, 268
Chancellor College, 146, 151–152, 156
Chichewa, 146–147, 151, 273
Chinweizu, 32, 277
Civilisation, 2, 19, 21–22, 24, 26, 35, 40, 92, 166, 176,
    205, 215, 233, 238, 253
Coloniality, 29, 76, 88, 108, 148, 153, 158–159
Colonial language, 161, 164–167, 173
Colonisation, 23, 25–26, 37–38, 45, 47, 57, 148,
    161–162, 166, 172, 183, 208, 224, 238, 269
Communalism, 2, 7, 14–16, 24, 30–32, 229
Community engaged research, 78
Conflict, 53–59, 61–63, 65–70, 73–74, 76–84, 86–90,
    108–111, 129, 131–132, 138, 140, 186–187, 267,
    269, 271–272
Congo, 21, 32, 62, 87–91, 93, 95–96, 107–112, 167, 172
Conscientisation, 224
Curriculum, 181–182, 198–200, 216–217, 269
  Africanised, 185, 193, 202–203, 217–219, 222
  apartheid, 174–175, 198
  development, 182, 187, 189–190, 195, 199, 217, 222
  internationalisation, 181–182, 185, 194–195, 197–198,
    200
  public health, 181–182, 189–190, 192–194

D

Decoloniality, 76, 85, 271
Decolonisation, 23, 25, 27, 29, 32, 36, 38–40, 43–47,
    147–149, 171–172, 176, 221–222, 224–225, 239,
    277
Democracy, 2, 6–7, 15–16, 18–19, 22, 40, 43, 46, 48,
    156–157, 173, 177–178, 259, 272–273, 278
Duende, 237, 239, 247–248, 250

E

Education, 21–22, 27–33, 117–119, 121–128, 145–146,
    148–159, 161–165, 167–171, 173–176, 178–179,
    181–214, 216–222, 229–235, 267–269, 272–276
Egypt, 64, 131, 134–135, 137–138, 142–143, 277
English, 27–28, 37, 83, 99, 127, 146–157, 159, 161–178,
    214–215, 231, 240, 244, 273

Essentialism, 10, 61, 115
Ethnophilosophy, 2, 9, 24, 26–27, 33

F

Familyhood, 30, 229
Feminism, 99, 106, 111–112, 115–117, 122, 124,
    126–127, 272
Francophone, 148–149
Freedom Charter, 269

G

Gender equality, 87, 93–94, 98–99, 103, 107, 109–112,
    114, 117, 122, 126–128, 272
Ghana, 39, 41, 54, 57, 68–69, 154, 184, 272
Globalisation, 68, 70, 108–109, 122, 128, 173, 176,
    178–179, 181, 183, 201, 203, 235, 253, 255

H

Heart of Darkness, 21, 28, 32–33, 167, 177
Hegemony, 22, 59, 91, 100, 102, 110–111, 139, 171–173,
    218, 235
Higher education, 22, 24, 27–28, 145, 148–149,
    170–171, 181–211, 213–214, 216–219, 221–222,
    224, 231–234, 268, 272–276
Homer, 132
Hor, 129–130, 132–138, 140–141
Humanness, 205, 207, 212

I

Identity, 21–24, 53–70, 77, 82, 103, 110, 112, 161,
    163–165, 177, 186–187, 202–203, 225–226,
    229–231, 236–239
Igbo, 41–43, 130, 277
Imbizo, 237, 254, 264
Interconnectedness, 84, 208
Internationalisation, 170, 181–186, 192–198, 200
Isata, 129–131, 135, 137
IsiXhosa, 118, 124, 164, 175, 237, 239–243, 247, 254
IsiZulu, 149, 163–164, 173, 175, 231–232, 237, 240, 244

J

Judeo-Christian, 12

K

King of the Dead, 131
KMT, 129–135, 137–140, 142

L

Leadership, 31, 36, 41, 43, 46–50, 54–57, 61–64, 66–68,
    70, 115, 117, 121, 189–191, 257–266, 268–269
Lekgotla, 264
Liberalism, 6–7, 13
Literacy, 117, 123, 165, 170, 177, 209, 242, 254

M

Malawi, 146–147, 149, 151–156, 158–159
Masculinity, 87–97, 99–101, 103–105, 107–112
Maskanda, 237–243, 245–247, 250, 253, 277
Maskandi, 237, 239–247, 249–250, 252–254
Mfecane, 266
Modernism, 6, 11
Mother tongue, 146, 151–154, 156–159, 167, 169–176,
    215, 231, 240
Multilingualism, 158–159, 162, 165, 169–170, 173–174,
    178, 234, 276
Mutilation, 107
Mythology, 133–134, 142–143, 233
Mzilikazi, 267

N

New Kingdom, 129, 131, 137, 141
Niger Delta, 35–36
Nigeria, 35–39, 41–51, 64, 127, 129, 142, 184, 277–278

O

Old Kingdom, 129, 132, 136
Osiris, 129, 131, 133, 139, 141–143
Ottoman Turkey, 136

P

Pan-Africanism, 28–29, 35, 38–39, 41, 46–51, 54, 56–59,
    61, 63–64, 67, 69–70, 228–229, 232, 236, 272
Pa Nsaka, 264
Patriarchy, 95, 100, 108–109, 111–112, 115–116, 264

Pharaoh, 133

Philosophy, 1–5, 9–10, 17–19, 21–33, 46–47, 142, 183,
    199, 205, 220, 225–226, 228–230, 232–234, 238,
    271–277

Portuguese, 36–37, 80, 146, 149, 165

Postmodernism, 10–11

Poverty, 28, 35, 49–50, 62, 113–115, 117, 119, 121–127,
    202, 209, 214, 216, 224–225, 232, 235

Public Health, 85–86, 108, 181–182, 187, 189–195,
    199–200

R

Racialisation, 74

Rationality, 4–9, 11, 14

Revolution, 6, 18, 37, 63, 97–98, 168, 176, 197, 225, 235

S

SADC, 39, 106, 154, 265

San, 73, 79–84, 143

Science, 3, 5–6, 9–14, 17–18, 33, 81, 85, 111–112, 148,
    153, 157, 211, 221, 269, 271

Setekh, 129–133, 135–141

Shaka, 139, 238, 264, 267

Shona, 261, 264–266, 268

Slave Coast, 35–36

Slave Trade, 35, 37, 41, 55, 59

Soweto, 150, 162, 228

Sudan, 142, 190

Sustainable Development, 109, 120, 124, 127–128, 153

T

Tanzania, 30, 32–33, 57, 59, 172, 225, 229

Technology, 2–3, 5–6, 13, 111, 150, 153, 185, 254, 271

Things Fall Apart, 167, 230, 236, 268

Tradition, 2–18, 22, 74, 76, 99, 129–130, 132, 134, 136,
    139, 141, 154, 172, 244, 257

Tsotsitaal, 164, 177

U

Ubuntu, 14, 16, 19, 32, 121, 232, 234, 260, 276

Ujaama, 57, 229–230

Underdevelopment, 21, 30, 35, 49, 62, 107, 153, 188,
    214, 224

UNESCO, 19, 114, 126, 151–152, 154, 157, 159, 178,
    184, 197, 253, 269

W

Western modernity, 2, 4–5, 10, 12–14

Wisdom, 15, 26, 28, 83, 147, 155, 202, 216, 258, 260,
    263–264, 267–268

Womanhood, 115, 272

Wsir, 129–141

X

Xhosa, 237, 241, 243, 254

Y

Yoruba, 27, 42, 129, 135–136, 140, 142–143

Youth, 22, 41–42, 44, 47, 64–65, 90, 93, 103, 110, 169,
    177, 223–225, 259, 266

Z

Zimbabwe, 112, 154, 258, 261, 264–265

Zulu, 139, 166, 177, 237–239, 241, 264

[Created with **TExtract** / www.Texyz.com]

www.ingramcontent.com/pod-product-compliance
Lightning Source LLC
Chambersburg PA
CBHW080605270326
41928CB00016B/2934